The dominant moral philosophy of nineteenth-century Britain was utilitarianism, beginning with Bentham and ending with Sidgwick. Though once overshadowed by his immediate predecessors in that tradition (especially John Stuart Mill), Sidgwick is now regarded as a figure of great importance in the history of moral philosophy. Indeed, his masterpiece, *The Methods of Ethics* (1874), has been described by John Rawls as the "most philosophically profound" of the classical utilitarian works.

In this volume a distinguished group of philosophers reassess the full range of Sidgwick's work, not simply his ethical theory but also his contributions as a historian of philosophy, a political theorist, and a reformer.

The volume will be of interest to philosophers, political theorists, intellectual historians, and any scholar concerned with Victorian studies.

ESSAYS ON HENRY SIDGWICK

Essays on
Henry Sidgwick

Edited by
BART SCHULTZ
University of Chicago

The right of the
University of Cambridge
to print and publish
all kinds of books
was granted by law
in 1534.
The University has printed
and published continuously
since 1584.

CAMBRIDGE UNIVERSITY PRESS

CAMBRIDGE

NEW YORK   PORT CHESTER   MELBOURNE   SYDNEY

Published by the Press Syndicate of the University of Cambridge
The Pitt Building, Trumpington Street, Cambridge CB2 1RP
40 West 20th Street, New York, NY 10011, USA
10 Stamford Road, Oakleigh, Melbourne 3166, Australia

© Cambridge University Press 1992

First published 1992

Printed in Canada

Library of Congress Cataloging-in-Publication Data
Essays on Henry Sidgwick / edited by Bart Schultz.
p.   cm.
Includes bibliographical references and index.
ISBN 0-521-39151-2
1. Sidgwick, Henry, 1838–1900 – Congresses.   2. Ethics,
Modern – 19th century – Congresses.   I. Schultz, Bart.
B1649.S44E77   1991
192 – dc20   91–3300
                                                      CIP

A catalog record for this book is available from the British Library.

ISBN 0-521-39151-2 hardback

*In memory of J. David Greenstone
and Alan Donagan,
who kept faith*

Contents

Foreword

Sidgwick studies do not give the appearance of great activity at the moment – at least not in comparison with the studies of other British philosophers. We now have a superb modern edition of the works of John Stuart Mill, the Locke edition is moving rapidly, a Hobbes edition has begun, we are to expect a Hume edition, and there are several volumes of the Bentham edition. There is a Hobbes journal, a Locke journal, a Hume journal, and a journal for Bentham–Mill studies. Hobbes, Hume, Bentham, and Mill produced enough philosophical discussion to win places in a series of books studying their arguments, and Locke joins the others in being honored as a past master. Sidgwick has not attracted this kind of attention. Happily, *The Methods of Ethics* and the *History* are again in print (and *The Elements of Politics* may be reprinted), but no one seems to be planning a variorum edition of the *Methods*, the rest of the books are unobtainable, the essays and reviews have never been completely collected, and the only biography is the one put out just after Sidgwick's death by his wife and brother.

The conference that was the occasion for the present volume was, its organizer claimed, the very first meeting ever devoted solely to Sidgwick. He was in all probability right. What the fact indicates, however, is not so much neglect of Sidgwick as something about the way in which we are able to benefit from him. He has generally made his meaning so evident that we can usually engage with him, take from him, controvert him, or go on from him without the kind of critical apparatus and painstaking exegesis called for by philosophers who are more remote historically or who failed to present clearly a position as consistent as Sidgwick's. The papers and discussions at the conference sessions as well as the other essays in this volume remind us that Sidgwick has never wholly dropped out of our philosophical conversation. They give ample evidence that Sidgwick's work continues to provide a fruitful and provocative focus for systematic as well as historical examination of central issues of moral philosophy. Bart Schultz's Introduction points to further ways in which Sidgwick's influence is to be found in contemporary theorizing.

Despite the absence of a large cadre of editors and commentators, then, Sidgwick has a secure place in the ongoing inquiries of philosophers. I hope this volume will enable those who have not yet benefited from close study of Sidgwick to see how available he is and how useful. I hope it will also encourage further work on his texts and his contexts to deepen our understanding of his thought.

J. B. SCHNEEWIND

Acknowledgments

The beneficence of many is reflected in this volume. I should of course like to thank all of the contributors, whose aid, cooperativeness, and punctuality made the editorial work as pleasant as possible. But special thanks must go to Russell Hardin and J. B. Schneewind, whose counsel and encouragement were invaluable throughout the planning and production of this work. Martha Ward's extraordinary efforts on behalf of the book and its editor were also indispensable. In addition, thanks are due to Merry Oates, Evelyn Perry, Reynolds and Marian Schultz, William Frankena, John Rawls, Joshua Cohen, Jon Elster, Marcus Singer, and the late Alan Donagan, one of this book's dedicatees. Terence Moore, of Cambridge University Press, was wonderfully helpful and encouraging; it was a delight working with him, and with the production editor, Janis Bolster, and copyeditor, Barbara Palmer.

After this volume was in process, I organized a conference called "Henry Sidgwick as Philosopher and Historian" to give the contributors an opportunity to exchange ideas. This conference, held at the University of Chicago from May 18 through May 20, 1990, was sponsored by the Department of Philosophy, the Social Science Collegiate Division, and the Center for Ethics, Rationality, and Society. For their help with the conference, my thanks to those institutions, and to John Boyer, Dan Garber, Alan Gewirth, Stephen Darwall, Jeanne Templeton, Mary Kinahan, and Tom Christiano. Once again, special thanks must go to Russell Hardin, J. B. Schneewind, and Martha Ward.

BART SCHULTZ

Contributors

DAVID O. BRINK
Department of Philosophy
20 D-213
MIT
Cambridge, MA 02139

THOMAS CHRISTIANO
Department of Philosophy
University of Arizona
Tucson, AZ 85721

STEFAN COLLINI
Faculty of English
Cambridge University
9 West Road
Cambridge CB3 9PD
UK

JOHN DEIGH
Department of Philosophy
Bretano Hall
Northwestern University
Evanston, IL 60208

ALAN DONAGAN (deceased)
Formerly Division of the
    Humanities and Social Sciences
    101–40
California Institute of
    Technology
Pasadena, CA 91125

WILLIAM K. FRANKENA
Department of Philosophy
University of Michigan
Ann Arbor, MI 48109

RUSSELL HARDIN
Departments of Philosophy and
    Political Science
University of Chicago
Chicago, IL 60637

T. H. IRWIN
Sage School of Philosophy
Cornell University
218 Goldwin Smith Hall
Ithaca, NY 14853

JAMES T. KLOPPENBERG
Department of History
Brandeis University
Wellesley, MA 02181

J. L. MACKIE (deceased)
Formerly Reader in Philosophy
    and Fellow of University
    College
Oxford University
Oxford OX1 2JD
UK

J. B. SCHNEEWIND
Department of Philosophy
The Johns Hopkins University
Baltimore, MD 21218

BART SCHULTZ
Social Sciences Collegiate
    Division
University of Chicago
Chicago, IL 60637

MARCUS G. SINGER
Department of Philosophy
University of Wisconsin
5185 Helen C. White Hall
Madison, WI 53706

NICHOLAS P. WHITE
Department of Philosophy
University of Michigan
Ann Arbor, MI 48109

Abbreviations

References to and citations of Sidgwick's major works are given parentheticlly in the text using the following abbreviations. All works were published by Macmillan and Co., London, except for *Practical Ethics*, published by Swan Sonnenschein, London, and *Ethics of Conformity and Subscription*, published by Williams and Norgate, London. The last editions of *The Methods of Ethics* and *The Outlines of the History of Ethics for English Readers* have recently been reprinted by Hackett Publishing Co., Indianapolis, though in the case of the former, the pagination of the prefaces was changed, and references will consequently be to the Macmillan edition, unless otherwise stated.

DEP   *The Development of European Polity*, ed. Eleanor Mildred Sidgwick, 1903

ECS   *The Ethics of Conformity and Subscription*, 1870

EP   *The Elements of Politics*, 1st ed., 1891; 2d ed., 1897; 4th ed., 1919

GSM   *Lectures on the Ethics of T. H. Green, H. Spencer, and J. Martineau*, ed. E. E. Constance Jones, 1902

LPK   *Lectures on the Philosophy of Kant and Other Philosophical Lectures and Essays*, ed. James Ward, 1905

M   *Henry Sidgwick: A Memoir*, ed. Arthur Sidgwick and Eleanor Mildred Sidgwick, 1906

ME   *The Methods of Ethics*, 1st ed., 1874; 2d ed., 1877; 3d ed., 1884; 4th ed., 1890; 5th ed., 1893; 6th ed., 1901; 7th ed., 1907

MEA   *Miscellaneous Essays and Addresses*, ed. Eleanor Mildred Sidgwick and Arthur Sidgwick, 1904

OHE   *Outlines of the History of Ethics for English Readers*, 1st ed., 1886; 2d ed., 1888; 3d ed., 1892; 4th ed., 1896; 5th ed., 1902; 6th ed., enl., 1931

PE   *Practical Ethics: A Collection of Addresses and Essays*, 1st ed., 1898; 2d ed., 1909

PPE   *The Principles of Political Economy*, 1st ed., 1883; 2d ed., 1887; 3d ed., 1901

PSR   *Philosophy, Its Scope and Relations: An Introductory Course of Lectures*, ed. James Ward, 1902

A comma separates abbreviation and page number. If the reference is to an edition other than the last, the number of the edition is placed immediately after the abbreviation and before the comma. For example, "*ME*1, 7" refers to *The Methods of Ethics*, 1st ed., p. 7.

Introduction
Henry Sidgwick today

BART SCHULTZ

1. Biography and reputation

Henry Sidgwick, who was born on May 31, 1838, and died on August 28, 1900, lived his entire life within the reign of Queen Victoria and his entire adult life within the confines of Cambridge University, ultimately achieving, in 1883, the status of Knightbridge Professor of Moral Philosophy. Although he began his academic career as a classicist, by 1865 he was examining in philosophy and by 1867 teaching it; in the seventies he added political philosophy and political economy, and in the eighties law and legislation.

His career at Cambridge, where he was also educated – in significant measure through his membership in the discussion group the Apostles – suffered only one interruption, and this in 1869, when he resigned his fellowship because he could no longer in good conscience subscribe to the Thirty-nine Articles of the Church of England as required. Such was Sidgwick's stature with his colleagues that his resignation was promptly met with the creation of a special position, one that did not require subscription, and thus his career continued apace, as did his tireless work in university politics and reform. In 1876 he married Eleanor Mildred ("Nora") Balfour, with whom he collaborated in a number of areas, but especially on psychical research and women's education. Henry was a founder and the first president of the Society for Psychical Research, and with Nora engaged in numerous investigations of mediums, psychics, ghosts, and so forth – his "ghostological studies." And together they helped found Newnham College (Cambridge's first college for women), of which Nora became the second principal. In university reform generally, he advocated such things as an increased emphasis on the sciences and modern literature and less emphasis on classics, as well as greater independence for philosophy and less reliance on lecturing, which he thought a relic from the days before printing.

Once, in a characteristic fit of despair over his writing, he remarked: "Still man must work – and a Professor must write books" (*M*, 481).

This he did, publishing during his lifetime *The Methods of Ethics* (1874), *The Principles of Political Economy* (1883), *Outlines of the History of Ethics for English Readers* (1886), *The Elements of Politics* (1891), and a collection of essays entitled *Practical Ethics* (1898), as well as countless reviews and essays ranging across endlessly diverse topics – Shakespeare, the poetry and prose of A. H. Clough, classical education, religious conformity, hallucinations, luxury, the trial scene in the *Iliad*, Tennyson, bimetallism, and Tocqueville, along with those previously mentioned and many more. Significantly, he published as a pamphlet his *Ethics of Conformity and Subscription* (1870), which gave the philosophical rationale behind his resignation from his lectureship.[1] Posthumously published were his *Philosophy, Its Scope and Relations: An Introductory Course of Lectures* (1902), *Lectures on the Ethics of T. H. Green, H. Spencer, and J. Martineau* (1902), *The Development of European Polity* (1903), *Miscellaneous Essays and Addresses* (1904), and *Lectures on the Philosophy of Kant and Other Philosophical Lectures and Essays* (1905). Sidgwick's *Memoir* (1906), compiled by his widow and brother, is composed mostly of extracts from his letters and journal.

His work, his character, and his life all testify to the accuracy of some lines that he borrowed for his self-assessment:

Though without much fame, he had no envy. But he had a strong realism. He saw what it is considered cynical to see – the absurdities of many persons, the pomposities of many creeds, the splendid zeal with which missionaries rush on to teach what they do not know, the wonderful earnestness with which most incomplete solutions of the universe are thrust upon us as complete and satisfying. (*M*, 395)

Indeed, his character, which by all accounts was luminously fair and impartial, may have been his finest accomplishment, leading Brand Blanshard to write that Sidgwick was the nearest thing he knew to a "fully reasonable temper."[2] Arthur Balfour, his brother-in-law, wrote of him: "Of all the men I have known he was the readiest to consider every controversy and every controversialist on their merits. He never claimed authority; he never sought to impose his views; he never argued for victory; he never evaded an issue." Balfour adds: "Whether these are the qualities which best fit their possessor to found a 'school' may well be doubted" (*M*, 311). And as W. R. Sorley wrote, "his teaching was a training in the philosophical temper – in candor, self-criticism, and regard for truth."[3] He was, in sum, a philosopher notable for his sanity rather than his lunacy, his good will rather than his cantankerousness. Whether or not such a temper is paradigmatically philosophical, it has certainly always been a rare enough thing.

At this date, now within a decade of the centenary of his death, it is still safe to say that of all the great nineteenth-century utilitarians Sidgwick has suffered the most neglect. Although recent decades have seen some excellent studies of his ethical philosophy – the *Monist* symposium of 1974 and, most importantly, J. B. Schneewind's masterly *Sidgwick's Ethics and Victorian Moral Philosophy*[4] – the secondary literature on Sidgwick is quite sparse compared to that on Bentham and John Stuart Mill. And this is especially true of work on other aspects of Sidgwick's thought than the ethical philosophy embodied in his undisputed masterpiece, *The Methods of Ethics* (first published in 1874, seventh and last edition in 1907), for example, his views on the history of ethics, on political theory and political economy, on the scope and method of philosophy, and on the social sciences, not to mention his literary criticism, practical ethics and politics, theory of education, studies of Kant, and so on.

Thus, the object of this collection is not only to press forward with serious work on Sidgwick's ethical theory, coming to grips with Schneewind's work, the further development of Sidgwickian themes by John Rawls and Derek Parfit, and the continuing influence of *The Methods of Ethics* on the utilitarian program, but also to extend the scope of Sidgwick studies to get a better sense of his thought as a whole. Consequently, although the preponderance of the essays collected here are concerned with Sidgwick's ethics – and justifiably so, given the enduring value of his work on the subject – this volume also attempts a broader, indeed, more interdisciplinary, approach. In particular, it reflects a recognition of the importance of Sidgwick as a historian of ethics and classicist (see, especially, the essays by William Frankena, Marcus Singer, and T. H. Irwin) and as a political theorist and practical reformer (see the essays by Alan Donagan, Stefan Collini, and James Kloppenberg). To be sure, much remains to be done. Recovering the importance even of Sidgwick's second-most-important book, *The Elements of Politics* (1891), for his thought and times – it was required reading for the Cambridge political science exam through the late 1920s, Sidgwick being regarded as one of the masters of political science (not that one would have any inkling of this today) – is no small task and, indeed, has scarcely been broached, with the exception of the seminal work of Stefan Collini and James Kloppenberg.[5] And much the same could be said for most of Sidgwick's work, which recent decades have treated with a neglect that is baffling given Sidgwick's prominence during his lifetime, his importance as a scholar and academic discipline builder, and the degree to which his works continue to repay the effort (though the often dry and always undogmatic nature of his work undoubtedly explains something). This collection of essays will have achieved its purpose if it makes at least some progress in demonstrating the historical importance and continuing relevance of Sidgwick's work in these other areas, along with his profound accomplishments as an ethical theorist.

In the remainder of this introduction, I shall sketch some of the predominant themes of Sidgwick's work and its historical context and significance, explaining their bearing on the essays in this volume in particular and recent philosophical work in general. In doing this, I shall move back and forth across Richard Rorty's genres of rational reconstruction, historical reconstruction, and *Geistesgeschichte*, while trying not to lapse into doxography. But perhaps it should be stressed at the outset that this volume reflects the belief that it is important to understand philosophical works in their historical context, even if, as Schneewind remarks of *The Methods of Ethics*, the work is "the prototype of the modern treatment of moral philosophy" and "so modern in tone and content, and so lucid in style, that it has not seemed to call for any historical or exegetical study."[6] Indeed, Schneewind's book succeeds brilliantly in setting out the mid-Victorian filiations of Sidgwick's ethical work, and the article reprinted here (Chapter 2) encapsulates some of the crucial themes of his larger study.[7] And many of the pieces in the present volume, especially those by Singer, Donagan, Frankena, Irwin, Collini, and Kloppenberg, further develop the story. The others, those by J. L. Mackie, David Brink, Thomas Christiano, Nicholas White, John Deigh, and Russell Hardin, aim primarily at rational reconstruction, though they also frequently engage in historical reconstruction. The rather daunting job of *Geistesgeschichte* – canon building, history with a moral – may fall mainly to this introduction.

2. Moral theory: preliminaries

The following incident relative to Professor Sidgwick's own view of his work is told me by Mr. Oscar Browning.

Sidgwick had just completed his "Methods of Ethics." There lay the manuscript, accepted by Messrs. Macmillan. The author looking upon it said to Mr. Browning: "I have long wished and intended to write a work on Ethics. Now it is written. I have adhered to the plan I laid out for myself; its first word was to be 'Ethics,' its last word 'Failure.' "

The word "Failure" disappeared from the second and succeeding editions, but I doubt whether Sidgwick ever acquired a faith in the possibility of a perfectly satisfactory ethical system.

F. H. Hayward

That was what was so remarkable in Henry Sidgwick – the perpetual hopefulness of his inquiry. He always seemed to expect that some new turn of argument, some new phase of thought, might arise and put a new aspect upon the intellectual scenery, or give a new weight in the balance of argument. There was in him an extraordinary belief in *following reason* – a belief and a hopefulness which continued up to the last.

Canon Gore

Let me begin, in this and the next two sections, by giving a broad exegetical overview of Sidgwick's ethical position, with special reference to the interpretations of Schneewind, whose work is virtually canonical on many points, and of Rawls, whose appeal to Sidgwick has been influential, though controversial. Perhaps I should add that given the subtlety of Sidgwick's work, and the way in which he drew inspiration from a diversity of sources – Mill and Butler, Aristotle and Kant – it is often easy to sympathize with F. H. Hayward's somewhat exasperated comment that the "point upon which I would mainly insist is not that Sidgwick should be classified as this or that, but that it is extremely difficult to classify him at all."[8]

In his preface to the Hackett edition of the *The Methods of Ethics*, Rawls maintains that the book represents a twofold achievement. First, it is "the clearest and most accessible formulation" of classical utilitarianism, Sidgwick being "more aware than other classical authors of the many difficulties this doctrine faces" and attempting "to deal with them in a consistent and thorough way while never departing from the strict doctrine, as, for example, did J. S. Mill" (*ME*, Hackett ed., v). Second, the book is "the first truly academic work in moral philosophy which undertakes to provide a systematic comparative study of moral conceptions, starting with those which historically and by present assessment are the most significant," and Sidgwick's "originality consists in his conception of moral philosophy and of the way in which a reasoned and satisfactory justification of any particular moral conception must proceed from a full knowledge and systematic comparison of the more significant moral conceptions in the philosophical tradition" (*ME*, Hackett ed., v).

The connection between these two achievements might seem somewhat problematic, since the supposedly neutral and impartial position of the second could undercut any defense of a particular position such as utilitarianism. But as Schneewind, especially, has insisted, it is in fact "a mistake to view the book as primarily a defense of utilitarianism." In *The Methods of Ethics*, Sidgwick does work out a way of supporting utilitarianism and at times indicates that it is the best alternative, and it is clear from his other works that he was a utilitarian, but "it does not follow that the *Methods* itself should be taken simply as an argument for utilitarianism."[9] As Schneewind demonstrates in the essay reprinted herein, the book is in various respects a departure from classical utilitarianism, since it "centers on an examination of the accepted moral opinions and modes of thought of common sense," rejects empiricism and "dismisses the issue of determinism as irrelevant," tries to reconcile

utilitarianism with its traditional opponents, finds ethical egoism to be
equally reasonable, and winds up arguing that, "because of this, no full
reconciliation of the various rational methods for reaching moral decisions is possible and therefore that the realm of practical reason is
probably incoherent."

As Schneewind goes on to argue, and as Singer also demonstrates in
his erudite contribution to the present volume, Sidgwick shared a number of the assumptions and concerns of the philosophers whom he was
most concerned to criticize – namely, the Cambridge moralists, figures
such as F. D. Maurice, William Whewell, and John Grote, who represented the intuitionist alternative to utilitarianism, an alternative that,
with Whewell in particular, involved a straitlaced endorsement of such
traditional principles of duty as veracity, promise keeping, justice, and
so on. Indeed, Sidgwick was an intuitionist, at least of a certain type,[10]
and like the Cambridge moralists, he was, at least in part, examining
morality in the hope of finding some support in it for religious views,
for a belief in progress and moral freedom and insight that might call
for a religious, preferably Christian, interpretation. This he did not find.
In fact, on his analysis, the direction of moral development would seem
to be positively at odds with a Christian interpretation, more utilitarian
and less intentionalist, less concerned with the rightness of a "man's
heart before God." In consequence it is not inaccurate to view *The
Methods of Ethics* as containing "the negative results of a theological
investigation" (Schneewind, Chapter 2, herein).

However, as all of these commentators emphasize, Sidgwick's investigation was anything but a piece of failed special pleading, theological
or utilitarian. A fundamental point for Sidgwick, and one that is perhaps
especially understandable in light of the tardy separation of philosophy
and religion in the Cambridge curriculum and English academics generally, is "to put aside temporarily the urgent need which we all feel of
finding and adopting the true method of determining what we ought to
do; and to consider simply what conclusions will be reached if we start
with certain ethical premises, and with what degree of certainty and
precision" (*ME*, v). Sidgwick believed that the desire to edify had
"impeded the real progress of ethical science," which would benefit
from "the same disinterested curiosity to which we chiefly owe the great
discoveries of physics" (*ME*, vi), and he repeatedly stressed that the
reader should focus less on practical conclusions and more on the methods themselves. His object was "to expound as clearly and fully as my
limits will allow the different methods of Ethics that I find implicit in
our common moral reasoning; to point out their mutual relations; and
where they seem to conflict, to define the issue as much as possible."

That is, the book is "an examination, at once expository and critical, of the different methods of obtaining reasoned convictions as to what ought to be done which are to be found – either explicit or implicit – in the moral consciousness of mankind generally: and which, from time to time, have been developed, either singly or in combination, by individual thinkers, and worked up into systems now historical" (*ME*, v).

Schneewind and Rawls are surely correct in holding that this is what gives Sidgwick's work much of its modern tone. Indeed, despite the intuitionism at work in Sidgwick's approach, he and Rawls have much in common on this score, especially since the tasks of clarification and systematic comparison form an important part of Rawls's method. As Rawls explains in "Kantian Constructivism in Moral Theory," Sidgwick's "originality lies in his conception and mode of presentation of the subject and in his recognition of the significance of moral theory for moral philosophy."[11] "Moral theory," for Rawls, refers especially to substantive moral theory, as opposed to a metaethical concern with questions of moral language and justification, which he calls moral philosophy. As he observes in "The Independence of Moral Theory," it is "the study of how the basic notions of the right, the good, and moral worth may be arranged to form different moral structures," and it "tries to identify the chief similarities and differences between these structures and to characterize the way in which they are related to our moral sensibilities and natural attitudes, and to determine the conditions they must satisfy if they are to play their expected role in human life."[12] In such works as "Kantian Constructivism," and "The Independence of Moral Theory," Rawls has stressed the need to develop substantive moral theories in sufficient detail, and in systematic comparison with the alternatives, as a necessary preliminary to progress on metaethical problems; this endeavor, he urges, can be largely pursued independently of such areas as metaphysics, epistemology, and philosophy of language, which may well require progress in moral theory for their own advance. In this respect, Sidgwick and Rawls share, to a very considerable extent, a belief in the autonomy or independence of ethical theory from other parts of philosophy (and of course theology), as a field capable of progress on its own, a field in need of systematic theorizing.[13]

Sidgwick's construction of ethical theory on an independent basis, with non-ethical commitments – for example, theological or metaphysical – kept to a minimum, is evident in a number of areas.[14] He is not much concerned with the origin of the moral faculty or the object of moral knowledge, and he holds (against the Cambridge moralists) that the issue of free will versus determinism is largely irrelevant to moral issues. Perhaps most importantly, he maintains (with most of the Cam-

bridge moralists) that the basic concept of morality is unique and irreducible to any descriptive propositions derived from other disciplines.
Morality is sui generis; it is a fundamental mistake to try to derive
"ought" from "is."[15]

Indeed, according to Sidgwick, there is an absolutely simple, fundamental notion common to such ideas as "right" and "ought," one which
"is too elementary to admit of any formal definition" (*ME*, 32). This
notion is distinct from factual or descriptive notions, simple and un-
definable, and yet precisely the thing that makes the propositions in
which it figures a matter for rational consideration. Though the basic
notion cannot be reduced to any simpler notion, it can be "exhibited"
in various ways, by setting out its relations to other notions. As Schneewind puts it, the basic notion is, "roughly, the notion of a demand made
by reason on action, or, more generally, the notion of a requirement
which our own rationality presents to our desires and volitions."[16] Thus
"right" acts are objectively so, not because such acts have some sort of
property but precisely because right acts are rational – they simply are
what we have most reason to do. Reason, on Sidgwick's view, is certainly
not inert. And as John Deigh shows in his careful analysis and critique
of the introspective and common-sense method by which Sidgwick arrives at this view, Sidgwick holds that we are all familiar with this basic
notion, if only from the experience of goading ourselves to be rational
in pursuing our own greatest (individual) good.

This side of Sidgwick's view certainly struck a number of his contemporary critical commentators as one of the things that set him apart
from the earlier utilitarians and as perhaps a result of his (at the time
unusual) fluency in German philosophy. Thus, in his response to the
criticisms of Sidgwick's student, E. E. Constance Jones, Hayward maintained (with some hyperbole) that

Sidgwick's identification of "Right" with "Reasonable" and "Objective"; his
view of Rightness as an "ultimate and unanalysable notion" (however connected
subsequently with Hedonism); and his admission that Reason is, in a sense, a
motive to the will, are due to the more or less "unconscious" influence of Kant.
Miss Jones appears to think that these are the common-places of every ethical
system, and that real divergences only arise when we make the next step in
advance. I should rather regard this Rationalistic terminology as somewhat
foreign to Hedonism. I do not think that Miss Jones will find, in Sidgwick's
Hedonistic predecessors, any such emphasis on Reason (however interpreted).[17]

A fuller sense of Sidgwick's basic notion can be gained by considering
it in relation to the concept of ultimate goodness, a tangled area that
has exercised many of the contributors to this volume.[18] Roughly put,

for Sidgwick, the same basic notion, as involving a requirement of rationality, figures in both rightness and goodness, though the former has to do with our active powers and the latter with the sentient side of our nature. Sidgwick wants to resist definitions of the good that simply reduce it to pleasure or desire; goodness is a comparative notion, not some quantum of pleasure, and at any rate it should be significant, not merely tautological, to say for example that pleasure (or, as Sidgwick eventually wants to claim, desirable consciousness) is the good. Ultimately, Sidgwick maintains that good "is what it is reasonable to seek to keep, or aim at getting; and Evil is what it is reasonable to seek to get rid of or avoid" (*GSM*, 331), and, more specifically, that ultimate good on the whole is "what one would desire if one's desires were in harmony with reason and one took oneself to have an equal concern for all existence" (*ME*, 112), though he allows that this a bit too baroque to advance as a piece of ordinary usage. Because judgments of good are comparative, they do not involve, as judgments of right do, a definite categorical dictate to do this or that or, as with "right," the suggestion that we are capable of this or that. Judgments of right decree that we do, and can do, the acts judged right. Right conduct, indeed, is the best conduct that is in our power. But conduct can have a certain goodness even if it is not right. Thus, in "the recognition of conduct as 'right' is involved an authoritative prescription to do it: but when we have judged conduct to be good, it is not yet clear that we ought to prefer this kind of good to all other good things: some standard for estimating the relative value of different 'goods' has still to be sought" (*ME*, 106). However, as one approximates what is genuinely ultimately good on the whole, the rational dictate to aim at it grows, melding, insofar as action is a possibility, into the notion of right. Schneewind provides a good summary:

The concepts of goodness and rightness then represent differentiations of the demands of our own rationality as it applies to our sentient and our active powers. Seeing this helps give us a better understanding of what Sidgwick takes the basic indefinable notion of practical rationality to be. It is what is common to the notions of a reason to desire, a reason to seek or aim at, a reason to decide or choose, a reason to do; it does not involve an authoritative prescription to act where there is barely reason to desire something, or even where there is fairly strong reason, but only where there is stronger reason to desire one thing than to desire anything else, and that one thing is within our powers. At this point it becomes the through-and-through "ought" or "right" of definite dictates claiming to give authoritative guidance to our conduct. If any "metaethical" answer to the question of the nature of the object of moral judgements is implicit in Sidgwick's position, it is that moral judgements embody the fact that we are reasonable beings who feel and act. In judging what is right or good, we are following out the implications of our rationality for the practical aspects of our nature.[19]

Thus, sometimes moral notions involve the constraints of reason on the active side of human nature, and sometimes they involve constraints of reason on the sentient or feeling side of human nature. But again, in either case there is, according to Sidgwick, no question that it is, at least prima facie, a plain, unvarnished demand of reason that is at stake, a reason to do or aim at something; ordinary language demonstrates the absurdity of supposing that two flatly contradictory moral judgments made by different persons could both be true, as they could be if they were merely matters of feeling, expressions of emotion, and so on.

As remarked, Sidgwick's account of ultimate good is scrutinized by many of the contributors to this volume. Thomas Christiano, in his challenging contribution, grapples with the problems posed by Sidgwick's strictures on ultimate good and by his arguments that in fact the best (though still highly problematic) candidate for ultimate good is a hedonistic one – namely, happiness, conceived as "Consciousness on the whole desirable" (*ME*, 397). Christiano's rational reconstruction of Sidgwick's arguments carefully plays down the intuitionist elements in Sidgwick's account. Relatedly, William Frankena, in his masterly essay, sheds further light on the question by considering how Sidgwick uses the notion of the good in distinguishing between modern and classical ethics. Sidgwick, broadly in line with many historical accounts of the development of ethical theory, held that modern ethics had been primarily inclined to take the (more jural) notion of right as fundamental, whereas classical thought focused primarily on a somewhat undifferentiated notion of the good, with important exceptions such as the Stoics, whom Sidgwick viewed as transitional to Christian ethics and on whom, along with the Sophists, he did some of his best historical work. T. H. Irwin's essay and Nicholas White's also insightfully bring out how Sidgwick's intuitionistic views on ultimate good, and his hedonistic interpretation of it, affected his view of moral theory and his construal (and in large part, dismissal) of classical thought.[20] Sidgwick's treatment of perfectionism, of Aristotelian virtue ethics, a view that he thought all too easily lapsed into vacuity and circularity, was also carefully (though sympathetically) scrutinized in two extremely important earlier articles by Frankena: "Sidgwick and the Dualism of Practical Reason" and "Concepts of Rational Action in the History of Ethics," which are complementary pieces to his essay in this volume.[21] Frankena, too, had noted, in an early piece, the authoritative element in Sidgwick's account of "good" and argued that this would seem to mean that the good cannot be wholly reduced to a naturalistic definition in terms of the facts, actual or hypothetical, about desire.[22]

As Schneewind pithily remarks, on Sidgwick's way of doing moral philosophy "we are concerned with what it is reasonable to desire, to seek, and to do." However, it seems that Sidgwick does not actually have too much to say in this connection about how reason can be practical or, for that matter, about reason as such, though he obviously supposes that it involves both noninferential and inferential components, moves at higher levels of generality, and so on. Thus, "what little he says," Schneewind states, "he puts in commonplace terms." Calling moral judgments "dictates of reason" does not mean that they are "given by 'the dictation of reason' or obtained by conscious reasoning . . . but only that they bear the characteristic marks of judgments which are subject to rational support and critique. They can be contradicted, their truth or falsity is objective in the sense that what any one person thinks, if he thinks correctly, cannot be denied without error by others, and reasons for and against them can be given."[23]

It is striking, as Schneewind continues, with what easy assurance Sidgwick supposed that moral judgments can be fully rational. "Such confident rationalism seems to belong to the Victorian age, which, however troubled it may have been with religious doubt, does not appear to have been nearly as troubled as later periods by various forms of doubt about the reasonableness of morality."[24] In fact, as we shall see, it is arguable that the results of Sidgwick's inquiry contributed to the doubts of later periods to no small degree. Further reflections on the differences between Sidgwick and his more skeptical successors are given in John Deigh's article, which contains a wide-ranging, critical discussion of Sidgwick's view of practical reason and judgment as matters of objective truth, a discussion that certainly bears on the problems involved in judgments of both right and good.

Whatever weaknesses or obscurities may attend Sidgwick's notion of reason, it is fundamental to his work. As Schneewind states, "the central thought of the *Methods of Ethics* is that morality is the embodiment of the demands reason makes on practice under the conditions of human life, and that the problems of philosophical ethics are the problems of showing how practical reason is articulated into these demands."[25]

In line with the independence of moral theory, Sidgwick hoped that this account of ethical terms would be more or less neutral between different moral conceptions and would not prejudge the choice between them. The account of goodness in terms of intrinsic desirability, without requiring any specific, actual desire, and the account of rightness as involving a rational directive to act, without specifying any particular dictate or reason, do make the analysis at least relatively formal, since the only halfway substantive point made is that rightness involves maximizing goodness. Moreover, on his view, it does not follow that right actions necessarily maximize good consequences, as opposed to some other form of goodness; he does not suppose that definitions can say much about how goodness or rightness is determined. His account, as we shall see, is not even meant to rule out egoism as a method of ethics.[26] Thus, though Sidgwick certainly places great stress on the importance of clarifying terms, the choice between substantive moral views is not to be settled, in any truly significant way, by definitional or linguisitic considerations.

A similar vindication of the autonomy or independence of ethics can be seen in Sidgwick's focus on "methods." It is unfortunately not altogether plain just what Sidgwick means by a "method" of ethics, or what is the difference between a method and a principle. Some, such as Singer, have argued that he gives no consistent definition of a method.[27] However, Schneewind, quoting Sidgwick's statement that a method is a rational procedure for determining what it is right to do, argues that

a principle asserts that some property which acts may or may not possess is an ultimate reason for the rightness of acts. A method is a regular practice of using some property of acts as the property from whose presence or absence one infers that specific acts are or are not right. Since a principle says nothing about a procedure for reaching conclusions about the rightness of specific acts, and a method says nothing about the ultimate reason justifying the use of the property through which such conclusions are reached, each plainly requires the other.[28]

However, the relationship between a method and a principle with which Sidgwick is concerned is a direct, or logical one; the property appealed to by the method is not merely evidential or criterial but is the right-making property. Thus, if, say, the principle is that right acts are those which produce general happiness, the method must involve identifying the presence of that property, and not merely some indicator of it. On this point, and in the general concern with methods, the advantage of Sidgwick's approach is that it neutralizes many of the problems posed by factual disagreement over the specific contents of moral judgments or over general assumptions, perhaps religious, that would carry us outside of the domain of ethics. Thus, in dealing with methods, Schneewind observes, "we deal with the rational determinant of moral judgements which is, aside from the ultimate principles themselves, the most purely moral." And this consequently gives us "the best hope of finding out to what extent the distinctively moral aspect of common-sense morality can be systematized."[29]

Now, for Sidgwick (as, of course, for Rawls), the object is to study these methods not merely historically but as

alternatives between which – so far as they cannot be reconciled – the human mind seems to me necessarily forced to choose, when it attempts to frame a complete synthesis of practical maxims and to act in a perfectly consistent manner. Thus, they might perhaps be called natural methods rationalised; because men commonly seem to guide themselves by a mixture of different methods, more or less disguised under ambiguities of language. (*ME*, 12)[30]

Common-sense morality is confused, a jumble of different methods. This is consequently where much of Sidgwick's critical, synthesizing apparatus comes in; it is of a piece with the systematic comparative approach, which in Sidgwick's work involves a sort of dialectical unfolding of the phases of the civilized mind, of which his own is – with some justice – taken as a paradigm.

3. Moral theory: construction and progress

The greater part of the *The Methods of Ethics* is given over to an examination of three methods of determining right conduct: ethical egoism (that one ought to pursue one's own greatest good), "dogmatic" intuitional morality (which, as Marcus Singer sharply argues, Sidgwick somewhat ambiguously treats as broadly continuous with its looser and rougher form in common-sense morality), and universal hedonism, or utilitarianism (that one ought to pursue the greatest good for all). Very controversially, Sidgwick's rather eclectic (and admittedly tentative) account of hedonism as desirable consciousness provides the value theory common to both ethical egoism and utilitarianism, since it is only some such theory, Sidgwick holds, that shows even the faintest possibility of systematizing the vast run of human activities, ideals, and so on, into a coherent system suitable for practical reason.[31] Also very controversial is his assimilation of perfectionist or virtue ethics to the second method, which he justifies on the grounds that what is typically at issue here, insofar as there is a real issue, is moral excellence. Intuitional morality, "the view of ethics which regards as the practically ultimate end of moral actions their conformity to certain rules or dictates of Duty unconditionally prescribed [e.g., veracity, promise keeping, justice, etc.]" (*ME*, 96), which also holds that "we can discern certain general rules with really clear and finally valid intuition" (*ME*, 101), would seem mostly to cover the deontological alternatives to consequentialism, egoistic or utilitarian, though there is some confusion here precisely because of his assimilation of perfectionism, surely a teleological theory, to this method. Again, the cogent complaint that in setting out the different methods Sidgwick was blinded by his intuitionism and hedonism and was thus incapable of appreciating the nonhedonistic teleological alternative, such as Aristotle's perfectionism, is aired by the essays in Part III. (A parallel complaint, equally cogent, can be made about his treatment of Kantianism, as we shall see.)

Now, on Sidgwick's account, the intuitional method crucially involves critical reflection on common-sense morality, attempting to render it consistent in order to determine whether we even have veridical intuitions. The dogmatic intuitionist, by which Sidgwick meant someone like William Whewell (so scorned by J. S. Mill), holds that general moral rules

are implicit in the moral reasoning of ordinary men, who apprehend them adequately for most practical purposes, and are able to enunciate them roughly; but that to state them with proper precision requires a special habit of contemplating clearly and steadily abstract moral notions. It is held that the moralist's function then is to perform this process of abstract contemplation, to arrange the results as systematically as possible, and by proper definitions and explanations to remove vagueness and prevent conflict. (*ME*, 101)

Indeed, common-sense morality, Sidgwick explains, is his "own morality as much as it is any man's," and he is not attempting "mere hostile criticism from the outside" (*ME*, x). In rationalizing these methods, however, Sidgwick thought that he could demonstrate an important result: namely, that dogmatic intuitional morality – common-sense morality in a relatively cleaned-up, systematized version, as found in the Whewellian view – was in the end unsatisfactory to the philosophic mind and not really an independent method at all. Common-sense morality might seem like a reservoir of self-evident truths; many have so taken it. But, in fact, common-sense morality is somewhat vague and incomplete, only apparently a fund of such truths. Although it may be good enough to give guidance in many cases, and it is certainly important for both learning and teaching morality, as soon as the attempt is made to sharpen it, the "self-evidence" of its rules evaporates and the need to complete it by a truly exceptionless principle becomes manifest. Dogmatic intuitional morality, even in its best estate, cannot deliver the goods, cannot produce really self-evident principles. Indeed, what Whewell had tried to palm off as a system was, for Sidgwick, at bottom just an invocation of the status quo, warts intact.

In their contributions to this volume, Singer, Schneewind, and Donagan are all more or less in accord on the point that Whewell was not quite the feckless mouthpiece for things as they are that Mill and Sidgwick made him out to be but was in fact a subtle ethical theorist with a sophisticated grasp of the philosophy of science. Again, when it came to the justification of moral judgments, Sidgwick in fact shared a number of assumptions with the Cambridge moralists (though, in Donagan's view, he did not share nearly enough of them).

This is a crucial point, if a difficult one. For Sidgwick, "really self-evident" principles are those which can withstand careful reflection (that is, they derive solely from rational insight, not from our local and temporal prejudices), are clear and precise (their application must be absolutely precise), mutually consistent (with other self-evident principles anyway), and capable of eliciting agreement from all competent judges (one must, as Russell Hardin urges, take seriously the contrary views of those who should be in a position to know). Now, Sidgwick maintained that common-sense morality, when scrutinized in the light of these conditions, could be shown to be incomplete on its own, unless supplemented by the utilitarian principle (*ME*, 101). Utilitarianism can, it turns out, sustain the approximate validity of common-sense moral judgments, explaining the exceptions to them and providing a principle for working them into a complete and harmonious system. Indeed, the utilitarian method retains common sense as its starting point. Consequently, Sidgwick claimed that the common antithesis (and, as Schneewind and Singer show, it was *the* antithesis of mid-nineteenth-century English moral theory) between intuitionists and utilitarians should be discarded. The intuitional or common-sense moralities need a utilitarian foundation – in fact, common sense is inchoately or unconsciously utilitarian. What is more, "such abstract principles as we can admit to be really self-evident are not only not incompatible with a Utilitarian system, but even seem required to furnish a rational basis for such a system" (*ME*, 496).

Thus, Sidgwick does not reject all forms of intuitionism. Utilitarianism, or universal hedonism, requires a rational intuition (or a set of them) to the effect that one should act for the happiness of all. If common sense must have a utilitarian basis, utilitarianism rests on an intuitional basis, or "philosophical" intuitionism, as Sidgwick calls it. In this way, and also because of its completeness as a method, it might hope to equal the compellingness of egoistic hedonism, which Sidgwick thought frequently underestimated or sanitized by earlier utilitarians. As Sidgwick explains, the "utilitarian method – which I had learnt from Mill – could not, it seemed to me, be made coherent and harmonious without this fundamental intuition," namely, that it is rational or "right for me to sacrifice my happiness for the good of the whole of which I am a part" (*ME*, xvi).

To consider more precisely the nature of philosophical intuitionism, and the difficult issue of the relation between egoistic and universal hedonism, more should be said about the reconciliation of dogmatic intuitionism or common sense and utilitarianism, since Sidgwick regarded this as one of his most important accomplishments, and indeed, his characterization of common-sense morality is roundly regarded as superb, "the best work of the kind since Aristotle's," according to Broad.[32] Here, one of the central questions has been: What sort of synthesis has been effected, and how do the critique and reconstruction of common-sense morality add to the justification of utilitarianism, which might seem to require nothing more than its intuitively evident first principles?

Sidgwick does not suppose for a moment that it is at all easy to show that some proposition is really self-evident – mere subjective certainty is not enough. In fact, the human mind is prone to error when it designates the obvious; critical reflection is absolutely essential to the process of ascertaining such truths. But there is something of a puzzle here as to how one goes about arguing for first principles that are presumably, as such, incapable of proof. To deal with this difficulty, Sidgwick accepts Aristotle's distinction between logical priority and priority in the knowledge of a particular person – the naturally prior and the prior for us. In an important note on "The Establishment of Ethical First Principles," he urges that we "are thus enabled to see that a proposition may be self-evident, i.e., may be properly cognisable without being viewed in connexion with any other propositions; though in order that its truth may be apparent to some particular mind, there is still required some rational process connecting it with propositions previously accepted by that mind." He argues that there are only two ways of doing this: by showing how "some limited and qualified statement" that is taken as self-evident is actually only part of a "simpler and wider proposition," on which the limitations turn out to be arbitrary, and by establishing some general criteria "for distinguishing true first principles . . . from false ones," which are then used to "construct a strictly logical deduction by which, applying their general criteria to the special case of ethics, we establish the true first principles of this latter subject."[33]

This is a considerable part of what he does in *The Methods of Ethics*. But it raises the question, posed by Sidgwick's contemporary, Henry Calderwood, as to why he should not have confined himself "to the consideration of Intuitionism in its most philosophical form," to which Sidgwick answers:

> But this would have led me at once to Utilitarianism: because I hold that the only moral intuitions which sound philosophy can accept as ultimately valid are those which at the same time provide the only possible philosophical basis of the Utilitarian creed. I thus necessarily regard Prof. Calderwood's Intuitionism as a phase in the development of the Intuitional method, which comes naturally between the crude thought of Butler's "plain man" and the Rational Utilitarianism to which I ultimately endeavor to lead my reader.[34]

In familiar fashion, Sidgwick explains that his object in *The Methods of Ethics* was not sectarian; his "endeavor was rather to unfold a method of reaching practical decisions which I find (more or less implicit) in the ordinary thought of the society of which I am a part, and to some extent in the natural processes of my own mind; and after tracing its different phases, to estimate carefully their scientific value." Thus, he begins by "taking the notions which I have to use as I find them in common thought as expressed in common language; and I let them become gradually more definite, as my discussion brings into view distinctions in the general objects which they represent." If we start with the plain man, it is tolerably clear, for Sidgwick, that the plain man's idea of moral intuition "does not exclude either universal abstract intuitions or particular concrete intuitions: but of the two, I think, he more often means the latter." This idea, of intuiting the rightness or wrongness of particular acts, is what Sidgwick calls "aesthetic intuitionism," and he dismisses it as plainly inadequate: "I have no doubt that reflective persons, in proportion to their reflectiveness, come to rely rather on abstract universal intuitions relating to classes of cases conceived under general notions; and I prefer the moral thought of the reflective few to that of the unreflective many."[35]

Calderwood is apparently among the reflective few, but he is not quite reflective enough, being, on Sidgwick's account, one of the dogmatic intuitionists. Now, to decide the issue between the dogmatic intuitionist and the utilitarian, Sidgwick remarks, the rigorously applied Cartesian test (of clarity and precision) would be enough to settle the matter on the utilitarian side, *if* he "could trust his own moral faculty alone." Thus,

> If I ask myself whether I see clearly and distinctly the self-evidence of any particular maxims of duty, as I see that of the formal principles "that what is right for me must be right for all persons in precisely similar circumstances" and "that I ought to prefer the greater good of another to my own lesser good": I have no doubt whatever that I do not. I am conscious of a strong impression,

an opinion on which I habitually act without hesitation, that I ought to speak truth, to perform promises, to requite benefits, &c., and also of powerful moral sentiments prompting me to the observance of these rules; but on reflection I can now clearly distinguish such opinions and sentiments from the apparently immediate and certain cognition that I have of the formal principles above mentioned. But I could not always have made this distinction; and I believe that the majority of moral persons do not make it: most "plain men" would probably say, at any rate on the first consideration of the matter, that they saw the obligations of Veracity and Good Faith as clearly and immediately as they saw those of Equity and Rational Benevolence. How then am I to argue with such persons? It will not settle the matter to tell them that they have observed their own mental processes wrongly, and that more careful introspection will show them the non-intuitive character of what they took for intuitions; especially as in many cases I do not believe that the error is one of misobservation. Still less am I inclined to dispute the "primitiveness" or "spontaneousness" or "originality" of these apparent intuitions. On the contrary, I hold that here, as in other departments of thought, the primitive spontaneous processes of the mind are mixed with error, which is only to be removed gradually by comprehensive reflection upon the results of these processes. Through such a course of reflection I have endeavored to lead my readers in chaps. 2–10 of Book III of my treatise: in the hope that after they have gone through it they may find their original apprehension of the self-evidence of moral maxims importantly modified.[36]

As these remarks illustrate, for Sidgwick, utilitarianism ultimately issues from a set of self-evident principles, as a base, along with common-sense morality. As Rawls has put it, Sidgwick typically viewed classical utilitarianism "as following from three principles each self-evident in its own right," namely, the principles of equity (two persons should not be treated differently merely because they are different persons), rational prudence (mere temporal difference should not matter in considering one's good), and rational benevolence (the good of one person is no more important than the good of another). From these three principles, "when combined with the principle that, as reasonable beings, we are bound to aim at good generally and not at any particular part of it," the principle of utility followed.[37]

However, the crucial point here is that these principles are, Sidgwick believes, on a different plane from those of common sense, though both the plain man and the dogmatic intuitionist have yet to realize it. Indeed, such are the perils of subjective certainty that, prior to his reflection on the matter, Sidgwick himself had not been able to discern the difference between these principles and those of common-sense morality. Having achieved greater insight into the matter, he hopes naturally enough, in reporting his findings, to lead his readers through a similar course of reflection and to similar conclusions. Thus, to illustrate, in *The Methods of Ethics*, Sidgwick argues that the

Utilitarian must, in the first place, endeavor to show to the Intuitionist that the principles of Truth, Justice, etc. have only a dependent and subordinate validity: arguing either that the principle is really only affirmed by Common-Sense as a general rule admitting of exceptions and qualifications, as in the case of Truth, and that we require some further principle for systematising these exceptions and qualifications; or that the fundamental notion is vague and needs further determination, as in the case of Justice; and further, that the different rules are liable to conflict with each other, and that we require some higher principle to decide the issue thus raised; and again, that the rules are differently formulated by different persons, and that these differences admit of no Intuitional solution, while they show the vagueness and ambiguity of the common moral notions to which the Intuitionist appeals. (*ME*, 421)

And Sidgwick wants to show

how Utilitarianism sustains the general validity of the current moral judgements, and thus supplements the defects which reflection finds in the intuitive recognition of their stringency; and at the same time affords a principle of synthesis, and a method for binding the unconnected and occasionally conflicting principles of common moral reasoning into a complete and harmonious system. If systematic reflection on the morality of Common Sense thus exhibits the Utilitarian principle as that to which Common Sense naturally appeals for that further development of its system which this same reflection shows to be necessary, the proof of Utilitarianism seems as complete as it can be made. (*ME*, 422)

Of course, the other side of Sidgwick's suggestion that common-sense morality is "a system of rules tending to the promotion of the general happiness" is that utilitarianism needs common-sense morality for guidance, "on the ground of the general presumption which evolution afforded that moral sentiments and opinions would point to conduct conducive to general happiness" (*ME*, xxi). In fact, Sidgwick holds, "no one doubts that it is, *generally speaking*, conducive to the common happiness that men should be veracious, faithful to promises, obedient to law, disposed to satisfy the normal expectations of others, having their malevolent impulses and their sensual appetites under strict control" (*ME*, 485). But, although Sidgwick is tempted by the view that "the apparent first principles of Common Sense may be accepted as the 'middle axioms' of Utilitarian method; direct reference being only made to utilitarian considerations, in order to settle points upon which the verdict of Common Sense is found to be obscure and conflicting" (*ME*, 461), he is cautious, recognizing that "it is one thing to hold that the current morality expresses, partly consciously but to a large extent unconsciously, the results of human experience as to the effects of actions: it is quite another thing to accept this morality en bloc, so far as it is clear and definite, as the best guidance we can get to the attainment of maximum general happiness" (*ME*, 463). Partly for reasons deriving from Adam Smith's account of the moral sentiments (which Sidgwick admires but thinks overestimates somewhat the role of sympathy), the ordinary moral consciousness, reflecting a balance between direct sympathy with the agent and indirect sympathy with those acted upon, may "easily be many degrees removed from the rule which Utilitarianism would prescribe" (*ME*, 463). Thus, although Sidgwick's view has much in common with the explanatory or contemplative utilitarianism of Hume and Smith, care must be taken not to overestimate the similarity of their conclusions. Certainly, although he allowed that utilitarianism must often work in an indirect fashion – that it is *not* always utilitarian to appeal directly to utility, as a conscious decision procedure in daily life, but necessary also to, say, cultivate certain beliefs and habits that do not directly appeal to utility – he did not go as far as Smith often did in thinking that human moral psychology (perhaps with divine aid) would yield norms happily coinciding with utility.[38]

However, against the notion that a systematic utilitarian could make a complete revision of common-sense rules to bring them into line with a perfectly utilitarian code, as urged by Bentham and James Mill, Sidgwick argues that "humanity is not something that exhibits the same properties always and everywhere: whether we consider the intellect of man or his feelings, or his physical condition and circumstances, we find them so different in different ages and countries, that it seems prima facie absurd to lay down a set of ideal Utilitarian rules for mankind generally" (*ME*, 467–8). Indeed, Sidgwick is so struck by the necessity of taking into account the particularities, the moral habits, impulses, tastes, and so on, of people as they are, that he denies that the utilitarian could, given existing knowledge,

possibly construct a morality de novo either for man as he is (abstracting his morality), or for man as he ought to be and will be. He must start, speaking broadly, with the existing social order, and the existing morality as a part of that order: and in deciding the question whether any divergence from this code is to be recommended, must consider chiefly the immediate consequences of such divergence, upon a society in which such a code is conceived generally to subsist. (*ME*, 473–4)

Given these (rather Hayekian) limits on utilitarian reason, the utilitarian, "if he keeps within the limits that separate scientific prevision from Utopian conjecture, the form of society to which his practical conclusions relate will be one varying but little from the actual, with its actually established code of moral rules and customary judgements regarding virtue and vice" (*ME*, 474). Russell Hardin, in his challenging essay, picks up this theme and offers what is essentially a contemporary version of a Sidgwickian account of what a usable method of moral reasoning must look like and of how the method involved in common-sense reasoning may be rational (and utilitarian) to a degree, though tightly bound to time and place.

Thus, rather ironically, Sidgwick the utilitarian critic of Whewell does ultimately endorse a conservative attitude toward common sense: "Adhere generally, deviate and attempt reform only in exceptional cases in which, – notwithstanding the roughness of hedonistic method, – the argument against Common Sense is decisive" (*ME*, xx). Still, even on this view, the basic utilitarian principle, as befits a comprehensive moral conception, is meant to be applied at least in some fashion across the board to all departments of moral and political practice – indeed, "one who values conduct in proportion to its felicific consequences, will naturally set a higher estimate on effective beneficence in public affairs than on the purest manifestation of virtue in the details of private life. . . . A sincere Utilitarian, therefore, is likely to be an eager politician" (*ME*, 495). In their contributions to this volume, Collini and Kloppenberg provocatively consider the ways in which Sidgwick's philosophical views translated into moral and political reform, or the lack thereof, with Collini stressing the inherently conservative nature of Sidgwick's approach (ultimately, he became "an Independent with Tory sympathies") and Kloppenberg suggesting its potential affinities with the pragmatist reformism of James and Dewey. Certainly, as the foregoing should suggest, and as Collini emphasizes, in Sidgwick's hands utilitarianism was far removed from its Benthamite roots in radical reform. The more conservative nature of Sidgwick's ethical and political theory, as it was developed not only in *The Methods of Ethics* but also (and quite importantly) in *The Elements of Politics*, was immortalized in a review of the latter work by David G. Ritchie, who observed that Sidgwick

nowhere arrives at any conclusion which would differ very widely from that of the average man of the professional and commercial middle-class at the present day. The method is Bentham's; but there is none of Bentham's strong critical antagonism to the institutions of his time, and the mode of thought is much more what we might expect from an end-of-the-nineteenth-century Blackstone, or from an English Hegel, showing the rationality of the existing order of things, with only a few modest proposals of reform. If this is Benthamism, it is Benthamism grown tame and sleek.[39]

Sidgwick of course allowed, in *The Elements of Politics*, that he was simply setting forth "in a systematic manner the general notions and principles which we use in ordinary political reasonings," which, as in his ethical work, he took to be fundamentally utilitarian (*EP*, 7). Thus, he held that he could claim "general – if not universal – assent for the principle that the true standard and criterion by which right legislation is to be distinguished from wrong is conduciveness to the general 'good' or 'welfare,' " where this meant "the happiness of the individual human beings who compose the community; provided that we take into account not only the human beings who are actually living but those who are to live hereafter" (*EP*, 38). The catch, naturally, was that, even when "we have agreed to take general happiness as the ultimate end, the most important part of our work still remains to be done: we have to establish or assume some subordinate principle or principles, capable of more precise application, relating to the best means for attaining by legislation the end of Maximum Happiness" (*EP*, 40) – principles of which English political experience offered a fund.[40] Sidgwick's utilitarianism, as Singer, Collini, and Kloppenberg show, was not about to resignedly meet its end because of the late nineteenth century's obsession with evolution and the progress of history, since in Sidgwick's view history and utilitarianism could work in harness. If history showed that different times and places were really quite different, then that was all the more reason why utilitarianism, in ethics and politics (and economics), was right to begin with the here and now.

But before we further explore the political implications of Sidgwick's theory and the question of his nascent pragmatism, more should be said about how it is precisely this view – that the principles of common-sense morality (and common-sense politics), duly clarified, round out and make concrete the utilitarian principle, and that the utilitarian principle provides a critical standard for common-sense morality – that marks out Sidgwick's position as an advance within the classical utilitarian tradition in its dialogue with intuitionism. Again, as Schneewind has argued both in the essay reprinted herein and in *Sidgwick's Ethics and Victorian Moral Philosophy*, the attempt to synthesize these two methods directly addresses the ethical controversies of Sidgwick's day: "common-sense morality had come by the middle of the 1860s to occupy a central place in the ethical controversies between the 'two schools' [intuitionist and utilitarian] of the early Victorian era. Both agreed in accepting it as valid and binding, at least to some extent and on some basis." And furthermore, Sidgwick's "methodological views support the conclusion thus suggested by historical developments."[41] Intuitively evident starting points are required for a complete rational system; many reflective, morally concerned people accept the dictates of common-sense morality, perhaps as self-evident; consequently, it is essential to examine the claims of common-sense morality carefully, trying to account for what consensus might exist among experts. Common-sense morality provides the data for theorizing, even if, on reflection, it cannot be fully rationalized.

What Schneewind demonstrates, however, is just how complex this historical relationship actually was. Sidgwick's approach to common-sense morality does not quite neatly align with either that of the Cambridge moralists or that of (the at least partly tamed utilitarian) J. S. Mill, whose attempts to accommodate principles of justice are not on the same scale. The issue here gets exceedingly intricate, but it is crucial for understanding just what kind of force Sidgwick attributes to common-sense morality. It is especially important to stress the complexity of Sidgwick's approach in order to avoid a misguided assimilation of it to various contemporary tactics. Sidgwick certainly places more importance on the examination of common-sense morality than, say, Hare or Brandt (who deny that "received opinion" has any probative force whatsoever), though he also shares with them an emphasis on the role of a moral code.[42] But his analysis of common-sense morality is tied to his intuitionism, and his times, in ways that both friends and foes of common sense have frequently failed to recognize.

As Schneewind reformulates it, there is a dual purpose to Sidgwick's examination of common-sense morality. First, there is the search for "really self-evident principles," as described; second, as the previously quoted passages illustrate, "there is the search for a principle superior in validity to other moral principles" – that is, a principle with superior moral (not epistemological) authority, which is what any complex moral code requires to determine the limits and exceptions of its component principles and be thoroughly rationalized. The latter has two stages: a negative stage, which appeals to the "dependence" argument (that the principles of common-sense morality have only a dependent and subordinate validity), and a positive stage, which appeals to the "systematization" argument (that the utilitarian principle sustains the common moral judgments and affords a principle of synthesis).[43] On the one side, Schneewind argues that for Sidgwick it is not "inevitable that a code of the kind which he takes to be a practical necessity in human life must have the characteristics of common-sense morality on which the dependence argument focuses attention." Indeed, he continues,

in view of Hare's objection to attributing any probative force to received moral opinion, it should be noted how little Sidgwick relies on common-sense morality. ... His conclusions stem from formal features of the accepted morality. If his reliance on received opinion biases the outcome of his search for a substantive first principle, it does so only by biasing his idea of the formal features such a principle must have.[44]

On the other side, the examination of common-sense morality forms at least part of the case for utilitarianism. "For it shows, among other things, that the factual characteristics which are treated by common-sense moral rules as indicating rightness cannot be ultimate right-making characteristics."[45] Thus, as Schneewind puts it in a crucial passage,

The dependence argument shows that certain features of received opinion which it would share with any equally complex code in an equally complex society, require us to go beyond its dictates to a different kind of principle. The appeal to self-evidence next yields rational principles of the kind required by the dependence argument. We then turn to see if these principles can systematize common sense. Since the first principles are obtained by a procedure not involving consideration of their systematizing power, the degree of their serviceability for this task provides an independent test of their acceptability. From the explanatory side of the systematization argument we learn that in so far as common-sense morality is already rational, the best explanation or model of its rationality is the utilitarian one. The rectificatory side of the systematization argument shows that in so far as received opinion still needs to be made rational, the best method of making it so is the utilitarian one. Thus the systematization argument is not meant to show that all our pre-theoretical moral opinions can be derived from the axioms. It is meant to show that the axioms provide an ideal or model of practical rationality which enable us to see that the kind of code we need for daily decision-making can be rational. The fact that one and the same ideal of rationality enables us to see that our actual code is to some extent rational and shows how it can have its rationality increased, provides stronger support for the ideal than any abstract argument about it could provide.[46]

It is true that Sidgwick thought of himself as following Aristotle in certain respects: If Aristotle had given us "the Common-Sense Morality of Greece, reduced to consistency by careful comparison," why not do the "same for *our* morality here and now, in the same manner of impartial reflection on current opinion" (*ME*, xix–xx)? But, crucially, he also thought this necessary in order to determine whether he even had the relevant intuitions; and the dialectical process that follows, showing the systematizing power and explanatory and rectificatory sides of the utilitarian principle, is meant to lead the reader through the same phases of reflection that he had gone through.[47] And for Sidgwick, "careful and systematic reflection on . . . Common Sense, as expressed in the habitual moral judgments of ordinary men, results in exhibiting the real subordination of these rules" to the genuinely self-evident principles that ground utilitarianism (*ME*, 497), and this is in part because of the demonstration of the actual demands of practical rationality, of reason when made genuinely and realistically practical.

Now, as many of the foregoing passages illustrate, for Sidgwick, the intuitionism – philosophical intuitionism – that grounds utilitarianism is not viewed as "a candidate for being a usable daily procedure for making moral decisions. It is brought in to make possible one kind of solution to the theoretical problems of synthesizing basic moral beliefs."[48] "Philosophical intuitionism" is not a method in the same sense as the others, its dictates not being specific enough to yield determinate practical conclusions, and it must therefore be distinguished from intuitional morality. Again, the faintly paradoxical point that Sidgwick makes about self-evident truths is that, although there are a number of them, they are in general too abstract to give much guidance and thus insufficient for a satisfactory method.

It would be disheartening to have to regard as altogether illusory the strong instinct of Common Sense that points to the existence of such principles, and the deliberate convictions of the long line of moralists who have enunciated them. At the same time, the more we extend our knowledge of man and his environment, the more we realise the vast variety of human natures and circumstances that have existed in different ages and countries, the less disposed we are to believe that there is any definite code of absolute rules, applicable to all human beings without exception. And we shall find, I think, that the truth lies between these two conclusions. There are certain absolute practical principles, the truth of which, when they are explicitly stated, is manifest; but they are of too abstract a nature, and too universal in their scope, to enable us to ascertain by immediate application of them what we ought to do in any particular case; particular duties have still to be determined by some other method. (*ME*, 379)

As remarked earlier, along with the proposition concerning the general happiness, the principle of benevolence, he allows that a version of the Kantian principle of universalizability, construed as justice or equity (treating similar cases similarly), is self-evident, as is a principle of prudence to the effect that one should have an equal concern for all parts of one's life. As with so many recent utilitarians, Sidgwick saw no difficulty at all in treating this largely formal version of the Kantian principle as compatible with the utilitarian one, since he "certainly could will it to be a universal law that men should act in such a way as to promote universal happiness" (*ME*, xx).

Sidgwick makes it plain that the self-evident element in these principles, "immediately cognisable by abstract intuition," depends "on the relation which individuals and their particular ends bear as parts to their wholes, and to other parts of these wholes" (*ME*, 382–3). This does not mean that the principles, or axioms, are obtained by mentally divining or gazing upon some new esoteric entity. As Schneewind explains, they function, in broadly Kantian fashion, "by requiring us to generalize whenever we assign a reason for an act or a desire." That is, they are "involved in providing ultimate warrants for transitions from premises to conclusions rather than as ultimate premises for arguments," and they work by prohibiting the "denial of certain types of inference."[49] Thus, for example, as with justice, what is a reason for one person must be allowed as a reason for anyone, *ceteris paribus*, and one cannot nonarbitrarily deny the legitimacy of treating a similar case similarly. Likewise, it would be arbitrary to hold that "mere difference of priority and posterity in time" is a ground "for having more regard to the consciousness of one moment than to that of another" (*ME*, 381). These axioms are principles of reasoning, to be sure; but "to call them axiomatic or intuitive is to say that they present requirements which are intrinsically reasonable, or which possess ultimate rational justification."[50] It is the apprehension, "with more or less distinctness, of these abstract truths" that he regards as "the permanent basis of the common conviction that the fundamental precepts of morality are essentially reasonable" (*ME*, 383).

The self-evident principles are framed, as Schneewind stresses, so that the key ethical notion is plainly manifest, with the "non-ethical concepts involved – concepts of action, self, other, earlier, later" being "so basic that to give a critical examination of them would require a digression on other branches of philosophy."[51] Still, the crucial point is that these principles are not on a par with those of dogmatic intuitionism; reached on reflection, they do not suffice for a practical method but approximate the ideal of "a law infinitely constraining and yet infinitely flexible" (*M*, 243). And again, Sidgwick's further development of this position is extremely advanced, producing a highly sophisticated version of indirect utilitarianism (and of egoism). Thus, as he parenthetically notes,

It should be observed, however, that the proposition that Universal Benevolence is the right *means* to the attainment of universal good, is not quite self-evident; since the end may not always be best attained by directly aiming at it. Thus Rational Benevolence, like Rational Self-Love, may be self-limiting; may direct its own partial suppression in favour of other impulses. (*ME*, 385; emphasis added).

Now, given this account of Sidgwick's intuitionism and analysis of common-sense morality, with its emphasis on the inescapable demands of a rational moral code and of system in practice, it should be fairly easy to see why Schneewind takes Sidgwick to be centrally concerned with "the demands reason makes on practice under the conditions of human life," which is after all part of what the emphasis on methods should amount to.

As I shall explain more fully in the final section, although Sidgwick was far more familiar with Kant's work than most of his contemporaries, and his own theory had marked affinities with the Kantian position at many points, his too narrow and formal treatment of Kantianism is today regarded as one of the most significant problems with his work. Some, such as Alan Donagan, have maintained that Whewell's rationalism (Whewell's view is, Donagan believes, better described as rationalism than as intuitionism, given its emphasis on the systemic and less than strictly deductive nature of morality) might have served as a tolerable stand-in for the Kantian view, but Sidgwick simply misinterpreted crucial features of rationalism, particularly with respect to how much disagreement among the experts it could bear. Thus, Sidgwick ended up largely begging the question against it.[52]

Others, such as Rawls, have argued that on the various forms of rational intuitionism "first principles, as statements about good reasons, are regarded as true or false in virtue of a moral order of values that is prior to and independent of our conceptions of person and society, and of the public social role of moral doctrines," and thus that "our agreement in judgment when properly founded is said to be based on the shared recognition of truths about a prior order of values accessible to reason." But any such view must be regarded as heteronomous from a Kantian perspective, since on intuitionism moral principles obtain by virtue of an objective order that "is not affected or determined by our conception of ourselves as reasonable and rational persons (as possessing the powers of practical reason), and of the public role of moral principles in a society of such persons." For Kant, the first principles of right and justice are "specified by a procedure of construction . . . the form and structure of which mirrors our free moral personality as both reasonable and rational."[53] Sidgwick's intuitionism led him to define his theoretical enterprise too narrowly, missing the significance of the constructivist alternative; focusing on first principles and methods that seek truth, Sidgwick said little about the conception of the person or the social role of morality, which are the component parts of Kantianism. His blinkered reading of Kant as offering only a formal principle naturally led him to overlook the constructivist alternative.

Though they differ in their interpretations of Kant and of just where Sidgwick went wrong in interpreting him, Donagan and Rawls are both

Kantians and are united in thinking that Sidgwick missed the true significance of Kantianism primarily because of his intuitionism, especially the way his focus on the first principles of methods led him to overlook other elements in a moral conception. The problem of the public nature of moral conceptions, which Rawls especially emphasizes, is of course a deep one for Sidgwick, and his failings on that score are related to many of the questionable aspects of his indirect form of utilitarianism, which according to critics is really "Government House" utilitarianism, a view that can too easily countenance the deceptions and paternalism characteristic of colonial administration because such policies might nevertheless be conducive to the greatest happiness. That is, it might be utilitarian to have the true morality remain esoteric.[54]

But, though it is plain enough that Sidgwick did not discern the full import of constructivism, it is important to reiterate that he surely had a keen sense of many of the difficulties confronting morality in its claims to provide an effective, usable code. Moreover, as regards the comparison with rationalism, Sidgwick's account of rational intuitionism was at least more receptive to the systemic and social dimensions of practical rationality than many other versions of that position. Locating Sidgwick's epistemology on the map of such (interminable) debates is a most intricate task.

Surely, as Schneewind and Kloppenberg stress, Sidgwick's version of intuitionism is really quite sophisticated, with a strong emphasis on epistemological fallibilism, consensus, and coherentism. Again, mere subjective certainty is not enough, on Sidgwick's view, since many beliefs that are fallible or even erroneous may be subjectively certain. In *The Methods of Ethics*, he frequently insists on the importance of consensus, allowing that he would "rely less confidently" on his claims about self-evident principles "if they did not appear to me to be in substantial agreement – in spite of superficial differences – with the doctrines of those moralists who have been most in earnest in seeking among commonly received moral rules for genuine intuitions of the Practical Reason" (*ME*, 384). In an important later work, the appendix to "The Criteria of Truth and Error" (in *LPK*), Sidgwick explains that he rejects the claims of both rationalism and empiricism to put forth a simple infallible criterion for determining ultimately valid, foundational knowledge. Instead, he settles for humbler, fallible, methods of verification – that is, methods for excluding error. Of these there are three: intuitive verification, which basically means careful examination to determine if the belief is really clear and distinct (an approach also used, he believes, in, e.g., mathematics); discursive verification, which involves considering the belief alongside others that might conflict and trying to impose system on the ensemble; and social or ecumenical verification, the agreement of relevant experts, those qualified to judge. Thus, for Sidgwick, "if we find that an intuitive belief appears clear and certain to ourselves contemplating it, that it is in harmony with our other beliefs relating to the same subject, and does not conflict with the beliefs of other persons competent to judge, we have reduced the risk of error with regard to it as low as it is possible to reduce it" (*LPK*, 465) – though it could still be wrong. All three methods are important, since none is completely free from error. But for the philosopher the second is of special importance, since "the ideal aim of philosophy is systematisation – the exhibition of system and coherence in a mass of beliefs which, as presented by Common Sense, are wanting therein" (*LPK*, 467). In fact, he cites his work on the conflicts within dogmatic intuitionism as an example of this approach. However, he immediately adds that "the special characteristic of *my* philosophy is to keep the importance of the others in view" (*LPK*, 467).

Despite his insistence on the irreducibility of ethics, and the importance of not confusing judgments of "ought" with judgments of "is," Sidgwick certainly allows that philosophy "can reduce somewhat" the difference between what is and what ought to be. From the philosophical point of view,

we regard the world of Duty and the world of Fact as objects of thought and – real or supposed – knowledge, and discover similar relations of thought in both, relations of universal to particular and individual notions and judgements, of inductive to deductive method, etc. Whatever differences between the two may appear from this point of view are of a subordinate kind, and not greater than the differences between different departments of Fact regarded as objects of thought and scientific method. (*PSR*, 246)[55]

Such passages illustrate that side of Sidgwick's thought that in good pragmatist fashion is concerned to soften or blur (if such words can be applied to Sidgwick) the differences between ethical and other forms of study and argument. Pragmatists, as Morton White once observed, are dispositionally opposed to dualisms: "Continuities and similarities between disciplines, kinds of reasoning, varieties of experience are sought with passion and celebrated by pragmatists, while differences and contrasts tend to be treated – if they are recognized at all – as negligible."[56] For all his careful, discriminating, analytical inquiry, Sidgwick could certainly also bring into view the larger "continuities and similarities." As remarked, Kloppenberg, in his essay herein, detects sturdy pragmatist shoots in this view of epistemology.

But in elaborating these features of Sidgwick's thought, it should also be stressed that, in *Philosophy, Its Scope and Relations*, cited above, Sidgwick certainly insisted that the "fundamental controversies in politics and ethics" turned on the problem of "the *ultimate end*, which gives the standard by which all particular rules and institutions are to be tested," and that this subject of controversy could not "be treated at all by a 'positive' instead of a metaphysical method. Ultimate ends are not 'phenomena' or laws or conditions of phenomena: to investigate them as if they were seems as futile as if one inquired whether they were square or round" (*PSR*, 220). Sidgwick makes these points largely by developing a critique of (mostly Comtean) progressivism, "which takes its stand on the admitted social fact of progress in knowledge, and especially points to the sciences which relate to the physical world as examples of right method attained after a long struggle through erroneous and confused methods." Sidgwick, with his steadfastly nonreductive approach to the different departments of knowledge, rejects this view

on account of the diversity of methods which the different sciences, impartially viewed, are found to require and use: – the method of mathematics is most importantly different from that of abstract physics, the method of abstract physics different from that of the concrete study of the inorganic world, and this again different from that of the history of the world of life, while the methods of the studies of human life and thought, individual and social, are still tentative and beset with difficulties in which the analogy of the physical sciences can only give very limited assistance. (*PSR*, 230–1)

Furthermore, progressivism should be rejected "on account of the fundamental difference between the task of special sciences dealing with partial and limited aspects of the Universe and the task of Philosophy dealing with the Universe as a whole" (*PSR*, 231) – that is, as concerned with the broad systematization of the most fundamental aspects of knowledge, with "putting together the parts of knowledge thus attained into a systematic whole" (*PSR*, 11), a pursuit that, for Sidgwick, the human mind finds irresistible. On this project, science "sets before us an ideal of a consensus of experts and continuity of development which we may hope to attain in our larger and more difficult work" (*PSR*, 231). But again, on the relationship between "Theoretical and Practical Philosophy" as it figures in this systematization, although Sidgwick (in typically undogmatic fashion) admits that it would be rash to claim that it is forever impossible to reduce matters of ought to matters of is, he is certainly not satisfied with any of the proposed reductions advanced so far. Thus, "questions of ends are indeed philosophical questions: but they are questions which it belongs to *Practical* Philosophy or Philosophy in its practical aspect to answer."[57]

Consequently, there is a sense in which practical philosophy is not to be subordinated to theoretical philosophy but rather subordinates it, since it too is a department of human activity. From another perspective, however, the propositions of "Practical Philosophy regarded as human thoughts or judgments or beliefs are seen to be parts of that sphere of cognisable existence with which Theoretical Philosophy is concerned," and "Theoretical Philosophy thus viewed – and made to include Practical Philosophy as subordinate – seems to become a study of the thoughts or beliefs of the human mind, with a view to their complete systematisation" (*PSR*, 34–5).

Such, at any rate, is what philosophy *aims* at, though Sidgwick laments that the experts are more often in disagreement than agreement when it comes to "the method and main conclusions of Philosophy" (*PSR*, 13). When the experts are thus disagreed, philosophical knowledge amounts to knowledge "of the confusions of thought to which the human intellect is liable when it begins to speculate on the questions of Philosophy: knowledge of how to state these questions so as to avoid to some extent confusions of thought: and knowledge of considerations that have some force, though not necessarily decisive force, for or against conclusions on disputed questions of Philosophy" (*PSR*, 12). This, I believe, is how he regarded much of his own work and teaching in the different areas of practical philosophy.[58]

As the foregoing remarks should suggest, Sidgwick's approach to moral theorizing is subtle, complex, and original to a degree, as is perhaps obliquely conceded in his retort to the hapless Calderwood that this "whole view of mine seems so new to Prof. Calderwood, that he can only reply that 'corrections of intuitions or of spontaneous utterances of conscience is impossible, and the proposal of it absurd' – a forcible statement, but hardly an effective argument."[59] In Sidgwick's hands, intuitionism was emphatically not simply a means for complacently putting a halt to argument, as Bentham had claimed. Indeed, in considering Sidgwick's conception of philosophical argument, it is instructive to recall his diagnosis of Bradley's failings as an ethical theorist. After observing that Bradley often lapses into "mere debating-club rhetoric" and that his apprehension of opposing doctrines is "rather superficial and sometimes even unintelligent," Sidgwick explains that this

last defect seems partly due to his limited acquaintance with the whole process of English ethical thought, partly to the contemptuous asperity with which he treats opposing doctrines: for really penetrating criticism, especially in ethics, requires a patient effort of intellectual sympathy which Mr. Bradley has never learned to make, and a tranquility of temper which he seems incapable of maintaining. Nor again, does he appear to have effectively criticised his own fundamental positions, before presenting them to the public.[60]

One could handily epitomize Sidgwick's ethical theorizing by remarking that it was the antithesis of Bradley's, at least as long as it was not supposed that the twentieth century has seen a higher synthesis.

The Cartesian aspects of Sidgwick's philosophical intuitionism, along with his hedonism, are received with very little sympathy today, for well-known reasons having to do with noncognitivism, on one side, and holism, that our beliefs do not stand or fall singly (or even in small packs), on the other. Of the contributors to this volume, none has actually picked up the defense of intuitionism, though David Brink, who has defended a form of moral realism, has suggested that the traditional view is not in fact as madly absurd as is commonly supposed, which is surely correct, at least in Sidgwick's case. And as we shall have occasion to see, Sidgwick's intuitionism has scarcely proved any barrier at all to the strange melange of utilitarians who have adopted (or adapted) parts of his program – for example, Brink, J. J. C. Smart, Alan Gibbard, and Russell Hardin.[61] However, as mentioned, Rawls's Kantian constructivism, with its emphasis on the ideal of the person and the public role of a conception of justice, is set in contrast to rational intuitionism, which Rawls holds led Sidgwick to define his inquiry too narrowly.

Moreover, intuitionism or no, it is this very attempt to do ethics as a form of systematic inquiry, bringing the different methods into a coherent and consistent whole, that antitheorists such as Bernard Williams and Annette Baier (and even to some extent such defenders of the irreducible complexity of common sense as Marcus Singer, in the essay included here)[62] are concerned to reject. Whereas rationalists and utilitarians are quite content with this feature of Sidgwick's approach – the former, such as Donagan, thinking that Sidgwick simply missed the better systematizing principles, the latter, such as Hardin, thinking that he got it about right – antitheorists deny that we should be searching for any such overarching principles. The Sidgwickian reply that want of system is unsatisfactory to the philosophic mind would be taken by such critics as an indictment of the philosophic mind.[63]

The perfectionist position, and the pragmatist one, can be shaded into the antitheory view. Thus, some such argument has been made by James Wallace, who, in his book *Moral Relevance and Moral Conflict*, defends a pragmatized, contextualized account of Aristotelian judgment, which is in fact developed through an extended critique of Sidgwick's intuitionism. For Wallace, establishing the relevance of a moral consideration and solving conflicts between relevant considerations are matters not for a decision procedure or an algorithm but for such things as "intelligent, calculated improvisation and the virtue of resourceful inventiveness in adapting our practical knowledge to unprecedented difficulties."[64] Not surprisingly, Wallace singles out Sidgwick as a prime example of a moral theorist who tried to impose an inappropriate philosophical gridwork over the flux of action. In response to the possibility of moral conflict, according to Wallace, the absolutist denies the possibility of it because different considerations must be in harmony, the utilitarian denies its possibility because there is only one moral consideration, utility, and the intuitionist denies the irreducibility of it because there is an intuitively correct solution in each particular case. For Wallace, Sidgwick, tainted by one or another (or all) of these misplaced ideas, ends up inadvertently revealing their inadequacy:

> Sidgwick has exhibited the implausibility of the notion that familiar maxims of morality can be made to play the role required of rules by the passive conception of rationality. The complexity of practical affairs and of the world defeats the attempt to formulate principles that in every case correctly tell us what we should do. Sidgwick's attempt to improve upon matters by adopting the single utilitarian principle is wrecked by the ineluctable plurality of the practical and by the fact that the claim that the GHP [general happiness principle] simply tells us correctly what to do is no more plausible when confronted with certain cases than the same claim made for such principles as "One should fulfill express promises and distinct understandings."[65]

Wallace is here pointing to the fact that Sidgwick did not manage a complete rationalization of practical rationality. As previously observed, for all his love of system and consistency, Sidgwick did not, in the end, claim to have effected a complete reconciliation of all the methods of ethics.

4. Moral theory: failure and crisis

Whatever defense of utilitarianism is to be found in *The Methods of Ethics*, it must be qualified by the fact that Sidgwick could not eliminate egoistic hedonism as a viable alternative. As he explained in an important commentary on his own book,

> Along with (*a*) a fundamental moral conviction that I ought to sacrifice my own happiness, if by so doing I can increase the happiness of others to a greater extent than I diminish my own, I find also (*b*) a conviction – which it would be paradoxical to call "moral," but which is none the less fundamental – that it would be irrational to sacrifice any portion of my own happiness unless the sacrifice is to be somehow at some time compensated by an equivalent addition to my own happiness. I find both these fundamental convictions in my own thought with as much clearness and certainty as the process of introspective

reflection can give: I find also a preponderant assent to them – at least implicit – in the common sense of mankind: and I find, on the whole, confirmation of my view in the history of ethical thought in England.[66]

Thus, the two species of hedonism cannot be reconciled, and practical reason would seem to be divided against itself. Sidgwick regarded this as a "fundamental contradiction in our apparent intuitions of what is Reasonable in conduct" (*ME*, 508), and indeed, as mentioned, in the first edition of *The Methods of Ethics*, he had dismally concluded that, unless a way be found to reconcile "the Individual with the Universal Reason," the "Cosmos of Duty is thus really reduced to a Chaos: and the prolonged effort of the human intellect to frame a perfect ideal of rational conduct is seen to have been foredoomed to inevitable failure" (*ME*1, 473). Although the methods of egoistic and universal hedonism might come to the same practical conclusions on many points, Sidgwick rightly held that there were also bound to be clear conflicts, as in cases where the general good would call for the sacrifice of one's life. The only way to overcome this "Dualism of Practical Reason," as he famously called it, is by means of a theological premise, an appeal to a Supreme Being to underwrite the moral order of the world and guarantee the coincidence of the two methods. At any rate, the problem was beyond the scope of a work on ethics and had to be tackled by "a general examination of the criteria of true and false beliefs" (*ME*, 509).

To be sure, Sidgwick was, personally, a utilitarian, as we have seen, and he was certainly capable of expounding the doctrine in compelling terms, proclaiming "Universal Happiness, desirable consciousness or feeling for the innumerable multitude of living beings, present and to come," as "an end that satisfies our imagination by its vastness, and sustains our resolution by its comparative security." Sidgwick's utilitarianism was unfailingly high-minded, giving great scope to the social and sympathetic side of human nature – "the selfish man misses the sense of elevation and enlargement given by wide interests. . . . He is made to feel in a thousand various ways, according to the degree of refinement which his nature has attained, the discord between the rhythms of his own life and of that larger life of which his own is but an insignificant fraction" (*ME*, 501). In this vein, he often sounds more like J. S. Mill than like the earlier utilitarians, with whom his sympathies were less than fully refined. Criticizing Bentham, he wrote:

While he is as confident in his power of constructing a happy society as the most ardent believer in the moral perfectibility of mankind, he is as convinced of the unqualified selfishness of the vast majority of human beings as the bitterest cynic. Hence the double aspect of his utilitarianism, which has caused so much perplexity both to disciples and to opponents. It is as if Hobbes or Mandeville were suddenly inspired with the social enthusiasm of Godwin. (*MEA*, 131)[67]

Sidgwick's difficulty was to render his allegiance to rational benevolence fully consistent and rational, leaving utilitarianism as the only theory in the field; this he could not do.

And so, finally, Sidgwick's attempt to render the methods of ethics consistent and fully rational ended in a draw; though dogmatic intuitionism and utilitarianism could be reconciled, egoism and utilitarianism could not. As Schneewind, Parfit, and others have observed, this recognition of the challenge posed by egoism certainly set Sidgwick apart from the earlier utilitarian tradition, which had tended to gloss over or underestimate this conflict, much as he had claimed.[68] And thus it was that in the end Sidgwick was driven, however unhappily, to believe that the autonomy of ethics could not be completely sustained; ethics is forced to go outside of itself in order to come to terms with the dualism of practical reason.

Sidgwick, however, believed that his views on dualism were confirmed by the history of moral thought in England and that in recognizing this dualism he was basically following Bishop Butler, though whether this is actually so is questioned by Frankena in his remarkable survey of this dualism in English moral theory. Frankena finds some important differences between Butler and Sidgwick on this issue and suggests that, for better or worse, Sidgwick may have been more original than he proclaimed himself to be. Among other things, Frankena points up the importance of Samuel Clarke, who had, as Schneewind has observed, figured more heavily in the first edition of *The Methods of Ethics* than in later editions.[69] Frankena's essay provides a careful analysis of just what Sidgwick means when he casts this dualism in terms of the "governing faculties" of reason, a formulation that is especially important when we consider how Sidgwick conceived the difference between ancient and modern ethics. Along with its companion essays, this piece gives a detailed rendering of how Sidgwick framed the dualism of practical reason, and this in a way that clarifies the issue of whether a theological premise could actually solve this dualism at the level of reason, as opposed to simply guaranteeing the coincidence of the methods in practice.

Further ambiguities are explored by David Brink and by John Deigh, who comments on Brink's suggestion that, in contrast to the internalist reading of Sidgwick that Frankena has defended, Sidgwick might be read as an externalist. That is, in an important article, summarized in his contribution to this volume, Brink considers the question of whether we should represent the dualism of practical reason as "(a) a conflict between *competing moral theories*, namely, between utilitarianism and *ethical* egoism, or as (b) a conflict between (the utilitarian's account of) *morality* and (an egoist theory of) *rationality*" and details how the choice between these alternatives "depends upon whether Sidgwick should be regarded (as we would say) as an internalist or as an externalist. (a) derives from an internalist reading of Sidgwick, while (b) requires an externalist reading."[70] For the internalist, questions of moral motivation or reasons for action – the action-guiding character of morality – are underwritten by the very concept of morality; the externalist, by contrast, holds that internalism fails to take seriously the challenge of amoralist skepticism and that the force of moral considerations is a matter of contingent psychological fact.

The main advantage of reading Sidgwick as an externalist is an epistemological one. Since Sidgwick thought that both utilitarianism and egoism were supported by rational intuitions, and yet one of the conditions for self-evidence was that the propositions in question be mutually consistent, which ethical egoism and utilitarianism are not, it would seem to follow that "neither can really be self-evident," at least on an internalist reading. On the externalist interpretation, however, there need be no inconsistency: "For even if there is a conflict between duty and interest, rational egoism can truly state the agent's reasons for action and utilitarianism can truly state his moral obligations. . . . Only the externalist reading, therefore, allows us to avoid attributing to Sidgwick a fairly significant inconsistency or confusion."[71]

Of course, how inconsistent such dualism actually is greatly depends on just how one interprets Sidgwick's intuitionism, that is, on just how much fallibilism it can countenance (or perhaps also, to what degree it does simply point up the inevitable limits of his method). And furthermore, it may in the end be the case that, given the way Sidgwick frames the issue (in terms of the basic notion of a demand of reason), it is simply impossible to tease his arguments into an externalist form, as John Deigh urges in his essay. That the internalist view, with its attendant ambiguities, was indeed Sidgwick's own is further supported by the way that some such view apparently colored his reading of the history of ethics, as Frankena demonstrates.

In his essay in this volume (Chapter 7), Brink is primarily concerned with another aspect of the dualism of practical reason, namely, preserving the plausibility of the egoistic side of it in the face of Derek Parfit's ingenious arguments to show that egoism is an unstable hybrid of temporal neutrality and agent relatively, one which (as Sidgwick seems to have recognized) might be undermined by a radically reductionist view of personal identity according to which a person is not a

simple enduring self but only various physical and psychological connections and continuities.[72] Parfit has developed this metaphysical Sidgwickian alternative to the theological tack, but Brink defends rational
egoism against any such maneuver. Mackie's insightful article (Chapter
5) sets the stage for this debate, defending Sidgwick's rendition of ethical
egoism against the criticisms of Moore.

It is worth expanding a little on Parfit's work in this connection, since
his *Reasons and Persons* surely draws much of its inspiration from Sidgwick, though in its own way it is even more heavily qualified and tentative
in the defense of utilitarianism. At any rate, consideration of it will lead
back around to the question of Sidgwick's pragmatism, raised in the
previous section.

It is not implausible to read Parfit as in very many ways picking up
Sidgwick's project, jettisoning much of the intuitionism and all of the
religious concern, remaining more agnostic about the nature of the good,
but retaining the emphasis on reasons for action and developing certain
points about the precise nature and connection of reasons (personal or
impersonal) and persons (irreducible or reducible) that Sidgwick noted
but left relatively unexplored.[73] Thus, Parfit, too, argues that common-
sense morality is unsatisfactory, and this in a way that points toward a
reconciliation of common-sense morality and consequentialism – a unified theory, and one that takes account of people's desires and dispo-
sitions. (However, Parfit states that, although he follows Sidgwick in
arguing that common-sense morality is indirectly self-defeating, his own
argument that it is directly collectively self-defeating, for reasons having
largely to do with the prisoner's dilemma, is less dependent on
intuitions.)[74]

Moreover, as mentioned, although he is very cautious in drawing out
the implications for moral theory, Parfit believes that the dualism of
practical reason may best be tackled by a metaphysical argument about
personal identity. That is, on the basis of what Parfit believes is the true
view of personal identity, a highly reductionist, Humean view, the standard egoistic theory of self-interest or prudence[75] and various moral
views such as those concerning distributive justice may well be undermined in a way that could ultimately support some more impersonal
moral theory such as utilitarianism – for example, because on the nonreductionist view one's relation to one's future selves is less deep and
not that different from one's relation to other people, which thus down-
plays the significance of the separateness of persons as construed by
distributivists.[76] Parfit observes that Sidgwick had in fact broached the
question of personal identity and of how egoism seems to rest on a
nonreductionist theory, though he did not pursue it.[77] But, of course,

we might think that, if Sidgwick would have allowed a theological premise or epistemological considerations to help in dealing with the dualism
of practical reason, then why not a metaphysical argument?

Although Parfit thinks that the classical theory of self-interest or prudence should be rejected, he admits that there is some force to the claim
that it cannot be entirely undermined. Thus, he speculates that it might
also be possible to show how there is a three-sided draw among morality,
self-interest, and the "Present-aim Theory," which relativizes reasons
to the time of action and is thus based on what one most wants at the
present moment instead of what is in one's long-term interest. In that
case, we might at least be able to break the tie, if two sets of reasons
lined up against one; thus, when morality conflicts with self-interest, we
might, contra Sidgwick, have more reason to follow one or the other.[78]
(It should be remarked that, like Sidgwick, Parfit also ends up with an
unresolved problem of great significance, though this one is within the
house of beneficence and has to do with policies toward future
generations.)

In advancing such arguments (and many others), Parfit believes that
he is largely avoiding the "High-Road" of metaethics and, to at least a
certain extent, also the "Low-Road" of mere appeal to (not necessarily
cognitive) intuitions. Arguments that shows how a moral theory is self-
defeating, or how the moral significance of certain facts has been overlooked, or what a theory really implies, or how a theory is structurally
weak, or the implications of a metaphysical claim – these hold out the
prospect of a middle way and of genuine progress in moral theory.
Nonreligious ethics is comparatively young. Though Hume and Sidgwick
were (according to Parfit) atheists who made ethics a main part of their
life's work, there have not been too many of these, especially because
the first part of the twentieth century was mostly preoccupied with
metaethics. Thus, "Non-Religious Ethics has been systematically studied, by many people, only since about 1960. Compared with the other
sciences, Non-Religious Ethics is the youngest and the least advanced."[79]

In these claims about progress in ethical theory, Parfit takes himself
to be following Rawls and Nagel, with Sidgwick and Hume as intellectual
forefathers, and this is obviously appropriate to some extent. But it is
in truth very difficult to determine to just what degree Parfit's work falls
within the same tradition or even to what degree this is a coherent
tradition. Parfit's approach often seems closest to a more eclectic version
of Nagel's view, which Rorty has classified as "intuitive realist" – a
traditional capital-P Philosophical affair enamored with the "essence"
of philosophical problems, showing to "what ineffable depths, what limit
of language," they lead.[80] At any rate, although Parfit's battery of ar-

guments is, I believe, more diverse, his approach is at least as resolutely antihistoricist when it comes to describing its philosophical problems, though of course the deep truth about the self that he discovers is that there is no self, as traditionally conceived.

Nagel's vision of the independence of philosophy, which places less stress on the importance of developing substantive ethical theory as a necessary preliminary to metaethical work, admittedly has always been rather different from Rawls's, and it may have become more so in recent years.[81] Certainly, as a practical political view, Rawls's recent theory seeks to avoid controversial metaphysical arguments about realism versus antirealism of the kind one sees in Nagel's work.[82] It also seeks to avoid controversial metaphysical arguments about the self (since they could just as well be theological arguments about the self and thus inappropriate for a conception of public reason dealing with constitutional essentials) of precisely the kind that Parfit counts as making for progress in ethical theory and that he would apparently want to see translated in a more straightforward manner into political practice. Indeed, although the evolution was complex, Rawls's practical political conception of his theory is a direct outgrowth of his general notion of the independence of moral theory, which was in part framed precisely in opposition to Parfit's arguments for the relevance of personal identity to moral theory.[83] And surely, in comparison with Rawls or Sidgwick, Parfit's work is quite weak on the systematic, comprehensive comparison of the main alternative ethical theories.

As we have seen, Sidgwick's ethical theory, although it obviously represents a comprehensive moral conception (and an intuitionistic, hedonistic, mostly utilitarian one at that) rather than an expressly political theory, tends, in parallel fashion, to avoid undue reliance on other areas of philosophy, theology, and so forth. Curious as it may seem, and it should seem at least somewhat curious, there are a number of broad structural similarities between Sidgwick's approach and Rawls's theory of justice, especially when it comes to avoiding metaethical, metaphysical, and theological precommitments. These are, I suggest, largely attributable to their conception of moral theory and to the sophisticated, non-Cartesian elements at work in Sidgwick's arguments.[84] And in fact, if Schneewind, Rawls, and Collini are correct, the similarities may not be as curious as all that, since various strands of Sidgwick's thought conspired to preserve the independence of the sphere of political reflection and argument and to focus on a conception of the person largely in accord with reflective common sense. As Collini has argued, "in effect Sidgwick was denying the much-touted supersession of political theory by some version of the 'science of society,' and restoring it to its traditional home in moral philosophy." This, however, did not mean that "he believed that actual moral and political questions could be settled *a priori*, without reference to concrete historical details." Quite the contrary, as we have seen, he insisted that "the formulation of any meaningful moral or political judgements demanded close attention to the unique details of a particular time and place." His starting point was "analytical reasoning itself," and he argued that "the essential method of the moral sciences was the method of philosophy, 'i.e. the method of reflection on the thought we all share, by means of the symbolism which we all share, language' " – which for Sidgwick typically meant, as Collini shows, drawing on "the ordinary experience of civilized life," especially with regard to human nature.[85] In his hands, ethics, politics, and economics all took their point of departure from the normal man as the civilized world then found him. The vicissitudes of historical development, the methods of fledgling inquiry, and the demands of utilitarianism were in accord on this.[86]

By contrast, Parfit's metaphysical arguments are rather akin to those about freedom of the will, and so on, that Sidgwick, to a considerable extent anyway, tried to elide or elude when doing ethical theory. Thus, Parfit's notion of progress in ethical theory would seem, at least in practice, to appeal *from the start* to more eclectic (and external) foundations. There is perhaps a little irony in the fact that Sidgwick the intuitionistic utilitarian attended far more scrupulously to the demands of common sense and shared experience than Parfit, whose ingenious conceptual revisionism is rather the philosophical equivalent of Bentham's reformism. For Parfit, most people in Western culture – even *most of the most reflective people in Western culture* – are flatly (indeed, wildly) wrong about the nature of the self, wrong in ways that by his own admission are extraordinarily difficult to root out. Most people, he correctly holds, believe the nonreductionist view, and even believers in reductionism find it a very difficult position to adhere to consistently. Obviously, Parfit thinks that the results of psychic research on the self are pretty much in, as are (relatedly) those on religion. And unlike Sidgwick, who hoped to find support for religious belief from ethical theory and was distressed to find instead that ethical theory might require the support of (unsupported) theology, Parfit holds that it is the very elimination of theological premises in ethics that is promising – the dualism of practical reason is tackled precisely by demonstrating the non-existence of anything resembling a soul, not by the evidence for personal survival and the consequent buttressing of (ethically relevant) religious belief of a Christian or theist variety.

Consequently, Parfit's sharply controversial view of the self does not strike one as a promising beginning in the search for a language of public reason. Although Parfit is of course not at all tempted by Nietzsche's view that metaphysics and theology are just fraudulent attempts to sell altruism as rational, his views do, as Rorty might put it, gravitate toward problems of self-creation in ways that make for serious problems in political theory.[87] For a variety of reasons, some of them perhaps also having to do with a temperament that could find some truth in every point of view, Sidgwick's ethical and political thought always remained, in this area at least, rather closer to the common understandings of the ordinary educated citizen of his day, as Collini demonstrates. Indeed, Parfit would seem to concede this point, after a fashion anyway. He notes that Sidgwick accepted the "Common-Sense View" about personal identity and "believed that Hume's view was false." Thus, "it is not surprising that he did not develop his suggested challenge to the Self-Interest Theory."[88] Also, "the separateness of persons seemed to Sidgwick deep enough to support a Self-interest Theorist's rejection of the claims of morality. I wish that we could ask Sidgwick why this deep fact did not, in his view, support the claims of just distribution."[89] I agree. It would also be instructive to ask him how much store he would put in Parfit's way of arriving at such conclusions about personal identity and how, even if converted to the reductionist view, he would conceive of the problem of translating such views into moral and political practice – especially given his belief that "the mind of England" is "Protestant to the core."[90] If there is irony in Sidgwick the hedonistic utilitarian sharing the culture's presuppositions about the deep nature of the self, there is a double irony in Sidgwick the "Government House" utilitarian having a real feel for the public nature of reasoned justification in politics.

Of course, given that Sidgwick was the most uncompromisingly academic of philosophers, a foundationalist who believed in ethics as a (potential) department of cognitive knowledge replete with moral experts, and in the great value of philosophy as a special discipline and of philosophers as political teachers, one must avoid any suggestion, however oblique, that he was a Rortyan advocate of post-philosophical culture. Perhaps it would be better to say that he was a very diffident advocate of post-theological culture. Surely, he was driven to his approach to an independent ethical theory (and to psychical research) in part by the failures of theology and metaphysics, in their grand but premature and faulty forms. After all, in his *Ethics of Conformity and Subscription*, an extremely important work that, as Schneewind and Donagan have stressed, contains the seeds of much of his later thought, Sidgwick had observed that it "is sometimes said that we live in an age that rejects authority. . . . it is true that we only accept authority of a particular sort; the authority, namely, that is formed and maintained by the unconstrained agreement of individual thinkers, each of whom we believe to be seeking truth with single-mindedness and sincerity, and declaring what he has found with scrupulous veracity, and the greatest attainable exactness and precision." The sciences are of course the models of such collegial inquiry. But unfortunately, Sidgwick adds, with respect to most theologians "we have hitherto been able to feel no such security."[91] Theology and ethics had been marred by the same notable absence of dispassionate discussion.

No doubt there is much to this. But Sidgwick proposes the same cure for both disciplines, and with equally unpromising early returns. Indeed, for Sidgwick, the results of independent ethical inquiry were so explosive that they redounded back on the inquiry itself in a way that threatened to wreck the project at an early stage. Shortly before publishing *The Methods of Ethics*, he wrote that "Ethics is losing its interest for me rather, as the insolubility of its fundamental problem is impressed on me." He thought that "the contribution to the *formal* clearness and coherence of our ethical thought which I have to offer is just worth giving: for a few speculatively-minded persons – very few" (*M*, 277).

Worse than that, he felt that he had to take great care in dealing even with the speculative few. As he explained in a letter written in 1878, one which gives a good sense of the boundaries of his notion of ethical theory, there "are some minds to whom the great difficulty is to know how to *act*; how in this mixed world (however it has come to be so mixed) the ideal of Duty (of whose ideal reality they feel no general doubt) is to be concretely realised here and now – there are so many competing methods and so much to be said on both sides of so many questions." Somewhat surprisingly, given the academic nature of his enterprise, he goes on to say that his book was primarily designed for this class of persons. But, he explains, this is not because he pretends "to give them immediate practical guidance in any special difficulties they may have" but because he tries "to contribute towards an ultimate reconciliation and binding together of all the different lines of moral reasoning that have gone on mingling and contending with each other since men first began to reflect on their wellbeing and their duty." However, this is followed by the admission that "I know very well that there is another class of minds, with which I have also strong sympathy, who have never really felt troubled about practical questions. . . . What *they* long to know is not so much what Duty is, but how Duty comes to be there in conflict with inclination; why the individual is so often sacrificed to the general; why both in the single life and in the race good is so imperfectly triumphant over evil, etc., etc." And for such speculative minds,

these questions are, no doubt, more profoundly interesting than the others. Sometimes they become absorbingly so to me, but I rather turn aside from much contemplation of them, because I not only cannot answer them to my satisfaction, but do not even know where to look for the answer that I want. I am sincerely glad that so many of my fellow-creatures are satisfied with the answers that they get from positive religions; and the others – philosophers – find a substitute for the satisfaction of an answer found, in the high and severe delight of seeking it. I cannot quite do either; and therefore I hold my tongue as much as I can! (*M*, 337–8)

Now, it may well seem that even in these passages Sidgwick's tongue does not have a very long leash, since it is clear that he agonized over the issue a great deal and regarded his work on psychic research and general philosophy as relevant to it. Indeed, in terms of Sidgwick's inner life, his academic career was really a prolonged crisis of conscience, a continuation by other means of the crisis of faith that caused him to resign his fellowship. If the shape of the first was determined by his independence from theology, the shape of the latter was analogous – though the resulting action more measured. Thus, in 1888, when struggling with his conscience over his position in the university, he wrote:

Ethics seems to me in a position intermediate between Theology and Science, regarded as subjects of academic study and profession, in this way: – No one doubts that a Professor of Theology, under the conditions prevailing in England at least, is expected to be in some way constructive; if not exactly orthodox, at any rate he is expected to have and to be able to communicate a rational basis for some established creed and system. If he comes to the conclusion that no such basis is attainable, most sensible persons would agree that he is in his wrong place and better take up some other calling. On the other hand the professor of any branch of science is under no such restriction; he is expected to communicate unreservedly the results to which he has come, whether favourable or not to the received doctrines: if (e.g.) he were the solitary Darwinian in a society of Creationists, that would be no reason for resigning his chair – rather for holding on. Now my difficulty is to make up my mind which of these analogies I ought to apply to my own case – and I have not yet done so. (*M*, 485)

The heresy at stake, of course, was the dualism of practical reason; insofar as ethics leaned toward theology (even if only in fact rather than sound theory), could he teach ethics in good conscience? In another journal entry, he laments that none of his critics has even tried to answer his claim that the Cosmos of Duty has been reduced to a chaos and wonders, "am I to use my position – and draw my salary – for teaching that Morality *is* a chaos, from the point of view of Practical Reason; adding cheerfully that, as man is not after all a rational being, there is no real fear that morality won't be kept up somehow" (*M*, 472).

As the *Memoir* makes amply clear, such tensions colored most of Sidgwick's intellectual and practical concerns. The problem went beyond that of meeting (or giving a reasoned justification for failing to meet) the institutional expectations of his role. His overwhelming, lifelong concern with the viability of religious belief (theist if not Christian), which found its outlet first in biblical criticism and then in psychical research, was a reflection of his fear of egoism, his fear that only a divine moral order could insure the rational supremacy of benevolence or at least the coincidence of benevolence and egoism. Although, as his painstaking moral theorizing makes clear, he would allow no easy answers or shortcuts in inquiry, his entire life manifested the most intense Victorian concern over the fate of morality should religious belief fail; to find a rational basis for duty or to find a basis for religious belief – these were the poles of philosophical and social stability for Sidgwick. But after his work in ethics the suspicion always gnawed at him that "the alternatives of the Great Either–Or seem to be Pessimism or Faith" (*M*, 340). And his work in psychic research did not help. In a crucial journal entry from 1887, the period leading up to the dilemma concerning his position just described, he confesses that he is "certainly drifting towards" the conclusion that "we have not, and are never likely to have, empirical evidence of the existence of the individual after death." Upon reaching such a conclusion, he continues, "it will probably be my duty as a reasonable being – and especially as a professional philosopher – to consider on what basis the human individual ought to construct his life under these circumstances." For, he goes on,

Some fifteen years ago, when I was writing my book on Ethics, I was inclined to hold with Kant that we must *postulate* the continued existence of the soul, in order to effect that harmony of Duty with Happiness which seemed to me indispensable to rational moral life. At any rate I thought I might *provisionally* postulate it, while setting out on the serious search for empirical evidence. If I decide that this search is a failure, shall I finally and decisively make this postulate? Can I consistently with my whole view of truth and the method of its attainment? And if I answer "no" to each of these questions, have I any ethical system at all? (*M*, 466–7)

His philosophical conclusions were personally disturbing and, he felt, potentially dangerous. It was not solely a belief in the academic nature of philosophy – much as he did believe in its academic status – that led him to write: "I would not if I could, and could not if I would, say

anything which would make philosophy – my philosophy – popular."
He thought of his view "as an inevitable point in the process of thought"
but one he took "as a soldier takes a post of difficulty"; he could not
"take the responsibility of drawing anyone else to it" (*M*, 354). He
worried about the corrosive effect that his skeptical intelligence might
have on others and was indeed glad, and for utilitarian reasons, that his
fellow creatures were more easily satisfied:

In fact, the reason why I keep strict silence now for many years with regard to
theology is that while I cannot myself discover adequate rational basis for the
Christian hope of happy immortality, it seems to me that the general loss of
such a hope, from the minds of average human beings as now constituted, would
be an evil of which I cannot pretend to measure the extent. I am not prepared
to say that the dissolution of the existing social order would follow, but I think
the danger of such dissolution would be seriously increased, and that the evil
would certainly be very great. (*M*, 357)

If ethics required theology in order to be rational and the social order required it in order to be stable, small wonder that Sidgwick, whatever his
scruples about free and critical inquiry, was inclined to hive off such subjects rather than proclaim their bankruptcy. Perhaps, if he went into
ethics hoping to find an independent support for theology, he emerged
from his later study of theology cum psychic research thinking it better
for both if the relationship remained distant. Sidgwick may have been
Blanshard's truly reasonable man, the pure white light, but he certainly
did not think of himself as the bearer of good tidings. He confessed that
about the only youthfulness of spirit in his outlook on life was that of a
"pessimistic undergraduate." It was this preoccupation that led J. M.
Keynes to say of Sidgwick that he never did anything but worry about
whether Christianity was true, show that it wasn't, and wish that it was.

There is every reason to think that Sidgwick did find his conclusions
genuinely agonizing and thus that he would probably not have taken
much comfort in Wallace's suggestion that he had stumbled across a
good argument for pragmatism – much less in Rorty's view that philosophers are part of the problem. For

the fact is that while I find it easy enough to *live* with more or less satisfaction,
I cannot at present get any satisfaction from *thinking* about life, for thinking
means – as a philosopher – endeavoring to frame an ethical theory which will
hold together, and to this I do not see my way. And the consideration that the
morality of the world may be trusted to get on without philosophers does not
altogether console. (*M*, 475)

However, on the other side, if Sidgwick's problem was whether "to
teach Ethics without a basis," it is noteworthy that he did continue to

teach it. And perhaps, as Kloppenberg urges, his exasperation could have led to a more fully pragmatist turn. After all, he was searching. "But the point is that I have tried *all* methods in turn – all that I found pointed out by any of those who have gone before me; and all in turn have failed – revelational, rational, empirical methods – there is no proof in any of them. Still, it is premature to despair, and I am quite content to go on seeking while life lasts" (*M*, 472–3). And as Kloppenberg shows, the revised last line of *The Methods of Ethics* did point up the possibility that if "in our supposed knowledge of the world of nature propositions are commonly taken to be universally true, which yet seem to rest on no other grounds than that we have a strong disposition to accept them, and that they are indispensable to the systematic coherence of our beliefs, – it will be more difficult to reject a similarly supported assumption in ethics, without opening the door to universal scepticism" (*ME*, 509). This is at least suggestive of the idea that Sidgwick was beginning to suspect that the problem might be his notion of proof itself, perhaps even capital-*P* Philosophy. Pragmatist views of justification as reasonable belief may well have afforded him a most welcome refuge.

Moreover, true to form, he was not prepared to say that his fears concerning the dissolution of the social order would be equally justified "some centuries hence." In this diagnosis, too, he had been attending to the details of things as they then stood. And, in fact, he thought that there was strong ground "for believing that it will *not* be equally true, since the tendency of development has certainly been to make human beings more sympathetic; and the more sympathetic they become, the more likely it seems to me that the results of their actions on other human beings (including remote posterity) will supply adequate motives to goodness of conduct, and render the expectation of personal immortality, and of God's moral order more realised, less important from this point of view" (*M*, 357–8). Indeed, improving the average person's sympathetic capacities is "likely to increase the mundane happiness for men generally, and to render the hope of future happiness less needed to sustain them in the trials of life" (*M*, 358). Perhaps a better-vindicated observation, however, was that "the political results of the coming generation will be determined by considerations very unlike those that come to the pen of a theoretical person writing in his study" (*M*, 504).

Thus, if Sidgwick envisioned a post-theological culture, it was a post-theological culture "but not yet." Parfit may well have grasped the spirit of some crucial elements in Sidgwick's thought, especially the hope for ethical progress in a post-theological world. Sidgwick discovered a deep fissure in the ordinary understanding of morality when it came to reasons; Parfit discovered such a fissure when it came to persons. And surely it is ingenious to carry Sidgwick's skepticism one step farther, to show that not only is there no soul for an afterlife but there is no self for this one, and by so doing to offer a guarded brief for utilitarianism. Morality would then indeed have risen from the ashes. But it is a mean paradox, suggestive of the changing times, that for Sidgwick the hard truth about the self that imperiled morality was frightfully believable; for Parfit, the hard truth about the self that might salvage morality is frightfully unbelievable – hardly "an inevitable point in the process of thought," at least for most people for the foreseeable future. Parfit welcomes most of his results; Sidgwick regretted most of his. Is it significant that in later years Sidgwick increasingly turned to problems of epistemology and metaphysics, on the one hand, and to political reasoning, on the other – *two* directions in which escape might be sought?

It is difficult to say just what turn Sidgwick's work might have taken. Certainly, his thought did develop; he went on seeking. And, as Marcus Singer explains in his essay, in the later periods of his life Sidgwick was more taken up with the challenges of evolutionism and "Kanto-Hegelianism" (as he called it) than of Whewellism. Indeed, the developments in Sidgwick's work are explored by many of the contributions to this volume – Irwin's chapter examines the important relationship between his views and the philosophy of his friend, T. H. Green, as does Kloppenberg's, and, again, Collini and Kloppenberg shed light on his political development and connections to the pragmatist movement.

Possibly it was after all the Victorian faith not to succumb to despair but to remain hopeful, or at least to move in cycles of despair and hope, the tension between the "emancipated head and the traditional heart," as Walter Houghton put it.[92] Sidgwick wrote, in *Philosophy, Its Scope and Relations*, that the most important lesson that science held for philosophy and theology was the vague one of patience and hope. At least we can say that, if Sidgwick's utilitarianism rested on faith, he also believed that faith was utilitarian. He had "hankerings after Optimism" (*M*, 508) and continued to the end to allow himself "the indestructible and inalienable minimum of faith which humanity cannot give up because it is necessary for life; and which I know that I, at least so far as the man in me is deeper than the methodical thinker, cannot give up" – namely, that expressed in Tennyson's extraordinarily influential poem "In Memoriam," the final lines of which read, "And out of darkness came the hands, That reach through nature, molding men" (*M*, 541).

Schneewind remarks that such views show how Sidgwick maintained a balance between thought and feeling, how he "neither allows the philosophic mind to stifle the longings and insights of the natural man, nor permits the man's emotions to achieve gratification at the cost of reason."[93] Times have changed, no doubt. But one need not be among the Victorian faithful to appreciate this quality in Sidgwick's life and thought. As Broad observed, Sidgwick succeeded in "seeing life steadily and seeing it whole."

Notes

1 Sidgwick, *The Ethics of Conformity and Subscription* (London: Williams and Norgate, 1870). The title page has a quotation from St. Paul: "Let every man be fully persuaded in his own mind." This was one of Sidgwick's mottoes.

2 See Blanshard's engaging study of Sidgwick in his *Four Reasonable Men* (Middletown, CT: Wesleyan University Press, 1984), pp. 181–243, a shorter version of which appeared in *Monist* 58 (1974).

3 Sorley, "Henry Sidgwick," *International Journal of Ethics* 11 (1900–1): 171.

4 Schneewind, *Sidgwick's Ethics and Victorian Moral Philosophy* (Oxford: Oxford University Press [Clarendon Press], 1977), is indisputably the single most important work on Sidgwick. However, as I shall record throughout the course of this introduction, recent years have also seen a number of important articles on Sidgwick, especially by William Frankena and Marcus Singer, as well as the crucial treatments by Rawls and Parfit.

5 See Collini, Donald Winch, and John Burrow, *That Noble Science of Politics*: *A Study in Nineteenth-Century Intellectual History* (Cambridge: Cambridge University Press, 1983), from which his contribution to this volume is adapted, and Kloppenberg, *Uncertain Victory*: *Social Democracy and Progressivism in European and American Thought, 1870–1920* (New York: Oxford University Press, 1986). On Sidgwick's politics, a very important and somewhat neglected book is Christopher Harvie, *The Lights of Liberalism* (London: Lane, 1976). And W. C, Harvard's *Henry Sidgwick and Later Utilitarian Political Philosophy* (Gainesville: University of Florida Press, 1959) also contains some useful information on Sidgwick and utilitarian political reformism.

6 Schneewind, *Sidgwick's Ethics*, p. 2.

7 It should be noted that other works by Schneewind are also extremely valuable in this regard. See, for example, *Backgrounds of Victorian Literature* (New York: Random House, 1970); "First Principles and Common Sense Morality in Sidgwick's Ethics," *Archiv für Geschichte der Philosophie* 45, no. 2 (1963); "Henry Sidgwick," *The Encyclopedia of Philosophy*, vol. 7, ed. P. Edwards (New York: Macmillan and Free Press, 1967); "Whewell's Ethics," *Studies in Moral Philosophy*, American Philosophical Quarterly Monograph Series, no. 1 (1968); and "Moral Problems and Moral Philosophy in the Victorian Period," *Victorian Studies*, supp. to vol. 9 (1965). For an insightful review of some fairly recent works on the relevant period, see Stefan Collini, "Political Theory and the 'Science of Society' in Victorian Britain," *Historical Journal* 23 (1980): 203–31. This essay stresses Sidgwick's role in defending po-

litical science against what had been the utilitarian tendency to envelop it under the general science of sociology.

8 Hayward, "A Reply," *International Journal of Ethics* 11 (1900–1): 361. Hayward's "Reply" is to a commentary (in the same issue) by E. E. Constance Jones on his "True Significance of Sidgwick's 'Ethics.' " The exchange between them is vigorous and illuminating, dealing with many of the problems that have continued to figure in Sidgwick studies. However, it should be noted here that my introduction must unfortunately be highly selective. Although I shall occasionally use older writings on Sidgwick for illustrative purposes, no attempt will be made to deal at all adequately with the pre-1970s material – the works by, for example, Hayward, Albee, Seth, James, Havard, and, most importantly, Moore and Broad, not to mention the many critics who responded to the early editions of Sidgwick's work. It is, I believe, correct to say, with Schneewind, that a great many of Sidgwick's earlier commentators and critics failed to appreciate the systematic nature of his enterprise, the overall logic of his approach, often mistakenly viewing him as simply presenting a brief for utilitarianism.

9 Schneewind, *Sidgwick's Ethics*, p. 192.

10 As Schneewind explains, Sidgwick was at first skeptical of intuitionism, thinking it mystical; he was only converted when he came to believe that even mathematics must rest on intuitions.

11 Again, *The Methods of Ethics* is "the first truly academic work in moral theory, modern in both method and spirit. Treating ethics as a discipline to be studied like any other branch of knowledge, it defines and carries out in exemplary fashion, if not for the first time, some of the comprehensive comparisons that constitute moral theory" (Rawls, "Kantian Constructivism in Moral Theory," *Journal of Philosophy* 77 [1980]: 555–7).

12 See "The Independence of Moral Theory," *Proceedings and Addresses of the American Philosophical Association*, 1974–5, p. 5.

13 See "Kantian Constructivism" and, especially, "The Independence of Moral Theory." "Independence" may not be the best word here, since what Rawls often has in mind is something more like mutual dependence, simply a denial that philosophy has a foundational, pyramidal structure, with philosophy of language or epistemology (or whatever) at the base. Thomas Nagel, in some of the essays in *Mortal Questions* (Cambridge: Cambridge University Press, 1979), also defends a version of this view, as does Derek Parfit in *Reasons and Persons* (Oxford: Oxford University Press [Clarendon Press], 1984), pp. 447–54, though there are important differences among these three, especially as concerns the nature of political versus ethical theory. I shall briefly comment on these differences later in the text. It should be noted however that some lively work has been inspired by the comparison between Rawls and Sidgwick. Thus, Peter Singer, in "Sidgwick and Reflective Equilibrium" (*Monist* 58 [1974]: 490–517), has argued that Rawls's appeal, in *A Theory of Justice* (Cambridge, MA: Harvard University Press, 1971), to Sidgwick's

approach to moral theory is misplaced. According to Singer, Sidgwick's intuitionism is clearly not akin to Rawls's method of reflective equilibrium between considered judgments; furthermore, Sidgwick's approach is better, since Rawls's collapses into relativism. Unfortunately, however, most of Singer's arguments are either outdated or were misguided to begin with. He plainly misses much of the redeeming subtlety of Sidgwick's arguments and many crucial elements in Rawls's notion of wide and general reflective equilibrium – indeed, the very point of the method as a way of investigating "the substantive moral conceptions that people hold, or would hold, under suitably defined conditions." These conceptions could, for all we know in advance, "turn out to be based on self-evident first principles," unlikely as this may seem. Rawls's method simply suspends consideration of the problem of moral truth, requiring only that we try "to see how people would fit their various convictions into one coherent scheme, each considered conviction whatever its level having a certain initial credibility," and that we "investigate what principles people would acknowledge and accept the consequences of when they have had an opportunity to consider other plausible conceptions and to assess their supporting grounds" ("Independence," pp. 7–8). Naturally, though Rawls fully acknowledges his indebtedness to Sidgwick, he wants moral theory to proceed on "a broader front," since Sidgwick "gave little attention to perfectionism or to the sort of conception represented by Kant." Thus, "these two moral conceptions, or methods of ethics, must also be included in the systematic comparisons essential to moral theory. Making these comparisons is a task, for the most part independent from the rest of philosophy, that we should be able to accomplish; and until it is further along, the problem of moral truth admits no definitive resolution" ("Independence," pp. 9–10). Rawls and Sidgwick were more insightfully contrasted in Marcus Singer, "The Methods of Justice: Reflections on Rawls," *Journal of Value Inquiry* 10 (1976): 286–316. For a fairly recent treatment of Rawls versus Singer on Sidgwick, see Steven Sverdlik, "Sidgwick's Methodology," *Journal of the History of Philosophy* 23 (1985): 537–53. Of course, in recent years, Rawls has increasingly stressed the practical and political nature of his constructivist approach, and it has become correspondingly clearer that his theory of justice is not meant as part of a particular comprehensive moral theory and is thus not on all fours with the theories that Sidgwick examines. And, in such works as "Kantian Constructivism," he has emphasized how Sidgwick's rational intuitionism led him to define the methods too narrowly as methods that seek truth. I briefly consider some of the relevant issues later in the text and in other notes. For a superb quick overview of recent developments in Rawls's theory, see the new preface to Norman Daniels's *Reading Rawls* (Stanford: Stanford University Press, 1989).

14 Schneewind also stresses the way in which Sidgwick tends to put ethics on an independent footing, noting that "Sidgwick's ways of handling problems seem as if they were designed according to a policy of keeping the non-ethical commitments of moral philosophy to an absolute minimum," though

he is not certain that this was always a fully conscious policy on Sidgwick's part. Thus, he notes that such a policy "might arise from the methodological principle of aiming at general agreement, since the fewer the extra-moral involvements of a theory, the fewer the opportunities it provides for dissent. Whether they were consciously designed to do so or not, Sidgwick's procedures and arguments generally – though certainly not always – lead him to think that the moral philosopher is not required to say much, if anything, about non-moral issues" (Schneewind, *Sidgwick's Ethics*, p. 204). As the line about aiming at general agreement should suggest, for all of the differences between Rawls and Sidgwick on substantive moral theory, the independence thesis generates important broad structural similarities between their views; in Rawls's recent work, the emphasis on independence has been transmuted into a more self-consciously practical and political approach that, among other things, especially stresses the need for a companion conception of shared, public reason to go with the conception of justice. The avoidance of controversial metaphysical issues, more often framed earlier as a requirement for progress in moral theory, is now cast as a practical political demand. Of course, this transition in Rawls's view was made possible by the fact that his overriding concern has always been with justice rather than morality in general, whereas Sidgwick's utilitarianism is a perfect example of a comprehensive moral conception. But, though complex, the affinities between Rawls and Sidgwick are nonetheless quite marked. See my "Knowledge to Practice: Rawls on the Independence of Moral Theory," unpublished manuscript, and remarks later in the text.

15 This point was admirably treated in A. N. Prior's *Logic and the Basis of Ethics* (Oxford: Oxford University Press [Clarendon Press], 1949).

16 Schneewind, *Sidgwick's Ethics*, p. 221.

17 Hayward, "Reply," p. 361. There is perhaps some irony in the suggestion that Sidgwick, who held that common-sense morality was unconsciously utilitarian, was himself an unconscious Kantian. However, I include Hayward's remark merely to point up, in dramatic fashion, the larger claim made by Schneewind, that Sidgwick's view is importantly different from the earlier utilitarian tradition. The issue of Sidgwick's relationship to Kant will be discussed later. It is considered in some detail in the contributions herein by Singer, Schneewind, Frankena, and Deigh.

18 For some helpful background material, especially on Sidgwick's views as compared to Moore's, see the essay by J. L. Mackie (Chapter 5, herein). For a quite recent treatment, see Roger Crisp, "Sidgwick and Self-interest," *Utilitas* 2, no.2 (November 1990): 267–80.

19 Schneewind, *Sidgwick's Ethics*, p. 226. See also the discussion by Parfit in *Reasons and Persons*, esp. pp. 493–502.

20 Of course, virtue ethics has enjoyed an extraordinary vogue during the last two decades, though fortunately this has, with only a few exceptions, taken a rather more toothless (and clawless) form than Aristotle would have countenanced. For a good critical review of the (now quite extensive) literature,

see Schneewind, "The Misfortunes of Virtue," *Ethics*, in press. T. H. Irwin's remarkably erudite work, *Aristotle's First Principles* (Oxford: Oxford University Press [Clarendon Press], 1988), admirably brings out the complexities of Aristotelian ethics and the extraordinary difficulties involved in the question of its dependence on Aristotelian metaphysics. It is perhaps worth noting that G. E. M. Anscombe's clarion call for the revival of virtue ethics, in "Modern Moral Philosophy" (*Philosophy* 33 [1958]: 1–19), was performed with Sidgwick's work serving as the horrible example of what modern ethics had come to. For a recent treatment of Sidgwick along these lines, see Alasdair MacIntyre, *Three Rival Versions of Moral Enquiry* (Notre Dame: University of Notre Dame Press, 1990), esp. chap. 8.

21 See Frankena, "Sidgwick and the Dualism of Practical Reason," *Monist* 58 (1974): esp. 464–5; and "Concepts of Rational Action in the History of Ethics," *Social Theory and Practice* 9 (1983): 165–97.

22 See Frankena, "Henry Sidgwick," in *The Encyclopedia of Morals*, ed. Vergilius T. Ferm (New York: Philosophical Library, 1956), pp. 539–44. However, Frankena, at least in this piece, does not allow that, for Sidgwick, the notion of right involves that of maximizing the good. For an important and highly relevant set of remarks, see Parfit, *Reasons and Persons*, p. 500.

23 Schneewind, *Sidgwick's Ethics*, p. 229.

24 Ibid., p. 230.

25 Ibid., pp. 303–4. In the book, this statement is presented in slightly qualified form, on the condition that other claims about Sidgwick's self-evident axioms are true. However, since Schneewind does seem to endorse these other claims, he would also seem to endorse the quoted statement.

26 Here I follow Schneewind (ibid., p. 229).

27 Singer, "The Many Methods of Sidgwick's Ethics," *Monist* 58 (1974): 420–48.

28 Schneewind, *Sidgwick's Ethics*, p. 197. As Schneewind notes, Sidgwick does not in fact rule out the possibility of a method involving more than one principle, providing that this does not produce conflicting results in particular cases.

29 Ibid.

30 In Rawls's case, "necessarily forced to choose" is perhaps too strong, since he has never insisted that there must be a unique reflective equilibrium.

31 Again, see the contributions herein by Mackie, Christiano, and Irwin, in particular. The problem, as Sidgwick sees it, is partly this: "For we have a practical need of determining not only whether we should pursue Truth rather than Beauty, or Freedom or some ideal constitution of society rather than either, or perhaps desert all of these for the life of worship and religious contemplation; but also how far we should follow any of these lines of endeavour, when we foresee among its consequences the pains of human or other sentient beings, or even the loss of pleasures that might otherwise have been enjoyed by them" (*ME*, 406). For a brisk summary of Sidgwick's hedonistic value theory, and an equally brisk dismissal of it, see James

Griffin, *Well-Being* (Oxford: Oxford University Press [Clarendon Press], 1986), pp. 9–10.

32 See Broad, *Ethics and the History of Philosophy* (New York: Humanities Press, 1952), p. 64. Prior to Schneewind's work, the most important treatment of Sidgwick's ethical theory was Broad's in *Five Types of Ethical Theory* (London: Routledge and Kegan Paul, 1951).

33 Sidgwick, "The Establishment of Ethical First Principles," *Mind* 4 (1879): 106–7. Irwin, in *Aristotle's First Principles*, questions the plausibility of the first type of argument; see esp. p. 533 n. 9; chap. 7 of this work gives an extremely helpful account, with several references to Sidgwick, of Aristotle on intuition and dialectic.

34 Sidgwick, "Professor Calderwood on Intuitionism in Morals," *Mind* 1 (1876): 564.

35 Ibid., pp. 563–4. See also the discussion of aesthetic intuitionism in Irwin's chapter 10, herein.

36 Sidgwick, "Calderwood on Intuitionism," p. 565.

37 Rawls, "Kantian Constructivism," p. 558. There has been some controversy over just how many self-evident truths Sidgwick actually advances. Frankena, in "Henry Sidgwick," argued that there were eight; Schneewind, in chap. 10 of *Sidgwick's Ethics*, plumps for four.

38 On contemplative utilitarianism, see the important work by T. D. Campbell, *Adam Smith's Science of Morals* (London: Allen and Unwin, 1971). For relevant discussions of the explanatory side of Sidgwick's analysis, see Alan Gibbard, "Inchoately Utilitarian Common Sense: The Bearing of a Thesis of Sidgwick's on Moral Theory," and A. John Simmons, "Utilitarianism and Unconscious Utilitarianism," both in *The Limits of Utilitarianism*, ed. H. B. Miller and W. H. Williams (Minneapolis: University of Minnesota Press, 1982). The above passages naturally raise the old question of whether Sidgwick was an act or a rule utilitarian. Schneewind's discussion of the matter, in *Sidgwick's Ethics*, pp. 34–9, is excellent. See also R. G. Frey, "Act-Utilitarianism: Sidgwick or Bentham and Smart?" *Mind* 86 (1977): 95–100. For an important discussion that sets out Sidgwick's view as a form of indirect utilitarianism, see John Gray, "Indirect Utility and Fundamental Rights," in Gray, *Liberalisms: Essays in Political Philosophy* (London: Routledge, 1989), pp. 120–39. According to Gray, although Sidgwick did not fully grasp that maxims different from, and more specific than, the utility principle would be necessary even in a world of perfectly enlightened utilitarians, he was nevertheless an important expositor of indirect utilitarianism because he acknowledged that "efficacious pursuit of the utilitarian goal entails according to aspects of our ordinary moral life a measure of immunity to utilitarian appraisal and criticism" (p. 128). As Gray urges, the indirect approach of Sidgwick and, especially, Mill is much superior to the often vacuous twentieth-century debates about rule versus act utilitarianism. That the act/rule debate is indeed moribund forms a common point of departure for much recent utilitarian work, which seems to be flourishing. See, for example,

R. M. Hare, *Moral Thinking* (Oxford: Oxford University Press [Clarendon Press], 1981), and the collection of essays devoted to it, *Hare and Critics*, ed. D. Seanor and N. Fotion (Oxford: Oxford University Press [Clarendon Press], 1988); Fred Berger, *Happiness, Justice, & Freedom: The Moral and Political Philosophy of John Stuart Mill* (Berkeley: University of California Press, 1984); Russell Hardin, *Morality within the Limits of Reason* (Chicago: University of Chicago Press, 1988); David Brink, *Moral Realism and the Foundations of Ethics* (Cambridge: Cambridge University Press, 1989); and Alan Gibbard, *Wise Choices, Apt Feelings* (Cambridge, MA: Harvard University Press, 1990), a work that contains some extremely interesting reflections of Sidgwick. For a stimulating overview of some utilitarian controversies, one appropriately dismissive of the act/rule debate, see James Griffin, "Modern Utilitarianism," *Revue Internationale de Philosophie* (1982). Of course, it was precisely the indirect side of Sidgwick's utilitarianism that allowed Bernard Williams to label it "Government House" utilitarianism, a position happily suited to colonial administrators. See the oft-cited discussion in Bernard Williams, *Ethics and the Limits of Philosophy* (Cambridge, MA: Harvard University Press, 1985), esp. pp. 105–10. The problem of publicity is, of course, part of what is at stake here, as always in discussions of utilitarianism. I shall consider the problem in more detail later in the text, when discussing Rawls's Kantian constructivism.

39 Ritchie, "Review: *The Elements of Politics*, by Henry Sidgwick," *International Journal of Ethics* 2 (1891–2): 255.

40 Though Sidgwick took as most fundamental an "individualistic principle," namely, that "what one sane adult is legally compelled to render to others should be merely the negative service of non-interference, except so far as he has voluntarily undertaken to render positive services; provided that we include in the notion of non-interference the obligation of remedying or compensating for mischief intentionally or carelessly caused by his acts – or preventing mischief that would otherwise result from some previous act" (*EP*, 42). For an interesting and important discussion of how Sidgwick's notion of liberty may have led to certain unclarities in Rawls's conception of justice, see H. L. A. Hart, "Rawls on Liberty and Its Priority," in Daniels, *Reading Rawls*, pp. 230–52. It should also be remarked that the whole texture of Sidgwick's treatment of self-evident principles and their relation to the demands of practice weighs against a too light, anti-Kantian dismissal of his view on the grounds that moral principles "only have a point insofar as they incorporate tacit reference to a whole range of institutions, practices, and vocabularies of moral and political deliberation" (see Rorty, *Contingency, Irony, and Solidarity* [Cambridge: Cambridge University Press, 1989], p. 59). But see the discussion at the end of this section.

41 Schneewind, *Sidgwick's Ethics*, pp. 192–3.

42 See, for example, Hare, *Moral Thinking*, and R. B. Brandt, *A Theory of the Good and the Right* (Oxford: Oxford University Press [Clarendon Press], 1979). This debate has often been cast in the form of objections

to Rawl's method of reflective equilibrium. Again, see Daniels, *Reading Rawls*.

43 See Schneewind, *Sidgwick's Ethics*, pp. 264–5.
44 Ibid., p. 284.
45 Ibid., p. 285.
46 Ibid., p. 350.
47 Again, see Irwin, *Aristotle's First Principles*, chap. 7, for an account of the links between dialectic and intuition.
48 See Schneewind, *Sidgwick's Ethics*, pp. 201–21.
49 Ibid., p. 303. Sidgwick hopes to make a similar inference work in the case of going from one's own ultimate good to the good of all, but here he runs into difficulties, as discussed in Section 4.
50 Ibid., p. 302.
51 Ibid., p. 297.
52 Besides the piece reprinted herein (Chapter 3), see Donagan, *The Theory of Morality* (Chicago: University of Chicago Press, 1977), esp. pp. 19–24; "Whewell's *Elements of Morality*," *Journal of Philosophy* 71 (1974): 724–36; and "Justice and Variable Social Institutions," in Midwest Studies in Philosophy vol. 7: *Social and Political Philosophy*, ed. P. French et al. (Minneapolis: University of Minnesota Press, 1982).
53 See Rawls, "Themes in Kant's Moral Philosophy," in *Kant's Transcendental Deductions*, ed. E. Forster (Stanford: Stanford University Press, 1989), pp. 95–7. See also Rawls, "Kantian Constructivism."
54 This charge as well as the familiar claims that as a form of classical utilitarianism Sidgwick's theory both ignores distributivist concerns and might justify indefinite increases in population growth are of course the stock objections to Sidgwick's substantive theory. See, for example, Rawls, *Theory of Justice*, and Williams, *Ethics*. For a (highly Sidgwickian) utilitarian response, see Brink, *Moral Realism*, chap. 8, sec. 11.
55 The last lines of this work read: "Further, we must recognize that even in the case of our thought about 'what is,' though error may lie in want of correspondence between Thought and Fact, it can only be ascertained and exposed by showing inconsistency between Thought and Thought, i.e. precisely as error is disclosed in the case of our Thought about 'what ought to be' " (*PSR*, 247).
56 Morton White, *Toward Reunion in Philosophy* (New York: Atheneum, 1963), p. 25. This work, though first published in 1956, contains an extremely valuable discussion of pragmatism, especially in its relations with analytical philosophy as developed by Sidgwick's students, Russell and Moore. Its remarks on the various forms of disciplinary independence and autonomy, and on the disputes over the "scientific" nature of ethics in the periods following Sidgwick's struggles with the matter, are still quite illuminating.
57 Unfortunately, as James Ward states in the editorial note to *PSR* (vii), it was impossible to reconstruct the texts that Sidgwick had apparently intended to use to give a fuller account of the divisions of practical philosophy. Ward

cites *ME*, book 1, chap. 2, and *EP*, chap. 13, as supplying some relevant additional material. He might also have mentioned, among other works, *PPE*, introduction, chaps. 1–3, and book 3, chaps. 1 and 9. I remark on some of this material in Section 4.

58 And this perhaps helps explain why one can find delicately balanced in Sidgwick's approach elements that would yield both the Moorean emphasis on the distinctions found in common sense (and eventually Austin's view of ordinary language as the "beginning all" of philosophy) and the emphasis on both technical development and systematizing human knowledge in the large that characterized Bertrand Russell's work, despite its later demotion of ethics to the realm of the noncognitive. Perhaps Moore and Russell learned more from Sidgwick than they let on, especially about the merits of patient, detailed inquiry. At any rate, on knowledge in ethics, Sidgwick once wrote to a friend, "though I hold strongly that the Right is knowable, if not 'absolutely' . . . yet as an ideal, a standard to which we may indefinitely approximate, I by no means assert that it is *known*, that our general rules are even nearly the best possible" (*M*, 243). This was in 1871; but in 1896 it was still the case that ethics had yet to enjoy the comforts of "normal" science: "I feel that in all branches of Moral Sciences there is at present a danger that every energetic teacher will want to write his own book and make it as unlike other people's books as he can. But after all this is a sign of intellectual life, and I suppose that we shall some time or other begin to converge towards agreement" (*M*, 547). As I make clear in the text, although Sidgwick certainly held out the ideal of systematic theorizing in both practical and theoretical philosophy, he was sober and cautious in the extreme when it came to carrying out the project, and, as I shall show in the next section, he was not as sanguine about the prospects as the last passage suggests.

59 Sidgwick, "Calderwood on Intuitionism," pp. 565–6.

60 Sidgwick, "Review: *Ethical Studies*, by F. H. Bradley," *Mind* 1 (1876): 545.

61 J. J. C. Smart's famous contribution to Smart and B. Williams, *Utilitarianism: For and Against* (Cambridge: Cambridge University Press, 1973), was in large part an attempt to present Sidgwick in "modern dress" – that is, minus the intuitionism. Brink's *Moral Realism*, which novelly defends a realist metaethics but with a coherentist epistemology, and Alan Gibbard's *Wise Choices*, which defends an extremely sophisticated form of noncognitivism (norm expressivism), both manage to say quite charitable things about Sidgwick's intuitionism. Gibbard gives a provocative sketch of how the conditions on self-evident principles might play a valuable role in effecting the coordination involved in societal norms; see esp. pp. 316–25.

62 See also Singer's very valuable article, "Ethics and Common Sense," *Revue Internationale de Philosophie* 158 (1986): 221–58. As this article makes plain, Singer is clearly not opposed to all ethical theory; he simply wants to insure that it is moored in common sense.

63 For a recent sampler, see *Anti-theory in Ethics and Moral Conservatism*, ed. S. G. Clarke and E. Simpson (Albany: SUNY Press, 1989). There is of

course an extraordinary range of opinion on just how much system is acceptable – obviously, "theory" in ethics need not always means full-blown rationalism.

64 James Wallace, *Moral Relevance and Moral Conflict* (Ithaca: Cornell University Press, 1988), pp. 92–3. For a cogent discussion of the role of principles in moral decisions, see Schneewind, "Moral Knowledge and Moral Principles," in *Revisions: Changing Perspectives in Moral Philosophy*, ed. S. Hauerwas and A. MacIntyre (Notre Dame: University of Notre Dame Press, 1983).

65 Wallace, *Moral Relevance*, p. 48.

66 Sidgwick, "Some Fundamental Ethical Controversies," *Mind* 14 (1889): 483. Another article worth noting for its bearing on Sidgwick's ethical theory is "The Establishment of Ethical First Principles."

67 This passage is from Sidgwick's essay "Bentham and Benthamism" (*MEA*), a piece that should disabuse anyone of the notion that he was incapable of sprightly prose, though he did rather disarmingly note that "it is the first thing that I have written for years in which I have aimed at all at literary effect" (*M*, 327).

68 See Schneewind, Chapter 2, herein, and Parfit, *Reasons and Persons*, p. 529, n.4. But see also Frankena's exceptionally interesting remarks (Chapter 6, herein) on the paradoxical way in which Bentham figures in Sidgwick's conception of the historical development of ethics.

69 See Schneewind, *Sidgwick's Ethics*, p. 300.

70 Brink, "Sidgwick's Dualism of Practical Reason," *Australasian Journal of Philosophy* 66 (1988): 291. For Frankena's interpretation, see his "Dualism of Practical Reason" and "Concepts of Rational Action."

71 Brink, "Sidgwick's Dualism," p. 305. It should be noted that Brink actually allows that Sidgwick's texts support both interpretations and thus that neither reading can be decisively defended.

72 See Parfit, *Reasons and Persons*, esp. pp. 137–42, where he analyzes p. 418 of *The Methods of Ethics*. Parfit's work is very much inspired by Sidgwick's views on progress in ethical theory, though he tends to believe that this will often depend on metaphysical arguments of the kind that Sidgwick did not care to elaborate. The bearing of theories of personal identity on ethical egoism is a good case in point.

73 As Parfit stresses, his "two subjects, reasons and persons, have close connections. I believe that most of us have false beliefs about our own nature, and our identity over time, and that, when we see the truth, we ought to change some of our beliefs about what we have reason to do. We ought to revise our moral theories, and our beliefs about rationality" (ibid., p. ix). For Parfit, reason can certainly be practical, and he argues that even desires can be rational or irrational, as did Sidgwick. Again, see Parfit's remarks on p. 500.

74 This still quite Sidgwickian form of immanent critique has become rather popular in recent moral theory, of course. Common-sense morality comes

in for a similar drubbing in Shelly Kagan's book, *The Limits of Morality* (Oxford: Oxford University Press [Clarendon Press], 1989), which tries to show how various of its anticonsequentialist elements, those aimed at determining a ceiling on moral requirements, do not work; Kagan thus believes that he has provided at least a negative argument for consequentialism. Though not overtly utilitarian, such treatments of common-sense morality certainly provide aid and comfort to that position, especially if, as in Russell Hardin's work, utilitarianism fundamentally amounts to consequentialism. Michael Slote's *Common-Sense Morality and Consequentialism* (London: Routledge and Kegan Paul, 1985) also provides a highly Sidgwickian critique of common-sense morality, though Slote is also critical of consequentialism and ends up leaning toward a Kantian position. For an overview of some of the theoretical issues at work in the conflict between common-sense morality and utilitarianism on the issue of demandingness, one that makes special reference to Sidgwick, see Paul Gomberg, "Self and Others in Bentham and Sidgwick," *History of Philosophy Quarterly* 8 (1986): 437–48. And for somewhat more generous views of the broad role of common sense in moral theory, see the previously cited works by Marcus Singer (nn. 13, 27, 62).

75 At the level of theories of rationality, Parfit argues for the "Critical Present-aim" theory, which, he allows, is not Sidgwick's principle of benevolence and is in some respects even more personal than the self-interest theory.

76 Parfit's arguments about the significance of the reductionist view for our theories of rationality and morality are intricate and cannot be fully summarized here. They are admittedly mostly considerations of relative force, for example, to the effect that utilitarianism (or perhaps negative utilitarianism) is more plausible on the reductionist view than on the nonreductionist view. Again, Brink's essay herein surveys a number of Parfit's claims.

77 Parfit, *Reasons and Persons*, pp. 137–44. According to Parfit, Sidgwick may have confused the argument for the full relativity of reasons (linked to the present-aim theory) with the argument for the (absurd) "hedonistic egoism of the present" view, requiring one to aim at one's greatest happiness now. This would be another way in which Sidgwick's hedonism led him astray.

78 Ibid., p. 462.

79 Ibid., p. 453.

80 See Rorty, *Consequences of Pragmatism* (Minneapolis: University of Minnesota Press, 1982), pp. xxix–xxxvii. In his work on personal identity, however, Parfit tries to base some of his arguments on various forms of brain research and research into the possibility of personal survival, literature which Nagel has also considered. See, for example, Nagel, *Mortal Questions* (Cambridge: Cambridge University Press, 1979), chap. 11. Perhaps the most controversial aspects of Parfit's argument have to do with his use of bizarre puzzle cases to determine the significance of the reductionist view for theories of rationality and morality – cases of the sort that Rawls's theory, from its very inception, has regarded as inadmissible.

81 See Nagel, *Mortal Questions*, chaps. 9 and 10, for some of their early differences.

82 As Rawls explains, his "view that philosophy in the classical sense as the search for truth about a prior and independent moral order cannot provide the shared basis for a political conception of justice . . . does not presuppose the controversial metaphysical claim that there is no such order. . . . The reasons I give for that view are historical and sociological, and have nothing to do with metaphysical doctrines about the status of values. What I hold is that we must draw the obvious lessons of our political history since the Reformation and the Wars of Religion, and the development of modern constitutional democracies" (Rawls, "The Idea of an Overlapping Consensus," *Oxford Journal of Legal Studies* 7 (1987): 13, n. 21. Perhaps the point in the text could be put, in part, by saying that Sidgwick too was anxious to draw out the obvious lessons of our shared political experience, which he saw both as consistent with, indeed the preliminary to, the search for truth and as the only realistic, responsible way for philosophy to inform political debate. To illustrate just one further relevant point, in a late article, "Public Morality," Sidgwick argued that there were "two distinct ways of treating ethical questions," the first of which involved "establishing fundamental principles of abstract or ideal morality" and working "out deductively the particular rules of duty or practical conceptions of human good or well-being," and the second of which involved contemplating "morality as a social fact" and endeavoring "by reflective analysis, removing vagueness and ambiguity, solving apparent contradictions, correcting lapses and supplying omissions, to reduce this body of current opinions, so far as possible, to a rational and coherent system." Sidgwick observes that these methods are "in no way antagonistic" and that it is reasonable to think that "they must lead to the same goal – a perfectly satisfactory and practical ideal of conduct." But he also allows that, "in the actual condition of our intellectual and social development, the respective results of the two methods are apt to exhibit a certain divergence which, for practical purposes, we have to obliterate – more or less consciously – by a rough compromise" (*PE*, 53).

83 On all these points, see Rawls, "Justice as Fairness: Political Not Metaphysical," *Philosophy & Public Affairs* 14 (1985): 223–51. See also the penetrating discussion, from a Kantian perspective, in Christine Korsgaard's "Personal Identity and the Unity of Agency: A Kantian Response to Parfit," *Philosophy & Public Affairs* 18 (1989): 101–32. Again, for an excellent overview of Rawls's recent work and its political interpretation, see the new preface to Daniels, *Reading Rawls*.

84 To some, it may seem that, between *A Theory of Justice* and "Kantian Constructivism in Moral Theory," Rawls went from regarding Sidgwick as an early fellow practitioner of the method of reflective equilibrium, with a few insignificant intuitionist leanings, to regarding him as, along with Ross and Moore, a "rational intuitionist" and thus part of the very school against which Rawls seeks to define his constructivist view. Thus, Rawls's work

opposes Sidgwick's on a number of (related) dimensions: It is Kantian and
deontological rather than utilitarian and teleological and affirms a plurality
of conceptions of the good rather than one rational (much less hedonistic)
good; it is practical and political rather than comprehensive; and it is constructivist rather than intuitionist. It should also be mentioned that for Sidgwick ethics has to do with determining right individual conduct even under
far from ideal circumstances, whereas Rawls is primarily concerned with
determining principles of justice for a more or less ideal institutional arrangement, though in chapter 2 of *The Methods of Ethics* Sidgwick allows
that the province of "Political Theory" is "Ideal Law." The differences
between Rawls's theory of justice and Sidgwick's utilitarianism are of course
obvious enough, and I have certainly not been concerned to deny them. My
claim is simply that certain points of similarity on such matters as the importance of moral theory for moral philosophy have not been sufficiently
stressed, and in spelling them out I have in fact appealed to Rawls's more
recent work, rather than *A Theory of Justice*. As noted earlier, the defense
of Sidgwick's method against Rawls's that is given in Peter Singer's "Sidgwick
and Reflective Equilibrium" suffers from numerous misinterpretations.
Again, for an excellent overview of Rawls's development, see the new preface to Daniels, *Reading Rawls*. For superb work on the constructivist approach, see Onora O'Neill's *Constructions of Reason: Explorations of Kant's
Practical Philosophy* (Cambridge: Cambridge University Press, 1989), and
Rawls, "Themes." The latter contains an important, somewhat altered, contrast between constructivism and rational intuitionism.

85 See Collini, "Political Theory," p. 221, and similar passages in the work
included here (Chapter 12).

86 I shall not here tackle "Das Henry Sidgwick Problem," as Collini has dubbed
the difficulty of reconciling Sidgwick's views on the relationship between
analytical and deductive theory, on the one side, and historical and inductive
theory, on the other. Importantly, as Eleanor Sidgwick explained, Sidgwick
believed "that a threefold treatment of politics is desirable for completeness:
– first, an exposition analytical and deductive, such as he attempted in his
work on the *Elements of Politics*; secondly, an evolutionary study of the
development of polity within the historic period in Europe, beginning with
the earliest known Graeco-Roman and Teutonic polity, and carried down
to the modern state of Europe and its colonies as the last result of political
evolution; thirdly, a comparative study of the constitutions of Europe and
its colonies in connexion with the history of what may be called the consti-
tution-making century which has just ended" (*DEP*, v). However, it is worth
remarking again that Sidgwick did "not think that the historical method is
the one to be primarily used in attempting to find reasoned solutions of the
problems of practical politics." History cannot in itself determine the ultimate
end of conduct, and besides, there is the fact "of the continual process of
change and development through which political societies move, which renders the experience of the past – unless it be a comparatively recent past –

largely inapplicable to the present needs of the most advanced communities" (*DEP*, 4–5). Plausibly, a roughly similar balance between directly addressing the reader here and now, without being too specific about the time frame, and providing historical perspective on what we believe, on reflection, can be found in Rawls's work.

87 See Rorty, *Contingency, Irony, and Solidarity*, p. xiii.
88 Parfit, *Reasons and Persons*, p. 139.
89 Ibid., pp. 520–1, n. 109.
90 *Ethics of Conformity*, p. 6.
91 Ibid., pp. 14–15.
92 Houghton, *The Victorian Frame of Mind, 1830–1870* (New Haven: Yale University Press, 1985). Sidgwick's mind figures prominently in this still very helpful overview.
93 Schneewind, *Sidgwick's Ethics*, p. 379.

Part I

Common-sense morality, deontology, utilitarianism

1

Sidgwick and nineteenth-century British ethical thought

MARCUS G. SINGER

Ethics in nineteenth-century Britain opens with Bentham and ends with Sidgwick and thus both opens and closes with utilitarianism, though utilitarianism of markedly different varieties. The major figure in the middle of the century was John Stuart Mill, and the middle period of the century was dominated both by utilitarianism and by disputes about utilitarianism. Thus, utilitarianism was in many ways the dominant moral philosophy of the century – and there is certainly something typically British about it – but it was by no means the only one. Cambridge rationalism was still strong, especially in the work of William Whewell, who, even though his work has in large measure dropped from sight, was not just another intuitionist, as he came to be regarded by so many, but an acute and knowledgeable thinker who had an ethical theory of some complexity. Idealism, influenced in varying degrees by the philosophies of Kant and Hegel, was especially strong, and especially pronounced in the work of T. H. Green – presently a very underrated philosopher – and F. H. Bradley, who lived well into the twentieth century and whose virtuosity as a dialectician was so strong as to create for him an indelible reputation as a keen philosophical thinker, whose work – as with the paradoxes of Zeno – is to be taken seriously even when it is most incredible. The outstanding new development of the century was the development of the theory of evolution and of natural selection by Darwin and Wallace and its anticipation in the work of Herbert Spencer, who gave a naturalistic and evolutionary account of ethics in a work that foreshadowed the theory of biological evolution

This essay is essentially an amalgamation and revision of two others: portions, considerably expanded, of "Nineteenth Century British Ethics," forthcoming in the Garland *Encyclopedia of Ethics*, ed. Lawrence C. and Charlotte Becker; and portions, somewhat revised, of the first two sections of "Common Sense and Paradox in Sidgwick's Ethics," *History of Philosophy Quarterly* 3, no. 1 (1986): 65–78. I must express my gratitude to the appropriate editors and publishers for permitting their use in this form. I am also pleased to express my appreciation to Bart Schultz for first seeing and then painstakingly pointing out to me how they could effectively be combined into one, something I did not at first see.

by almost ten years. Spencer also developed a philosophical system, based on evolutionary theory, of immense scope and range, in which ethics played an essential but subordinate part.

At the beginning of the century, then, there were three or four strands of thought vying with one another: theological ethics, based somehow and in some way on the will or the nature of the deity and on the promise of a life to come; utilitarianism, earlier in its theological form (represented first by Gay and near the end of the eighteenth century by Paley) and then in its secular form established by Bentham; egoism, strong in the British tradition ever since Hobbes and despite pious acclamations against it; and various form of intuitionism or moral sense theory. In mid-century, naturalism, the attempt to base ethics on nature or on human nature, was revived by the work of Spencer and Darwin, and from the 1860s on a good deal of debate was expended on the supposed antagonism between evolution and theism, science and religion. All moral philosophers had to come to terms with evolutionary theory, whether they accepted it or not, and ethics in turn came to be thought of as something evolving, for if species evolve so does society. Some attempted to combine evolution theory with utilitarianism; others attempted to work out an evolutionary ethics independently of utilitarianism; and some were convinced that the theory of evolution had no special relevance to ethics. Near the end of the century evolution theory was still going strong, but rationalism had made something of a comeback, influenced partly by the work of Sidgwick, whose *Methods of Ethics* remained a dominant work from its first edition, in 1874, through its fifth edition, published in 1893, and also influenced by the attention being paid to the work of Kant. The form moral philosophy assumed in the early twentieth century was the form it took in this period, until the development of logical positivism, the emotive theory, relativism, and other forms of moral skepticism influenced by developments in sociology, anthropology, historical studies, linguistics, and the physical sciences.

What follows is a compressed overview of the development of nineteenth-century British ethical thought through Sidgwick, focusing, once we get there, on the validity and coherence of Sidgwick's analysis of common-sense morality and his contribution to the developing concern with the history of ethics, which started in that century.

1

Although Bentham's most famous work, *An Introduction to the Principles of Morals and Legislation*, was published in 1789 and thus in the eighteenth century, in manner, authority, and influence it was a work of the nineteenth, and this is the work with which ethics in nineteenth-century Britain began. Indeed, it was not actually widely read until its second edition of 1823. But Bentham's main interest was in jurisprudence, more specifically legislation, with the question of how it can be determined what laws ought to be passed, revised, or repealed and how to effectuate this determination. What Bentham called "private ethics" played only a subordinate part in it.[1] Bentham's discussion of private ethics – so far as it is Bentham's and not the editor's – is contained in the *Deontology* of 1834 (two years after Bentham's death), arranged and edited by John Bowring, with a number of Bowring's own interpolations.[2] Its authenticity is disputed. J. S. Mill held a very low opinion of it, insisting that it was not genuinely Bentham's: "The style proves it to have been so entirely rewritten, that it is impossible to tell how much or how little of it is Bentham's."[3] In part, Mill held this view because the book's treatment of private ethics is so inferior to Mill's idea of how Bentham would or should have treated it. On the other hand, in the preface to the third edition of his *Outlines of the History of Ethics for English Readers* (1892), Sidgwick remarked that he was "now disposed to accept the ... *Deontology* of Bentham, as giving a generally trustworthy account of his view as to the relation of Virtue to the virtuous agent's Happiness" (*OHE*3, x).

Bentham very early started from the principle, which he took as axiomatic, that "it is the greatest happiness of the greatest number that is the measure of right and wrong,"[4] where happiness is understood to consist of a balance of discrete pleasures over discrete pains. This is one formulation of the central principle of utilitarianism, which was formulated in various ways by Bentham and others. But Bentham's main contribution was not in originating utilitarianism (though he may have originated its name), nor is it in the hedonic calculus (which had been anticipated by Hutcheson). It lies in the dictum, "Each to count for one and none for more than one," which is vital in impartially applying the hedonic calculus and the utility principle and which thus sharply marks off Benthamite utilitarianism from pre-Bentham varieties. It also lies in the detailed and exhaustive working out of the application of the principle of utility, especially with respect to legislation and the criminal and civil codes.

Bentham had a number of disciples who were instrumental in transforming utilitarianism from a philosophical doctrine into a political and social movement. Among them were James Mill, father of John Stuart, and John Austin. James Mill's *Essay on Government* of 1820 was the object of a fierce criticism by Macaulay in the pages of the *Edinburgh*

Review (1829), which in turn generated a sharp controversy between Macaulay and anonymous authors in the *Westminster Review* (started by Bentham in 1824), in which some searching criticisms of utilitarianism as political doctrine and as ethical theory are to be found.[5] The elder Mill's main contribution to ethics proper consists in the 431-page *Fragment on Mackintosh*, a defense of utilitarianism and Bentham by way of an attack on Mackintosh's *Dissertation on the Progress of Ethical Philosophy* (1830).[6] Mackintosh had said that "It is unfortunate that Ethical Theory . . . is not the province in which Mr. Bentham has reached the most desirable distinction"; that "Mr. Bentham preaches the principle of utility with the zeal of a discoverer. Occupied more in reflection than in reading, he knew not, or forgot, how often it had been the basis, and how generally an accepted part, of moral systems"; and also, "He is too little acquainted with doubts to believe the honest doubts of others, and he is too angry to make allowance for their prejudices and habits."[7] Mackintosh's 29 pages on Bentham are dissected and excoriated in 181 pages of the *Fragment on Mackintosh* in a manner that echoes Bentham's ferocious demolition, in *A Fragment on Government*, of a few sentences in Blackstone's *Commentaries*. James Mill was also the organizing force behind the development of Benthamism as a philosophical movement and program of reform.

John Austin played a different role. Austin developed what was basically Bentham's thought on jurisprudence into a comprehensive and penetrating philosophy of law, in his *Lectures on Jurisprudence*, published posthumously in 1863, preceded and prefaced by his *Province of Jurisprudence Determined* of 1832, both works that fell stillborn from the press.[8] In this work Austin introduced an interpretation of utilitarianism that amounted to a departure from orthodox Benthamism, though that was not perceived at the time. Austin introduced what has come to be called rule or indirect utilitarianism. (In this he had been preceded by Paley, though this innovation by Paley was also not noticed for over a hundred years.) Austin maintained that "we must not contemplate the act as if it were single and insulated, but must look at the class of acts to which it belongs. We must suppose that acts of the class were generally done or omitted, and consider the probable effect upon the general happiness." On the view Austin is advancing, "our conduct [should] conform to *rules* inferred from the tendencies of actions, but . . . not be determined by a direct resort to the principle of general utility. Utility [is] the test of our conduct, ultimately, but not immediately: the immediate test of the rules to which our conduct [should] conform, but not the immediate test of specific or individual actions. Our rules [should] be fashioned on utility; our conduct, on our rules" (*Jurispru-*

dence, vol. 1, lecture 3, pp. 113–14). Since Austin's *Province* went unnoticed for years, it is not surprising that this twist of doctrine did so as well. It was later revived (especially but not solely near the end of chapter 2 of *Utilitarianism*) by J. S. Mill (who had attended Austin's lectures in 1828), though without any reference to Austin. It may even be that the younger Mill did not regard this interpretation as any sort of departure from Benthamite utilitarianism.

John Stuart Mill did not write any systematic ethical treatise, as he did in logic and political economy, and his developed views on ethics have to be gleaned from a number of sources. However, his *Utilitarianism* (1863) is one of the most widely read works in the history of ethics and is usually understood (even though it is not always correctly understood) as representing Mill's ethical theory. In it, Mill attempted to defend utilitarianism from various objections that had been leveled against it and misunderstandings to which it had been subject. In the process he added what some critics regarded as various misunderstandings of his own. Perhaps his most pronounced departure from Bentham, apart from the one just mentioned, is the idea that in determining the value of distinct pleasures the quality of the pleasures must be considered, not just the quantity. "It would be absurd that while, in estimating all other things, quality is considered as well as quantity, the estimation of pleasures should be supposed to depend on quantity alone" (*Utilitarianism*, chap. 2, par. 4). This distinction, and the accompanying idea that some pleasures are of such a quality as to be higher and therefore better than others, was not generally accepted, and a consensus developed that in moving in this direction Mill had actually abandoned hedonism, although without intending to. It was not until fairly recently that the idea began to be considered on its merits and not simply on the ground of whether it is consistent with hedonistic utilitarianism. It is also just beginning to be noticed that in *Utilitarianism* Mill developed a conception of happiness different from the simple hedonistic conception of happiness as pleasure and freedom from pain, such that the achievement of the utilitarian end espoused by Mill would entail a radical reordering of society and of the typical outlook of individuals (chap. 2, pars. 12–14, 18; chap. 3, pars. 10–11). "The present wretched education and wretched social arrangements are the only real hindrance to [its] being attainable by almost all" (chap. 2, par. 13), and Mill refers over and over again to "the comparatively early state of human advancement in which we now live" (chap. 3, par. 11). Some features of the improvement in social order and individual life and of the revolution in human feelings and attitudes that Mill envisaged are developed in *On Liberty* (1859) and *The Subjection of Women* (1869).

Mill's ethical views were outlined in the last chapter of his *System of Logic* and were also presented in some of the essays collected in his *Dissertations and Discussions*. Some of them are highly polemical, such as his "Whewell on Moral Philosophy" (1852). Whewell represented for Mill the example par excellence of the a priori intuitionist whose doctrine is to be combated at all costs, since it is regarded as essentially reactionary in practice, an implicit defense of the status quo and an attempt to defend "the present wretched social arrangements" that make for unhappiness, mass misery, and a backward state of society. And Mill's emphasis on the importance of rules to apply the principle of utility by (*Utilitarianism*, chap. 2, pars. 24–5) is echoed in his "Inaugural Address" of 1867:

You will find abundance of people to tell you that logic is no help to thought, and that people cannot be taught to think by rules. Undoubtedly rules by themselves, without practice, go but a little way in teaching anything. But if the practice of thinking is not improved by rules, I venture to say it is the only difficult thing done by human beings that is not so. . . . Wherever there is a right way and a wrong, there must be a difference between them, and it must be possible to find out what the difference is; and when found out and expressed in words, it is a rule for the operation. (*Dissertations and Discussions*, 4: 373)

Whewell, who wrote extensively and originally on the philosophy and history of science, also wrote extensively and originally on ethics. His most important ethical works are his *Elements of Morality* (1845); *Lectures on Systematic Morality* (1846), a commentary on and explanation of the *Elements*; and *Lectures on the History of Moral Philosophy* (1852; 2d ed., 1862, the lectures having been delivered originally in 1838). The *Elements* is the best known of these works, but it is easily misunderstood, and it has appeared to some to be simple-minded. Thus it was taken by both J. S. Mill and James Martineau. Some recent commentators, in particular Schneewind and Donagan, have found more sense and substance in it.[9] Whewell regarded his *Elements* as setting out a system of morality, not a moral philosophy; it was his view that between morality and moral philosophy there is a relationship analogous to that between geometry and the philosophy of geometry, with the difference being that, whereas geometry was already well understood, there was not sufficient understanding of actual morality, which the *Elements* were designed to bring about. Whewell was a rational intuitionist who emphasized the importance of understanding and conforming to common sense: "No scheme of morality can be true, except a scheme which agrees with the Common Sense of Mankind, so far as that Common Sense is consistent with itself" (*Elements*, 2d ed., preface). One implication of this is that first principles of morality, which Whewell goes on to describe, cannot be applied apart from a social context, and one of the essential features of that context is the law of the land. Thus, on Whewell's view morality depends on law, in the sense that there are moral precepts that can be understood only by reference to the law of the land. One instance given is the precept that it is wrong to steal, which presupposes the concept of property, and it is the law that determines what is property and whose property it is. Whewell was probably the first philosopher since Aristotle to attempt to give an account of the morality of common sense and to systematize and coordinate it, and Whewell was thus an unacknowledged forerunner of Sidgwick's attempt to analyze the morality of common sense. Whewell held that a system of morality is a "body of moral truths, definitely expressed and rationally connected" (*Lectures on Systematic Morality*, pp. 20–1), all shown to be subordinate to practically necessary first principles. He aimed to "construct a deductive system in which a comprehensive and consistent set of precise moral rules would be rationally derived from practically necessary first principles"[10] and from which, given adequate knowledge of the facts, the solutions to problems of conscience could be derived. In this respect, as in others, Whewell's views differed drastically from those of Spencer and Darwin and other evolutionary naturalists.

2

T. H. Green's *Prolegomena to Ethics* was published posthumously in 1883, his *Lectures on the Principles of Political Obligation* in 1886.[11] Though both are incomplete and unfinished, they are remarkable works, related to each other somewhat as Aristotle's *Ethics* relates to his *Politics*. Each conceives of politics as necessary for the completion of ethics. Green was an acute philosophical critic, an opponent of empiricism, an idealist influenced more by Kant than by Hegel, who talked uncommonly good sense about that with which he was dealing. He was a liberal idealist who took philosophy seriously as a guide to life, not simply as ex post facto commentary on it. In his practical philosophy he sought to provide a foundation for a liberal theory of society that would succeed in coming to terms with contemporary life in a way in which, he was convinced, utilitarianism had failed. Green held that the good could not be identified with pleasure and argued against the main tenet of psychological hedonism, that pleasure is the object of every desire. Although the good is what satisfies desire, the satisfaction must be an *abiding* one, not transitory; "there can be no such thing as a state of feeling made up of a sum of pleasures" (*Prolegomena*, sec. 221), and "a sum of pleasures is not [itself] a pleasure." Moral good is "that which satisfies a moral agent" (sec. 171). Moral agency is to be found in the willing of a good will, in and for a complex of a common good (possibly the first time that the concept of the common good formally entered ethical discourse). "Man has bettered himself through institutions and habits which tend to make the welfare of all the welfare of each" (sec. 172), Green held, and he attempted to explain how "the idea in man of a possible better state of himself, consisting in a further realisation of his capabilities, has been the moralising agent in human life" (sec. 180). Green takes it as "an ultimate fact of human history . . . that out of sympathies of animal origin, through their presence in a self-conscious soul, there arise interests as of a person in persons" (sec. 201), from which he deduces the necessity of a common good as both a reality and a moral ideal. Since "society is the condition of the development of a personality" (sec. 191), politics is necessary for the completion of ethics. "There can be no right without a consciousness of common interest on the part of members of a society" (*Political Obligation*, sec. 31). Green's political liberalism is illustrated by his argument that society has

the moral duty . . . to make its punishments just by making the system of rights which it maintains just. The justice of the punishment depends on the justice of the general system of rights . . . on the question whether the social organisation in which a criminal has acted is one that has given him a fair chance of not being a criminal. (*Political Obligation*, sec. 189)

Thus Green was akin to Mill in his liberalism, despite being so opposed to utilitarianism, and these two had the most liberating and inspiring social vision of all the thinkers mentioned in this survey.

Bradley's *Ethical Studies* (1876) was, as its author said, "mainly critical."[12] It is sharply and fiercely critical of egoism, hedonism, utilitarianism, the theory of "duty for duty's sake," and also of its own views. It is in influence, manner, and presentation Hegelian and dialectical: Each chapter modifies the doctrine of the preceding chapter, which is admitted to be partial and "one-sided." "They must be read in the order in which they stand." Bradley's positive doctrine is one of self-realization, but since on his metaphysics the self is itself evolving in the process of attempting to realize itself, the doctrine here takes on a form different from that in practically every other writer. Perhaps the most famous chapter is the one called "My Station and Its Duties," which Bradley takes as representing the minimum required by morality: One's duties are determined by one's station, and one's station is determined by the social and moral order that one develops into and is a result of.

There is no self, no individual, independent of society. But the morality of "my station and its duties" is itself only preliminary, not complete. One must realize one's self by overcoming its obstacles and generating a true self in which self-sacrifice will be seen to be identical with self-interest. "Selfishness and self-sacrifice are equally selfish" (essay 7) is just one example of Bradley's provocative rhetoric. Bradley's fiercest assaults are reserved for casuistry and the idea that philosophy can serve as a guide to life. "There cannot be a moral philosophy which will tell us what in particular we are to do. . . . moral philosophy has to understand morals which exist, not to make them. . . . ethics has not to make the world moral, but to reduce to theory the morality current in the world" (essay 5, p. 193). Thus, in his fashion, Bradley was attempting to give an account of the morality of common sense. And, although he was a philosophical idealist, as was Green, in politics and practical philosophy he was a reactionary, "the implacable enemy of all utilitarian or liberal thinking,"[13] and in this respect there was greater affinity between Green and Mill, the great liberals of the age, than between Green and Bradley, the great idealists.

3

Herbert Spencer's *Social Statics* (1851) preceded by eight years the publication of Darwin's *Origin of Species*. Nonetheless, a theory of evolution is presupposed and foreshadowed in it, even though the word "evolution" hardly occurs in it; the term Spencer used was "adaptation." Spencer's post-Darwinian work in ethics, the *Principles of Ethics* of 1892–3, was the culmination of his massive System of Synthetic Philosophy; and the first part of the *Principles*, *The Data of Ethics*, appeared separately in 1879. Although there were of course changes in view and in emphasis over this long period of time, the view as a whole manifests remarkable consistency of doctrine. From the start Spencer set out to found ethics on natural facts, in which the facts of natural adaptation were taken as paramount. "The human race . . . has been, is, and will long continue to be in a process of adaptation" (*Social Statics*, chap. 2, sec. 3). And part 2 of *Social Statics* is devoted to a remarkable derivation and application of a "first principle," the Law of Equal Freedom, – "Every man has freedom to do all that he will, provided he infringes not the equal freedom of any other man", – "the law on which a correct system of equity is to be based" (chap. 6, sec. 1). (Spencer was unaware that this was equivalent to Kant's principle of justice.) Another distinctive feature of Spencer's ethics is that it is an ethics of the ideal, of "the straight man"; it is not intended to apply in the imperfect actual world. It specifies the state toward which humanity is inevitably tending. Since "all imperfection is unfitness to the conditions of existence," and since "it is an essential principle of life that a faculty to which circumstances do not allow full exercise diminishes, and that a faculty on which circumstances make excessive demands increases," it follows that "the ultimate development of the ideal man is logically certain. . . . Progress, therefore, is not an accident, but a necessity" (chap. 2, sec. 4). On this view,

morality is essentially one with physical truth . . . a species of transcendental physiology. That condition of things dictated by the law of equal freedom; that condition in which the individuality of each may be unfolded without limit, save the like individualities of others . . . is a condition toward which the whole creation tends. (Chap. 30, sec. 12)

"Moral truth . . . proves to be a development of physiological truth . . . the moral law is in reality the law of complete life" (chap. 31, sec. 6). This doctrine was taken to be, as Spencer meant it to be, an argument for as little state interference in the social order as possible, since such interference is interference with the natural struggle for existence and would circumvent the development and the survival of the fittest – the ideal person. Unfortunately, the specifically ethical features of the doctrine were as a consequence relatively ignored, and the Law of Equal Freedom (later called the formula of absolute justice) has not been subjected to the sort of examination typically leveled at claimants to the title of ethical first principle.[14]

In the preface to the *Principles of Ethics*, forty-one years later, Spencer said that his primary purpose had been "to show that . . . the principles of ethics have a natural basis." Though, he said, full use is made in the later work of "the general doctrine of evolution . . . the ethical doctrine set forth is fundamentally a corrected and elaborated version of the doctrine set forth in *Social Statics*." This should not be taken to imply that there are no differences in doctrine. Spencer's agnosticism appears in the later work, not the earlier, and the doctrine of a moral sense, developed at some length in the earlier work, is distinctly deemphasized in the later. But it is a pity that ideological fashion, which led the works of Spencer to be so much overemphasized in the nineteenth century, has led to their almost total neglect in the twentieth. Spencer's system of philosophy was a remarkable construction, still worthy of study.

Spencer quite manifestly denies that *ought* implies *can* (although that was not at that time an idea that was the subject of much debate):

If men cannot yet entirely obey the law, why, they cannot . . . but it does not follow that we ought therefore to stereotype their incompetency by specifying how much is possible to them and how much is not . . . a system of morals which shall recognize man's present imperfections and allow for them cannot be devised, and would be useless if it could. (*Principles of Ethics*, chap. 32, sec. 2)

"It is only by perpetual aspiration after what has been hitherto beyond our reach that advance is made." Spencer adds that even though he "once espoused the doctrine of the intuitive moralists . . . it has become clear to me that the qualifications required practically obliterate the doctrine as enunciated by them. . . . It is impossible to hold that men have in common an innate perception of right and wrong" (part. 2, chap. 14, sec. 191).

The outstanding intellectual development in nineteenth-century Britain, amounting to a revolution in thought, was the publication in 1859 of Darwin's *Origin of Species*, which advanced the doctrine, supported by an immense mass of observations, of evolution by natural selection. In the later *Descent of Man* (1871), Darwin tried to give an evolutionist account of the moral sense. Darwin had long accepted the doctrine that the moral sense has a "rightful supremacy over every other principle of human action,"[15] which he had learned from his conversations with and his reading of Mackintosh. Darwin was here attempting to provide a naturalistic basis for Mackintosh's theory of the moral sense.[16] Darwin considered the moral sense a species of social instinct – not a developed or acquired capacity – which evolved out of the process of social selection, itself a species of natural selection. Since instinctive actions are not calculated actions, Darwin regarded the moral sense theory so understood as altogether distinct from egoism, hedonism, and utilitarianism. And Darwin did have a theory of morality. Darwin took as "the standard of morality the general good or welfare of the community, rather than the general happiness," where "general good [is] defined as the rearing of the greatest number of individuals in full vigour and health, with all their faculties perfect, under the conditions to which they are subjected" (*Descent of Man*, chap. 4, par. 40; Modern Library ed., p. 490). Darwin added that when a person "risks his life to save that of a fellow-creature, it seems . . . more correct to say that he acts for the general good, rather than for the general happiness." Darwin's moral theory was thus "a biologizing of Mackintosh's ethical system" (Richards, *Darwin*, p. 116). Though Mackintosh regarded "the *moral sense* for right conduct" as distinct from "the *criterion* of moral behavior" (something for which he was severely fragmented by James Mill), Mackintosh "could not satisfactorily explain the coincidence of the moral motive and the moral criterion."

He could not easily explain why impulsive actions might nevertheless be what moral deliberation would recommend. Darwin believed he could succeed where

Mackintosh failed; he could provide a perfectly natural explanation of the linkage between the moral motive and the moral criterion. Under the aegis of community selection, men in social groups evolved sets of instinctive responses to preserve the welfare of the community. . . . What served nature as the criterion for selecting behavior became the standard of choice for her creatures as well. (Richards, *Darwin*, pp. 116, 601)

This feature of Darwin's view – his attempt at the formulation of a moral theory – was not adequately appreciated or understood at the time. Yet it is apparent that Darwin was a pioneer not only in biology but also in moral theory and in attempting to understand the relative roles played in the progress of society between the egoistic and the altruistic impulses and the overriding character of the moral sense (something that even Butler could only assert but could not explain). Even though Sidgwick may have been correct in his claim that the theory of evolution provides no "argument for or against any particular ethical doctrine,"[17] if this interpretation be correct then Sidgwick was not correct in his claim that "the theory of evolution . . . has little or no bearing upon Ethics," a point argued in rebuttal by Frederick Pollock.[18]

4

The neglect of Darwin and evolutionary theory (although Spencer comes in for some notice in it) may be the single greatest gap in Sidgwick's monumental *Methods of Ethics* (1874) – a gap that Sidgwick tried to fill with his 1876 article (see n. 17) – the main achievement of which is generally taken to be the detailed account given of the intuitive morality of common sense, on the model provided by Aristotle. The methods referred to are those of egoism, intuitionism, and hedonistic utilitarianism, and Sidgwick's argument is that common sense is unconsciously utilitarian, in that it appeals to utilitarian considerations to resolve conflicts that arise between common-sense rules. Sidgwick thus attempted to show that utilitarianism itself rests on an intuitionistic basis. But Sidgwick reached an impasse in trying to decide between the ultimate rationality of egoism and utilitarianism, since they seem in unavoidable conflict with each other, neither seems more rational than the other, and each taken by itself seems intrinsically rational and to rest on a self-evident principle. Sidgwick called this ultimate conflict the "dualism of practical reason," and he never in a lifetime of thought was able to resolve it, without bringing in theistic assumptions. Nonetheless, Sidgwick's work of synthesis and the close careful analysis it involved set ethics off on a new course. Sidgwick was actually building on the work of Whewell in his discussion of common-sense morality, though he neglected to ac-

knowledge this (perhaps because Whewell was an acknowledged opponent of utilitarianism), and he built also on the work of Bentham,
J. S. Mill, Clarke, Butler, and Kant. Indeed, the sort of work in which he
engaged required a wide and deep knowledge of the history of ethics.

What I want to do now is examine Sidgwick's account of common-
sense morality, critically and also sympathetically. This will, I think,
have some utility.

Sidgwick assays no precise definition of common-sense morality, and
it is actually dubious that a precise account can be given. That would
be a reasonable inference from a prime maxim of common sense in
ethics, which is not to demand more precision or certainty than the
subject is capable of. Nonetheless, Sidgwick provides some statements
that enable us to identify the subject, and a definition of more than
ordinary interest.

Sidgwick tells us that the morality he examines is as much his own
morality as it is anyone's: "it is . . . the 'Morality of Common Sense,'
which I only attempt to represent in so far as I share it: I only place
myself outside it either (1) temporarily, for the purpose of impartial
criticism, or (2) in so far as I am forced beyond it by a practical consciousness of its incompleteness." And he goes on to say that he has
"criticized this morality unsparingly" (*ME*, x). Again, Sidgwick tells us
that what Aristotle "gave us was the Common Sense Morality of Greece,
reduced to consistency by careful comparison: given not as something
external to him but as what 'we' – he and others – think, ascertained
by reflection." Thus, what Sidgwick aimed to do was to "imitate this:
do the same for our morality here and now, in the same manner of
impartial reflection on current opinion" (*ME*, xix–xx). "Common Sense
Morality" is here characterized as the morality we all share, which is,
so far as can be ascertained, prephilosophical if anything is, hence the
data for ethical inquiry. It is to be taken "quite empirically, as we find
it in the common thought expressed in the common language of mankind" (*ME*, 229). Although the language here is vague, it is not indefinite, and we can identify readily enough the phenomenon to which
Sidgwick is referring, since we share this morality as well. Differences
of moral outlook on particular points are not to the point.

But Sidgwick also provides a more precise account, in a context in
which he draws a distinction between positive morality and the morality
of common sense. Both, he says, consist of general rules, "as to the
validity of which there would be general agreement at least among moral
persons of our age and civilization, and which would cover with approximate completeness the whole of human conduct"; knowledge of
such rules is to be attained by "reflection and observation of men's

moral discourse" (*ME*, 214–15). Such a collection, "regarded as a code imposed on an individual by the public opinion of the community to which he belongs [is] the Positive Morality of the community; but when regarded as a body of moral truth, warranted to be such by the *consensus* of mankind . . . it is more significantly termed the morality of Common Sense" (*ME*, 214–15). The ground of the distinction drawn here, then, is this: that whereas Positive Morality is a code imposed by public opinion, hence enforced by social sanctions, Common Sense Morality is – or is regarded as – a body of moral truth, or rules that make a claim to moral truth, thought to be so warranted by a human consensus, not merely the traditions and usages of a given community.

I think myself that this account too closely connects positive morality with public opinion, and that this is unfortunate, given the perennially shifting and transitory character of public opinion and the relative stability of positive morality. But that is of no moment. Of special interest is the idea that the morality of common sense is a set of rules regarded as a body of moral truth. Given the conception of common sense as "the rational and moral manifestation of a common human nature experiencing a common world,"[19] a conception I accept as sound, this makes very good sense indeed, for it is actually part of common sense that it is something common and something true and that it serves to unite rather than to divide. Such a conception can help distinguish the morality of common sense, regarded as something common to humanity, from the morality of a particular community, which is something manifestly variable and diverse.

Still another point of interest in Sidgwick's account, but for other reasons, is his identification of common-sense morality with "Intuitive Morality," that is, with the philosophical theory of intuitionism. Sidgwick takes this transition so much for granted that for the most part he simply slides back and forth between the two without notice. Occasionally the identification is nearly explicit, as when he says that he is "not trying to prove or disprove Intuitionism, but merely by reflection on the common morality which I and my reader share, and to which appeal is so often made in moral disputes, to obtain as explicit, exact, and coherent a statement as possible of *its* fundamental rules" (*ME*, 216; emphasis added). To what does this "its" refer, to intuitionism or to common morality? I think it is clear from this sentence that in Sidgwick's thinking it can refer to either, indifferently. Now this, I am convinced, is one mistake Sidgwick made about common-sense morality, and it has some interesting consequences.

My argument is this: (1) Sidgwick neglects to distinguish commonsense morality from intuitionist ethics, treats them for the most part as indistinguishable. Thus, he tends to treat common-sense morality as a system of intuitionist ethics, which is expected to come up with a definite and precise intuitive answer to every practical question that arises or that a philosopher can formulate. Thus, arguing that intuitionist ethics falls short of appropriate standards of adequacy, Sidgwick concludes that this is true also of common-sense morality. (2) But Sidgwick also fails to see that the rules of common-sense morality must be taken together. Instead, he examines them individually and in isolation, and in consequence, despite the brilliance and profundity of his analysis, he tends to create or discover paradoxes and difficulties where there are none. (3) This links with his tendency to think that all sorts of unde-cidable questions – undecidable because they are too general to be answered as they stand – can be answered by the utilitarian method. But reducing these questions to problems of hedonistic comparison, as Sidgwick tends to do, is no help; no method or principle can decide what is undecidable.

Consider the sorts of questions Sidgwick raises in his examination of "common-sense morality." He asks "how far the promise of aid to a friend ought to override the duty of giving one's children a good edu-cation" (*ME*, 305) and speaks of the "moral question how far a promise is binding if any material concealment is shown to have been used to obtain it" (*ME*, 306). He raises the question "whether the requital of a benefit ought to be proportionate to what it cost the benefactor, or to what it is worth to the recipient" (*ME*, 349). Sidgwick's purpose in raising these questions is to show that common-sense morality is inca-pable of deciding them, that hence there are questions "common sense" is incapable of deciding. For instance, he says:

Suppose that I have promised A to do something, which, before I fulfil the promise, I see reason to regard as likely to injure him. The circumstances may be precisely the same, and only my view of them have changed. If A takes a different view and calls on me to fulfil the promise, is it right to obey him? Surely no one would say this in an extreme case. . . . But if the rule does not hold for an extreme case, where are we to draw the line? At what point ought I to give up my judgment to A, unless my own conviction is weakened? Common Sense seems to give no clear answer. (*ME*, 308)

Sidgwick assumes throughout his discussion that such questions as these are actually decidable in the form in which they are raised. But it seems clear enough that they are not. These questions cannot be answered in general. It cannot be said, for instance, that the promise of aid to a friend ought always to override the duty of giving one's children a good education, nor can it be said that it ought never to do so. All that can be said is, it depends – in some cases it ought to and in some cases it ought not to. Such questions as these need further clarification in order to be answerable. As they stand they are too general to be decided.

At certain points Sidgwick does recognize that such questions as these cannot be answered in general one way or the other, that the answers to them will depend on and vary with particular circumstances. This occurs where he criticizes the view, expounded by James Martineau in *Types of Ethical Theory*, that there is a scale of motives, such that a higher motive should always take precedence over a lower one. Sidgwick here insists that it is "impossible to assign a definite and constant ethical value to each different kind of motive, without reference to the particular circumstances under which it has arisen, the extent of indulgence that it demands, and the consequences to which this indulgence would lead in any particular case"; and he adds, "it seems to me in the highest degree paradoxical to lay down that each class of motives is always to be preferred to the class below it, without regard to circumstances and consequences" (*ME*, 369). Sidgwick says that, "supposing a conflict between 'Compassion,' which is highest but one in Dr. Martineau's scale, and 'Resentment,' which he places about the middle, it is by no means to be laid down as a general rule that compassion ought to prevail" (*ME*, 371).

Although Sidgwick's statements here are framed in terms of motives and refer to cases of conflict between motives, they can readily be reformulated to apply to actions and to conflicts between rules of conduct. Sidgwick points out that

The view of Common Sense appears . . . to be that most natural impulses have their proper spheres, within which they should be normally operative, and therefore the question whether in any case a higher motive should yield to a lower one cannot be answered decisively in the general way in which Dr. Martineau answers it: the answer must depend on the particular conditions and circumstances of the conflict. (*ME*, 370)

If this is the view that common sense takes about conflicts of motives, as it appears to be, then it is manifest that it takes a corresponding view about conflicts of duties. The statement can readily be paraphrased: The view of Common Sense appears . . . to be that moral rules have their proper spheres, within which they should be normally operative, and therefore the question whether in any case one rule should yield to another rule cannot be answered decisively in the general way in which Sidgwick demands that it be answered; the answer must depend on the particular conditions and circumstances of the conflict.

The demands Sidgwick makes upon ordinary moral rules – the rules of common-sense morality – are neither legitimate nor appropriate. The standard against which he tests them is that of "scientific axioms . . . to be available in clear and cogent demonstrations" (*ME*, 215). He appears to want these rules to "be so defined as perfectly to fit together and cover the whole field of human conduct, without coming into conflict and *without leaving any practical questions unanswered*" (*ME*, 102; emphasis added). And these rules are criticized for their failure to come up to this standard. Thus, he says that

the rule of Veracity, as commonly accepted, cannot be elevated into a definite moral axiom: for there is no real agreement as to how far we are bound to impart true beliefs to others: and while it is contrary to Common Sense to exact absolute candour under all circumstances, we yet find no self-evident secondary principle, clearly defining when it is not to be exacted. (*ME*, 317)

Although what Sidgwick says here is perfectly true, it is not an appropriate criticism of "the rule of Veracity" or of the morality of common sense generally. There is no reason to look for a self-evident principle, as part of common-sense morality, "clearly defining" just when one need not tell the truth – though common sense commonly has more of sense to say on this score than is commonly imagined. Common sense does not purport to provide principles or procedures for precisely and with certainty answering every question of morality.

The problem Sidgwick is confronting here arises, in my judgment, from his failure to distinguish intuitionism from the morality of common sense, a mistake on a par with supposing that common-sense beliefs about perceptual powers and situations are equivalent to the epistemological theory called "naive realism." Intuitionism is a philosophical theory. Common sense is not, nor is the morality of common sense. The morality of common sense is not an ethical theory; it provides the data and the springboard for philosophical inquiry, and it is a further philosophical claim, one not made by common sense itself, that common sense is an ultimately satisfactory philosophy. The reason why Sidgwick, whose description of common-sense morality is still unrivaled in scope and accuracy, gets into this conundrum would make for an interesting further inquiry into Sidgwick's ethics, but will not be explored here. All that we need notice is the fact of difference. As Sidgwick himself describes it, the morality of common sense, considered substantively, consists of the ensemble (*ME*, 480) of ordinary moral rules, not precisely stated or formulated, ascertained by "reflection and observation" on ordinary moral discourse (*ME*, 214). But these rules do not themselves claim to be self-evident, absolute, and independent of one another, as Sidgwick in this mood sometimes supposes. That is to foist on them the preconceptions of the philosophical theory entitled "intuitionism," and they do not fall short of being what they are supposed to be or of doing what they are supposed to do because they fall short of the requirements of these preconceived standards. It is essential, all the more because it is not easy, to distinguish common sense from a philosophical theory about common sense.

(It is worth noting that intuitionism and the morality of common sense are identified in the index [in the entry under "Morality of Common Sense," *ME*, 523]. It is true that index was compiled not by Sidgwick himself but by E. E. Constance Jones [starting with the fourth edition, of 1890]. But Constance Jones was his editor and collaborator, and Sidgwick must be supposed to have at least looked over the index, even if he did not compile it. And the index is often a clue to Sidgwick's thought and interconnections of ideas, as, for instance, that of the interdependence of method and end [see under "end," *ME*, 519].)

Sidgwick speaks of common sense being perplexed on certain points, of its being divided or conflicting or even perhaps inconsistent. But this is a misconception of common sense. All that can be meant by this is that there are questions that common sense does not answer and does not pretend to answer, for they are not common-sense questions. Sidgwick says: "If we ask . . . how far our promise is binding if it was made in consequence of false statements, on which, however, it was not understood to be conditional; or if important circumstances were concealed . . . we see that Common Sense is clearly divided as to the answer" (*ME*, 353; cf. pp. 281, 315, 321). But this is not so. What is so is that common sense provides *no* answer to the question; it is not, as it stands, a question for common sense. Sidgwick reaches the conclusion he reaches because "different conscientious persons would answer these . . . questions . . . in different ways." That is so, but that does not mean that common sense is divided against itself. It only means, what is already obvious, that opinions differ, even the opinions of sensible people. At any one time in any complex society there are a great many issues on which opinion is divided, on which there are different factions and pressure groups, as there are different parties with different views and programs. But it is not common sense that is divided or conflicting on these issues, nor is it common sense to think so.

As Sidgwick himself observes, and it is an important part of his invaluable inquiry into the morality of common sense,

The notions of Benevolence, Justice, Good Faith, Veracity, Purity, etc., are not necessarily emptied of significance for us, because we have found it impossible to define them with precision. The main part of the conduct prescribed under each notion is sufficiently clear: and the general rule prescribing it does not necessarily lose its force because there is in each case a margin of conduct involved in obscurity and perplexity, or because the rule does not on examination appear to be absolute and independent. (*ME*, 360–1)

It is at this point that Sidgwick notices, though he appears not to draw the general consequences of so noticing, that there is an important distinction between intuitionism, a philosophical theory, and the morality of common sense. For he immediately adds: "the Morality of Common Sense may . . . be perfectly adequate to give practical guidance to common people in common circumstances: but the attempt to elevate it into a system of Intuitional Ethics brings its inevitable imperfections into prominence without helping us to remove them." But the attempt to elevate the morality of common sense into a system of intuitional ethics is not an attempt of common sense, even though it is an attempt of a common-sense philosopher. It is something Sidgwick set out to do. And nowhere in Sidgwick's incomparable work is there anything even resembling an attempt to justify this attempt at elevation.

5

A phenomenon that may partially have disabled Sidgwick on this matter was the dearth – practically the death – of studies in and of casuistry in nineteenth-century British ethics. Whewell devoted space to this matter, both in his *Elements* and in his *History*, but Whewell's example was not picked up by many, and in any event Whewell was not likely to be emulated by a utilitarian. In 1868 F. D. Maurice published *The Conscience: Lectures on Casuistry*, which seems to have been ignored by all except moral theologians (among whom the tradition of casuistry was kept alive), and its merits have yet to be discovered.[20] Frederick Pollock's *Essays in Jurisprudence and Ethics* (1882) contains three essays, one called "The Casuistry of Common Sense," of the first importance for the study of casuistry.[21] Still, with the development of the Ethical Societies in Britain as an outgrowth of the Ethical Culture movement, and the involvement in them of distinguished moral philosophers, some attention began to be paid to questions of practical ethics. Thus, Sidgwick's *Practical Ethics*, a collection of addresses on such topics, appeared in 1898. And in 1899 Lecky published *The Map of Life: Conduct and Character*, an illuminating discussion of a number of the ethical questions of life.[22] Although it was reprinted an unusual number of times, it does not appear to have had a wide technical readership. So by and large casuistry did not play a prominent role in nineteenth-century British ethics. Utilitarians tended to take the view that casuistical questions could all be decided by hedonistic calculation and the application of the greatest-happiness principle. Bradley was publicly nauseated by the idea, not only in his *Ethical Studies* but in his *Principles of Logic*,[23] and the power of his rhetoric, if not the power of his logic, may have proved intimidating to others. Also operating in this century was the idea that casuistry was an outgrowth of a theological ethics, not of a rational or utilitarian one, or of any that operated with a first or supreme principle or that claimed to be scientific in method or in substance.

6

It has now been observed that Sidgwick confronts common-sense morality with questions that cannot be answered in general, that as they stand are undecidable. But if a question is undecidable it is undecidable, and it cannot be decided by appealing to some more precise supreme principle, even a self-evident one. Sidgwick says that "the common principle of Gratitude" is "essentially indeterminate" because it cannot answer the question "whether the requital of a benefit ought to be proportionate to what it cost the benefactor, or to what it is worth to the recipient" (*ME*, 349). Yet that cannot be, for if it were it would follow that every principle whatever would be "essentially indeterminate," since no principle whatever can answer this question as so framed. What is needed with such a question is not a more determinate principle but a more determinate question. The question framed in this way is not a question that can arise in practice, and no practical question depends on it. In other words, it is not a question of common sense; it can arise only in a philosophical context.

A number of the questions Sidgwick raises in his criticism of common-sense morality arise only because he is taking ordinary moral rules, the rules of common-sense morality, in isolation from one another. But a rule that appears vague and indefinite in isolation may not be so when taken in context, and this is the way such rules must be taken. Thus, Sidgwick undertakes to "examine the propositions 'that law ought to be obeyed' and 'that promises ought to be kept' . . . as independent principles" (*ME*, 295). But that is a mistake at the outset. They are not independent principles. They are independent neither of each other nor of other rules, the rules that make up the complex of common-sense morality. Sidgwick claims that "the duty of Fidelity to promises is . . . commonly conceived as independent of any injury that might be done to the promisee by breaking it: for . . . men ordinarily judge that promises to the dead, though they are beyond the reach of injury, ought to be kept" (*ME*, 295). But this argument is fallacious. The most it could show is that the duty to keep a promise to a dead person is independent of any injury that might be done to the promisee by breaking it. It could not show that the obligation to keep promises in general is independent of any injury that might be done to the promisees by breaking them. And in fact it is not. If no injury at all would be done to a promisee by the breaking of a promise and if, in addition, the promisee does not care one way or another whether it is kept, the obligation to keep the promise practically disappears and is easily overridden by a conflicting consideration. The duty to keep promises to dead people is connected with other factors. Living people might be harmed by the failure to keep them, people are enabled to provide for their children after their death, and so on. Just as "the whole Law must be taken together" if we are to understand any part of it,[24] the whole body of moral rules that make up common-sense morality must be taken together if we are to understand any one of them and any part of it.

Another instance in which Sidgwick isolates a rule of common-sense morality from other rules, and thus comes to regard it as more vague and questionable than it actually is, is provided by his examination of "the duty of parents to children":

We have no doubt about this duty as a part of the present order of society, by which the due growth and training of the rising generation is distributed among the adults. . . . If, however, we consider the duty of parents by itself, out of connection with this social order, it is certainly not self-evident that we owe more to our own children than to others whose happiness equally depends on our exertions. To get the question clear, let us suppose that I am thrown with my family upon a desert island, where I find an abandoned orphan. Is it evident that I am less bound to provide this child, as far as lies in my power, with the means of subsistence, than I am to provide for my own children? (*ME*, 346–7)

The answer is, certainly not. On a desert island the situation is very different, and relevantly different, from what it normally is. And if the complexion of society were to be greatly changed, this too might change the situation with respect to this duty. The point is that *in general* we have a greater obligation to care for our own children than for the children of others, because *in general* our own children are more dependent on us than on others. As our own children become less dependent on us our obligation to care for them is lessened. On the same grounds, one who adopts or becomes the guardian of a child has the obligation to care for it as one's own. If the parent becomes dependent on the child for support, then the child has the obligation to support the parent. No appeal to self-evidence is required to see this; common sense is enough.

The moral of this story is that it is a mistake *ab initio* and in general to consider this rule or any other "out of connection with the social order" of which it forms a part. I do not mean that it is a procedural mistake. It can be enlightening, as it is in Sidgwick's treatment of the matter, to consider the rule in isolation for the sake of exploring its implications in isolation (supposing it has any) and determining its place in the social order or way of life of which it is a part. But to suppose that the deficiencies of the rule in isolation are deficiencies of the rule in its natural home in the social order, or to suppose that because in isolation it is unable to answer certain hypothetical questions that rarely if ever arise in practice it therefore cannot answer such questions in its natural setting, is a mistake of enormous magnitude. It is owing to Sidgwick's enormous labor and acumen in examining these rules that we are able to see this. It is unfortunate that Sidgwick did not himself see this and was led to foist some supreme principle on the morality of common sense under the misapprehension that common sense is unconsciously utilitarian and unconsciously presupposed the utilitarian method of answering those questions. This is just not so, as the arguments just given bring out. For, although appeal was made to consequences – certainly an essential component of common-sense morality, as it is an essential component of common sense – appeal was not made to any one principle or to utilitarian*ism*. Appeal to consequences is not a monopoly of utilitarianism. It is an essential component of common sense, which also considers motives and intentions, though it has no ready or rigid formula for balancing these considerations. The balancing is left to judgment, which is good sense in action.

"Systematic reflection upon the morality of Common Sense," Sidgwick says, "exhibits the Utilitarian principle as that to which Common Sense naturally appeals for the further development of its system which this same reflection shows to be necessary" (*ME*, 422). But common sense is no system and has no system, in the sense intended; hence, there is nothing that needs to be further developed.[25] This is not to say that common sense by itself is all-sufficient or infallible or incorrigible or irrefragable or unchangeable. It is none of these things, and it does require supplementation. What it does not require is to be remade into the model of some ethical system, which would be to misinterpret and distort it. Note that the conundrum Sidgwick raised as to the common-sense duty of parents to children was resolved by appeal to common sense itself, not by appeal to some higher or supreme or ultimate principle. Common sense never goes to extremes, as common sense defines extremes. And the appeal to one single overriding principle is such an extreme.

7

It remains to be noticed that Sidgwick's work had considerable impact very early on. The discussion of this work, and of course of the work of others as well, was facilitated by the founding in 1876 of *Mind*, the first philosophical journal to be published in Britain. This provided a forum for philosophers and featured what by current standards must be regarded as rapid discussion of philosophical issues, ideas, and books. Most of the well-known thinkers of the period contributed to it. It was followed in 1887 by the publication of the *Proceedings of the Aristotelian Society* and in 1890 by the publication (in the United States, but with many British authors represented in it) of the *International Journal of Ethics* (now simply *Ethics*), and these periodicals added a new dimension to the development of ethics in the nineteenth century in Britain and the English-speaking world generally.

The nineteenth century was also the first in which there was concentrated study of the history of ethics. The first such history appears to have been the article on the "history of the science of morals" in the third edition of the *Encyclopaedia Britannica* (1797), contributed by George Gleig, though this history manifestly had a didactic purpose.[26] Thomas Brown's *Lectures on Ethics*, delivered not long before Brown's death in 1820 but not published until 1846, delve in part into the history of ethics, from Mandeville through Hume and Adam Smith to Hutcheson, Cudworth, and Price; though it is not exactly a history, it is a forerunner.[27] Dugald Stewart had planned a history of ethics as part of his "Dissertation on the Progress of Philosophy," prepared as a supplement to the *Encyclopaedia Britannica*, but Stewart died (1828) before completing more than a preliminary sketch of the section on ethics. The first book-length history of ethics in Britain was Mackintosh's *Dissertation on the Progress of Ethical Philosophy*, published in 1830 as a supplement to the *Encyclopaedia Britannica* and issued separately in 1837 with a valuable preface by Whewell. This is the work that aroused such ideological ire in James Mill and stimulated Darwin to fundamental ethical inquiry. Whewell's own *Lectures on the History of Moral Philosophy* were delivered in 1838, published in 1852, and reissued with a supplement containing additional lectures in 1862.[28] W. E. H. Lecky's *History of European Morals from Augustus to Charlemagne* (1869) attempted in its first chapter to integrate an account of the development of moral theory with the development of morals and is one of the first attempts in that direction.[29] A work that has retained its status as a classic is Sidgwick's *Outlines of the History of Ethics for English Readers*, which first appeared as an *Encyclopaedia Britannica* article in 1878 and was published separately in 1886; though brief – *Outlines* is an accurate title – it covers the whole subject and is a genuine history. James Martineau's learned *Types of Ethical Theory* (1885) intersperses its presentation of Martineau's own "idiopsychological ethics" with historical discussions.[30] Sidgwick, as we have seen, thought its doctrines worthy of close scrutiny, and its historical discussions are genuine history, not a form of historical demolition. One final work worth mentioning is volume 1 of *The Principles of Morals* by John M. Wilson and Thomas Fowler, which, though printed in 1875, owing to the ill health and then the death of Wilson was not published until 1886; this first volume contains preliminary studies that are mainly historical.[31]

Thus, a distinctive feature of nineteenth-century ethics was the felt need to take account of the history of the subject. To what extent this felt need resulted from the influence of the historical school, represented for example by Henry Maine's *Ancient Law* of 1861, and to what extent it was stimulated by the general idea of unfolding, evolution and transformation, is a speculative question not to be examined here. But a question worth keeping in mind is this: How does the appearance of a noteworthy history of a subject affect the later development of the subject? In particular, to what extent was the development of ethics itself affected by, and to what extent did ethics in turn affect, these studies in the history of ethics? Leslie Stephen's massive three-volume work, *The English Utilitarians*, was published at the end of the century, in 1900; but it was more an account of Bentham and the two Mills than an account of utilitarianism itself.[32] And Ernest Albee's more comprehensive, if less massive, *History of English Utilitarianism* appeared about the same time, in 1901.[33] The end of the century also saw the publication of L. A. Selby-Bigge's classic collection *British Moralists* (1897), which made the writings of British moral philosophers of the eighteenth century more readily accessible. No one was more ahistorical than Bentham. The interest in the history of ethics (and of politics and law) was much greater at the end of the century than it was at the beginning. And it is of course much greater now than it ever was.

Those who have done the most important work in ethics did not usually burn daylight complaining of their predecessors and contemporaries but built on the work of the tradition, improving, modifying, sometimes thoroughly revamping, but always aware of and respecting the tradition, even if not every thinker in it. As has been observed by a twentieth-century philosopher paradoxically best known as a critic, "The notion that we can dismiss the views of all previous thinkers surely leaves no basis for the hope that our own work will prove of any value to others."[34] This, apart from its intrinsic interest, apart from its play

as drama, and apart from the stimulus it provides to more fruitful thinking, is surely the great value of increasing our awareness of the history
of our subject. Occasionally, we get a revised view of some important
figure, such as I have attempted to provide here with respect to Sidgwick,
and this can sometimes lead to a revised view of our subject itself. And
every once in a while an important yet totally ignored thinker turns up
to provide added dividends. This would appear to be the case with
Alexander Smith, discovered – rediscovered – by Schneewind,[35] though
in the present state of our knowledge he can hardly be said, yet, to have
turned up.

Notes

1 Jeremy Bentham, *An Introduction to the Principles of Morals and Legislation*
(1789; 2d ed., 1823), chaps. 1–2; chap. 17, sec. 1.
2 Bentham, *Deontology; or, The Science of Morality*, ed. John Bowring, 2
vols. (London: Longmans, 1834).
3 J. S. Mill, "Bentham," in *Dissertations and Discussions*, 4 vols. (New York:
Holt, 1874), 1:390.
4 Bentham, *A Fragment on Government* (1776; Oxford: Blackwell, 1960),
preface.
5 *Utilitarian Logic and Politics: James Mill's "Essay on Government," Ma-
cauley's Critique, and the Ensuing Debate*, ed. Jack Lively and John Rees
(Oxford: Oxford University Press [Clarendon Press] 1978).
6 James Mill, *A Fragment on Mackintosh: Being Strictures on Some Passages
in the Dissertation by Sir James Mackintosh, Prefixed to the Encyclopaedia
Britannica* (London, 1830, 1835).
7 James Mackintosh, *Dissertation on the Progress of Ethical Philosophy,
Chiefly during the Seventeenth and Eighteenth Centuries*, 2d ed., with a preface by W. Whewell (Edinburgh: Adam and Charles Black, 1837), pp. 291,
292, 286.
8 John Austin, *The Province of Jurisprudence Determined* (London, 1832),
pt. 1 of *Lectures on Jurisprudence; or, The Philosophy of Positive Law*,
2 vols. (London, 1863), 5th ed., ed. John Campbell (London: Murray,
1885).
9 J. B. Schneewind, "Whewell's Ethics," in *Studies in Moral Philosophy*,
American Philosophical Quarterly Monograph Series, no. 1 (1968): 108–41;
Alan Donagan, Chapter 3, herein.
10 Donagan, "Whewell's *Elements of Morality*," *Journal of Philosophy*, 71
(1974): 735.
11 Thomas Hill Green, *Prolegomena to Ethics*, ed. A. C. Bradley (Oxford:
Oxford University Press [Clarendon Press], 1883); *Lectures on the Principles
of Political Obligation*, ed. R. L. Nettleship (London: Longmans, 1886),
delivered in 1879.

12 F. H. Bradley, *Ethical Studies* (1876; 2d ed., Oxford: Oxford University Press [Clarendon Press], 1927), p. viii.
13 Richard Wollheim, *F. H. Bradley* (Harmondsworth: Penguin, 1959), p. 14.
14 But see Sidgwick, *GSM*, pt. 2, lectures 8 and 9; and D. G. Ritchie, *Natural Rights* (London: Swan Sonnenschein, 1895), chap. 7.
15 Charles Darwin, *The Descent of Man and Selection in Relation to Sex* (New York: Modern Library, n.d.), chap. 4; quoting Mackintosh, p. 231.
16 See Robert J. Richards, *Darwin and the Emergence of Evolutionary Theories of Mind and Behavior* (Chicago: University of Chicago Press, 1987), pp. 115–17. I am grateful to Michael McFall for calling this book to my attention. It is a marvelously illuminating study.
17 Sidgwick, "The Theory of Evolution in Its Application to Practice," *Mind* 1 (1876): 54.
18 Frederick Pollock, "Evolution and Ethics," *Mind* 1 (1876): 336 ff.
19 Hans J. Morgenthau, *The Purpose of American Politics* (New York: Knopf, 1960), p. 224.
20 F. D. Maurice, *The Conscience: Lectures on Casuistry* (London: Macmillan, 1868).
21 Frederick Pollock, *Essays in Jurisprudence and Ethics* (London: Macmillan, 1882).
22 W. E. H. Lecky, *The Map of Life: Conduct and Character* (London: Longmans, 1899).
23 F. H. Bradley, *The Principles of Logic* (1883; 2d ed., Oxford: Oxford University Press, 1922), 1: 268–71.
24 John Chipman Gray, *The Nature and Sources of the Law*, 2d ed. (New York: Macmillan, 1921), p. 106.
25 The point here is paraphrased from Singer, "The Many Methods of Sidgwick's Ethics," *Monist* 58 (1974): 441.
26 George Gleig, "Moral Philosophy, or Morals," *Encyclopaedia Britannica*, 3d ed. (1797), 12: 272–318, esp. pp. 273–9.
27 Thomas Brown, *Lectures on Ethics* (Edinburgh: Tate, 1846).
28 William Whewell, *Lectures on the History of Moral Philosophy in England*, 2d ed. (Cambridge: Deighton, Bell, 1862).
29 W. E. H. Lecky, *History of European Morals from Augustus to Charlemagne*, 2 vols. (London: Longmans, Green, 1869).
30 James Martineau, *Types of Ethical Theory*, 2 vols. (Oxford: Oxford University Press [Clarendon Press], 1885).
31 John M. Wilson and Thomas Fowler, *The Principles of Morals*, 2 vols. (Oxford: Oxford University Press [Clarendon Press], 1886, 1887); vol. 2 is solely by Fowler; vol. 1, on history, is a joint work.
32 Leslie Stephen, *The English Utilitarians*, 3 vols. (London: Duckworth, 1900).
33 Ernest Albee, *A History of English Utilitarianism* (London: Allen and Unwin, 1901).
34 Morris R. Cohen, *Reason and Nature* (New York: Harcourt, Brace, 1931), p. x.

35 J. B. Schneewind, *Sidgwick's Ethics and Victorian Moral Philosophy* (Oxford: Oxford University Press [Clarendon Press], 1977), esp. pp. 81–8. The reference is to Alexander Smith, *The Philosophy of Morals*, 2 vols. (London: Smith, Elder, 1835), not a work one sees referred to with any frequency, and one that even Sidgwick appeared ignorant of.

2

Sidgwick and the
Cambridge moralists

J. B. SCHNEEWIND

> In thinking of the history of moral philosophy, we are rather inclined to
> forget to how great a degree, especially in more recent times, moral phi-
> losophy is embodied in religion. If we do not keep this in mind, but look
> at the history of moral philosophy only as it is contained in avowedly ethical
> treatises, the history can never be to us more than a matter of literature;
> and the point of much the greatest consequence about it, which is, the
> relation of the ethics of any period to the general thought of that period, is
> a matter which we shall not be in a condition to speak of.
>
> John Grote[1]

Sidgwick is usually considered to be a utilitarian, and with good reason.
In an autobiographical fragment he tells us that his "first adhesion to a
definite Ethical system was to the Utilitarianism of Mill," and that after
a variety of intellectual changes he became "a Utilitarian again, but on
an Intuitional basis."[2] He refers to himself in other works and in letters
as a utilitarian, and he was so viewed by his contemporaries. Hence it
is understandable that Albee should view *The Methods of Ethics* as "an
independent contribution to the literature of Utilitarianism," labeling
it "the last authoritative utterance of traditional Utilitarianism,"[3] and
that almost everyone who discusses the book should agree with this
classification of it. Yet Sidgwick did not himself say that the *Methods*
is a defense or a restatement of utilitarianism. On the contrary: He was
from the first at pains to disavow any intention of proving a system of
morality and to insist that he is presenting only an examination of "the
different methods of obtaining reasoned convictions as to what ought
to be done which are to be found . . . in the moral consciousness of
mankind generally."[4] In the preface to the second edition he bemoans
the misunderstanding which led critics to suppose that he was "writing
as an assailant of two of the methods" he examines. One critic, he
complains, thought he was giving "mere hostile criticism" of intuitionism, another "has constructed an article on the supposition that my
principal object is 'the suppression of Egoism.' "[5] Yet a third critic, he

This essay is reprinted by permission from the *Monist* 58, no. 3 (July 1974): 371–404.

remarks dryly, referring to a savage attack by F. H. Bradley, "has gone to the length of a pamphlet under the impression (apparently) that the 'main argument' of my treatise is a demonstration of Universalistic Hedonism. I am concerned," he comments, "to have caused so much misdirection of criticism"; and he goes on to reiterate his position about the two forms, egoistic and universalistic, of hedonism: "I do not hold the reasonableness of aiming at happiness generally with any stronger conviction than I do that of aiming at one's own."[6]

For many purposes it is quite adequate to think of Sidgwick as a classical utilitarian, but to think of him only in this way makes a number of facts about his main treatise on morality quite puzzling. There is not only the matter of his repeated explicit denial, in the text as well as in the prefaces, that the book is intended as a defense of utilitarianism: Several aspects of the book itself, even without these comments by its author, would suggest that there is more to it than a restatement of that view. The *Methods* departs from classical utilitarianism in a number of ways. It centers on an examination of the accepted moral opinions and modes of thought of common sense. It involves a rejection of empiricism and dismisses the issue of determinism as irrelevant. It emphasizes an attempt to reconcile positions seen by utilitarians as deeply opposed to each other. It finds ethical egoism as reasonable as utilitarianism; and it concludes with arguments to show that, because of this, no full reconciliation of the various rational methods for reaching moral decisions is possible and therefore that the realm of practical reason is probably incoherent. In this essay I try to show that an explanation of these markedly nonutilitarian features of the *Methods* is suggested by relating its argument to the views of Sidgwick's predecessors in moral philosophy at Cambridge.

The main writers I shall consider are S. T. Coleridge, F. D. Maurice, William Whewell, and John Grote. Coleridge was at Cambridge only as a student, but his views were adopted and developed by a number of important Cambridge teachers. Among them was Julius Hare, who taught at Trinity College from 1822 to 1832 and who was a friend of Whewell's. Maurice was one of Hare's pupils, and later became related to him by marriage.[7] Whewell, Grote, and Maurice, in that order, held the Knightbridge Professorship of Moral Philosophy, to which Sidgwick eventually succeeded; and Sidgwick was acquainted with all of them, and with their works. Neither Whewell nor Grote was an avowed follower of Coleridge, as Maurice was, and none of the three was unoriginal enough to have been simply a follower of anyone. But their views, different in many respects though they are, have important similarities. Two themes, in particular, are of importance. They are defending a spiritual and religious, and so far as possible a specifically Christian, outlook, and they see opposition to any utilitarian view of morality as part of this defense; and they are all strongly opposed to philosophical empiricism, which they see as being, among other things, at the root of antireligious doctrine. While views like these were common during the Victorian era, the forms they took at Cambridge were largely a result of the influence of Coleridge.

1

Coleridge's chief concern is to lay the groundwork for a defense of Christian doctrine against the advance of science and of critical examination of the Bible. His strategy, which had a profound influence on theology in Britain, is to interpret the doctrines of Christianity as the best explanations available of human experience construed in a very broad sense. The doctrines themselves are not irrational. Their discovery, indeed, may have been beyond human ability: Our first grasp of them may have come with God's help. But revelation and inspiration are not to be viewed as wholly mysterious and incomprehensible processes. They are our insights, usually dim and indistinct, often partial and one-sided, into truths about the constitution of the universe; and any of us can check and test them. This view emerges most clearly in Coleridge's well-known theory of biblical inspiration. "In the Bible," he claims,

there is more that *finds* me than I have experienced in all other books put together . . . the words of the Bible find me at greater depths of my being; and . . . whatever finds me brings with it an irresistible evidence of its having proceeded from the Holy Spirit.[8]

The spirit that worked in the various writers of the books of the Bible works in us too,[9] and because it does, we can see for ourselves where they were rightly guided by it and where, being human, they went astray. We need not take every word and syllable as divinely given, as if God were some sort of ventriloquist. We can sort out the inspired from the uninspired for ourselves, using the testimony of the ages and our own intelligence. The point at issue in considering inspiration, Coleridge says, is this: Either we hold that the Bible is inspired of God and therefore must be accepted as true, holy, and in all parts unquestionable; or we hold that we can see that the Bible contains more true, holy, and unquestionable wisdom than any other book and we conclude that it is therefore inspired by God.[10] By defending the second alternative persuasively, Coleridge gave new impetus to the belief that the essential points of religious teaching can be checked against, and can rest on, experiential evidence.

The major part of this experiential evidence comes, on Coleridge's view, from the conscience. The works of God in the world, and the adaptation of means to ends, remind me of God's existence; but they presuppose that I have the notion of God, and this notion, Coleridge says, which is "essential to the human mind," is "called forth into distinct consciousness principally by the conscience."[11] "The one great and binding ground of the belief of God and a hereafter is the law of conscience," Coleridge says, and like Kant he connects this closely with an awareness of our being morally responsible agents possessing free wills.[12] There are other respects in which Coleridge's view is similar to Kant's: For example, his description of conscience uses, at times, directly Kantian language:

That I am conscious of something within me peremptorily commanding me to do unto others as I would that they should do unto me; – in other words a categorical . . . imperative; – that the maxim . . . of actions . . . should be such as I could, without any contradiction arising therefrom, will to be the law of all moral and rational beings; – this, I say, is a fact of which I am no less conscious . . . than I am of any appearance presented by my outward senses . . . knowing that consciousness of this fact is the root of all other consciousness . . . we name it conscience.[13]

This consciousness or conscience, for Coleridge, springs from or perhaps is the Reason (in his technical sense of that term) and is neither a feeling, a sense, nor a special faculty. Its presence in all men is shown by the universality of "the inward experience of the diversity between regret and remorse . . . so long as reason continues, so long must conscience exist."[14] In addition to being the core of our personal identity, and the main source of our notion of God and of our evidence for His existence, conscience is also the channel through which God communicates with us: "The will of God is revealed to man through the conscience."[15]

What conscience tells us has two characteristics of interest. First, its deliverances are of a unique kind, not reducible to or explicable in terms of the kind of information given us by any other cognitive capacity. Criticizing someone who identified the good with the pleasant and the desirable, Coleridge says:

there is an equivocation in the main word of the definition, viz., *desirable*, by means of which you assume all that ought to be proved. . . . For *desirable* means either that which actually I do desire, or that which I know I ought to desire. . . . You preassume, I say, that *Good* is nothing more than a reflex idea of the mind after a survey and calculation of agreeable or delightful sensations. . . . Now this I utterly deny. *I know – intuitively know* – that there is a power essential to my nature, and which constitutes it human nature, the voice of which is I ought, I should, I ought not, I should not, and that this voice is original and self-existent, not an echo of a prior voice.[16]

The uniqueness of the deliverances of conscience is plainly shown in the distinction our language makes between utility or prudence and morality:

The sum total of moral philosophy is found in this one question, Is *Good* a superfluous word, – or mere lazy synonyme for the pleasurable and its causes. . . . Or the question may be . . . stated thus, Is *good* superfluous as a word exponent of a *kind?* If it be, then moral philosophy is but a subdivision of physics. If not, then the writings of Paley and all his predecessors and disciples are false and *most* pernicious.[17]

Elsewhere Coleridge objects to Epicureanism on the grounds that a philosopher of that persuasion has no business using the words "right" and "obligation," because he means by them only "power" and "compulsion." Only the religious man – who, presumably, admits the intuitive abilities of conscience – can use moral terms in their proper senses.[18] The second point about the deliverances of conscience, not surprisingly, is that they are opposed to hedonism, utilitarianism, and, more generally, to consequentialism. Ethics contemplates action, Coleridge says, "in its originating spiritual source. . . . Not the outward deed . . . not the deed as a possible object of the sense, – is the object of Ethical Science," but rather the character of the will from which the deed springs.[19] Even if actions dictated by and done from self-love were the same as actions dictated by and done from "Christian principle," there would be a difference – a difference "in that, for which all actions have their whole worth and their main value, – in the agents themselves."[20]

Coleridge's anticonsequentialism is so strong that at times he denies that Paley is a moralist at all, since Paley is concerned only with outward effects of acts.[21] But this is not all he has to say about such views. Because of his conviction that our understanding of the truths first revealed through the Bible grows and develops, he holds that views long and deeply believed by a society or a profound thinker have something important to teach us: They contain some aspect of the truth we have not seen ourselves.[22] Egoistic and utilitarian moralists – and like many others at this time, Coleridge does not distinguish the two carefully – have grasped something that needs to be included in a full understanding of morality:

the outward object of virtue being the greatest producible sum of happiness of all men, it must needs include the object of an intelligent self-love. . . . Hence, you cannot become better (that is, more virtuous), but you will become happier.[23]

We assume that the physical world is a unity and a harmony; we must not less assume that the spiritual world of free and intelligent agents is one as well, and that true happiness for each will be the outcome of virtue.[24]

On Coleridge's view the data found in our moral experience form a substantial part of the evidence to which we must appeal to test the hypotheses about the universe and our place in it which are first suggested to us by the revelation and which our testing will show to be truly inspired. Part of the confirmation is provided by the very existence of unique and irreducible moral judgments: They show our distinctive place within the universe, as possessors of powers of intuition, and of free will. Another part of the confirmation is provided by the content of the deliverances of conscience: By commanding us at times to act in opposition to our animal needs and desires, and by stressing the inner worth of agents rather than the outer values of consequences, the dictates of conscience confirm the teachings recorded in the Bible. Presumably it is fair to infer from Coleridge's view that moral experience generally will show these features and that the morality of common sense will increasingly be explicable only in terms of the religious outlook. These general points suggest themes of great importance for the Cambridge moralists who preceded Sidgwick, and for Sidgwick as well.

2

As early as 1856 a major Victorian moralist noted the influence of Coleridge at Cambridge. "No one talks of a 'Cambridge Theology,' " James Martineau wrote,

There is such a thing, nevertheless; – at least there is a theology, perfectly distinct and characteristic of the age, formed by Cambridge men and born with the impress of Cambridge studies. . . . Coleridge . . . learned at Jesus College: and the men through whom chiefly his Platonic gospel has passed into the heart of our generation, Julius Hare and Frederick Maurice, acknowledged the same *alma mater*. To those who are familiar with the writings of these eminent teachers it will not appear fanciful if we trace the origin of the school to intellectual revolt against their academic textbooks, Locke and Paley. Empirical psychology and utilitarian ethics were the permanent objects of Coleridge's hostility. . . . it was reserved for Professors Sedgwick and Whewell, at a later time, to dethrone upon the spot the two established potentates in philosophy.[25]

The Cambridge theologians were one segment of those who came to be referred to as the "Broad Church" group of Anglicans. Like others who were included under this name, they held a wide variety of views on most topics, and were unified mainly by their very Coleridgean beliefs that religion need not fear and should, indeed, welcome the advance of science, that the dogmatic commitments required for membership in the Church of England should be reduced to a minimum, and that the church should try to include as many devout people as possible. Only thus, they felt, could the church survive in an age which was bound to see an increase of scientific study of the Bible.

The liberal Anglicans,[26] at Oxford and elsewhere as well as at Cambridge, were united not only by their rejection of empiricism and utilitarianism but by a denial of the view of progress that often went along with those positions in the early decades of the nineteenth century. They neither believed in nor wished for endless improvement in man's material lot: On the purely secular level, their view of history was rather that of Vico than of Condorcet. They saw secular history as primarily a matter of nations, and they held that nations go through regular stages of growth, maturation, decay, and death. Laws of this process may be derived, they thought, from the study of history and used to give guidance for political action. The relativism and apparent determinism involved in this view of history were countered by their Christian insistence on God's providence, and on the free will of men as the ultimate agent in historical change. For the other side of their denial of a materialistic kind of progress was an affirmation of the existence of spiritual and moral progress. Later ages, they claimed, begin their slow procession through the cycles of national history at a higher intellectual and ethical level than earlier ages. The agency in bringing about moral progress was at first God, whose direct revelation was decisive for all later times; but since then man's own nature has enabled him to grow in stature as a spiritual and moral being. This is the only true progress. "Accordingly," says J. C. Hare, "the philosophical idea of the history of the world will be, that it is to exhibit the gradual unfolding of all the faculties of man's intellectual and moral being . . . the purpose and end of the history of the world is to realize the idea of humanity."[27] Hare goes on to say that we must take seriously the commandment to be perfect as God is perfect. "These words," he remarks, "declare that the perfect renewal of God's image in man is not a presumptuous vision . . . but an object of righteous enterprise, which we may and ought to long for and to strive after."[28] Conscience, the voice of God within us according to Hare, is a testimony to the finer original nature we had before the fall: It is also the means by which we achieve moral knowledge. Like Coleridge, Hare connects the conscience with the Reason and denies that the conscience is utilitarian: "when the calculating, expediential Understanding has superseded the Conscience and the Reason, the Senses soon rush out from their dens, and sweep away everything before them."[29]

Motivated in large part by their desire to accept the advances of biblical scholarship, the liberal Anglicans developed a theory of "accommodation," which is a central point of their theology. Many of them were historians, and the theory of accommodation is in some sort a historical view. It holds that divine revelation at any time in history is adapted to the faculties and to the stage of spiritual and moral development of the men and the nation to whom the revelation is made. They drew from this view the conclusion that much of what is in the Bible must be understood not as conveying directly and literally some central truth but as indicating the truth in a way that could have been plainly enough understood by the relatively primitive nation to whom it was revealed, and that must be recovered through historical study now. Religious insight and understanding develop as man develops; and as our insight grows, we see more and more the ways in which divine providence is at work in the universe. The same is true in the moral realm, though here the advance is slower and more painfully achieved than in the sciences of the natural realm. But the result is assured:

> Though Chaos may only have been driven out of a part of his empire as yet, that empire is undergoing a perpetual curtailment; and in the end he will be cast out of the intellectual and moral and spiritual world, as entirely as out of the material.[30]

For Hare and his colleagues, then, we may conclude, morality, properly studied, reveals a progressive development toward a harmonious and coherent religious and spiritual standpoint; and the fact that it does is evidence of the spiritual structure of the universe.

F. D. Maurice, whose active career spanned the professorships of both Whewell and Grote, agrees with this general outlook. There is a theology, he says, and it is clearly his own, which

> suppose[s] the Infinite to be goodness and wisdom . . . and to be guiding men by various processes, in various regions and ages, into the apprehension of that which by their constitution they were created to apprehend. The history of Moral and Metaphysical Philosophy, is, as I think, the History of this Education.[31]

The knowability of God is a key point in Maurice's theology. He strongly rejects empiricism on the grounds that the doctrine is a barrier to human communication with God. "Ever since the position was adopted . . . that there is no knowledge but that which comes to us through the senses, the idea of a communion between the Divine Word and the heart and conscience and reason of men has been of course rejected," he writes in his major early work, *The Kingdom of Christ* (1838).[32] He also rejects the kind of antiempiricism represented by H. L. Mansel, which would place limits in principle on our ability to understand God. He holds that God is always and really accessible to us, and that knowledge of God is essential for all other knowledge. "The only possible doctrine for an age of Science," he remarks in a discussion of Comtean positivism, is

that God *can* be known; that the knowledge of Him is the root of all other knowledge; that we are only capable of knowing our fellow-creatures, and of knowing the world of nature, because we are more directly related to Him than to them; because His knowledge of them is imparted in a measure to the creatures whom he has made in His image. . . . Science demands God, as its foundation.[33]

At the basis of this view of the knowability of God is Maurice's fundamental conviction that God is not to be thought of as somehow distant from us, and that the kingdom of Christ is not to be envisaged as something which will come at some indefinite future date. So far as any temporal or spatial terms are appropriate to them, God and his kingdom are here and now – only we do not see them. Terms like Heaven, Hell, and Eternity refer to the way in which each of us relates to God and to every other person. Hell is willful and sinful self-isolation from God; Heaven is our closer union with him.[34] Social order on earth, like the order of the physical world, is an image of and is sustained by the divine order which is in and of the universe now, and which includes us all. What prevents us from seeing this more fully and from realizing it more completely than we do is our own selfishness.

Is not the world God's world? Is not the order which we see, His order? . . . Assuredly, it is God's world, God's order; . . . *how* has disorder come into this order? for that it is there, we all confess. It has come from men falling in love with this order, or with some of the things in it, and setting them up and making them into gods.[35]

God is forever reaching out to us, trying to help us to understand him; and in different ages and countries, from different intellectual backgrounds, men have tried in various ways to express and to teach what they have learned of him. Maurice is a true Coleridgean in his insistence that there is something of value to be learned from the deepest views of any thinker on religious matters. Each in his own way has seen a part or an aspect of the truth. So far as each has done so, each is right: It is only their denials, Maurice teaches, that are wrong. This attitude pervades Maurice's writings and leads him always to attempt to reconcile opposing views and to search for the truth embodied in the most diverse social schemes, religious opinions, and philosophical writings, as well as in the sects and religions of the world.[36]

If selfishness is the cause of our ignorance of God's order, conscience is the means through which we most directly come to know of it. Selfishness is a deliberate and sinful[37] failure to be what God means us to be: Conscience, which Maurice like Coleridge associates closely with our real self, tells each of us what he ought or ought not to be.[38] Maurice dismisses questions of the origins of conscience as irrelevant to an understanding of it. It cannot be reduced to simpler elements in sense experience,[39] nor is it simply feeling or even reason. It is the voice of God speaking within us.[40] Maurice takes this to mean that conscience is not an authority on its own (he thinks he is here disagreeing with Bishop Butler): Rather, it transmits to us God's authoritative law, which is the law of love. Conscience gives neither rules nor subsidiary laws to guide us,[41] for love expresses itself in different ways in different times and places. We see in Jesus Christ the perfect paradigm of human love, and we are called on to be like him; but we can only even begin to do this through God's working within us. Our selfishness shows itself in our opposing God's guidance. It has the effect of destroying order:

no man . . . no society, can stand upon selfishness. It must stand upon the opposite of selfishness. . . . Its root must be in love. That is the one binding force. . . . So far as any family or any nation has ever been held together, it has been held by the might not of selfishness but of sacrifice.[42]

Maurice is thus claiming that while conscience reveals the law of love to us, its dictates come in the form of specific judgments about specific situations. Selfishness blinds us to the presence of God and distorts though it cannot stifle the voice of conscience. Maurice does not argue for his views in any direct way; but if he is correct, then the judgments of conscience will show, over the ages, a developing pattern of increasing conformity to the law of love.

Whewell does not share the admiration felt by many of the liberal Anglicans for Coleridge,[43] but he holds many similar views. First, he is an intuitionist, holding that moral knowledge requires principles which cannot be proven and through the development of which all the remainder of morality is to be obtained. Though he uses the notion of conscience and identifies conscience as a means by which God's will is known to us,[44] he does not see it as a separate faculty. Moral judgments are deliverances of reason, and conscience is simply reason exercised on moral subjects. Moral concepts, however, are not reducible to or definable in terms of any other kind of concept, and this fact, Whewell thinks, may have led to the postulation of a special faculty for determining moral truths. His own view, by contrast, is that "we do not require that this Faculty or those Faculties by which man thus judges of right and wrong should be anything peculiar and ultimate, but only that the distinction should be a peculiar and ultimate one."[45] Second, Whewell strongly denies that consequentialism of any sort can be a full and accurate theory of morality. He offers numerous criticisms of utilitarianism, but underlying them all is his conviction that it is misguided from the start. Morality deals only secondarily with what utilitarianism makes basic, external actions and their results. It deals primarily with motivation. "The character of actions as right or wrong, considered with reference to the internal Springs of Action from which they proceed, is their *Moral* character."[46] Third, like Coleridge and Maurice, Whewell is a reconciliationist, even about utilitarianism. We all desire general happiness as our own ultimate aim; moreover, "it is quite true that we ought to act so as to increase as much as possible our own happiness and the Happiness of others" – but from this truth we cannot derive rules of action.[47] Such rules, which are essential to morality, Whewell thinks, must be obtained in quite another way; and since they are derived without reference to production of happiness there is a serious question as to whether happiness – our own or that of others – will be promoted by acting on the rules and doing our duty. Whewell insists strongly that "there can be no harmony in our being, except our Happiness coincide with our Duty" and that doing the latter will in fact lead to the former. But he allows that we require religion to be convinced of this.[48]

These Coleridgean commonplaces do not occupy a major place in Whewell's writings on ethics. His energies are mainly devoted to showing how the moral knowledge which mankind has so far acquired can be systematized and cast into the form of a scientific theory. At the basis of this endeavor is his theory that there is progress in knowledge. We acquire more details concerning facts or duties; more significantly, we increase the degree and extent of our understanding of the necessary, a priori, intuitively grasped truths which are the foundations of all knowledge. "There are scientific truths which are seen by intuition," Whewell writes, "but this intuition is progressive"[49] and the same is true of intuitively known moral truths. Moral conceptions,

in the progress of nations, gradually become clearer and clearer among men. We may suppose that, at first, man's social and moral faculties are very imperfectly developed . . . his moral conceptions are dim and vague. . . . As the intellectual culture of the nation proceeds . . . the conceptions . . . grow clearer in men's minds . . . nor can we say to what extent this intellectual and moral progress may proceed.

The intellectual progress of individuals follows nearly the same course, in these respects, as that of nations . . . the two careers are of the same kind; – a constant advance from the material to the abstract; from the particular to the general; but, in what is abstract and general, advance from the dim and vague to the distinct and precise.[50]

Our intuitions are directed upon Ideas in the mind of God, according to Whewell,[51] and though we never fully understand those Ideas because of the immeasurable difference between the human and the divine mind, we do nonetheless gain some genuine knowledge of God through our knowledge of his Ideas. Hence, as our knowledge of science and of morality progresses, our understanding of God progresses along with it, and in addition, every new discovery gives us a new assurance of "the Divine nature of the human mind."[52] Now Whewell sees two reasons for attempting to systematize common-sense morality. Systematization of existing knowledge, in terms of such grasp of the necessary truth as our ability to intuit gives us, is a central mode of making progress in knowledge: It helps increase our intuitive insight into the Idea or Ideas involved, as well as improving our understanding of the organization of the details. This is the procedure of the sciences, and Whewell thinks it crucial to show that morality proceeds in the same way. For he thinks that Christian morality is threatened by a hedonistic, secular outlook. In face of the kind of attack mounted by Hobbes, Christian moralists have so far been unable to defend their morality from the charge of being essentially dependent upon outmoded and antiscientific methods of thought,[53] while the antireligious moralists, following Hobbes, have come close to convincing the public that science and a hedonistic morality are allied. It is therefore, Whewell thinks, important for the future of civilization to show that Christian morality can be defended by rational methods of the same kinds as those used in the sciences, and this is what his systematization of common-sense morality is meant to do.

His mode of systematizing is complicated, and we need not concern ourselves here with the details.[54] It may be enough to say that he tries to present common-sense morality as the result of the application of gradually increasing intuitive insight into the divine Ideas of justice, benevolence, personality, and so on, to the changing circumstances of human life. He also tries to show that common-sense morality, as it develops independently of any specifically Christian revelation, is the basis out of which our demand for and understanding of Christian morality itself develops.[55] Common-sense morality, he argues, shows itself fit to be taken up into the religious view, in which the dictates of conscience are understood as the will of God and immorality becomes sin. Whewell presents, then, in a systematic and carefully structured fashion, the liberal Anglican version of the view that the evidence present in morality as we now know it points strongly toward a universe governed by a deity of the Christian description.

We come, finally, to John Grote, whose two books on ethics, both published posthumously, give us a good idea of what he must have been teaching during his tenure of the Knightbridge professorship from 1855 to 1866. Grote is at pains, from time to time, to dissociate himself from the views of his Cambridge predecessors, but the general tenor of his moral philosophy is completely consonant with theirs. He is, to begin with, as insistent as any of them on the difference in kind between moral concepts and beliefs and factual ones. Observational, or "positive," knowledge is certainly needed for morality, he holds, but what he calls the "ideal" is at least as important. "Moral philosophy," he tells us, "involves the notion of an ideal, of something which . . . *ought to be*, as distinguished from what is":[56] It is the besetting error of modern ethics to try to derive knowledge of the ideal from positive knowledge of fact. Like Coleridge and Whewell, Grote connects our knowledge of the ideal with intuition, and with reason. Though he discusses the conscience, he argues that it is only a feeling. It is distinctive in that it brings before us the idea of what we ought to do.[57] But the thought that we ought to do something, Grote says, is the thought "that there is *reason* why one sort of action . . . should be preferred to other sorts," just as the "ought to be" involved in ideals "really means that there exists reason why one . . . of these ideals is better than another."[58] The claim that an intuitively known ideal is necessarily involved in any morality is developed by Grote in a significant direction. The Benthamites, he points out, need an intuition of an ideal or of what ought to be if they are to make their interest in general happiness more than a purely personal concern. If, following Bentham, they say they cannot imagine anyone denying the greatest happiness to be the all-important ideal, then, he says, they are "placing the foundation of moral philosophy where . . . it ought to be placed, on . . . intuitivism."[59]

This gesture toward reconciling apparent opponents is as typical of Grote as it is of the other Cantabrigians. Grote thinks utilitarianism mistaken but not *simply* mistaken. It is not true that the production of happiness or pleasure (quite aside from the serious error of supposing that happiness is only a sum of pleasures)[60] provides the only good

reasons there can be for actions. But it is true that production of goodness, or of happiness properly understood, is a necessary condition of
goodness in actions, and Grote seems to think that no one really disputes
this. Hence, he claims, there is a "utilitarianism which is common to all
moral philosophy"; but this sort of utilitarianism does not warrant Mill
in setting his views in opposition to those of others, for this utilitarianism
"is not condemnatory of various other philosophies" in the way Mill
thinks it is.[61] For a full understanding of morality we must see that man
is more than simply a sentient creature, seeking gratification: We must
see that he is also an active creature, with "a work to do." The laws of
the distribution of "action for happiness," as well as the conceptions of
being worthy of happiness, are rooted in this aspect of human nature
and in the ideals appropriate to it, as the proper concept of a *summum
bonum* is rooted in our sentient nature and the ideals appropriate to
it.[62] In a complete moral philosophy, therefore, utilitarianism has a
proper but subordinate place. It is the science of "eudaemonics," or
what satisfies us as sentient beings. But "aretaics," or the study of how
we ought to distribute good, and of the actions that "would be worth
having in the universe" regardless of consequences, is "the principal of
the two sciences which [constitute] moral philosophy."[63]

Grote says less about religion than his Cambridge predecessors, and
almost nothing about progress, moral or otherwise, except to deny that
utilitarianism is the morality of progress.[64] But like Whewell he thinks
that morality leads us to a point at which we feel a need for the truths
religion alone can give us.[65] And he shares with Whewell the view that
if we are to act on our moral convictions an essentially religious assumption is needed: the assumption that the moral universe is harmonious. The ideas of virtue and duty cannot be resolved into the ideas
of utility or happiness, but they must point to the same lines of action.
We can see for ourselves that this must be so, "because human nature
is one, and is reasonable"; but

the belief which we must more or less entertain, that they are really and entirely,
upon the whole, consistent, that they coincide as to the line of action which
they point out, is in fact the belief that the moral universe is *one*, and good,
and the work of reason and design; a belief which . . . carries us . . . very deeply
and powerfully towards ideas of religion.[66]

Grote also thinks that we must suppose, "in order to reason to any
purpose about morals at all," that "what we ought to do and what we
wish to enjoy or have, our duties and our wants, will in the end be found
in harmony with each other." Without this, Grote sees no possibility of
morality.[67] How would it be, he asks, "if the different *goods* or purposes

of action which our intelligence suggests to us" had no relation to each other?

We have got to choose whether we will do our own pleasure, or others' pleasure, ...or the...rationally just, or the apparently natural, each of which things seem *good* to be done but seem also to lead us different ways: so far as this is so, there is moral chaos: there is absence of reason for acting any one way.[68]

We must therefore have "faith in the goodness and orderliness of the *moral* world...of the good that suggests itself, as what we should act for, being homogeneous, harmonious, consistent."[69]

3

A composite portrait of the views of the Cambridge moralists[70] would show us something like this. Morality provides the crucial evidence for the view that the best explanation of the universe as we experience it is a theistic, and very probably a Christian, one. The facts that we have the ability to obtain, however imperfectly, an intuitive grasp of moral truths, which are unlike any other sort of truth and not derivable from any other knowledge; and that we are free and responsible agents, as is shown by our having moral obligations and duties, testify to our unique status in the universe and to our having contact with a divine being. The content of the morality accessible to us all also suggests a religious interpretation. For common-sense morality shows the growth of an increasingly clear and penetrating grasp of the morality taught by the best religious leaders, and consummately by Christ, but not derivable from worldly considerations. One-sided and partial views of morality, such as the utilitarian view, are not to be rejected as completely false: They have grasped an aspect of truth, and in a full moral philosophy they too will have a place. The demands of our morality point toward the view that the universe is harmonious not only in its physical laws but also with respect to the various goods and duties it presents as guides to human action. Since this point is not decisively established by purely secular considerations, however, the confirmation it receives from the teachings of the Christian religion is good news indeed.

Sidgwick's *Methods of Ethics*, I suggest, presents an extremely careful examination of this kind of position. The question is whether the data of morality taken alone call for a Christian, or more generally a theistic, interpretation. Sidgwick was personally very sympathetic to the religious views of the Cantabrigians, and his epistemology is very close to theirs. In particular, he has no objections in principle to the kind of argument they try to produce. This is made clear in a review, published in 1871, of a book of essays by R. H. Hutton, a literary critic and popularizer of religious philosophy. Sidgwick comments here, as he does in other early reviews, on the importance of attention to method and clarity in theological argument:

If we are to argue from the facts of man's nature ascertained by observation of his thought and feelings, to the most profound and comprehensive judgments as to the essence of the universe, its origin and end – and I agree with Mr. Hutton, in opposition to many careful thinkers, that such argument is legitimate – we must surely take extreme heed to get our psychological premises as irrefragable and our principle of inference as clear and definite, as possible.[71]

"Such argument" – argument of the kind used by the Cambridge moralists – "is legitimate": The question then is simply what it actually leads to. Sidgwick's results are negative. Approaching the data without question-begging religious assumptions, he finds that the conclusions about religion drawn from them by the Cambridge moralists are simply not sustained; and in some respect he finds opposing conclusions suggested.

The evidence for this claim about Sidgwick's intentions in *The Methods of Ethics* is of two kinds. There is first the fact that this view of the work sheds considerable light on aspects of it which remain puzzling if we take it simply as the last expression of classical utilitarianism. The centrality of the examination of common-sense morality, the position with respect to determinism, the method of argument, the refusal to see any more rational basis for utilitarianism than for egoism, the concern about the disarray in which this leaves practical reason – all of these make very good sense if the *Methods* is an examination of the position that morality provides evidence for Christianity. The second kind of evidence is biographical; and although these two kinds of evidence quickly run together, I shall begin by presenting the available data about Sidgwick's early intellectual development, since it shows quite clearly that while the religious concerns of the Cambridge moralists were very much Sidgwick's concerns, from the beginning he was equally concerned about the soundness of their arguments.

Sidgwick, born in 1838, was the son of an Anglican clergyman and had a good religious upbringing. When he went to Rugby, which was still teaching along the lines set for it by the great liberal Anglican Thomas Arnold, he came under the influence of E. W. Benson, who was eventually to become archbishop of Canterbury as well as Sidgwick's brother-in-law. Sidgwick went up to Cambridge in 1855, just four years after Whewell had established the moral sciences tripos, and the year Grote first taught from the Knightbridge chair.[72] Within two years he had begun to "fall under different influences" from those of home and

Rugby, and to be less dominated by Benson.[73] Though he initially taught classics when he completed his degree in 1859, he was studying philosophy at the same time, particularly the writings of J. S. Mill, who did not encourage him to expect positive answers to basic religious questions. But, he tells us,

I was by no means then disposed to acquiesce in negative or agnostic answers. In fact I had not in any way broken with the Orthodox Christianity in which I had been brought up, though I had become sceptical with regard to many of its conclusions, and generally with regard to its methods of proof.[74]

The published correspondence shows that during the same period he had begun thinking about ethics, without losing his concern about religion. In August of 1861, he tells his close friend Henry Graham Dakyns that the deep problem that interests him now is "the great one of reconciling my religious instinct with my growing conviction that both individual and social morality ought to be placed on an inductive basis."[75] By March of the following year he writes that he is "revolving a Theory of Ethics. . . . I think I see a reconciliation between the moral sense and utilitarian theories." At the same time he is explaining to another friend that he is startled to find how "paralysed" his religious beliefs and sentiments have gradually become; but, he adds, "I cling to the hope of a final reconcilement of spiritual needs with intellectual principles."[76] In April 1862, he says he has "not advanced much in my 'Reconciliation of Ethical Systems.' " One of the problems he puts as follows:

Bain is the only thoroughly honest Utilitarian philosopher I know, and he allows self-sacrifice . . . to constitute a 'glorious paradox,' whereas Comte and all practical Utilitarians exalt the same sentiments into the supreme Rule of life. These are the views I am trying to reconcile.[77]

Not surprisingly, his views were still very much in flux: In May he writes that he has "given up a good deal of my materialism and scepticism, and come around to Maurice and Broad Church again," probably to move on, but wanting first to "learn all they have to teach."[78]

Sidgwick tells us elsewhere that while his early friends had varying religious views, "what was fixed and unalterable and accepted by us all was the necessity and duty of examining the evidence for historical Christianity with strict scientific impartiality."[79] In 1862 he began the study of Hebrew and Arabic as an aid to historical research on this topic. After working away at languages and allied subjects for three years, he came to feel that "the comparative historical study which I had planned would not give any important aid in answering the great questions raised by the orthodox Christianity from which my view of the Universe had been derived."[80] Hence he turned increasingly to philosophy, which the correspondence during the years of his immersion in historical studies shows he never really abandoned. Late in 1862 he says he has doubts as to the utility of Semitic languages, "so I am falling back . . . into philosophy." The same letter confesses a longing to accept "mystical beliefs," a longing so strong that "I am gradually developing my intuitive theories." And then Sidgwick says:

You know that I want intuitions for Morality; at least one (of Love) is required to supplement the utilitarian morality, and I do not see why, if we are to have one, we may not have others. I have worked away at the selfish morality, but I cannot persuade myself, except by trusting intuition, that Christian self-sacrifice is really a happier life than classical insouciance. . . . You see, I still hunger and thirst after orthodoxy: but I am, I trust, firm not to barter my intellectual birthright for a mess of mystical pottage.[81]

It seems plain that as early as 1862 Sidgwick had come a long way toward shaping the outlines of his moral philosophy: The reconciliation of utilitarianism and intuitionism by showing that the former needs an intuition at its base, and the problem of bringing egoism into line with the synthesis thus achieved, are already much on his mind. The connection of "intuitions" with "mysticism" – with traditional, authority-based faith – is still bothersome: He seems to be looking for a purely rational account of morality which will not depend on religion so much as help to support it. Within a year and a half the problems were becoming acute. "I cannot even get my moral sense right," he writes in May 1864:

I have been setting to work on a book that was to be called "Eudaemonism Restated": and just when I have demonstrated on paper the absolute preferability of complete self-devotion, I find myself disbelieving it. . . . I will hope for any amount of religious and moral development, but I will not stir a finger to compress the world into a system, and it does not at present seem as if it was going to harmonize itself without compression.[82]

By 1865 he had abandoned his Semitic studies, and in the following year he was expressing increasing doubts about religion to his friends. In 1867 he began to devote his teaching time fully to philosophy, as a result of a Cambridge decision to strengthen the moral sciences tripos. He was also at this time beginning serious debate with himself about whether or not to resign his fellowship, on the grounds that he could not sincerely give the required subscription to the articles of faith. This was not only a question of great practical importance for him, it was one in which he felt his own personal integrity was at stake. He tried, he says, "to decide the question methodically on general principles. . . . it was while struggling with the difficulty thence arising that I went through a great deal of the thought that was ultimately systematised in the *Methods of Ethics*."[83] In June 1869, he resigned his fellowship.

It seems clear, then, that religious doubts and moral philosophy were intertwined in Sidgwick's mind from the time he began thinking independently. If we examine the *Methods* against the background of Sidgwick's early views, we can see how much it incorporates his religious as well as his ethical concerns. We may begin with two relatively minor points – the significance of Sidgwick's intuitionism, and the point of his chapter on free will. The Cambridge moralists argue that the fact that ordinary moral judgments are *sui generis*, not reducible to empirical or any other sort of nonmoral judgment, is evidence of our intuitive powers, which reveal the divinity of our nature, and perhaps the existence of a deity who addresses us through the voice of conscience. While Sidgwick agrees concerning the nature of moral judgments, he disagrees with the inference: He detaches intuition, and the correlative irreducibility of moral concepts, from any special connection with the religious outlook. As early as 1871 his own views on this subject had reached fairly definite form. In an article entitled "The Verification of Beliefs," he argues that we must rely on intuitions of apparently clear and self-evident truths as the basis of all knowledge, not only moral knowledge. Skeptical doubts of a general nature may be ignored, he says, because the skeptic cannot rationally defend them without limiting himself. The empiricist qualms about intuitions relate in part to "the origin of our belief in these principles," but Sidgwick dismisses this as irrelevant. He takes "intuitive" to be opposed, not, as the empiricists think, to "innate," but to "discursive" or to "demonstrative." Aside from this matter, the empiricists themselves accept particular judgments as in this sense intuitively evident: Why do they reject universal intuitions? The reason they give is that the latter are sometimes mistaken. Sidgwick does not deny this: "it must farther . . . be admitted that we cannot hope to get an intuitive criterion in so perfect a form as entirely to exclude the possibility of error." But errors may be found even in apparent particular intuitions, if by this phrase we refer to more than the barest experiencing of feelings, for any cognitive claim about experience implies comparison and contrast and may go wrong. Hence the empiricist is self-condemned by his reason for denying universal intuitions. Moreover, it is impossible to see how "he can establish upon his foundation the conclusions of science. . . . individual premises, however manipulated, cannot establish a universal conclusion," and yet we all agree that such conclusions can be established. The moral Sidgwick draws is significant:

One may say generally that as the intuitive verification cannot be made entirely trustworthy, it requires to be supplemented by a discursive verification – which consists generally in ascertaining the harmony between the proposition regarded as intuitively certain and other propositions belonging to the same department of fact, and of which the Baconian verification [by survey of particulars] is the most important, but by no means the only species.

Intuition is simply a requirement for any sort of knowledge or reasoning at all – not a special mark of our moral insight or divine nature. It is needed for matter-of-fact knowledge, for mathematics, for logic, and for science as well as for morality. But if this is so then plainly the fact that intuitions are needed in morality does nothing special to support a theistic view.[84]

Sidgwick's treatment of the Cantabrigian claim that our free will is an indication of our special place in a divinely ordered universe has a similarly negative result. He confesses himself completely and totally unable to give any answer to the speculative question, whether man possesses free will.[85] But he argues that the whole issue is basically irrelevant to morality; and the significance of this move, in the context set by the Cambridge tradition, is considerable. Sidgwick's claim is that the contents of the plain man's moral beliefs would not need to be much affected one way or another by the kind of speculative resolution of the free-will issue which neither he nor, apparently, anyone else seems to be able to reach. In other words, morality, for the most part, does not somehow mirror either our having or our not having free will. There is only one class of exceptions to this. In considering justice, Sidgwick thinks that the notions of merit and demerit, reward and punishment, seem to depend fundamentally on free will. Hence it seems that "on the Determinist theory, 'ought,' 'responsibility,' 'desert,' and similar terms, have to be used, if at all, in new significations." Sidgwick does not disagree with this; but he points out that a determinist can give perfectly clear senses to all these terms.

True, the meaning of punishment is altered: it is no longer properly retributory, but reformatory and preventive: but it may fairly be said that this is the more practical view, and the one toward which civilization – quite apart from the Free-will controversy – seems to tend. And so of the moral feelings and judgments.[86]

The Cambridge moralists are not in a position to argue that such a change of meaning in key moral terms must be ruled out as improper and immoral: They put too much stress on the growth and development of man's insight into the moral ideas and into the progress of revelation through the development of civilization to make such a move. Sidgwick's conclusion is then that the deliverances of common-sense morality do not require us to suppose, for their explanation, that we have the sort of free will the Cantabrigians took to be evidence for the religious view of the universe. We shall see that another major point in the moral psychology of the Cantabrigians is undercut by Sidgwick's examination of the plain man's beliefs about what we ought to do.

The *Memoir* puts the writing of the *Methods* after Sidgwick's resignation of his fellowship, and Sidgwick himself, in an Autobiographical fragment, tells us that the examination of common-sense morality which forms book 3 was the first part of it to be written.[87] In the same fragment Sidgwick associates the writing of this part with a challenge to Whewell, whom he takes to be claiming that there is "a whole intelligible system of moral intuitions."[88] The association is not surprising. The examination of common-sense morality was certainly not at the heart of the utilitarian tradition. James Mill and John Austin were willing to concede that common-sense morality might be of some help in dealing with the problem of calculating the consequences of action, and John Stuart Mill incorporated this view of positive morality somewhat more firmly into his ethics, but the utilitarians view common-sense morality primarily as something that needs reforming. Sidgwick himself pointed this out in an early review:

In Hume's hands utilitarianism, presented as a mode of *explaining* morality, was felt to have a destructive tendency and fell under suspicion; but it was not till Bentham that it was offered as a method for determining conduct, absolutely complete in itself, the conclusions of which were to overrule all traditional precepts and supersede all existing sentiments. Herein lies the originality of Bentham.[89]

But from the point of view of the Cambridge tradition, a careful examination of common-sense morality would be a crucial step in determining whether or not the deliverances of conscience offer evidence of a developing insight into a harmonious structure of Christian or of theistic moral norms. And Whewell had presented a far more detailed and comprehensive study of the plain man's morality from this point of view than anyone else. Sidgwick's autobiographical notes as well as his letters make it plain that by the time he came to write out the material for book 3 he had already devoted seven or eight years of intense thought to the general issues of moral philosophy. His examination of common sense and of Whewell, then, must have been written to answer specific questions which rested on basic views worked out in some detail. His own method is, ironically enough, extremely Whewellian: He is turning from a dim apprehension of the basic truths to a study of the data they are meant to organize, in the hopes of improving his grasp of both. But it should be clear that the point of such a study of common-sense morality need not be to attack or to defend the moral principles revealed in it. The point could be to determine, with greater care than Whewell, just what principles *are* revealed in it or, in other words, to see what theory of morality offers the best account of the plain man's unsystematized convictions. And this, of course, is precisely what Sidgwick claims he does in his examination of our ordinary moral convictions.[90]

Sidgwick suggests a comparison of his examination of common sense with books 2–4 of Aristotle's *Nichomachean Ethics*, in which the common-sense morality of Greece is presented in systematic fashion.[91] The historical perspective thus emphasized is not insignificant. For if there is progress in our insight into moral truth, surely our present-day moral convictions ought to be noticeably more Christian, or at least monotheistic, than those of Aristotle's day. Julius Hare says as much:

Courage may be considered as purity in outward action; purity as courage in the inner man. . . . The ancients . . . look to the former; the moderns have rather fixt their attention on the latter. . . . whence comes this superiority of ours in delicacy and reflexion? The cause is to be found in Christianity, and in Christianity alone. Heathen poets and philosophers may now and then have caught fleeting glimpses of the principle which has wrought this change: but as the foundation of all morality, the one paramount maxim, it was first proclaimed in *the Sermon on the Mount.*[92]

Sidgwick, in contrast, remarks that while the origin of moral notions and feelings lies buried in obscurity the evidence does not suggest that the further back in history we go, the closer we come to conscious utilitarian views. On the contrary:

It is . . . not as the mode of regulating conduct with which mankind began, but as that to which we can now see that human development has always been tending, as the adult and not the germinal form of Morality, that Rational Utilitarianism must claim the acceptance of Common Sense.[93]

The Cambridge moralists would obviously have taken such a conclusion about common-sense morality as showing that a Christian outlook was *not* developing within it. There is clear evidence that Sidgwick shares this view of the conclusion. It comes from a review, published in 1866 and summarizing the position to which Sidgwick had come as a result of his years of philosophical and historical studies.[94] The review devotes much space to criticizing the methodology used in the book and rejects any arguments based on alleged miracles; but the part of importance to us is Sidgwick's presentation of the moral teaching of Christ. The author of the book, he says, has given what, in a sermon, we might not complain of as a summary of general Christian ethics. He has not, however, helped us "to see Jesus as he appeared to his Jewish contemporaries." He has been too unhistorical. It may be that "we cannot assert that any virtue may not be found at least in germ in the teaching of Jesus," but we must distinguish the germ from the fully grown plant.[95] If in Jesus' teaching "all the subsequent development of Christianity is implicitly contained," the evolution of it was still gradual. There follows immediately a passage sketching what Sidgwick takes Christ's moral doctrine to be:

The one thing important to Jesus in man was a principle so general that faith, love, and moral energy seem only different sides of it. It was the ultimate coincidence, or rather, if we may use a Coleridgean word, *indifference* of religion and morality. It was "the single eye," the *rightness*, of a man's heart before God. It was faith in the conflict with baser and narrower impulses, love when it became emotion, moral energy as it took effect on the will.[96]

The principle has four consequences. First, it deepens the importance of obligation. No outward right act can be produced except from right inward impulses; and those in the right inner state will desire perfection. Second, it leads, properly understood – and Sidgwick adds, "in Christianity as at present understood" – to the view that "the degree in which a man possesses this inner rightness of heart fixes his rank in the Kingdom of God at any time." Neither external position nor even good works, if the spirit in which they were done is lacking, are of any account. Third, when morality is "made to depend on the state of the heart," the ceremonial law loses its importance. And finally, "if man's position in the universe, or, more religiously, in the sight of God, depends upon his rightness of heart," then anyone may enter the kingdom of God – a conclusion drawn, Sidgwick thinks, only by Paul.[97]

These brief passages, in addition to suggesting that Sidgwick was influenced by the developmentalism of the liberal Anglicans, present a clear picture of his understanding of Christian morality. He sees it, not as Paleyan theological utilitarianism, but as an intentionalism, a view in which not the results of action but their inner source in the human heart or will is the basic, prime, bearer of moral value. There is moreover no suggestion of hedonism in what he sees as Christian ethics. In the absence of any reason to suppose that his views about Christian ethics changed, we must take the conclusion of the *Methods* that the plain man's morality is utilitarian as being tantamount for him to the conclusion that the plain man's morality is not Christian.

Sidgwick's view that egoism is as rational and authoritative a guide to action as utilitarianism would, of course, be unacceptable to the Cambridge moralists. His reasons for holding the view, moreover, and its implications, reveal yet further problems with the Cantabrigian position in general. The Cantabrigians, with the exception of Maurice, stress the claim that the moral faculty is essentially the reason, concerning itself with one area of thought. The acts one ought to do are the ones for which there are good reasons (or perhaps the best reasons). But if this is, as they suggest, the only consideration, then insofar as we find reasons based on self-interest for doing certain acts, so far as we ought to do those acts. Sidgwick's assumptions about what it is to give a reason, together with his examination of our ordinary beliefs as to what we ought to do, lead him to conclude that the set of prudential reasons for doing self-interested acts is as solid as the set of utilitarian reasons for doing disinterested acts. He therefore finds no grounds for rejecting moral egoism. The consequence is his well-known worry about "the dualism of practical reason." There are two equally valid, authoritative and rational systems of guidance for action, each involving a basic intuition. Unfortunately, Sidgwick holds, the two positions contradict one another, and this, in the concluding words of the first edition of the *Methods*, reduces the Cosmos of Duty to a Chaos. In terms of the larger question of the success of the Cantabrigian argument as a defense of religion, it shows that ordinary beliefs about what we ought to do, far from pointing toward a religious hypothesis as the best explanation of all of our experience, suggest the opposite very strongly. For if there were a rational mind at the core of the universe, structuring it and communicating with humans, then on Cantabrigian assumptions, our beliefs about what it is reasonable to do would reflect not a chaos but a cosmos.

Why then should Sidgwick not do what Gizycki[98] and others suggest, simply argue that egoism is not a method of *ethics* at all? For if the principle on which egoism rests is not a moral principle, then there can be no contradiction between egoism and morality, no matter how widely their dictates may diverge. Sidgwick is in fact very hesitant about suggesting that egoism systematizes the plain man's *moral* convictions, and he might well agree that what we call "morality" must by definition involve concern for the good of everyone alike, while what we call "prudence" or "egoism" involves only concern for the agent. But he cannot see in such a nomenclatural point any solution to his basic problem. The difficulty is again rooted in the Cantabrigian position and was pointed out by John Grote. Criticizing Bishop Butler's account of the two superior principles in man, conscience and self-love, Grote says that Butler

gives no reason why *moral* principle, or conscience, should be superior to intellectual principle, or prudence. The account which he gives of the supremacy of conscience is applicable to all of that which I have called principle [i.e., to all rational reflective modes of determining what one ought to do] and we want to know why moral reflection has authority over other kinds of reflection.[99]

Sidgwick cannot answer this question because for him the authority of morality derives solely from its rationality, and he thinks, as I have said, that the same sort of rationality is to be found in egoism. If we have any grounds on which to claim overriding authority for the dictates of reason which demand disinterested or moral action, we have the same kind of grounds on which to claim overriding authority for the dictates of reason demanding interested or prudential action. Name calling, or name withholding, would not help.

Sidgwick's views on ethical egoism have, finally, important critical bearing on the moral psychology of the Cantabrigians. Sidgwick agrees with them that psychological egoism is mistaken: Our nature contains disinterested as well as interested impulses and motives. The Cantabrigians however are inclined to suggest that one set of motivations is somehow more real or more basic than the other; and here Sidgwick disagrees. His claim is that both types of motivation, not the disinterested type only, can be taken up into a coherent and rational pattern of living. This is directed in part of F. D. Maurice's claim that selfishness is the source of disorder and incoherence in the moral world. It is also aimed at a position that Coleridge and Whewell[100] seem to want to hold: that conscience is simply reason but also that conscience is especially connected with one's true self, which is one's moral or unselfish self. If Sidgwick is correct, then this position cannot be defended as they wish to defend it. Our self-interested desires cannot be shown by any internal incoherence to stem from a false or bad self. If we confine ourselves to common-sense beliefs about what we ought to do, and do not make a covert appeal to a priori doctrines derived from religion or metaphysics, then there is no reason to believe that we can get rid of self-interest and still keep the man. Our ordinary morality, in other words, no more needs, for its explanation, a self or soul of the kind religion teaches us about than it needs a rational ruler of the universe.

Sidgwick argues, then, that the fact of intuition in morality is no evidence for religious views; that morality does not seem to require the assumption of free will and so again fails to support religious claims; that ordinary morality is hedonistic and consequentialist and so opposed to Christian views of morality; and that our ordinary beliefs about what we ought, rationally speaking, to do sustain two equally sound but contradictory interpretations and point, therefore, rather away from than toward any theistic view of the universe. In 1887, in a journal kept for his friend John Addington Symonds, Sidgwick wrote:

On one point J. A. S. has not caught my position; he says that he never expected much from *the* method of proof on which I have relied. But the point is that I have tried *all* methods in turn – all that I found pointed out by any of those who have gone before me; and all in turn have failed – revelation, rational, empirical methods – there is no proof in any of them.[101]

No proof of what? Sidgwick does not say, but I think the answer is plain: no proof of Christian or even of theistic views. There is of course much more to *The Methods of Ethics* than the presentation of the negative results of a theological investigation; but unless we see that it does present such results, we shall not fully understand it.

Notes

1 John Grote, *An Examination of the Utilitarian Philosophy* (Cambridge and London, 1870), pp. 237–8.
2 *ME*, xv, xx.
3 E. Albee, *A History of English Utilitarianism* (London, 1902), p. 358.
4 *ME*, v.
5 The references are to H. Calderwood, "Mr. Sidgwick on Intuitionalism," *Mind*, o.s. 1 (1876): 197–206, and to A. Barratt, "The 'Suppression' of Egoism," *Mind*, o.s. 2 (1877): 167–86.
6 *ME*, x, and cf. Sidgwick's reply to Barratt, *Mind*, o.s. 2 (1877): 411, where the same point is made.
7 See the two "Introductory Notices" to E. H. Plumptre's edition of J. C. Hare, *The Victory of Faith* (London, 1874). One notice is by Maurice, the other by Dean Stanley.
8 S. T. Coleridge, *Confessions of an Inquiring Spirit*, in *Aids to Reflection*, etc. (London, 1913), p. 296.
9 Ibid., pp. 316–17.
10 Ibid., pp. 323 ff.
11 S. T. Coleridge, *Omniana*, in *The Table Talk and Omniana*, ed. T. Ashe (London, 1896), pp. 429–30.
12 Ibid., pp. 418, 429; and cf. *Aids to Reflection*, pp. 44, 91.
13 "Essay on Faith," in *Aids to Reflection*, p. 341.
14 Ibid., p. 342.
15 Ibid., p. 348.
16 S. T. Coleridge, *Philosophical Lectures*, ed. Kathleen Coburn (New York: Philosophical Library, 1949), pp. 152–3.
17 *Table Talk*, p. 155.
18 *Aids to Reflection*, pp. 90–1.
19 Ibid., pp. 196–7.
20 S. T. Coleridge, *The Friend* (London, 1863), 2: 139.
21 Cf. *Aids to Reflection*, pp. 196–7, and *Church and State* (London, 1839), p. 380 n.

22 Cf. *The Friend*, 2:143–4.

23 *Aids to Reflection*, p. 30.

24 Ibid., pp. 40–1; cf. 31 ff.

25 James Martineau, *Essays, Reviews, and Addresses* (London, 1890), vol. I, "Personal Influences on Our Present Theology," p. 224. Sedgwick, whom I do not discuss, delivered in 1832 an attack on Locke, Paley, and utilitarianism generally in his *Discourse on the Studies of the University*. A geologist, he was a friend of Whewell and Hare.

26 I am indebted to Duncan Forbes, *The Liberal Anglican Idea of History* (Cambridge: Cambridge University Press, 1952), for much of the material in this paragraph and the next. Although Forbes does not discuss Whewell, it was his book which suggested to me that it might be profitable to think of Whewell as the philosopher and historian of science of the Broad Church group.
   Whewell is generally thought to have been rather conservative; but on church matters he was viewed at the time as a liberal. See N. Gash, *Reaction and Reconstruction in English Politics*, 1832–1852 (Oxford: Oxford University Press, 1965), pp. 93, p. 95, n. 2. For further data on his academic and religious views, see the various letters to Hare in Mrs. Stair Douglas, *Life of William Whewell*, 2d ed. (London, 1882), and J. Willis Clark, *Old Friends at Cambridge* (London, 1900), pp. 91, 106, 123–4.

27 *Guesses at Truth*, by Two Brothers (1838; London, 1897), pp. 334–5. J. C. Hare wrote the book with his brother Augustus.

28 Ibid., p. 347.

29 Ibid., p. 80.

30 Ibid., p. 506.

31 F. D. Maurice, *Moral and Metaphysical Philosophy* (1862; London, 1872), 1:xxix; cf. *Theological Essays* (1853; London, 1891), p. 300.

32 Maurice, *The Kingdom of Christ* (1838; London, 1891), 1:44–5.

33 Maurice, *The Epistles of St. John* (1857; London 1893), p. 344.

34 Maurice, *Theological Essays*, pp. 405 f.

35 *Epistles of St. John*, pp. 120–1; cf. 61, 126–7.

36 See *Moral and Metaphysical Philosophy*, 1:xxx; *Theological Essays*, p. 384; *Kingdom of Christ*, 1:227; 2:88 ff., and *Social Morality* (London and Cambridge, 1869), esp. chap. 18, in which Maurice tries to show how we can learn vitally important religious lessons even from philosophers like Hobbes; *Epistles of St. John*, p. 93.

37 See Frederick Maurice, *The Life of Frederick Denison Maurice* (New York, 1884), 2:538–40.

38 Maurice, *The Conscience* (London and Cambridge, 1868), pp. 31, 3 f.

39 Ibid., pp. 32, 51, 165.

40 Ibid., p. 73; *Epistles of St. John*, p. 212.

41 *The Conscience*, pp. 104 ff., 113, 125.

42 *Epistles of St. John*, p. 264; cf. *Social Morality*, pp. 385 ff.

43 Cf., e.g., his lecture on Coleridge in *Lectures on the History of Moral Philosophy*, A New Edition (1862), pp. 119–30 of the second set of pages.

44 William Whewell, *Elements of Morality, including Polity*, 4th ed. (Cambridge, 1864), p. 288; cf. pp. 151–2.
45 Whewell, *Lectures on the History of Moral Philosophy*, p. 234. These lectures were originally given in 1838.
46 *Elements of Morality*, p. 67.
47 Ibid., p. 243.
48 Ibid., p. 241.
49 Whewell, *Philosophy of Discovery* (London, 1860), p. 344.
50 *Elements of Morality*, pp. 202–3.
51 See *Philosophy of Discovery*, pp. 359 ff.
52 Ibid., p. 374; cf. pp. 380 ff.
53 See the *Lectures on the History of Moral Philosophy*, lectures 1–4 of the original series.
54 For a fuller account, see my "Whewell's Ethics," in *Studies in Moral Philosophy*, American Philosophical Quarterly Monograph Series, no. 1 (1968).
55 *Elements of Morality*, pp. 288–9.
56 Grote, *Examination*, p. 269; cf. p. 162, and chap. 11.
57 John Grote, *A Treatise on the Moral Ideals*, ed. Joseph Bickersteth Mayor (Cambridge and London, 1876), p. 167.
58 Ibid., pp. 79, 45.
59 Ibid., p. 20; cf. pp. 44–5.
60 *Examination*, chap. 2.
61 Ibid., p. 79; cf. *Treatise*, pp. 70–1.
62 *Treatise*, chaps. 1–3; *Examination*, chap. 6.
63 *Treatise*, pp. 76–8.
64 *Examination*, chap. 20.
65 Ibid., pp. 217–8.
66 Ibid., pp. 162–3.
67 Ibid., p. 349.
68 *Treatise*, pp. 518–9.
69 Ibid., pp. 517–18.
70 Thomas Rawson Birks succeeded Maurice as Knightbridge professor in 1872; but he was an "Evangelical" or "Low Church" divine, rather than a member of the "Broad Church" group, and his writings prior to 1872 did not deal with moral philosophy. I therefore do not consider him here.
71 *The Academy*, July 1, 1871, p. 325.
72 Whewell's *Elements of Morality* was a set book in the moral sciences tripos, and Grote held regular discussions of philosophy with a few of the younger fellows, Sidgwick among them. F. D. Maurice attended some of these, and Sidgwick, who knew him in other contexts as well, seems to have been very knowledgeable about his career. See *M*, 42, 134–38, 205, n. 2.
73 *M*, 11.
74 *M*, 36.
75 *M*, 68. Mill's *Utilitarianism* was published that autumn.
76 *M*, 75.

77 *M*, 77–8.
78 *M*, 79.
79 *M*, 40.
80 *M*, 37.
81 *M*, 90.
82 *M*, 107–8.
83 *M*, 38.
84 The quotations in this paragraph are from "The Verification of Beliefs," *Contemporary Review*, 1871, esp. pp. 583–90.
85 *ME*1, 45.
86 *ME*1, 49–50.
87 *ME*, xx.
88 *ME*, xix.
89 *The Academy*, July 1, 1872, p. 251.
90 See my "First Principles and Common Sense Morality in Sidgwick's Ethics," *Archiv für Geschichte der Philosophie* 45, No. 2 (1963).
91 *ME*, xix.
92 *Guesses at Truth* (1826; London: Macmillan, 1897), p. 179.
93 *ME*1, 427; cf. *ME*, xx.
94 *M*, 37. The book, published anonymously, was *Ecce Homo*, by John (later Sir John) Seeley.
95 *MEA*, 18–19, and cf. p. 15.
96 *MEA*, 23.
97 *MEA*, 23–6.
98 Georg von Gizycki, Review of *Methods*, 3rd ed. in *Vierteljahrsschrift für wissenschaftliche Philosophie* 9 (1885–6): 104–12.
99 *Treatise on the Moral Ideals* p. 142; cf. p. 146.
100 Cf. *ME*1, 44–5, critizing Whewell for holding this kind of view.
101 *M*, 472. See also *M*, 608–15, esp. pp. 612 ff., where Sidgwick explains what the rational, revelational, and empirical methods are and explicitly criticizes a line of argument like that which I have attributed to the Cambridge moralists.

3

Sidgwick and Whewellian intuitionism
Some enigmas

ALAN DONAGAN

Sidgwick's *Methods of Ethics*[1] appears to defend a revised utilitarianism against both egoism and intuitionism, while conceding that the practical results of enlightened egoism largely coincide with those of utilitarianism, and that the utilitarian greatest-happiness principle can be justified only as a fundamental intuition. It is true that Sidgwick was distressed by the description of his treatment of intuitional morality as "mere hostile criticism from the outside" and protested that that morality "is my own . . . as much as it is any man's; it is, as I say, the 'Morality of Common Sense,' which I only attempt to represent so far as I share it" (*ME*, x). However, he could not well have denied that, in *The Methods of Ethics*, the endorsement tentatively accorded to intuitional morality as a system is in the end withdrawn. Ultimately it is concluded that utilitarianism can define and correct what intuitional morality is vague or mistaken about, and can complete what common sense does not venture to treat at all. Hence the teaching of *The Methods of Ethics* appears to be that, at the final stage of moral thinking, utilitarianism *replaces* intuitional morality, even though it incorporates, on a new basis, many intuitional precepts.

Yet, closer reading of Sidgwick's ethical writings throws doubt both on whether he was consistent in reaching these conclusions and on whether he held them firmly. These doubts are strengthened by comparing what he wrote about what he called "dogmatic intuitionism" with what Whewell, the principal "dogmatic" intuitionist he had in mind, wrote about it, and by considering what he had to say about his own relation to Whewell's work.[2] And they are further strengthened by studying the grounds on which he resigned his fellowship at Trinity over the

My research has been supported by the John Simon Guggenheim Memorial Foundation, by the Center for Advanced Study in the Behavioral Sciences (through a grant from the National Science Foundation), and by the University of Chicago, to all of whom I desire to express my gratitude. I also desire to express my gratitude to J. B. Schneewind for correcting some early follies of mine about Sidgwick, for helping me by his writings and in correspondence to such understanding of Whewell and Sidgwick as I have attained, and for proposing many of the themes of this essay. This essay is reprinted by permission from the *Canadian Journal of Philosophy* 7, no. 3 (September 1977): 447–65.

controversy about subscription to the Thirty-nine Articles, and his own general pronouncements on the question in his pamphlet, *The Ethics of Conformity and Subscription.*[3]

What did Sidgwick really think about "dogmatic" or Whewellian intuitionism? And did he, in *The Methods of Ethics*, succeed in saying what he thought about it? I can answer neither question. The following observations are submitted in the hope that they may help others to do so.

What Sidgwick found to say in *The Methods of Ethics* about "the intuitional method" is complicated. Its chief points are as follows.

Each of the diverse methods by which right and wrong are determined "in ordinary practical thought" presupposes acceptance of an end (*ME*, 6). Only two ends appear to be accepted by "the common sense of mankind" as rational and ultimate: namely, happiness and the excellence or perfection of human nature (*ME*, 9). Of these ends, the former "leads us to two *prima facie* distinct methods, according as it is sought to be realised universally, or by each individual for himself alone" (*ME*, 9); the latter, since "no one has ever directed an individual to promote the virtue of others except . . . as . . . involved in the complete realisation of Virtue in himself" (*ME*, 11), leads to a single method. The two methods which take happiness as the ultimate end are egoistic hedonism, or egoism, and universalistic hedonism, or utilitarianism. The single method which takes human excellence or perfection as the ultimate end "will *prima facie* coincide to a great extent with that based on what I called the Intuitional view" (*ME*, 11).

In his introductory chapter on intuitionism (*ME*, book 1, chap. 8), he characterized the intuitional view as "that which regards as the practically ultimate end of actions their conformity to certain rules or dictates of Duty unconditionally prescribed" (*ME*, 96). Strictly, this view gives rise to three methods.

The first is that of those persons, some of them philosophers, who think that they can "discard as superfluous all modes of reasoning to moral conclusions," because in any particular situation, if a particular action is right or wrong, it can be immediately perceived to be so (cf. *ME*, 98–9). Sidgwick dismissed as "ultraintuitional" rather than intuitional the view that underlies this method – "if," he scrupulously added, "we may extend the term 'method' to include a procedure that is completed in a single judgment" (*ME*, 100). Not even those who hold the ultraintuitional view, if they are reflective, consider all their particular intuitions to be "indubitable and irrefragable"; nor "do they always find when they have put an ethical question to themselves in all sincerity [a question, that is, about what to do in a particular situation] that they are always conscious of clear immediate insight in respect of it" (*ME*, 100).

By contrast with the method derived from the ultraintuitional view, "Christian and other moralists" have "represented the process of conscience as analogous to one of jural reasoning" (*ME*, 100). This second method is what is most familiarly called intuitional.

[Its] fundamental assumption [Sidgwick wrote] is that we can discern certain general rules with really clear and finally valid intuition. It is held that such general rules are implicit in the moral reasoning of ordinary men, who apprehend them adequately for most practical purposes, and are able to enunciate them roughly; but that to state them with proper precision requires a special habit of contemplating clearly and steadily abstract moral notions. It is held that the moralist's function then is to perform this process of abstract contemplation, to arrange the results as systematically as possible, and by proper definitions and explanations to remove vagueness and prevent conflict. (*ME*, 101)

This is what Whewell, in his *Elements of Morality*, took to be the intuitional method; and Sidgwick was justified in asserting that "such a system as this . . . seems to be generally intended when Intuitive or a *priori* morality is mentioned" (*ME*, 101).

But a third intuitional method naturally arises out of this second, or "dogmatic" method. Even if they accept the general rules obtained by reflecting on "the ordinary thought of mankind," and even granting that "these rules can be so defined as perfectly to fit together and to cover the whole field of human conduct, without ever coming into conflict and without leaving any practical questions unanswered," philosophic minds will nevertheless seek for some deeper explanation of why these rules hold (*ME*, 102). They will therefore try to formulate "one or more principles more absolutely and undeniably true and evident, from which the current rules might be deduced either just as they are commonly received or with slight modifications and rectifications" (*ME*, 102). This third species or phase of the intuitional method Sidgwick called "philosophical intuitionism."

In accordance with this preliminary analysis, of the fourteen chapters of *The Methods of Ethics* devoted to intuitionism, Sidgwick allotted no fewer than ten to the second of his two intuitional methods – that of the morality of common sense (book 3, chaps. 2–11). His findings in those chapters are, in the main, adequately summed up in the last of them, which he entitled "Review of the Morality of Common Sense" (chap. 11). They are as follows: A maxim or precept is intuitively known if and only if it satisfies four conditions: (1) that it is clearly and precisely formulated (*ME*, 338); (2) that its self-evidence is ascertained by careful reflection (*ME*, 339); (3) that it is consistent with other propositions received as intuitively evident (*ME*, 341); and (4) that experts in the subject do not dissent from it (*ME*, 341–2). However, careful inquiry into each of the various departments of morality shows that, even in those which have been thoroughly investigated, like veracity and keeping promises, the precepts which really are commonly accepted fail to satisfy condition (1), that they be clearly and precisely formulated; and those enunciated by moralists, although they may satisfy conditions (1) and (3), of clarity, precision, and consistency with one another, are too controversial to satisfy condition (4). Hence, although the morality of common sense may be "perfectly adequate to give practical guidance to common people in common circumstances," to attempt "to elevate it into a system of Intuitional Ethics" will merely bring "its inevitable imperfections into prominence without helping us to remove them" (*ME*, 361).

As Sidgwick originally delineated it, the third or "philosophical" intuitional method was to begin by assembling results obtained by the second or "dogmatic" one: namely, a set of general rules derived from reflection on the ordinary moral thought of mankind. It was then to seek for one or more ultimate principles that would provide a foundation from which those rules might be deduced. His negative criticism of the dogmatic method, however, persuaded him that it cannot yield the set of general rules which the employment of the third method presupposes. Yet he believed that a place remains for an intuitional method that might be called "philosophical." For there are "certain absolute practical principles, the truth of which, when they are explicitly stated, is manifest," although "they are of too abstract a nature, and too universal in their scope, to enable us to ascertain by immediate application of them what we ought to do in any particular case" (*ME*, 379). These principles are not part of the morality of common sense; but, once explicitly stated and understood, those who live by that morality will acknowledge their truth.

Sidgwick recognized three principles as obtainable by this "philosophical" method. The first, the Principle of Impartiality, is "an important element in the common notion of justice"; strictly stated, it "must take some such negative form as this: 'it cannot be right for A to treat B in a manner in which it would be wrong for B to treat A, merely on the ground that they are two different individuals, and without there being any difference between the natures or circumstances of the two which can be stated as a reasonable ground for difference of treatment' " (*ME*, 380). The second, or Principle of Prudence, affirms that "mere difference of priority and posteriority in time is not a reasonable ground for having more regard to the consciousness of one moment than to that of another"; or, more concisely, that "Hereafter *as such* is to be regarded neither less nor more than Now" (*ME*, 381). Finally, just as the Principle of Prudence was reached by comparing and integrating the different goods in the successive states of a sentient individual, so it is necessary to compare and integrate the goods in all sentient individuals. Two rational intuitions seem to be inescapable: "that the good of any one individual is of no more importance . . . than the good of any other"; and that each person, "as a rational being, [is] bound to aim at good generally" (*ME*, 382). From these intuitions, a third principle follows: namely, "that each one is morally bound to regard the good of any other individual as much as his own, except in so far as he judges it to be less, when impartially viewed, or less certainly knowable or attainable by him" (*ME*, 382). Sidgwick called it the Principle of Rational Benevolence.

Not surprisingly, Sidgwick concluded that the results of philosophical intuitionism coincide with those of utilitarianism. "[T]he common antithesis between Intuitionists and Utilitarians," he declared, "must be entirely discarded: since such abstract moral principles as we can admit to be really self-evident are not only not incompatible with a Utilitarian system, but even seem required to furnish a rational basis for such a system" (*ME*, 496). And so he could describe one result of his inquiry in *The Methods of Ethics* as that "I was a Utilitarian again . . . but on an intuitional basis" (*ME*, xx).

In addition, he believed that even the morality of common sense tends to coincide with utilitarianism. First of all, "although there are other rules [besides the three principles of philosophical intuitionism] which our common moral sense when first interrogated seems to enunciate as absolutely binding; it has appeared that careful and systematic reflection on this very Common Sense, as expressed in the habitual moral judgments of ordinary men, results in exhibiting the real subordination of those rules [to the three principles]" (*ME*, 497). Even common sense, in short, demands that its rules be applied flexibly, in accordance with the Principle of Rational Benevolence. And second, in his detailed exposition of the relation of utilitarianism to the morality of common sense (book 4, chap. 3), Sidgwick thought himself able to show

that the Utilitarian estimate of consequences not only supports broadly the current moral rules, but also sustains their generally received limitations and qualifications: that, again, it explains anomalies in the Morality of Common Sense, which from any other point of view must seem unsatisfactory to the reflective intellect; and, moreover, where the current formula is not sufficiently precise for the guidance of conduct, while at the same time difficulties and perplexities arise in the attempt to give it additional precision, the Utilitarian method solves these difficulties and perplexities in general accordance with the vague instincts of Common Sense, and is naturally appealed to for such solution in ordinary moral discussion. (*ME*, 425)

This "more positive treatment of Common Sense Morality," Sidgwick advised his readers, was "intended as an indispensable supplement of the negative criticism" elaborated in book 3, chapters 2–11 (*ME*, 361 n.).

Since he had not, in his negative criticism, questioned that the current moral rules, with their "generally received" limitations and qualifications, are "broadly" defensible, it is puzzling that Sidgwick should have described his qualified utilitarian endorsement of intuitionism as significantly "positive." All the specific objections to intuitionism are repeated: that it generates inconsistent results ("anomalies"), that its results are indefinite, that attempts to make them definite generate further anomalies, and that, when casuistical problems cannot be solved by the intuitional method because of those anomalies, recourse to the utilitarian method is not only "natural" but effective. And it is even more puzzling that these objections to the intuitional method depend on a simplified version of it which he had anticipated and corrected in his introductory exposition in book 1.

For example, in his first chapter on it (book 1, chap. 8) he had described what intuitionists like Whewell set out to do both accurately and without prejudice. He had acknowledged that they did not suppose that the moral maxims enunciated by ordinary men are other than vague, and that they held that only moralists with special theoretical capabilities could formulate the precepts underlying ordinary moral thought clearly and abstractly. Furthermore, implicitly conceding that the intuitionists recognized that, were the vague precepts of the morality of common sense to be carelessly given definite abstract form, they would undoubtedly be inconsistent with one another, he had correctly described intuitionism as imposing on moral theorists the tasks of "arrang[ing] the results [of their abstract formulation of what underlies common sense] as systematically as possible, and *by proper definitions and explanations* [of] remov[ing] vagueness and prevent[ing] conflict" (*ME*, 101; emphasis added).

He could not, indeed, seriously have supposed either that different intuitionist moralists would all propose the same definitions and explanations for removing vagueness and preventing conflict or that intuitionism presupposes that they would. True, intuitionism must have collapsed if intuitionist moralists had found their abstract formulations of what underlies ordinary moral thought to have nothing in common,

or their definitions and explanations to diverge haphazardly and unsys-
tematically. But they did not. Their formulations, definitions, and explanations for the most part varied in such ways as to admit of being
taken for approximations, in different degrees, to the true system they
were seeking; and to encourage them in the hope that by persevering
they might find it.

Sidgwick's demonstrations in book 3, chapters 2–11, that the deliverances of the ordinary moral consciousness are too imprecise and unclear to constitute precepts of an acceptable moral system, therefore
fully accord with intuitionism. And his further demonstrations that the
various formulations, definitions, and explanations of intuitionist moralists are too controversial for them to claim that the system they are
seeking has yet been found also accord with it. The intuitionists did not
claim that all the precepts of any system then existing fully satisfied the
four conditions Sidgwick laid down, but only that many of them ap-
proximated to doing so. And they might fairly have objected to Sidgwick's fourth condition as prejudicially rigorous: Even were the ideal
intuitionist system to be discovered, it might be expected that some
informed eccentrics would be found to dissent from parts of it.

Sidgwick's elaborate campaign against intuitionism was therefore mis-
directed. It gained its objectives; but they were not defended, and the
intuitionists were left unmolested in the positions they did defend. To
dislodge them, Sidgwick had to show, not that their method had not
yet led to the complete success they looked for, but that it could not.
And the only way in which he could have shown that was to have given
a better demonstration of their method than they themselves had, in
which it was seen to yield only the incoherent results he had predicted.
He himself seems to have recognized this when he outlined the plan of
his work: namely, to investigate the relations of the three principal
methods of ethics by expounding each of them "as clearly and fully as
[his] limits [would] allow" (*ME*, 14). When he found flaws in existing
treatments of any of the methods, his own plan demanded that he try
to correct them and forbade him to use them as objections to the method
in question. In his treatment of egoism and utilitarianism he adhered
to that plan, but not in his treatment of intuitionism.

This inequity becomes evident when his treatment of Whewell in book
3 is compared with his treatment of Mill in book 4. He fairly claimed
to have been unsparing in exposing error in both. But, when he detected
an error in Mill, he followed the plan of his book and tried to correct
it in terms of the utilitarian method by which Mill worked. By contrast,
when he found errors in Whewell (and comparison shows that Whewell
was in his mind when he wrote much of book 3, although his name is

seldom mentioned), he made no attempt to correct them in terms of the intuitional method but seized on them as objections to it.

The tone of the dismissals of Whewell in *Outlines of the History of Ethics*, and in a manuscript incorporated in the preface to the sixth edition of *The Methods of Ethics*, shows that Sidgwick had a deep antipathy to him, although an antipathy which did not preclude a strong influence.

In the *Outlines*, he wrote off four of Whewell's five principles of morality (those of benevolence, justice, purity, and order) as either tautological or vague and uncertain in application, and disparaged the fifth (that of veracity) as "evanescent on closer inspection" because subject to unstated exceptions – presumably a reference to Whewell's ill-formulated doctrine about cases of necessity (*OHE*, 233–4). Yet even this undeniably "hostile criticism from the outside" betrays something by what it does not say. Sidgwick objected that the application of the system to certain extreme cases is uncertain (when, for example, does the principle of order permit rebellion?) and that four of the five principles from which its specific precepts are professedly derived are too empty or vague to serve that purpose. But he did not deny that Whewell had furnished a set of specific precepts which in the main rendered the morality of common sense definite and coherent; and he could not have denied it. Yet, if the body of Whewell's system is thus to be left standing, intuitionists may reasonably hope to remedy Whewell's shortcomings in formulating its principles and in applying it to certain cases. Why then, does the *Outlines* treat Whewell's enterprise as refuted? We are left with an impression of hostility, the sources of which are not in view.

The autobiographical manuscript printed in the preface to the sixth edition of *The Methods of Ethics* gives us a glimpse of them. In it, Sidgwick discloses that his "first adhesion to a definite ethical system was to the Utilitarianism of Mill," in which he found

relief from the apparently external and arbitrary pressure of moral rules which I had been educated to obey, and which presented themselves to me as to some extent doubtful and confused; and sometimes, even when clear, as merely dogmatic, unreasoned, incoherent. (*ME6*, xv)

And he went on to add:

My antagonism to this was intensified by the study of Whewell's *Elements of Morality* which was prescribed for the study of undergraduates in Trinity. It was from this book that I derived the impression – which long remained uneffaced – that Intuitional moralists were hopelessly loose (as compared to mathematicians) in their definitions and axioms. (*ME6*, xv)

A page later, he alluded to his "early aversion to Intuitional Ethics, derived from the study of Whewell" (*ME6*, xvi).

Here also, Sidgwick was silent about the main body of Whewell's work and expressly criticized only his looseness in his definitions and axioms. But he did confess that, from the first, he read Whewell with a prejudice: He already adhered to Mill's utilitarianism. This prejudice he himself ascribed to the "relief" he found in Mill's system from the morality of common sense (that is, "the moral rules... I had been educated to obey"), which presented itself to him as arbitrary and irrationally oppressive. Now, not even Whewell's admirers consider his *Elements of Morality* a conciliatory work; and few who have read it in the state of mind Sidgwick describes can have found it anything but offensive.

When to antagonism thus intensified was added Sidgwick's conviction that the utilitarian principle of rational benevolence is intuitively evident, it is at least intelligible that he should have considered it unprofitable, as part of his study of intuitionism, to work out an improved dogmatic intuitionist system on Whewell's lines.

Yet the plan of *The Methods of Ethics* required no less. For, as is shown by his admission of an ultimate conflict between the methods of egoism and of utilitarianism, both of which have a basis in philosophical intuitionism, Sidgwick allowed it to be possible that intuitively sanctioned methods might be in conflict. It is therefore possible, despite the axiomatic status of the principle of rational benevolence, that applying the method of philosophical intuitionism to an improved system on Whewell's lines, obtained by the method of dogmatic intuitionism, might yield a further principle – perhaps a variation upon Whewell's principle of humanity – incompatible with both egoism and utilitarianism. For Sidgwick to have labored to improve upon Whewell in order to verify whether this is so or not would have been a feat of heroic disinterestedness. But Sidgwick was a man of heroic disinterestedness. And in the first and eighth chapters of *The Methods of Ethics*, book 1, he made clear to his readers that he had set himself standards which his treatment of the dogmatic intuitional method does not meet.

That Sidgwick's detailed objections to the dogmatic intuitional method rest on misconceptions which he himself had exposed, and that he did not, as his own enterprise demanded, work out for himself what the results of employing that method would be, are enigmas internal to *The Methods of Ethics*. In addition, one of its distinctive doctrines is externally enigmatic: namely, that the dogmatic intuitionist method leaves us in hesitation and perplexity in difficult cases, even of veracity and of contract, where it is clearest; and that what those cases are and how they are to be resolved are to be determined in accordance with the utilitarian principle (cf. *ME*, 442–4). How Sidgwick could have propounded such a doctrine is puzzling, in view of the following external facts which bear upon it.

First of all, he cannot have forgotten that Whewell offered resolutions of a number of the casuistical difficulties he mentions. In fact, although Sidgwick had no means of knowing it until the publication of Mrs. Stair Douglas's biography in 1881, Whewell claimed, as a practical advantage of his system, that by means of it he was able to find solutions of difficult cases of conscience, which had eluded him until he adopted it.[5]

A good illustration may be found in what Sidgwick wrote about promise keeping. Here he did acknowledge that by means of the intuitional method the following acceptable propositions have been refined out of ordinary moral thought: that a promise cannot override determinate prior obligations; that a promise is relative to a promisee and can be annulled by him; and that, subject to these conditions, a promise recognized as binding must be understood by promiser and promisee in the same sense (cf. *ME*, 304–5, 353). However, he went on to object that there is a class of cases for which these results are inadequate: namely, those in which a promise is made, without any expressed conditions, in consequence of some false statement believed by the promiser. A number of considerations, Sidgwick held, are pertinent to such cases: whether or not the promiser's false belief was produced by fraudulent representations, and, if so, by whom they were made; or whether it was produced by mere suggestion, or by the withholding of information; or whether it was held by both parties (cf. *ME*, 305–6).

In depicting intuitionist moralists as having been unable to lay down precepts for any promises except those understood by promiser and promisee in the same sense at the time of promising (*ME*, 304–6, 353), Sidgwick was oblivious of a subtlety in Whewell's study of the topic. He followed Whewell in taking the source of the promiser's obligation to be an understanding between him and the promisee; but he seems not to have remembered Whewell's demonstration that, even when promiser and promisee understand the terms of a promise differently, to the extent that they grasp what promising is, both must understand the promiser to be "bound in the sense in which he believes the Promisee to understand him" (*EMP*, 280, p. 155). Clearly, the promiser does not think that there is a common understanding that he will perform what he does not believe the promisee thinks him bound to perform, and not even the promisee can seriously claim that there is such an understanding. Inasmuch as a promisee claims more, he must do so on some ground other than the understanding common to him and the promiser. Whewell rightly held that common-sense morality rejects any such ground.

Whewell's exact formulation of the common understanding between promiser and promisee turns out, as intuitionist theory had predicted, to discriminate between difficult cases in an intellectually satisfying way. Consider the class of cases in which, on the testimony of a disinterested but mistaken third party, you and I both believe that my commuter train will be canceled tomorrow, and, much as I know you dislike carrying a passenger, you offer to take me to town tomorrow in your car. Later that evening, you learn that my train will run tomorrow after all. Are you entitled to inform me of this, and to treat your promise as void because a tacit condition of it is unfulfilled? Only if you honestly believe that I accepted it as made on that condition, so that, for example, I should not have been justified in making arrangements that depended unconditionally on the assumption that I was riding with you.

Where does the obligation lie when the promiser honestly but mistakenly believes his promise to have been accepted as having a tacit condition? Whewell's answer was that the fact that his belief is mistaken makes no difference. A promiser cannot be bound except in the sense in which he believes the promisee to understand his promise to bind him, even though his belief may be false. But, although he cannot be bound by his promisee's misunderstandings, he may be at fault for having inadvertently failed to make plain the conditions on which he believed his promise to have been accepted. When a condition of a promise is unexpressed,

it must be very difficult [wrote Whewell] for the Promiser to know how far his Promise is hypothetically understood. And therefore, to avoid the moral trouble which such doubts produce, it is wise in such cases to express the condition on which the Promise is given. (*EMP*, 281, p. 155)

He might have added that, if the situation is such that the promiser may well believe that his promise is understood as having an unstated condition, it is for the promisee to inquire whether he does or not.

Whewell's treatment of these cases, although brief, is virtually flawless. For it is not a flaw that it furnishes no method for reading the secrets of the promiser's heart. Courts of justice have need of procedures for deciding disputes about promises when it cannot be presumed that neither party is lying; but moralists, in describing the cases they consider, take the beliefs and intentions of the parties as given. In this connection, it may be observed that the considerations to which Sidgwick attached most importance in cases of promises made upon false beliefs but without expressed conditions, such as whether or not the false belief was produced by fraudulent representations, matter more in law than in morals. Nobody who has obtained a promise by means of a lie is in a position to impugn the promiser's affirmation that he believed his promise to have been accepted as conditional upon the truth of that lie. Even so, as Whewell pointed out, the promiser's affirmation may be false; and in that case, whatever the law may say, his promise binds him morally.

Sidgwick's suggestion that the utilitarian method can supply the qualifications and exceptions to the maxims of common sense about promising, which he maintained that the intuitional method cannot, is as surprising as his silence about the qualifications which Whewell supplied. There are two questions here: that of the grounds of qualifications to the simple maxims of common sense, and that of the grounds of exceptions to the qualified maxims.

The utilitarian calculations to which Sidgwick alludes are perfunctory in the extreme. The following specimen is representative.

It is obvious . . . that it is a disadvantage to the community that men should be able to rely on the performance of promises procured by . . . unlawful force, so far as encouragement is thereby given to the use of . . . force for this end. (*ME*, 443)

This may be set against Whewell's comment on the ill consequences of accepting a rule against keeping promises to pay ransom to bandits:

Is it probable that the banditti will give up their practice, simply because their captives, liberated on such promises, do not perform them? . . . Do we not, in making and adhering to such contracts, prevent their adding murder to robbery? [Until banditry is suppressed] may it not tend to preserve from extreme cruelties, those who fall into the hands of the robbers, that they should have some confidence in the payment of the ransom agreed upon? Even on the balance of probable advantage, it would seem that such a promise is to be kept. (EMP, 293; p. 161)

Perhaps without intending it, Whewell's ingenious sophistry shows where both it and Sidgwick's less obvious sophistry belong: in proceedings at a debating society, not in scientific discussion. Neither has the faintest pretense to being scientifically well founded.

The utilitarian position is even more curious when exceptions to duly qualified maxims are in question, rather than general qualifications. A representative specimen of Sidgwick's treatment of them is what he wrote about cases in which a promisee's expectations arise from a promise the conditions of which are disputed:

The Utilitarian view that the disappointment of natural expectations is an evil, but an evil which must sometimes be incurred for the sake of a greater good, is that to which Common Sense is practically forced, though it is difficult to reconcile it with the theoretical absoluteness of Justice in the Intuitional view of morality. (ME, 444)

But how common sense can be "practically forced" to such a view in the absence of any way of determining, in a given case, whether or not disappointing natural expectations will produce a greater good, he did not explain. Consider the class of cases specified above, in which one person promises another a ride, both being under the mistaken impression that a commuter train has been canceled. Is it not plain that, in the vast majority of such cases, the promiser will have no way at all of telling whether or not more good than evil will result from disappointing the promisee's expectation when their mistake is corrected?

It was because such necessary deductions cannot be made that Whewell had rejected any system which purported to be deduced solely from the principle of increasing human happiness. "The calculation," he had observed, "is too vast, vague and complex" (EMP, supp., chap. 2, sec. 2, p. 582). This position is not more than ordinarily hardheaded; and Sidgwick did not justify his rejection of it with persuasive specimens of utilitarian casuistry.

The absence of utilitarian casuistry from *The Methods of Ethics* is not more striking than its absence from Sidgwick's writings in connection with the controversy over the requirement that fellows of Oxford and Cambridge colleges subscribe to the Thirty-nine Articles of the Church of England, or from his thoughts, so far as they can be reconstructed, in resigning his fellowship at Trinity in 1869.[6]

In the Victorian age, as legal disabilities of dissenters and Roman Catholics were step by step attacked and removed, the conception of the universities of Oxford and Cambridge as part of the national ecclesiastical establishment, generally accepted since the Reformation, could not but be called in question. When Sidgwick was elected to a Trinity fellowship in 1859, while Whewell was still master, he subscribed to the articles in good faith. In the years that followed, however, he ceased to believe certain parts of the Apostles' and Nicene Creeds, which the articles affirm. He was not alone in his doubts; and he and others moved in the university and in their colleges for the abandonment of subscription. At the same time, private members' bills were being introduced in the House of Commons for the modification or abolition of religious tests in the universities. Although all these bills failed, parliamentary support for them grew; and when, at the general election in autumn

1868, the Liberal party won a majority of 112, and Gladstone became prime minister, the wiser opponents of reform saw that it was time to treat for terms.[7] But this made little difference within the university. In December that year, a movement within Trinity College to abolish all religious tests for fellowships, of which Sidgwick was a prime mover, was defeated.[8] Sidgwick thereupon announced that he would resign his fellowship, explaining to his brother-in-law, E. W. Benson, that he did so to free himself "from dogmatic obligations."[9] A few months later, a bill abolishing all religious tests for fellowships, introduced by the solicitor general as a private member, and endorsed by the prime minister, passed the House of Commons and was rejected by the Lords. Yet it was plain that the Lords were putting off the inevitable. An even stronger bill was introduced in the following year as a government measure; and after failing to amend it, in June 1871 the Lords finally acquiesced.

As to the effects of Sidgwick's resignation on the course of these events, D.E. Winstanley's verdict is irresistable.

It was the purely voluntary act of a high-minded and very scrupulous man who thought no sacrifice too great on behalf of honesty. But though it is impossible to exaggerate the moral splendour of his action, it is easy to exaggerate its effects; and there are no grounds for believing that "it exercised," as an admirer has asserted, "some real influence in procuring the abolition of University Tests." This might have been the case if the resignation had taken place a few years before; but by the summer of 1869 the battle had practically been won. The tests had been condemned by a powerful and united party in the House of Commons, which could rightly claim to enjoy the support of the nation; and though the House of Lords were able to delay victory, they could not possibly prevent it.[10]

That, in the extensive correspondence with his intimates preserved in *Henry Sidgwick: A Memoir*, Sidgwick nowhere mentioned its practical effects, even as partially justifying his resignation, is fairly strong evidence that he shared Winstanley's appraisal. And in a letter written to his friend H. G. Dakyns, he made it plain that he was far from convinced that the rule of veracity on which he had acted could itself be justified on utilitarian grounds.

Even my positivism is half against me [he wrote]. The effect on society of maintaining the standard of veracity is sometimes so shadowy that I feel as if I was conforming to a mere "metaphysical" formula. If I had been a hero and had perfect confidence in myself I might have been even as Harrison or Beesly. Or shall I say Jowett?[11] – but there is my excuse. I have endeavored to estimate, *lumine sicco*, the effect of Jowett's action. It seems to me mixed of good and evil; I attribute the evil to falseness of position and the good to fineness of character. It were wild arrogance in me to put myself in such a position. Little people should be at least harmless.[12]

In the pamphlet *The Ethics of Conformity and Subscription*, which he published in the year after his resignation, Sidgwick developed the nonutilitarian line of thought implicit in his letters to Benson and Dakyns. In it, he examined the moral obligations of both laity and clergy in the established church. He presupposed a liberal Protestant doctrine of the nature of the church, which (as he knew) was anathema to Anglo-Catholics and evangelicals equally: a doctrine according to which the teaching function of the clergy was not to study and expound a deposit of revealed truth but to investigate theological questions impartially, "with the single desire to be convinced of the truth," and to communicate their findings sincerely (*ECS*, 12–16). It would, of course, be extremely unlikely that a clergy committed to such a task would agree on all points, either with the established creeds and formularies or with one another. Yet not even a liberal Protestant church would exist without some agreement on doctrine. What agreement would such a church be entitled to exact? And how were the liberal Protestants in the church to act if they should fail to modify the established requirements in a liberal direction?

With regard to the laity, who were not, as adults, required formally to subscribe to any doctrines, those questions became: What doctrines were to be affirmed or implied in the prescribed services of a liberal Protestant church? And how were liberal laymen to act if the desired modifications of those services were not made? Most liberals, for example, could not accept every affirmation in the Apostles' Creed. But suppose it was to be retained? By 1870, as Sidgwick pointed out, nobody would have dreamed of seceding from the established church, or of expecting another to secede from it, merely because he dissented from certain clauses of the Apostles' Creed.

That a secession on such grounds alone [he wrote] would strike everyone as absurd, is the clearest possible proof that the common understanding in the Church of England is not that a man believes the whole of the Apostles' Creed, but that he has been taught the whole of it, and believes as much as he thinks necessary. (*ECS*, 20)

Not only was no definite rule laid down by common understanding as to what attendance at the services of the church committed one to assent to, but, in view of the variety of what such attendance signified to different worshipers, "it would be very inexpedient to lay down such a rule," presumably, because no agreement would be obtained (*ECS*, 23). In short, contrary to the Protestant ideal of worship, the Church of England service had become, to different degrees for different worshipers, a "ceremonial." But since, "if the religious life of the nation is to be in a healthy state, we ought continually to try and approximate to [the Protestant] ideal as far as possible" (*ECS*, 24), the Act of Uniformity ought to be modified, and each congregation be permitted some control over the services in which it participates, and dogmatic professions such as creeds be removed from formulas of worship and reserved for manuals of instruction (*ECS*, 25–6).

The clergy were in a different position. For, although the precise boundaries of what they were commonly understood to be committed to believe were not determinate, there were some doctrines disbelieved by many liberals and thought inessential by more, for example, that Jesus was born of a virgin, such that "the confidence of a congregation in the veracity of their minister would be entirely ruined, if he avowed his disbelief in this doctrine and still continued to recite the Creed" (*ECS*, 33). True, among "the liberal clergy and a certain small number of laymen who sympathize with their difficult position," there is a "tacit understanding" that a clergyman, when he recites the creed, may not mean by it what it is commonly taken to mean (*ECS*, 35–6). "But surely," Sidgwick observed, "if this esoteric morality is an evil anywhere, it is a disastrous evil in the profession whose function it is to propagate morality" (*ECS*, 36). Liberal Protestants may be apprehensive lest, if esoteric morality were to be condemned, and the traditional forms of service maintained, "no one [would] venture to be ordained except those who [were] too fanatical or stupid to doubt that they [would] always believe exactly what they believed at twenty-three" (*ECS*, 38). But although liberal Protestants could not willingly acquiesce in such a consequence, and should "strain every nerve to avoid it," Sidgwick adjured them to do so "by openly relaxing the engagements [the clergy must make], not by secretly tampering with their obligation" (*ECS*, 38–9).

There is, it is true, one passage in which Sidgwick appears to have allowed that a clergyman who disbelieved that Jesus was born of a virgin may continue to recite the creed–that is, to officiate as a clergyman; but even in that passage, Sidgwick declared that such a clergyman "can only justify himself by proving the most grave and urgent social necessity for his conduct" (*ECS*, 33). And since, in the passages already quoted, Sidgwick went on to deny that the social necessity of avoiding a clergy composed of fools and fanatics was sufficiently grave and urgent to justify it, and since he mentioned no other pertinent social necessity, the conclusion cannot be escaped that he held that, if a liberal clergy cannot honestly recite the formulas of the church in the sense in which they are commonly understood in their own time, and if they cannot get those formulas changed, then they are dishonest if they continue to officiate as clergy and are not entitled to plead urgent social necessity in excuse.[13]

What ethical "method" did Sidgwick follow in *The Ethics of Conformity and Subscription?* Despite the antipathy to Whewell which he recollected when he wrote the memoir included in the posthumous edition of *The Methods of Ethics*, I do not see how it can be denied that it was dogmatic intuitionism, or that, in form, his treatment exactly follows Whewell's application of his Principle of Truth to the obligations of those who take oaths to support the constitutive rules of institutions.

Whewell had recognized that such oaths, like the constitutive rules of institutions themselves, commonly change their sense through time: "each generation interpret[ing] the ancient Oath in good faith; and intend[ing] to fulfil it, as nearly as altered circumstances will permit . . . , in the sense of its Founders" (*EMP*, 631, p. 327). And Whewell's teaching about how to act in such cases has nowhere been better summed up than by Sidgwick himself, in *The Methods of Ethics:*

When the process [of changing the sense of an oath] is complete, we are right in adopting the new understanding as far as Good Faith is concerned, even if it palpably conflicts with the natural meaning of language; although it is always desirable in such cases that the form of the promise should be changed to correspond with the changed substance. (*ME*, 310; cf. *EMP*, 627–31; pp. 324–7; 638, p. 329)

When, however, there is a common understanding as to what the sense of an oath is, what is somebody to do who took the oath in good faith but at some later date has concluded that it would be wrong to do what he formerly engaged to do? Whewell's answer was unequivocal:

All such Oaths [that is, oaths of office, of allegiance, and the like] require of him who takes them, a sincere and unchanging purpose to do what he thus engages to do. . . . For instance, . . . if a man has entered upon an office engaging himself to a certain course of official conduct, and afterwards, thinks such conduct wrong; he is bound by Justice and Truth to give up his office. . . . The Oath of Office is the expression of a Contract between the Body and an individual. If he breaks the Contract, and keeps his share of the advantage which it gave, he is guilty of fraud and falsehood, aggravated by Perjury. (*EMP*, 622, p. 323)

It may be objected that these rulings do not exactly fit the case of the liberal clergy discussed in *The Ethics of Conformity and Subscription.* They have to do with an officeholder's engagement to pursue a certain course of official conduct, whereas subscribing to the Thirty-nine Articles, and reciting the Apostles' Creed in church services, would correspond to what Whewell called an "Oath of Assertion," the obligations arising from which he did not expressly consider.

I think that Sidgwick and Whewell would have agreed that this is a prevarication. An oath of assertion, taken as a condition of entering upon an office, binds whoever takes it to maintain what he has asserted, just as an oath of office binds him to follow a certain course of conduct. If he changes his mind about the truth of what he asserts, or the rightness of that course of conduct, he may attempt to have the conditions upon which he holds his office changed. But, if he fails, then he has no choice but to resign his office. To continue in a course of conduct he has come to believe wrong would of course be wrong; and to continue to profess to believe what he no longer believes would be "habitual unveracity"(*ECS*, 37).

If we turn from the case of the clergy described in *The Ethics of Conformity and Subscription* to that of a layman (like Sidgwick), who accepts an office of profit (a college fellowship), of which a condition of entry is that he subscribe to certain doctrines, may he remain in that office if he ceases to believe those doctrines, even though he is not required to repeat his subscription? Whewell's implicit argument that he may not is a powerful one. It might, perhaps, be held not to apply to those who refrain from denying in public what they have ceased to believe in private. Sidgwick undoubtedly considered himself bound, as long as he held his fellowship, not to attack the doctrines to which he had subscribed as a condition of holding it. And so, when he decided that it was a duty to attack them, he considered himself bound, in honesty, to resign. Otherwise, he would not have been free of dogmatic obligations.

In none of these transactions is there the slightest breath of utilitarianism. In *The Ethics of Conformity and Subscription* Sidgwick closely followed Whewell's application of the nonutilitarian Whewellian principle of truth. And, to judge by the reasons he gave in his correspondence, he likewise acted on Whewellian grounds in resigning his fellowship. Both in acting, and in defending his action, utilitarian considerations appear to have entered his mind only to be dismissed. Yet of none of this are there any traces in *The Methods of Ethics*. Or are there, and have I been blind to them?

Notes

1 Page references in the text are to Sidgwick's *Methods of Ethics*, 7th ed. (London: Macmillan, (1907) (*ME*); and *Outlines of the History of Ethics for English Readers*, 6th ed. (rpt., Boston: Beacon Press, 1960) (*OHE*).

2 In particular, his relation to William Whewell, *The Elements of Morality, including Polity*, 4th ed. (Cambridge: Deighton, Bell, 1864); hereafter cited as *EMP*. The first edition of *EMP* was published in 1845; the second in 1848; and the third, with an important supplement containing replies to critics, in 1854. In his *William Whewell D.D.: An Account of His Writings with Selections from His Literary and Scientific Correspondence*, 2 vols. (London: Macmillan, 1876), Isaac Todhunter gives the following information (1: 249): "[T]he work assumed in its second edition the form which it permanently retained. It will be sufficient to cite it by the numbers of the *Articles*, for this suits any edition after the first. Dr. Whewell regretted that the American booksellers [who were not obliged to respect copyright, and did not] stereotyped his first edition, and so would not adopt the improvements of his later editions." References to EMP will be by article and page (4th ed.): Thus "*EMP*, 97; p. 59" will mean "*EMP*, article 97, p. 59". The best introduction to Whewell's work in ethics is J. B. Schneewind, "Whewell's Ethics," *Studies in Moral Philosophy*, American Philosophical Quarterly Monograph Series, no. 1 (1968): 108–41.

3 Henry Sidgwick, *The Ethics of Conformity and Subscription* (London: Williams and Norgate, 1870); hereafter cited as *ECS*. For enabling me to use the original, and not the version republished by Sidgwick in *Practical Ethics: A Collection of Addresses and Essays* (London: Swan Sonnenschein, 1898), I thank J. B. Schneewind, who, after first drawing my attention to its importance, kindly supplied me with a Xerox copy of it.

4 In "Whewell's *Elements of Morality*," *Journal of Philosophy* 71 (1974): 724–36, esp. 731, I have tried to show that a less hostile reading of Whewell than Sidgwick's yields just such an "improved" theory.

5 Letter to F. Myers, Sept. 6, 1845, in Mrs. Stair Douglas, *The Life and Selections from the Correspondence of William Whewell, D.D.* (London: Kegan Paul, 1881), p. 328.

6 For what follows about the successful agitation for the abolition of religious tests at Oxford and Cambridge, I am chiefly indebted to D. A. Winstanley, *Later Victorian Cambridge* (Cambridge: Cambridge University Press, 1947). For Sidgwick's part in it, I have used *Henry Sidgwick: A Memoir* (*M*).

7 Winstanley, *Later Victorian Cambridge*, p. 63.

8 *M*, 172–3.

9 Letter of June 13, 1869, to E. W. Benson (*M*, 198).

10 Winstanley, *Later Victorian Cambridge*, p. 67.

11 In a letter of February 22, 1869, to James Martineau, Sidgwick wrote of Jowett: "he seemed to think (1) that Anglican clergymen ought to take the Church of England for their sphere of liberalising work; (2) that the union between enlightened Christians of all denominations, although very real, was too ethereal to be expressed in the concrete form of an association" (*M*, 191).

12 *M*, 199–200.

13 Sidgwick reaffirmed this opinion, with the same empty utilitarian gestures,

in a letter of May 16, 1881, to J. R. Mozley: "I am decidedly of opinion that no one who rejects [so definite and important a part of the Apostles' Creed as the virgin birth of Jesus] can hold any position of profit or trust, of which membership of the Church of England is a condition, without a grave breach of the ordinary rule of good faith. That such a breach is under all circumstances wrong a utilitarian like myself will shrink from affirming; but that it would require strong special grounds to justify it I feel no doubt" (*M*, 355).

4

Common sense at the foundations

RUSSELL HARDIN

Why do people have the morals they have? Despite superficial appearances, this is many questions, to which I have not enough answers. I wish to address only the general structure of the ordinary person's learning of morals. I will not address the moral theorist's program of justifying morality or a particular moral theory. Rather, I will focus only on the plausible nature of common moral reasoning. In rough outline, that reasoning must be quite similar to practical reasoning for other matters. It will turn on the moral knowledge available to the reasoner. That knowledge must have been gained in ways similar to the learning of any other knowledge.

A common move in much of contemporary moral theory and criticism is to test the theory under consideration against "our" moral beliefs. If the theory does not match the beliefs, intuitions, or so-called common sense, the theory is supposed to fail. In *The Methods of Ethics* Henry Sidgwick makes a nearly opposite move in his account of the method of utilitarianism. He supposes that common-sense morality has a utilitarian basis (*ME*, 423–59). Sidgwick's is a complicated sociological and psychological claim that neither he nor many others who have made it have backed with much compelling argument. I wish to test this claim from what might be called an economic theory of our knowledge about anything, including morals. To do so will require an analysis of the common-sense foundations of practical moral reasoning, which is to say, the foundations of ordinary persons' reasoning.

Immediately one may object that there are grievous difficulties in supposing there are foundations for such reasoning. An obvious major difficulty in the common-sense foundations of morality is the inherent

This essay has benefited from commentaries by David Brink, Paul Bullen, Philip Pettit, Bart Schultz, and Charles Silver, from discussions with participants in the conference, "Henry Sidgwick as Philosopher and Historian," University of Chicago, May 1990, and in the History of Ideas seminar at the Research School of the Social Sciences, Australian National University, August 1990, and the colloquim of the Department of Traditional and Modern Philosophy, University of Sydney, September 1990.

nature of practical reasoning in general, especially with respect to acquiring relevant knowledge. Another, which especially bothers theorists, is skepticism about the objectivity of morality. Another, which may be related to problems of objectivity at the level of theory but need not depend on it, is what Sidgwick calls the dualism of practical reason and motivation (*ME*, 507–509). Practical reasoning may give me a reason for acting in some way. If there are practical reasons for acting morally, as Sidgwick seems to believe there are, these may conflict with reasons for acting in one's self-interest. This is a problem that affects ethics in its practical application. But it may also affect the content of our moral knowledge, though it seems unlikely to affect many other kinds of practical knowledge.

I will focus on the nature of practical reasoning. To the extent it affects such reasoning, I will attend to Sidgwick's dualism of reason. There is, of course, an enormous contemporary literature on what constitutes a reason for acting, a literature that goes well beyond the relatively simple formulation of this issue by Sidgwick. I will not attempt to bring that literature to bear on Sidgwick's problem but will address his dualism in his terms as an aspect of moral reasoning by ordinary people. An economic account of moral reasoning that did not consider this dualism would be flawed just because the dualism is essentially a problem of motivation, which is the core of an economic account.

Throughout the discussion, note that in Sidgwick's views on commonsense moral knowledge the focus must be on our collective knowledge, not my knowledge or your knowledge or the knowledge of any one person. A conceptual account of the internal coherence and fit of my moral and my prudential knowledge cannot answer the issues addressed by an economic account of knowledge. Socially constructed knowledge and morals may be incoherent in various ways that may turn on the aggregation or blending of individual motivations. We might attempt to treat what Sidgwick calls the common man's views as merely a problem of the internal structure of an individual's views, but such an attempt is likely to involve a fallacy of composition. Again, if most of my knowledge is socially received, an internal analysis of my personal body of knowledge cannot get at the issues that bother Sidgwick. What we need is an external, social account.

1. Testing moral theories against common sense

Before turning to the general thesis on moral knowledge, let us consider first what is the nature of the contemporary claim that theories may be tested by their fit with common-sense morality. Perhaps the claim is based on an assumption that we have encoded within our minds some kind of true morality. This morality might be limited to a handful of rules or it might be quite extensive. That this inherited set of principles could be a complete moral theory was once a common view. For some, this view followed from the supposition that morality has a content analogous to that of mathematics or logic, about which our rational inquiry can lead us to correct results. For others, it followed from the – usually theological – supposition that humans were created with whatever faculties they have already in place. Among the most extreme variants of this view is that of H. A. Prichard, who supposes that we have a moral faculty that allows us simply to see the rightness or wrongness of various actions.[1] Sidgwick argues that the theory and broad understanding of evolution, which implies a long historical derivation of our instincts and capacities, undercut the theological view.[2] Without some remarkably inventive argument, such a view is not tenable for anyone who does not believe that a deity created us with such rules or principles in place.

A much more limited version of the view could follow from sociobiological claims about the development of action-guiding principles that might be genetically selected because they contribute to the survival of groups of humans. But such a set cannot be sufficiently articulate as to give useful tests of much more general and complete moral theories than what might have been selected. Moreover, it seems plausible that inconsistent rules would have been selected. For example, a strong instinct for self-interest must surely have been selected. In practice, this instinct might then conflict with any instinct for altruism or benevolence that might also have been selected. Even apart from their likely inconsistency with one another, the fact that action-guiding principles are selected by evolution does not make them right on any but a purely naturalistic theory.[3] It is obviously not such a sociobiological view that motivates the common-sense critics of moral theories.

Finally, a perhaps less limited version of the view could follow from social selection – not genetic selection – of principles. These may survive through being passed on to others by learning or through the creation of institutions that survive their original justifications.[4] This form of establishing the "truth" of moral principles, however, shades into something similar to the cognitive processes of working out a moral theory. And it has an air of relativism if it is conceivable that we could have developed different, contrary principles that would survive.

It seems unlikely that any of these positions can yield objections to any moral theory on the ground that it violates "our" intuitions. There is another way to put contemporary common-sense objections to moral theories, however, that may be more defensible in principle. That way is suggested by the sometime phrasing of the critics that a result of some theory runs counter to "our best-considered judgments." The chief difficulty with this phrasing is that most theorists might readily claim themselves to have come to their own best-considered judgments. If the critics mean this, they are merely conceited solipsists who claim, "*My* best considered judgment differs from yours and that proves you wrong." If the critics are making a claim that is worthy of attention, they must mean something with their invocation of "our."

What might be a compelling content for the common-sense criticism? One possibility is that the critics are saying something analogous to Sidgwick's view of the limits of reason in ascertaining what is moral:

On any theory, our view of what ought to be must be largely derived, in details, from our apprehension of what is; the means of realising our ideal can only be thoroughly learnt by a careful study of actual phenomena; and to any individual asking himself "What ought I to do or aim at?" it is important to examine the answers which his fellowmen have actually given to similar questions. (*ME*, 2)

Common-sense morality, and the apparent intuitions we have about rightness and goodness, may grow out of our moral debate, theorizing, and practice. In a sketch of the development of his own thinking, Sidgwick says that, because he was conscious of practical imperfection "in many cases of the guidance of the Utilitarian calculus, I remained anxious to treat with respect, and make use of, the guidance afforded by Common Sense in these cases, on the ground of the general presumption which evolution afforded that moral sentiments and opinions would point to conduct conducive to general happiness." But, he says, "I could not admit this presumption as a ground for overruling a strong probability of the opposite, derived from utilitarian calculations" (*ME*, xxi).

John Rawls calls his own such reasoning about morality the "method of reflective equilibrium."[5] That method involves little more than giving serious attention to the weight of prior collective wisdom on our subject while also attempting to bring theoretical order to it, letting neither theory nor collective wisdom always trump the other, but going back and forth between the two and letting each correct the other. This is the method of much of the greatest moral philosophy over the past few millennia. It is clearly outlined by Sidgwick in manuscript notes for a lecture on the development of his own thought (*ME*, xv–xxi) and is raised in context throughout his *Methods of Ethics*, although he does not call it a method.[6] The collective wisdom at issue is not merely that of past philosophers and writers on these subjects but that of social practices and norms that have arisen in various ways. Again, Sidgwick thinks the study of common-sense morality is attractive because our underlying morality is in fact utilitarian. If he is right, it is ironic that, in contemporary writings, common-sense morality is commonly invoked to prove utilitarianism false.

A striking feature of this view of the role of collective wisdom in moral thinking is that it is similar to the role of collective wisdom in practical reasoning more generally. Almost all of what I might claim to know rests on my accepting authoritative assertions by others. Some of these others know some of the same things I do but more nearly directly, at least in part. In the lives of many people, moral knowledge may have essentially the same character as any other practical knowledge.

Remarkably, such sloppiness in our practical reasoning and in our ground for belief may not get much in our way. Often the best reason for believing something is to know that almost everyone else believes it.[7] Many causal and other relationships we know only from experience. A causal account of most substantial things we "know" would demand far more theory than we can master. If we try radically to manipulate variables, we change the problem to one far beyond our present pragmatic understanding and we may lose all mooring (*ME*, 467–74).[8] Accepting what others believe is often smarter than attempting to bore deeper on our own.

Practical knowledge for most of us most of the time is inherently without foundations – or at least without anything that would count as foundations in a philosophical theory of knowledge.[9] If we are willing to accept certain things, then certain other things follow. At first consideration we might not, on this framing, wish to conclude that we then know those other things. We might suppose we know them only if the things we might be willing to accept are themselves known. But these things are in the consequent clauses, of other, similar if–then statements. There is no place to begin with any of our knowledge of the world. We merely do accept many things, and therefore we can get started on mastering other things.[10] Skepticism about knowledge that cannot be "better" grounded than such acceptance on faith is an artifact of theorizing. All of our knowledge is finally based on mere acceptance of some of its bases.

As Donald Davidson remarks, we cannot assign "beliefs to a person one by one . . . , for we make sense of particular beliefs only as they cohere with other beliefs, with preferences, with intentions, hopes, fears, expectations, and the rest. It is not merely . . . that each case tests a theory and depends upon it, but that the content of a propositional attitude derives from its place in the pattern."[11] Neither can an individual come by all beliefs one by one.

The general issue here may just sound like an ordinary person's problem. That it is not is suggested by the development of economics over the past century or so. Economics became an articulate, relatively successful enterprise when it became antifoundationalist. Marginal utility analysis takes place against a background of what we might call gross or absolute utility, except that it is not at all clear what gross utility could be. Given an acceptance of this background, however, marginal analysis makes very good sense and can be very powerful. It was in the long intellectual struggle to make sense of gross utility that the marginal theory was developed, but the marginal theory is itself the starting point for neoclassical economics.

If our practical knowledge cannot be traced back to clearly understandable foundations, then seemingly we must enter it laterally as much as hierarchically. It grows by sideways augmentation, the accretions overlapping extant knowledge. Moreover, we might be unable to take an overview of all of it to test it for coherence. We might quickly recognize that incoherence and inconsistency are problems when they do become evident, but we might often miss inconsistencies merely for want of effort, logical capacity, or sufficient completeness to make various connections.[12]

2. The economics of knowledge and belief

Consider two related questions. Why do we know what we know? How do we know it? Let us be concerned not with a theory of knowledge that might be applied to a science by philosophers but with the practical form that knowledge must take for us as ordinary people in everyday life when we wish to achieve our ends. For anyone concerned with practical reason rather than merely with knowledge per se or its justification, the question of why we know what we know may be more important than that of how we know or ought to know it. Much of philosophical writing on knowledge is directed at the latter question; little of it is directed at the former question. In quick summary, the answer to the question why we know what we know is that the content of what we know is adventitious. It is not completely out of control, however, because we are constrained in our possible knowledge by the kinds of considerations that arise in theories of how we know. Within this constraint we then come to know many things in common and many other things not at all in common.

Before proceeding, note that, on the economic account of practical reasoning, I face constraints, I do not choose them. If I could escape them, I would. One of the constraints on my actions this moment is the limit of my past investments in learning that could be applied to my choice of actions now. In some sense, I – or some past version of myself – did choose these constraints, but I did so in response to constraints that limited what investments I could make overall. It is therefore wrong to think of constrained optimization here on analogy with David Gauthier's constrained maximization. Gauthier's constraint is a deliberate choice of the agent to cooperate rather than defect in prisoner's dilemma interactions.[13] On the economic account of knowledge, common sense does not constrain my optimization. Rather, common sense is constrained in its striving to optimize.

Why do I know the things I know whereas you know other things? Principal reasons are that, in street language, the things I know came cheaper to me than many other things and they pay me better. As in Hume's and Smith's view of the greater productivity of the division of labor,[14] knowledge also grows faster if you pursue some things and I pursue others rather than having all of us pursue everything together. But division of labor in the production of knowledge requires acceptance on faith of what others have come to know if the advantage of division is not to be lost.

I know a great deal about putting words on paper. But actually to do it as I now do, with a computer and a printer, I have to depend on the radically richer knowledge of very many people who stand behind the machines I use. In this case, I can try out alternative equipment to decide intelligently that some set of machines is reasonably suitable for my task. Moreover, I can depend on social selection to produce relatively good devices, because social selection through market and other forces puts alternative devices to much better test than I can and because I can expect the incentives of many of the people involved in the social selection to fit my own interests. I can also depend on social selection to produce a lot of information on these devices, so that I may avoid testing everything or starting completely blind in my tests.

Suppose you grew up among the Azande in central Africa before the intrusion of anthropologists, and you have a collection of beliefs that anyone who has grown up in an advanced industrial state would consider incontrovertibly wrong.[15] Indeed, if you'd grown up in such a state and held such beliefs, we would hold them crazy. Yet it would be odd to call Azande beliefs crazy for the Azande. Why? Essentially because of the economics of belief. For an individual Zande the costs of knowing better might be egregious. More generally, we must suppose that individuals' intellectual histories matter for explanation of their views, knowledge, and theories. In various respects, the nature of such facts also matters for philosophical discussion.

The typical user's knowledge of morals must be similar in many respects to my knowledge of machines for producing my written documents. Such similarity is especially clear for the Azande, for whom moral and other practical considerations may be all of the same cloth. For us as children they may also have been heavily interwoven. Much of the guidance that adults give to children is expressed in moral terms but is about the children's interests, and vice versa. For example, children are told that lying or breaking promises is wrong and, in virtually the same breath, they may be told that being untrustworthy harms their longer-run interests. Both claims are arguably true for truth telling and promise keeping. This is fortuitous for morality, because in at least these cases it bridges the dualism of practical reason that bothers Sidgwick by simply being consistent with self-interest (*ME*, 508).

Or perhaps we should conclude that it was a sly bit of persuasive definition that put truth telling and promise keeping in the category of the moral. The overwhelming bulk of cases of truth telling and promise keeping may be sufficiently motivated by self-interest, especially as enlightened by consideration of longer-run effects on one's reputation and relationships.[16] If such commonplace problems of enlightened self-interest are given a moral gloss, morality may seem very attractive. Acting morally may even seem typically to fit the Socratic program of being shown to be identical with acting from self-interest. Then, in cases in which morality comes at a price, it may also come as a habit or an attitude that helps it override self-interest.

The great problem in morality is to justify to you that your very slight interest should not override a passing stranger's overwhelming interest. Simple reciprocity in ongoing relationships is not difficult to motivate either from morality or from self-interest (*ME*, 508). But self-interest would permit vicious disregard of the interests of another, especially a stranger, whereas morality would not. Law that is enforced can overcome vicious disregard in some contexts, such as, for example, in outlawing murder. But we may require morality to override self-interest in contexts in which law cannot align self-interest with the interests of others. And one may wonder whether we do not live in more or less constant vicious disregard of some large number of people, such as those suffering starvation in the Sahel.

3. The strategy of knowing

Practical knowledge may be viewed as a whole or piecemeal. Many of our judgments of actions, perhaps especially the actions of others, are made piecemeal. My car is slow to start and I flood it, ruining any chance of starting it. You may say this is an irrational response to the problem, which could have been resolved easily without creating a new, harder problem. In an important sense, you may be right, of course. The analytically correct response to my car's slowness may be as you say it is.

But in a larger, holistic sense, your criticism may be wrong. Yes, it would be better for me to do what you say, if only I knew it. But it might not be rational for me to know that in the first place. To know it requires happenstance experience with balky cars from which I might finally have learned how to diagnose and handle them. Or it requires deliberate effort to learn more about the way they work, effort that might not pay off for my limited needs. It may also involve the grievous difficulty of remembering what I've learned if it is not somehow readily deducible once I begin to understand the workings of car engines. If it is merely a rule or a list of procedures, I may remember it only if it has to be invoked very often.

In sum, we may suppose that repeated experience and the expectation of more to come might justify my taking some trouble to learn more about things such as the workings of my car and might help me to remember what I've once learned. Our knowledge is a bit like government classification of knowledge. We bother to know some things only on a need-to-know basis.

Once we take into consideration the costs of knowing certain things, we may readily conclude that it is not worthwhile. For example, we let doctors handle some of our problems, although we may begin to second-guess doctors for a problem that we suffer over a long time and that gets different treatments from different doctors. And most of us know very little about how the cars or other machines in our lives work. If it makes strategic sense not to invest in acquiring specialized knowledge because the investment will not pay, then, when I flood my car out of ignorance, it is perverse to say that my action is irrational as such.

Many of the subjects of vast numbers of experiments on rationality that seem to show people are irrational might better be seen as evidence that good reasoning is costly and not always worth mastering. Good reasoning with respect to a particular class of problems, such as dealing with cars that do not perform perfectly, may be harder to master for some than for others. It may be that some of those who perform badly in many experiments are more rational than those who perform well. They are more rational in a holistic sense that includes the costs of investing in specialized abilities. The English economist John Jewkes is credited with noting that to consider every case on its merits is not to consider the merits of the case. I may generally be rational to have some overview on how much one should be concerned with the details of the instant problem for decision. This is not to say that we should have general theories of how to decide. Even habits will help greatly in lowering our overall costs of decision.

That a formal decision theorist performs better than typical experimental subjects follows in large part for the simple reason that she has invested heavily in understanding the relevant class of problems. Her motivations for such investment are that it presumably pays, not in improving her capacity for rational decision but for its own sake in her career. It may be that she chose or happened into her career in part because she found the problems of decision theory especially interesting and because she had natural talents for dealing with them. Still, it is unlikely that much of her mastery of the issues was directly pragmatic in the sense that she learned what she needed for making better decisions in her own life. Most of us could not plausibly justify even a small part of her investment for ourselves.

The background or holistic consideration of whether it is worthwhile to learn something is in many respects a more important issue in our grasp of practical reason than is the large question of foundations and their justification. This is not to say that people actually reason through the costs and benefits of investing in knowledge about, say, how their cars work or what is morally right. We may more often merely happen into our particular range of knowledge when we are pushed by needs to know in various moments, when we are accidentally put in the way of knowledge of some things, or when we have more interest in consuming a particular kind of knowledge as an end in itself than in using it as a means to other ends.[17]

A general theory of justified belief might ground the strength of belief in x in the effort taken to justify believing x. But this is wrongheaded. What I must first decide, case by case rather than a priori for every case, is how much it is worth to invest in testing my belief in x. Because every belief is inherently grounded in efforts that are more or less costly and that must therefore trade off against efforts to ground other beliefs, it is perverse to construct a general theory of just any belief. It may be true that I would have less confidence in belief x just because I have not done much to test it whereas I have much greater confidence in belief y because I have done a lot to test it. But belief y may be only loosely related to other strongly held beliefs whereas x may be very tightly bound up with other beliefs.

4. The economics of moral motivation

Sidgwick concludes *The Methods of Ethics* on a note of grievous doubt. He notes that if we could assume a god of a kind that would punish wrongdoing and reward goodness, a utilitarian might reasonably suppose that the individual would then have motives of self-interest "to promote universal happiness to the best of his knowledge" (*ME*, 506). We may come by our moral knowledge as we come by any other knowledge. But acting on my knowledge of how to start a car without flooding it may immediately benefit me, whereas acting on my moral knowledge may often more likely cost me. This is Sidgwick's dualism of the practical or moral reasoning: Reason seems to provide us good grounds for making universal claims in moral theory while it also provides good grounds for first or even exclusive concern with self. If we suppose that motivation is not intrinsically determined by our recognition of the rightness of a moral theory, these considerations of practical reason leave us with a potential conflict of motivations. Following David Brink, we may characterize Sidgwick's "dualism of practical reason as a conflict between a utilitarian account of duty and an egoistic or prudential account of rationality."[18] Unfortunately for universalizing moral theory, motivation seems for most people to fit reasoned concern with the self much more forcefully than it fits concern with universal well-being.

The critical feature of the social evolution of practical knowledge that can serve the self-interest of those who learn it is that the knowledge can be tested in various ways. For example, I can use various computers and writing programs and discover which of them is best for my purposes. Although much of my knowledge is merely accepted from those around me or from the larger society, I am still the one who puts it to use on my behalf. The collective wisdom may be influenced by all of us who use bits of that wisdom to serve our separate interests. If what serves my interests is relatively similar to what serves others' interests, the result will be fairly systematic testing of our wisdom to improve it with use.

The economic incentives for gaining knowledge may be biased in favor of nonmoral practical knowledge, in part because we may have far more occasion to need nonmoral knowledge. This initial bias in favor of gaining nonmoral knowledge may lead to increasing bias as further knowledge builds on extant knowledge. The general reason for much of morality is that individual interests conflict in ways that recommend that some individuals yield their interests to others. But, if from nothing more than greater experience or practice in obtaining it, we may tend to see and seek to resolve issues in favor of our own interests to the neglect of others' interests.

If social selection of moral rules and institutions is affected in these biased ways by the dualism of practical reason, we may have less reason to trust it than we have to trust social selection of machinery for writing.

The drive for acquisition of knowledge about matters of mere self-interest is more nearly univalent than is the drive for acquisition of knowledge about moral matters. We might therefore expect the former kind of knowledge to be less likely to fall into confusion.

Even institutions to serve merely the self-interests of individuals fall prey to compositional problems in aggregating the effects of all our motivations. The actual structures of institutions that arise from individually motivated actions may be not only unintended but also perverse. There can be individually rational failures of collective action to generate collectively beneficial results. There can be individually rational failures of coordination that leave us repeatedly trapped in an inferior outcome. And there can be sensible resolutions of piecemeal problems that are not sensible resolutions of the overall collection of problems. All of these failings can result from strictly self-interested choices by all concerned.

If we now add motivations of universalistic concern of unequal strength across individuals, the impact of those motivations will depend not only on their average strength relative to self-interest and on the misfit between individually rational and collectively beneficial outcomes but also on the distribution of those motivations. If stronger universalistic motivations tend to be associated with leadership of institutions, they may be very effective. If they are randomly distributed, their effect may still be significant but less so.

To gain some purchase on understanding these issues, note that we may view the object of universalistic motivations in utilitarianism as a collective benefit that somehow aggregates individual interests. That is to say, collective and individual benefits or interests are not different in kind.

Suppose we are in a group that would benefit from universalistic actions by all of us. But we are afflicted by the dualism of practical reason because each of us individually would be better off acting from individualistic rather than universalistic concerns. The position of each of us is analogous to that of someone involved in a collective action problem of the provision of a collective benefit.

Suppose some of us have a greater relative concern for the collective benefit than do others who share an interest in its provision. This could happen either because we in fact directly benefit more or because we are more strongly motivated by universalistic considerations. The effect of either of these reasons will be the same, but our concern here is with the latter reason, the stronger universalistic motivation. That some of us have a stronger universalistic motivation means that it will often typically take fewer of us to act successfully for the collective interest, so that we are more likely to achieve the utilitarian result or at least to tend toward it. This is analogous to the provision of a straight collective good for which some of us have much more intense demand than others have. The group of intense demanders may face a less grievous problem of collective action than the overall group faces simply because it is a smaller group.[19]

This result may seem perverse: At the same average level, an unequal distribution of universalistic motivations may produce better results than an equal distribution. Having a few Sidgwicks may do more to improve the world than having a slight addition to the average person's utilitarian commitments.

On this brief account, the collective result is achieved by voluntaristic action by all of us. Often, however, we will have institutions to produce collective results and to organize individual contributions to them. For our governance, Hume supposes we require a small number of people who, "being indifferent persons to the greatest part of the state, have no interest, or but a remote one, in any act of injustice; and being satisfied with their present condition, and with their part in society, have an immediate interest in every execution of justice, which is so necessary to the upholding of society."[20] He further supposes that these few persons will be our governors and that most people would be too self-interested to serve us well as governors.

Hume gives no account of why just those persons would come to be our governors. How might the distribution of universalistic motivations in governing institutions be causally related to their strength relative to self-interest? In a quasi-democratic institution, those who display universalistic motivations may be trusted more than others and may therefore tend to be selected for leadership. But those who are more strongly motivated by self-interest may invest more in gaining leadership positions that are potentially rewarding. We might be better served by Pericles or Nicias, but Alcibiades or Cleon might successfully compete with them for leadership. There is no analytical answer to how the balance will tip in general.

In some ways Hume is optimistic: He expects the occasional Pericles to be available. In other ways he is pessimistic: He thinks we cannot manage without a Pericles. Contrary to his apparent view, there may be good reasons for expecting even basically self-interested officials to act reasonably universalistically with respect to some aspects of larger public interests.[21]

Even when motivations are more nearly universalistic than individual, they may still fall far short of universality. Reinhold Niebuhr remarks on the "ethical paradox" of patriotism, which "transmutes individual unselfishness into national egoism."[22] It may be that patriotism generally has beneficial effects on the whole, as Mandeville argues of individual egoism that "private vices beget public virtue."[23] Indeed, the so-called realist tradition that dominated Western international relations theorizing during most of this century arose in reaction to what the realists thought were destructive moral claims. In particular, the realists reacted against Woodrow Wilson's plans for remaking the world, which they thought moralistic and destructive.

To justify his claim about the tendency of our socially selected norms and our institutions to be utilitarian, Sidgwick must suppose that the differential effects of the motivations behind these is ultimately utilitarian. Alternatively, one might argue for social selection of institutions and norms that are more beneficial. Such an argument would have to be made at an aggregate level. In those groups or societies or nations that develop utilitarian norms and institutions, individuals thrive better than in those that do not. As a result, the group or whatever also thrives better. That is a complex argument that is likely to face insurmountable problems of factual accounting. It seems plausible that other forces for selection would swamp utilitarian forces, especially if selection involves survival in a contest between societies and not merely selection within an isolated society (*ME*, 470–4).

5. Authority and moral knowledge

Suppose we accept the account of the similarity between moral knowledge and other forms of knowledge. Nonmoral knowledge about how the world works is gained at costs that recommend economizing on how much we gain and, especially, relying on experts. As noted above, virtually all that I know may rest on my accepting authoritative assertions by others. In a society in which moral knowledge is typically enunciated by a single body or organization, such as the medieval Catholic church, one might expect relatively wide deference to authority on moral matters. In a society in which moral authority is in great dispute, as it is in many contemporary secular and multireligious communities, authoritative assertions may be less trusted as guarantors of correct views. It may then be only the most commonly held views that one may readily accept on "authority." For example, we may almost all accept the rightness of truth telling.

Suppose that an institutional authority, such as the earlier Catholic church, is widely accepted. Will its views tend to be utilitarian over time? Unfortunately, its individual officials will face their own personal dualism of practical reason. They are apt in many contexts to tend to push views that benefit themselves over strictly universalistic views. This may be true even though there may be a tendency to select these officials for reasons of their greater universalistic commitments. For example, the demand or even supposedly divine command that people tithe a tenth of their annual produce or income to support the church must surely represent a dualism of motivation on the part of church officials.

Other kinds of institutions, such as those that seek material gains, may often be constructed in such ways as to match official incentives with the interests of those whom the institutions are to serve. Such institutions need have little conflict of motivations other than the usual conflicts over whether to cheat under threat of penalty, either from the law or from loss of reputation. We who wish to economize on our knowledge may readily follow the lead of such institutions and let them be our authorities for certain kinds of knowledge.

Those who concede moral authority to various institutional leaders may, on the contrary, see the betrayal they suffer. For example, many early alternatives to the Roman church were groups, including such orders as the Jesuits and such renegades as Lutherans, who objected to the apparent luxury of the lives of many priests and, especially, of the papal regime in Rome. Some part of the intensity of feelings among East Germans toward Erich Honecker and his fellow governors and among Romanians toward the Ceausescus in 1989 must have come from the sense that these leaders of an egalitarian ideology had benefited more than equally.

This is a much too cursory account of the likelihood that institutionalized moral authorities may be as trustworthy and as trusted as institutionalized authorities over other realms of knowledge. But it seems implausible that Sidgwick's claims that our common-sense moral principles are driven by utilitarian concerns could be grounded in the special quality of institutionalized moral authority.

6. Concluding remarks

The foundations of the typical person's knowledge are in sand; there is no bedrock. For many people the claims of moral knowledge may be as compelling and valid as those of any other kind of knowledge. There is no more reason to put the theorist's scare quotes around "knowledge" when it is preceded by "moral" than when it stands alone, at least when we are speaking of the knowledge of ordinary people. Moral knowledge generally gives reasons for acting morally; other kinds of knowledge give reasons for acting both morally and self-interestedly.

This dualism in our reasons for action may be seen as a conflict between self-interest and morality in our motivations. The dualism may finally contribute to skepticism for ordinary people. If part of our tradition of moral knowledge picks out certain people or role holders as moral but our experience suggests they are morally deficient, our whole tradition may be cast into doubt. Moral commitments that are socially derived are at risk when social cues are mixed, as they must be if they come from individuals who are motivated by dual commitments.

Sidgwick recommends that we attend to the evidence of what is moral that may be derived from "a careful study of actual phenomena" (*ME*, 2).[24] But, because such evidence is fraught with problems of the foundations of ordinary practical knowledge and of the dualism of practical reason, we cannot place enormous confidence in it. Even though it may inform our theorizing, we certainly cannot suppose that common-sense knowledge trumps our theoretical reasoning in any but the very general sense that we must frame our theorizing against the background of our common-sense knowledge.

It is instructive that Sidgwick reaches a result analogous to that which economists also conceded toward the end of Sidgwick's own life:

I hold that the utilitarian, in the existing state of our knowledge, cannot possibly construct a morality *de novo* either for man as he is (abstracting his morality), or for man as he ought to be and will be. He must start, speaking broadly, with the existing social order, and the existing morality as part of that order: and in deciding the question whether any divergence from this code is to be recommended, must consider chiefly the immediate consequences of such divergence, upon a society in which such a code is conceived generally to subsist. (*ME*, 473–4)

The moral theorist or the moral chooser must be only a marginalist, taking the gross value of things as they are as a base on which to build outward.[25]

Notes

1 H. A. Prichard, *Moral Obligation and Duty and Interest* (1912; Oxford: Oxford University Press, 1968), p. 17.

2 Henry Sidgwick, "The Theory of Evolution in Its Application to Practice," *Mind* 1 (1876): 52–67, esp. p. 55.

3 As Sidgwick concludes in his criticism of Herbert Spencer (ibid.).

4 G. E. Moore argues for such a view in *Principia Ethica* (Cambridge: Cambridge University Press, 1903), esp. chap. 5; F. A. Hayek makes similar arguments, without recognizing that they are utilitarian, in various works,

including *The Constitution of Liberty* (Chicago: University of Chicago Press, 1960), p. 67. For a brief discussion, see Russell Hardin, *Morality within the Limits of Reason* (Chicago: University of Chicago Press, 1988), pp. 14–18.

5 John Rawls, *A Theory of Justice* (Cambridge, MA: Harvard University Press, 1971), pp. 20–1.

6 Also see Henry Sidgwick, "Professor Calderwood on Intuitionism in Morals," *Mind* 1 (1876): 563–6.

7 See further, Howard Margolis, *Patterns, Thinking, and Cognition* (Chicago: University of Chicago Press, 1987), p. 135.

8 See further, Hardin, *Morality,* pp. 22–9.

9 See further, David O. Brink, *Moral Realism and the Foundations of Ethics* (Cambridge: Cambridge University Press, 1989), pp. 100–22.

10 As Sidgwick says, "It is as true of the intellectual as of the physical life that living somehow is prior to living ideally well: and if we are to live at all, we must accept some beliefs that cannot claim Reason for their source" ("The Philosophy of Common Sense," *Mind* 4 [April 1895]: 145–58; quotation on p. 157).

11 Donald Davidson, "Mental Events," (1970), in *Actions and Events* (Oxford: Oxford University Press, 1980), p. 221.

12 This rough view may be Sidgwick's own (*ME*, 509).

13 David Gauthier, *Morals by Agreement* (Oxford: Oxford University Press, 1986), esp. pp. 157–89.

14 Poor Hume maladroitly speaks of "the partition of employments" and therefore loses paternity for our contemporary phrasing to Smith. David Hume, *A Treatise of Human Nature,* 2d ed., ed. L. A. Selby-Bigge and P. H. Nidditch (Oxford: Oxford University Press [Clarendon Press], 1978), book 3, pt. 2, sec. 2, p. 485.

15 E. E. Evans-Pritchard, *Witchcraft, Oracles, and Magic among the Azande* (Oxford: Oxford University Press, 1937).

16 Hardin, *Morality,* pp. 59–65.

17 For example, hobbyists and sports fans often consume the facts of their subjects because the consumption itself is pleasing or interesting.

18 David O. Brink, "Sidgwick's Dualism of Practical Reason," *Australasian Journal of Philosophy* 66 (1988): 291–307; quotation on p. 303.

19 For more extensive argument, framed for cases in which variation of direct individual benefits is the reason for differential actions, see Russell Hardin, *Collective Action* (Baltimore: Johns Hopkins University Press, 1982), pp. 67–75.

20 Hume, *Treatise,* book 3, pt. 2, sec. 7, p. 537.

21 Russell Hardin, "Constitutional Political Economy: Agreement on Rules," *British Journal of Political Science* 18 (1988): 513–30, esp. pp. 524–7.

22 Reinhold Niebuhr, *Moral Man and Immoral Society: A Study in Ethics and Politics* (New York: Scribner, 1932), p. 91.

23 Bernard Mandeville, *The Fable of the Bees,* 2 vols. (1705, 1714, 1723, 1728; Indianapolis: Liberty Press, 1988); see also Stephen Holmes, "The Secret

History of Self-Interest," in Jane J. Mansbridge, *Beyond Self-Interest* (Chicago: University of Chicago Press, 1990), pp. 267–86. Patriotism has few advocates among moral theorists, but see Alasdair MacIntyre, "Is Patriotism a Virtue?" Lindley Lecture (Lawrence: University of Kansas, 1984).

24 Passage quoted in full in Section 1.

25 Jack Smart suggests that the days of marginalist moral theory may be past in this era in which disasters can happen suddenly as the result of seemingly minor actions (in seminar, Australian National University, August 1990). Actions in the distant past that introduced devastating diseases to unwary peoples may have posed similar problems. Many of the disasters we potentially face may be the result of poor causal understandings.

Part II

Egoism, dualism, identity

5

Sidgwick's pessimism

J. L. MACKIE

But the fundamental opposition between the principle of Rational Egoism and that on which such a system of duty is constructed, only comes out more sharp and clear after the reconciliation between the other methods. The old immoral paradox, "that my performance of Social Duty is good not for me but for others," cannot be completely refuted by empirical arguments: nay, the more we study these arguments the more we are forced to admit, that if we have these alone to rely on, there must be some cases in which the paradox is true. And yet we cannot but admit with Butler, that it is ultimately reasonable to seek one's own happiness. Hence the whole system of our beliefs as to the intrinsic reasonableness of conduct must fall, without a hypothesis unverifiable by experience reconciling the Individual with the Universal Reason, without a belief, in some form or other, that the moral order which we see imperfectly realized in this actual world is yet actually perfect. If we reject this belief, we may perhaps still find in the non-moral universe an adequate object for the Speculative Reason, capable of being in some sense ultimately understood. But the Cosmos of Duty is thus really reduced to a Chaos: and the prolonged effort of the human intellect to frame a perfect ideal of rational conduct is seen to have been foredoomed to inevitable failure.

This splendid passage concludes the first (1874) edition of *The Methods of Ethics*. (Was Sidgwick thinking partly of the prolonged effort of his own 473 pages?) Taken by itself it is, of course, ambivalent. It asserts merely the conditional statement that *if* we reject the belief in a moral government of the universe, something like a God who will reward utilitarian virtue, *then* there will be an irreducible conflict within the rational principles of conduct, between rational egoism and social duty. And this conditional could be part either of a *modus ponens* or of a *modus tollens* argument: The implied continuation could be either "We must reject this belief, so the cosmos of duty is reduced to chaos" or "The cosmos of duty cannot be a chaos, so we must not reject this belief." Sidgwick himself seems also to have been ambivalent. A few

This essay is reprinted from the *Philosophical Quarterly* 26, no.105 (October 1976): 317–27, by permission of the *Quarterly* and of Mrs. Joan Mackie.

pages earlier he says that although "it is . . . a matter of life and death to the Practical Reason that this premiss [that the performance of duty will be adequately rewarded and its violation punished] should be somehow obtained," nonetheless "the mere fact that I cannot act rationally without assuming a certain proposition, does not appear to me, – as it does to some minds, – a sufficient ground for believing it to be true," and he rejects even more vehemently "the Kantian resource of thinking myself under a moral necessity to regard all my duties *as if they were* commandments of God, although not entitled to hold speculatively that any such Supreme Being exists 'as Real.' " Sidgwick "cannot even conceive the state of mind which these words seem to describe, except as a momentary half-wilful irrationality, committed in a violent access of philosophic despair." All this suggests the *modus ponens* continuation. But on the second-last page of the book, after speaking of "an hypothesis logically necessary to avoid a fundamental contradiction in a vast system of Beliefs: a contradiction so fundamental that if it cannot be overcome the whole system must fall to the ground and scepticism be triumphant over one chief department of our thought," he goes on, rather lamely, "The exact weight to be attached to this consideration, I cannot here pretend adequately to estimate. To do so would require a complete discussion of the Theory of Method, and of the ultimate basis of philosophic certainty." This suggests, though only very faintly, the *modus tollens* continuation. In the second (1877) and later editions this point is made more explicit.

Those who hold that the edifice of physical science is really constructed of conclusions logically inferred from self-evident premises, may reasonably demand that any practical judgments claiming philosophic certainty should be based on an equally firm foundation. If on the other hand we find that in our supposed knowledge of the world of nature propositions are commonly taken to be universally true, which yet seem to rest on no other grounds than that we have a strong disposition to accept them, and that they are indispensable to the systematic coherence of our beliefs, it will be more difficult to reject a similarly supported assumption in ethics, without opening the door to universal scepticism. (*ME*, 509).

Moreover, the concluding passage quoted at the beginning of this article was itself suppressed in the second and later editions, and in the preface to the second edition Sidgwick explains that in these and associated changes "I have yielded as far as I could to the objections that have been strongly urged against the concluding chapter" (*ME*, viii). But in this preface he makes it clear that he still adheres to the "Dualism of the Practical Reason," and since, as he says, he learned it from

"Butler's well-known Sermons," he is surprised that his critics are surprised by it (*ME*, x–xi). I shall discuss later the argument faintly hinted at in the first edition and more explicitly stated in the second; but for the present it is enough to note that in his earlier and, I think, better thoughts, before he yielded even partly to the pressure of his critics, Sidgwick was inclining toward the pessimistic or skeptical side.

These questions are raised in a chapter which in the first edition was entitled "The Sanctions of Utilitarianism," though the reorientation in the second and later editions changed this to "The Mutual Relations of the Three Methods." In book 4, Sidgwick is echoing at least the headings of Mill's chapters; not surprisingly, there are also two chapters entitled "The Proof of Utilitarianism" (2 and 3 in the first edition: chap. 3 was retitled in later editions). But his stress in chapter 6 on the "Sanctions" is due partly to what he regarded as the inconclusiveness of the "Proof." He takes account of the view of "others" who "will maintain that the proof offered in ch. 2, does not really convert them from Egoistic to Universalistic Hedonism; but only convinces them that, unless the two can be shown to coincide, Practical Reason is divided against itself." Since this position "is certainly very difficult to assail with argument," he is "led to examine the Egoistic inducements to conform to Utilitarian rules, in order to see whether an Egoist who remains obstinately impervious to what we have called Proof may be persuaded into practical Utilitarianism by a consideration of Sanctions" (*ME* 1, 460–1). Similarly, the final chapter in later editions begins by noting that "[the Egoist] may avoid the proof of Utilitarianism by declining to affirm [that his own happiness is not merely the rational ultimate end for himself but a part of Universal Good]" (*ME*, 497–8).

But what exactly is wrong with the "Proof"? With his usual combination of acuteness and honesty, Sidgwick has here got right something that many other moral thinkers have got wrong. I quote the key passage as it is given in the first edition. Referring to an argument addressed to egoism, Sidgwick says:

It should be observed that the applicability of this argument depends on the manner in which the Egoistic first principle is formulated. If the Egoist strictly confines himself to stating his conviction that he ought to take his own happiness or pleasure as his ultimate end, there seems no opening for any line of reasoning to lead him to Universalistic Hedonism as a first principle. In this case all that the Utilitarian can do is to effect as far as possible a reconciliation between the two principles: by expounding to the Egoist the *sanctions* (as they are usually called) of rules deduced from the Universalistic principle: that is, the pleasures and pains that will accrue to himself from their observance and violation respectively. It is obvious that such an exposition has no tendency to make him accept the greatest happiness of the greatest number as his ultimate end: but only as a means to the end of his own happiness. It is therefore totally different from a *proof* (as above explained) of Universalistic Hedonism. When, however, the Egoist offers, either as a reason for his Egoistic principle, or as another form of stating it, the proposition that his happiness or pleasure is objectively desirable or Good; he gives the ground needed for such a proof. For we can then point out to him that *his* happiness cannot be more objectively desirable or more a good than the similar happiness of any other person: the mere fact (if I may so put it) that *he is he* can have nothing to do with its objective desirability or goodness. Hence, starting with his own principle, he must accept the wider notion of Universal happiness or pleasure as representing the real end of Reason, the absolutely Good or Desirable: as the end, therefore, to which the action of a reasonable agent as such ought to be directed.

This is not changed substantially in later editions. At the end of the second sentence there is added, "it cannot be proved that the difference between his own happiness and another's happiness is not *for him* all-important"; in the sixth sentence "objectively desirable or Good" becomes "Good, not only *for him* but from the point of view of the Universe, – as (e.g.) by saying that 'nature designed him to seek his own happiness' "; below, "more objectively desirable or more a good" becomes "a more important part of Good, taken universally," and, regrettably, the very telling remark "the mere fact (if I may so put it) that *he is he* can have nothing to do with its objective desirability or goodness" is deleted. Other changes are minor and merely verbal. (See *ME*, 420–1.) Sidgwick is saying that a cogent *ad hominem* argument against the egoist can be constructed if, and only if, the egoist introduces into his view the notion of something's being objectively good, that is, objectively desirable, or "Good . . . from the point of view of the Universe." Once the egoist has claimed not merely that his own happiness is relatively good for him, something that it is reasonable for him to pursue, but that his being happy is intrinsically good – and perhaps that his desiring it, or his seeing it to be reasonable for him to pursue it, is evidence for its intrinsic goodness, being an apprehension of that goodness – then and only then can the utilitarian step in and point out the irrelevance, to such intrinsic goodness, of the happiness being *his*. This universalization follows the introduction of objective or intrinsic goodness-as-an-end. But, as Sidgwick sees, this move is not one which the egoist needs to make: In introducing objective goodness he is gratuitously compromising his position. Moreover, it is not ethical objectivity in general that has this effect, but specifically the objectivity of *good*. The objectivity of rightness or oughtness would not have the same effect. The egoist can assert that he absolutely and objectively ought to take his own happiness as his end, and there will still be no cogent *ad hominem* argument to make him adopt utilitarianism. In fact Sidgwick assumes from the start the objectivity of oughtness, and claims general agreement with this assumption. "That there is in any given circumstances some one thing which ought to be done and that this can be known, is a fundamental assumption, made not by philosophers only, but by all men who perform any processes of moral reasoning" (*ME*1, 6). And he argues that such ought-propositions are not merely hypothetical imperatives or counsels of prudence: Most of us would think that a man *ought* to seek his own happiness (*ME*1, 8). But he is more cautious about assuming the objectivity of goodness, partly because many moralists, including many intuitionists, "hold that our obligation to obey moral rules is not conditional on our knowledge of the end" (*ME*1, 3). "Hence it seems best not to assume at the outset that Ethics investigates an end at all, but rather to define it as the study of what ought to be done" (*ME*1, 4).

But why is there this curious difference between goodness on the one hand and either rightness or oughtness on the other? This Sidgwick does not explain; but it is a consequence of their formal logical features, essentially that " . . . is good" is a one-place predicate whereas " . . . is right for . . . " or " . . . ought to . . . " are two-place predicates. Whatever is objective must be universalizable over relevantly similar cases, but universalization works differently with one-place and with two-place predicates. If we start with "*A*'s being happy is (objectively) good" and universalize this with respect to all persons, or perhaps all sentient beings, relevantly similar to *A*, we can infer that *B*'s being happy is good, and *C*'s, and so on; in fact, that for all *X*, *X*'s being happy is good – where "for all *X*" is simply a quantifier: This is not to be read as saying that *X*'s happiness is good merely for *X*. It is in this way that, as Sidgwick says, the egoist can be brought to acknowledge that the happiness of others is good. On the other hand, if we start with the premise "*A* ought to seek *A*'s happiness" there are four ways in which universal quantification can be introduced: (1) For all *X*, *X* ought to seek *X*'s happiness; (2) for all *X*, *A* ought to seek *X*'s happiness; (3) for all *X*, *X* ought to seek *A*'s happiness; and (4) for all *X* and for all *Y*, *X* ought to seek *Y*'s happiness. Of these, only the first would be a valid universal generalization in modern formal logic: (4) would be a valid generalization from either (2) or (3), but neither (2) nor (3) would be a valid generalization from the premise. But the important question is whether they are morally cogent. If the identity of the seeker with the person whose happiness is sought is, or may be, a morally relevant feature of what the premise prescribes, the derivation of (2) or (3), and hence of (4), is noncogent;

it will be cogent only if it can be claimed confidently that this identity is irrelevant. But to claim this irrelevance is in effect to treat either " ... ought to seek *A*'s happiness" or "*A* ought to seek ... " as a one-place predicate; it is to say that *A*'s happiness is intrinsically seekable, that is, objectively good. As long as we keep consistently to a two-place-predicate interpretation of the "ought" in the premise we must allow that the identity of the seeker and the person whose happiness is sought may be morally relevant, and then (1) will be the only morally cogent universalization. And this, so far from refuting egoism, endorses a form of it. Equally, if we use the two-place predicate " ... is good for ... ," its universalization will be powerless to defeat the egoist. But when Sidgwick speaks of "objectively desirable or Good" or of "Good not only *for him* but from the point of view of the Universe," it is distinctively the one-place predicate that he is introducing.

Sidgwick's correct analysis here throws light on several less accurate discussions. Mill, in his notorious "proof" of the principle of utility, says:

No reason can be given why the general happiness is desirable, except that each person ... desires his own happiness. This, however, being a fact, we have not only all the proof which the case admits of, but all which it is possible to require, that happiness is a good: that each person's happiness is a good to that person, and the general happiness, therefore, a good to the aggregate of all persons. (*Utilitarianism*, chap. 4)

This looks like an argument in two steps, from "Each person desires his own happiness" to "Each person's happiness is desirable for that person" and then from the latter to "The general happiness is desirable for every person." The first step seems to move without warrant from "is" to "ought," while the second seems to involve a fallacy of composition. To yield a utilitarian conclusion, we must take "the aggregate of all persons" as equivalent to "every person" read distributively; but then the conclusion will not follow. Even with just two persons, "*A*'s happiness and *B*'s happiness are desirable for *A*, and are also desirable for *B*" does not follow from "*A*'s happiness is desirable for *A* and *B*'s happiness for *B*." The word "aggregate" would most naturally suggest a collective reading; for example, with two persons, "The happiness of the *A*–*B* collective is desirable for the *A*–*B* collective." This is plausibly analogous with "*A*'s happiness is desirable for *A*." But what it is for something to be desirable for a two-person or for a multiperson collective is obscure, and in any case this is not what a utilitarian is trying to establish.

Read thus, Mill's argument seems to be riddled with fallacies. But it can be read more charitably. Perhaps what he had at the back of his mind was that each person desires his own happiness because he realizes, or believes, that his own happiness is good – not just for him, but objectively – and that we can take each person's desiring of his own happiness as evidence that that happiness *is* good objectively. Then Mill's first step is not an invalid move from "is" to "ought" but a fairly plausible inference from the fact that judgments, of a certain sort, of objective value are widely believed to the truth of those judgments and hence to the corresponding evaluations – *A*'s happiness *is* objectively good, and so on. Then the second step becomes either the justifiable universalization from each of these evaluations to all the others – if *A*'s happiness is good, so is *B*'s, and so on – or else (as Mill himself claimed in a letter) it merely sums up all these separate evaluations so as to conclude that the general happiness, comprising the happinesses of *A*, of *B*, and so on, is also good. This would, no doubt, be too charitable as a reading of what Mill actually says. But it is more plausible to suppose that he had something of this sort in mind than that he committed the blatant fallacies of which critics have been too eager to accuse him.

G. E. Moore's criticism of egoism (*Principia Ethica*, pp. 97–104) turns upon the allegation that there is a confusion in the conception of "my own good":

> It is obvious . . . that the only thing which can belong to me, which can be *mine*, is something which is good, and not the fact that it is good. . . . I must mean either that the thing I get is good or that my possessing it is good. . . . The only reason I can have for aiming at "my own good" is that it is *good absolutely* that what I so call should belong to me.

Here Moore is simply asserting that any being good that can constitute a reason for anyone's aiming at something must be "absolute" – that is, that "good" must be a one-place predicate. But he has nothing to support this assertion except his extraordinarily limited views about the possible forms of meaningful linguistic constructions. Quoting from the passage in *The Methods of Ethics*, book 4, chapter 2, which I have quoted above, he asks: "What does Prof. Sidgwick mean by the phrases 'the ultimate rational end for himself' and '*for him* all-important'? He does not attempt to define them; and it is largely the use of such un-defined phrases which causes absurdities to be committed in philosophy" (p. 99). This, from the man who is best remembered as the defender of the view that "good" is indefinable! What effrontery! Or rather, what naivete, for Moore clearly thinks that an undefined one-place-predicate "good" can be straightforwardly meaningful, but a two-place-predicate "good for" or "all-important for" cannot. In fact Sidgwick would have had rather less difficulty in explaining these relations than Moore would have had in explaining his nonnatural quality. However, it is clear that if we assume, with Moore, that the only reason anyone can have for aiming at anything is that that thing is absolutely good, then we shall find egoism self-contradictory, whether it is expressed as "It is reasonable for everyone to aim only at his own happiness" or as "Each person's happiness is the sole good for him." But it is equally clear that this assumption is one which the egoist has no need to grant.

Moore also criticizes the suggestion in Sidgwick's final chapter that divine sanctions might avoid a contradiction in our apparent intuitions about what is reasonable:

Prof. Sidgwick here commits the characteristic fallacy of Empiricism – the fallacy of thinking that an alteration in *facts* could make a contradiction cease to be a contradiction. That a single man's happiness should be the *sole good*, and that also everybody's happiness should be the *sole good*, is a contradiction which cannot be solved by the assumption that the same conduct will secure both. (*Principia Ethica*, p. 103)

This is true, but Sidgwick never said it could. Sidgwick sees as clearly as Moore that if it were just a question about a sole (absolute) good, there would be no contradiction to solve, because egoism would have been refuted; but he also sees, as Moore does not, that the issue cannot be thus simplified, and that we are left with the competing apparent intuitions that it is rational for a man to seek his own happiness and that it is rational for a man to seek the general happiness. These are not in themselves contradictory: A contradiction arises only when we add to these two intuitions the factual statement that what best promotes a man's own happiness does not always coincide with what best promotes the general happiness. It is the facts that decide whether the two intuitions come into practical conflict or not. Moore fails to see that Sidgwick is keeping the questions of "proof" and of "sanctions" apart. Divine sanctions may come in not to complete a proof or to solve a contradiction between two intuitions but to resolve a contradiction that would otherwise arise from the conjunction of these intuitions with a factual truth.

Thomas Nagel recognizes the weakness of Moore's position:

nothing resembling an argument is offered for these claims. . . . They seem to him self-evident because he regards it as already established that "good" is a one-place predicate denoting a simple non-natural property. But that would not be granted by an egoist, whose fundamental evaluative concept would be a relation: "X is good for Y." (*The Possibility of Altruism* [Princeton: Princeton University Press, 1970], p. 86 and n.)

But Nagel proposes to "explain exactly what [Moore] assumes: that in order to accept something as a goal for oneself, one must be able to regard its achievement by oneself as an *objective* good." I cannot discuss Nagel's argument adequately, because its intricacies and obscurities make it hard to pin down. But it attempts to do what Sidgwick says cannot be done, that is, refute the egoist without first getting him to talk about objective good. Nagel deals not with good but with reasons for action. His crucial claim is that if we are to avoid "practical solipsism" – and the reasons for doing this are essentially those that support universalizability – we must be able to frame our practical judgments impersonally but "with motivational content": Objective principles, he thinks, will meet this requirement whereas subjective principles will not:

If I merely consider in impersonal terms the individual who I in fact am, I can conclude that there is, for him, subjective reason to do this or that, but this does not involve, and cannot even explain, any desire that he do so. The motivational content which forms an essential part of a first-person practical judgement is therefore missing entirely from an impersonal judgement about the same individual, if that judgement derives from a subjective principle. (P. 117)

But what in concrete terms does this mean? What Nagel calls a subjective principle would be, for example, the egoistic one that a man has reason to do what will avoid pain for himself. A derived impersonal judgment would be, say, that J.M. has reason for keeping his hand out of the fire. Nagel's thesis is that even though I am J.M. this judgment *qua* impersonal gives *me* no motive for keeping my hand out of the fire. This seems absurd. This judgment gives J.M. a motive, and since I *am* J.M., it gives me a motive. But presumably this obvious move violates Nagel's standard of impersonality. But then his demand for impersonality plus motivational content is equivalent to the demand that practical judgments should be of the form "For all X, X has reason to do S" – where S is some specific act such as "keep J.M.'s hand out of the fire" – or of some more general form from which this would follow, such as "For all Y and for all X, X has reason to do what will avoid pain for Y." He is dissatisfied with judgments of the form "For all X, X has reason to do what will avoid pain for X" because when the act component is instantiated to "keep J.M.'s hand out of the fire" the agent component will be correspondingly instantiated to "J.M." and we shall lose impersonal motivational content. But what ground is there for insisting on impersonality plus motivation thus interpreted? No general considerations in favor of the action-guidingness and universalizability of rational practical judgments will support this insistence, for they will be met by the obvious action-guidingness for J.M. of "J.M. has reason to keep J.M.'s hand out of the fire" and such universalizations of it as "For all X, X has reason to do what will avoid pain for X." In being dissatisfied with these, Nagel is just insisting on using the one-place predicate "For all X, X has reason to do . . . " which, for all its apparent difference in form, is equivalent to Moore's " . . . is good"; and Nagel has no more of an argument for this than Moore has.

R. M. Hare has endeavored to "establish a point of contact between utilitarianism" and his own universal prescriptivism, in effect to show that the latter method of moral argument will lead to some sort of utilitarianism:

The logical character of moral language, as I have claimed it to be, is the formal foundation of any such [utilitarian] theory. It is in the endeavour to find lines of conduct which we can prescribe universally in a given situation that we find ourselves bound to give equal weight to the desires of all parties (the foundation of distributive justice); and this, in turn, leads to such views as that we should seek to maximize satisfactions. (*Freedom and Reason* [Oxford: Oxford University Press, 1963], pp. 122–3)

But the phrase "lines of conduct which we can prescribe universally" conceals a vital ambiguity. Are these to be policies defined with reference to the agent – such as "X is to avoid pain for X" or "X is to look after X's children" – or are they to be attempts, by all the agents involved in some situation, to achieve some unitary goal? It is only with the latter interpretation that the endeavor to prescribe universally will lead toward some kind of utilitarianism. But there is nothing in the logical character of moral language to rule out the former interpretation. Even if egoism is suspect, what C. D. Broad has called self-referential altruism is not – that is, the doctrine that "each of us has specially strong obligations to benefit certain persons and groups of persons who stand in certain special relations to *himself*," such as parents, children, friends, benefactors, and fellow countrymen (see "Moore's Ethical Doctrines," in *The Philosophy of G. E. Moore*, ed. P. A. Schilpp [Evanston, IL: Northwestern University Press, 1942], pp. 53–5.) Self-referential altruism forms, and always has formed, a large part of common-sense morality. When William Godwin argued against its most central doctrines and in favor of utilitarianism – for example, that one should rescue Archbishop Fénelon from a fire rather than one's own mother – it was his view that seemed paradoxical or even outrageous (*Political Justice*, book 2, chap. 2; quoted and discussed by D. H. Monro, *Empiricism and Ethics* [Cambridge: Cambridge University Press, 1967], pp. 197–9). It would be quite implausible to say that the logical character of moral language excludes the universal prescription of such self-referentially altruistic principles. This shows at once that universal prescriptivism will not in itself lead to any kind of utilitarianism. Further, once self-referential altruism is allowed, egoism cannot be excluded by any appeal to the logical character of moral language: "For all X, X ought to avoid pain for X" is universally prescribable in the sense required by the logic of moral language. In order to arrive by this route at some kind of utilitarian conclusion we need to add some further restriction, for example, that what is to be prescribed universally is a single goal which all the agents involved should try to achieve, or some agreed distribution of benefits. Any such appropriate restriction will be a counterpart, within universal prescriptivism, of Moore's insistence on the one-place predicate "good"; but the egoist, or the self-referential altruist, is no more bound to accept such a restriction than, as Sidgwick shows, he is bound to talk in terms of an objective good.

I conclude, then, that Sidgwick was right to query the cogency of his own argument against egoism, and that various arguments produced by other moralists, before and after him, are not stronger than his. Rather, these thinkers have failed to bring out as clearly as he did the special assumptions or restrictions that are needed to make such arguments cogent. I shall therefore return to the argument about sanctions which, Sidgwick thought, arose naturally from the noted inadequacy of the "Proof." Briefly, this runs as follows. It is rational for each man to seek his own happiness. It is also rational for each man to seek the general happiness. In the natural course of events, the actions most fitted to promote the agent's own happiness will not always coincide with those most fitted to promote the general happiness. For perfect coincidence, therefore, we must postulate a moral government of the universe, something like a God who will adequately reward the performance of duty and adequately punish its violation. This hypothesis is "logically necessary to avoid a fundamental contradiction in one chief department of our thought," namely, practical reason. The question is whether this avoidance is an adequate ground for adopting this hypothesis.

An argument from two moral or practical premises to a factual conclusion is unusual, but there is nothing wrong with its logic. Similarly, there are valid arguments with two imperative premises and a factual conclusion – indeed, there must be, if there are, as is more commonly recognized, valid arguments with one imperative and one factual premise and an imperative conclusion. If "Do everything that father says" follows from "Do everything that mother says" in conjunction with "Everything that father says mother says too," then equally from the conjunction of "Do everything that mother says" with "Don't do everything that father says" it will follow that father says some things that mother does not.

But though such arguments can be made formally valid, moral or practical premises seem to provide not merely insufficient but also inappropriate grounds for factual beliefs. In the last sentence of the second and later editions Sidgwick suggests that factual and scientific "truths" "rest on no other grounds than that we have a strong disposition to accept them, and that they are indispensable to the systematic coherence of our beliefs"; if so, may not the systematic coherence of our practical judgments supply an equally respectable basis for factual (theological) truths? I think not. This sort of argument is back to front. What it is rational to do depends on how the facts are; we cannot take what we are inclined to think that it is rational to do as evidence that the facts are one way rather than another. As Sidgwick says in the first edition, "the mere fact that I cannot act rationally without assuming a certain proposition, does not appear to me . . . a sufficient ground for believing it to be true."

What, then, is the outcome of our discussion? Starting with a variety of apparent intuitions about rational conduct, Sidgwick thought that those of common sense and intuitionistic morality could be reconciled with and absorbed into a utilitarian view, but that this left unresolved the duality of egoist and utilitarian principles. He considered two procedures for reconciliation, "Proof" and "Sanctions." Whether or not we had a sanction, the objectivity of goodness would provide a proof; and so likewise would the centering of a moral system on some other appropriate one-place predicate, some counterpart of an objective good, for example, within a theory of good reasons for action or within universal prescriptivism. But egoism can coherently resist any such proof by adhering to the use of such two-place predicates as "right," "ought," and "good for": Objectivity and universalization with respect to these are powerless against it. Again, the existence of a moral government of the universe, of something like a God, would provide a sanction whether or not we had a proof; but there is no adequate independent case for this, and it is not reasonable to use these apparent moral intuitions themselves as evidence in favor of the hypothesis that would reconcile them. So, in the end, we have neither a proof nor a sanction: The fundamental apparent intuitions of practical reason remain obstinately unreconciled: The Cosmos of Duty is indeed a Chaos.

6

Sidgwick and the history of ethical dualism

WILLIAM K. FRANKENA

Some years ago I published a short systematic study of Sidgwick's dualism of practical reason;[1] here I propose to complement it with a study of his views about the history of that dualism, using both *The Methods of Ethics*, which contains many passages on the history of ethics, and especially *Outlines of the History of Ethics*. My two studies will, of course, overlap somewhat, and this one may embody some changes in my interpretations of Sidgwick (which I shall not spell out), since I mean to deal not only with his account of the history of ethical dualism before *The Methods of Ethics* but with the place of *The Methods of Ethics* in that history.[2]

1

In what is arguably his most interesting remark about the history of ethics Sidgwick writes as follows:

Butler's express statement of the duality of the regulative principles in human nature constitutes an important step in ethical speculation; since it brings into clear view *the most fundamental difference* between the ethical thought of modern England and that of the old Greco-Roman world. . . . [I]n Platonism and Stoicism, and in Greek moral philosophy generally, but *one* regulative and governing faculty is recognized under the name of Reason – however the regulation of Reason may be understood; in the modern ethical view, when it has worked itself clear, there are found to be *two* – Universal Reason and Egoistic Reason, or Conscience and Self-love. (*OHE*, 197 f.; emphasis added)

I recently quoted the second sentence of this passage at the head of another essay entitled "Concepts of Rational Action in the History of Ethics,"[3] which pays a good deal of attention to Sidgwick and also overlaps with this one, but did not there discuss it. By itself one might interpret it as saying that, whereas the ancients held that there is only one regulative faculty in us and were all agreed about what it was, the moderns take two (or more) different views about what it was. This is

how I was reading it when I wrote the article just referred to. But
Sidgwick's main point in the context in which it occurs is to say that
modern (British) moral philosophers are dualistic in a sense in which
the ancients were monistic – in the sense of (all?) holding that there are
two governing faculties in each of us, and not just one. Even so, however,
there are problems about its interpretation.

One is this: Are we to interpret the sentence as equating universal
reason with conscience and egoistic reason with self-love? It is easy to
equate egoistic reason and self-love (*cum* reason), but equating conscience and universal reason blurs the difference between the intuitionists and the utilitarians in modern British thought, a difference Sidgwick
is otherwise concerned to emphasize. Or are we to take him here as
meaning that modern moral philosophers (all?) believe in two regulative
faculties, but that some of them (the intuitionists) identify these as
conscience and egoistic reason whereas others (the utilitarians) identify
them as universal reason and egoistic reason? This would be more accurate, given Sidgwick's general picture of modern ethics and its methods
in *The Methods of Ethics*. One could also take "universal reason" to
mean non-egoistic reason, in which case it would cover both conscience
and utilitarian reason.

A second question about our sentence may ask what faculty Sidgwick
thinks the ancients were regarding as the one and only regulative and
governing faculty under the name of reason. Is it egoistic reason, universal reason, or conscience? He does not indicate here which, but
elsewhere it is clear that he thinks they recognized only egoistic reason
as a regulative and governing faculty in human nature. For example, he
writes in *The Methods of Ethics*,

Egoism in this sense [of holding that the ultimate end is the good of the indi-
vidual] was assumed in the whole ethical controversy of ancient Greece; that
is, it was assumed on all sides that a rational individual would make the pursuit
of his own good his supreme aim: the controverted question was whether this
Good was rightly conceived as Pleasure [hedonism] or Virtue [perfectionism]
or any *tertium quid* [e.g., knowledge]. (*ME*, 91 f.)

And, in a very interesting footnote to this passage, he implies that in
ancient ethics the proposition "My own Good is my only reasonable
ultimate end" is a "mere tautology," while asserting that in modern
thought it is not, "even though we define 'Good' as that at which it is
ultimately reasonable to aim."[4]

In the passage first quoted, Sidgwick hints that, although the ancients
regarded egoistic reason or self-love-*cum*-reason as the sole regulative
faculty or principle in us, they understood its operation in different ways.

One would have to read the first section of the introduction to the *Outlines of the History of Ethics* and all of chapter 1 to see what he has in mind, but for present purposes we may follow our second quotation and take him to mean that some of them conceived of its regulation along egoistic and hedonistic lines, others along egoistic and perfectionist lines, and still others along lines that are egoistic but neither hedonistic nor perfectionist.[5] One may, of course, ask whether the ancients were as egoistic in their psychology and ethics as Sidgwick takes them to be. Perhaps under his influence, I have always thought that they were, but I am less sure of this than I used to be. The question cannot be debated here, and for our purposes I shall assume that Sidgwick is at least roughly right.

My third question about our sentence concerns Sidgwick's saying that "*the* modern . . . view, *when it has worked itself clear*," recognizes that there are two regulative and governing faculties in us "*under the name of Reason*" (emphasis added). This suggests (1) that there is such a thing as *the* modern (or at least British) view on the number of such faculties in human nature, (2) that it was more or less inchoate in Butler's modern predecessors and "worked itself" clear in Butler, and (3) that, when worked out, it found that there are two and only two regulative faculties in human nature and put them under the name of Reason. Is this what Sidgwick thinks, and, if so, is he right? We must, I think, take Sidgwick's dictum with some salt, since he supplies much of its corrective elsewhere; he must have been on something of a rhetorical high, so to speak, when he penned it. To begin with, there is no such thing as *the* modern or even British view about the number of governing faculties found, not even on his own account; he himself describes Hobbes and Spinoza as egoists, that is, as finding, as the Greeks did, that egoistic reason is the sole governing faculty in us. Nor, according to Sidgwick, do all of the British put all of the faculties they regard as operative in us under *reason*, as he implies they do in our passage; he expressly cites Shaftesbury as the first to transfer "the centre of ethical interest from the Reason . . . to the emotional impulses that prompt to social duty," specifically to our moral *sense* and our disinterested and altruistic *feelings*, and portrays Hutcheson, Hume, and Adam Smith as following Shaftesbury's suit, as many others have.[6] I shall later try to show that ethical dualism, at least in the form in which Sidgwick accepts it, did not work itself entirely clear in Butler and did not do so until Sidgwick himself worked on it, if even then.

In any event, some modern moral philosophers were dualists about the number of regulative faculties in our natures and identified them either as egoistic reason and benevolent or utilitarian reason, *or* as egoistic reason and conscience (or intuitive reason or Kantian practical reason). I shall here go along with Sidgwick's claim that such dualistic views first appeared in early modern moral philosophy. So far, however, I have put everything in terms of Sidgwick's Butlerian talk about "regulative and governing faculties." What does such talk come to? What are we to understand by the statement that something, say X, is a regulative or governing faculty in human conduct? I think we can interpret it as asserting:

1. that X is something in us that actually regulates or governs our conduct, at least to some extent; in Butler's terms, it is something reflective and secondary, over and above our various primary appetites and passions (which need regulating), that has at least some *power* to influence our lives
2. that, also in Butler's words, X "naturally" claims and has *authority* or is *authoritative*, whatever its strength
3. that if X dictates a certain action, then the agent in question has an obligation to do it, apart from whatever (other) sanctions there may be bearing on that agent
4. that it is reasonable or rational to do what X dictates and unreasonable or irrational not to

Here, I take it that, in the talk in question, (2), (3), and (4) come to much the same thing. Then an ethical dualist will be saying that there are two things in us of which (1), (2), (3), and (4) are true, whereas an ethical monist will be saying there is but one.

2

Immediately following the passage first quoted, Sidgwick says again that "this dualism" was clearly recognized by Butler (1726), and also that it "appears confusedly" in Samuel Clarke's account of reasonable conduct (1706) and "implicitly" in Shaftesbury's account of the obligation to virtue (1711), and is "perhaps most closely anticipated" by William Wollaston (1722). Obviously, he is thinking here that the dualism he finds in modern British ethics worked itself clear in the thinking of these men. But before we review his discussions of the relevant parts of their thought,[7] we must note that Sidgwick may be somewhat confused about just who is a dualist. He tends to ascribe the view that egoistic reason is a regulative faculty in human nature to anyone who holds *either* (a) that one has a duty or obligation to, or ought to, pursue one's own good, happiness, or interest, *or* (b) that one should be virtuous or do the right because that is for one's happiness or at least not contrary to it. Thus he regards as a dualist anyone who asserts either (*a*) or (*b*) *and* (*c*), namely, that, besides egoistic reason, there is in us a non-egoistic regulative faculty, say conscience, universal reason, or rational benevolence. This is all right in the case of one who affirms (*b*) and (*c*), which one can do without affirming (*a*). Affirming (*a*) is another matter, for one could hold that conscience is the only faculty that should govern in our lives and also that conscience tells us, among other things, to look to our own good, at least if other things are equal. In effect, this is Richard Price's view. Then one's asserting (*a*) does not entail that there is a second regulative faculty besides conscience. Sidgwick, for all his perspicacity, does not seem to see this.

Now let us look at what Sidgwick says about Clarke. What is there about Clarke's account of reasonable conduct that leads Sidgwick to regard him as an ethical dualist? In what way is Clarke recognizing two regulative faculties in us, however confusedly? First of all, his view is that, given a clear grasp of "the natures and relations of things," our reason will see it to be self-evident that certain kinds of actions are fitting or unfitting, right or wrong, independently of any consideration of what is in our interest, or even what is for the general good, as well as of any commands or sanctions there may be.

from [the] different relations of different things . . . there necessarily arises a fitness or unfitness of certain manners of behaviour of some [beings] toward others. . . . some things are in their own nature good and reasonable and fit to be done. . . . Other things are in their own nature absolutely evil.

Having said this, Clarke then adds that "the judgement and conscience of a man's own mind, concerning the reasonableness and fitness of the thing . . . is the truest and formallest *obligation*. . . . The original obligation of all . . . is the eternal reason of things."[8] And he goes on to argue that four "rules of righteousness" are thus self-evident to reason or conscience: that of *piety* to God; that of *equity* toward fellow persons; that of *universal love* or *benevolence* (or promoting "the welfare and happiness of all men"); and that of *sobriety* (or preserving one's own being and being temperate). Thus Clarke is an intuitionist or, more accurately, a pluralistic deontological intuitionist, not a utilitarian. But notice that so far he has not said there is any regulative faculty in us besides intuitive reason or conscience; all of his duties are perceived by the same non-egoistic faculty. Nor has he said that one has a duty to consider or seek one's own welfare or happiness; this is not part of his rule of duty to ourselves. So far, then, there is no dualism about regulative faculties, though there is a pluralism about the rules of duty. In fact, it looks as if Clarke is insisting that we are simply to do what reason sees to be fitting to the natures and relations of things, period. As Sidgwick points out, however, he does not rest with this robust moral attitude, for he later writes as follows:

Men never will generally, and indeed *it is not very reasonable* to be expected they should, part with all the comforts of life, and even life itself, without expectations of any future recompense. . . . It is neither possible, *nor truly reasonable* that men by adhering to Virtue should part with their lives, if thereby they eternally deprived themselves of all possibility of receiving any *advantage* from that adherence. (Emphasis added)

Here Clarke seems to be saying that, even though we have no *duty* to seek our own advantage or happiness, still it is not *rational* for us to be virtuous or pursue righteousness if this is ultimately contrary to our own interests, thus implying that self-interest both is and should be a regulative principle in our lives, perhaps the supreme one. This is why Sidgwick rightly regards Clarke as "confusedly" a dualist in some sense after all, seeing him as believing in two kinds of obligation and reasonableness, one "from an abstract or universal point of view" and another "from the individual's point of view."[9] I wish to point out, however, that for Clarke our whole moral duty belongs to the former point of view, none of it to the latter; his duality is between duty and interest, or between two faculties "under the name of reason," that is, the moral faculty and egoistic reason – a point I shall return to when we look at Sidgwick's own dualism.[10]

As for Shaftesbury – in what way, according to Sidgwick, is dualism "implicitly" present in his account of the obligation to virtue? Well, for Shaftesbury, not only are there genuinely altruistic feelings in human nature – Sidgwick says Shaftesbury was the first moralist to make this the cardinal point in his system – there is also in us a "reflective" or moral sense, not under the name of reason, that approves and disapproves of conduct and character on a non-egoistic basis and also moves us, at least to some extent, to act accordingly. Thus, virtue consists, for him, of being so disposed as to promote the good of the whole "system" to which we belong. Our reflective sense is thus one faculty that plays a part in our lives. But, as Butler points out, Shaftesbury does not regard that sense as authoritative in the full sense explained above; indeed, he does not think that we have any obligation or reason to be virtuous as such or for its own sake, as Clarke does. For, having told us what virtue is, he then asks "*what obligation* there is to Virtue, or *what* reason to embrace it," and, as Sidgwick puts it, his answer assumes that "the ultimate appeal must be to the individual's interest. . . . it never occurs to him to answer . . . from any other than from an egoistic point of view;

his 'obligation' is the obligation of self-interest; his 'reasons' are entirely addressed to self-love" (*OHE*, 196). This is true, even though, in making a case for his claim that virtue is the good and vice the ill of everyone, he depends very considerably on his non-egoistic psychology.

If this is so, however, then Shaftesbury is not a dualist in Sidgwick's sense; he is not really holding that there are two regulative faculties in us, certainly not under the name of reason. For his moral sense is not actually authoritative; all authority for him belongs finally to self-love, altruistic as his view of human nature is. He does recognize two faculties in us, moral sense and egoistic reason, but he appeals to the former only in determining *what* virtue is, not at all in showing *that* or *why* we should embrace it. Again, Sidgwick does not seem to see this.

Sidgwick regards Wollaston as most closely anticipating Butler's dualism because in his book, "for the first time, we find 'moral good' and 'natural good' or 'happiness' treated separately as two essentially distinct objects of rational pursuit and investigation" (*OHE*, 198). I see no reason for objecting to this statement as it stands. Sidgwick supports it by saying that Wollaston holds happiness to be a "justly desirable" end at which every rational being ought to aim, presumably along with moral good, and Wollaston does indeed maintain, as Clarke did not, that "To make itself happy is a duty, which every being, in proportion to its capacity, owes to itself."[11] But he thinks that its being a duty is "self-evident" to the same abstract and non-egoistic reason that perceives our other duties, just as Clarke would have if he had thought it was a duty. As far as I can see, Wollaston's regarding it as a duty does not entail his thinking of self-love as a second regulative faculty, though he does remark, in the rest of the sentence quoted, that every intelligent being "may be supposed" to aim at its own happiness. It also does not entail that Wollaston thinks, as Clarke did, that, if duty ever does certainly conflict with self-interest, then it is only reasonable that self-interest should prevail. Thus, it does not seem to me that Wollaston is actually a dualist in Sidgwick's sense, not even as much as Clarke was. It is true that Wollaston holds that duty and self-interest cannot ultimately conflict, just as Clarke and Butler did, though Sidgwick is mistaken when he writes that Wollaston takes their harmony "as a matter of religious faith, not moral knowledge." For, although Wollaston may not regard it as a matter of *moral* knowledge, he does believe that it can be established by natural theology and so is a matter of philosophical knowledge, not merely one of faith.

This brings us to Joseph Butler, who so greatly influenced Sidgwick and is central to his history of modern British ethics. Just what form did Butler's "clear recognition" of ethical dualism, which Sidgwick re-

gards as an "important step" in ethical theory, take? We may begin by
noting that Sidgwick first contends that, for Butler, general or rational
benevolence is not a third naturally secondary and regulative principle,
in addition to conscience and self-love (or reasonable self-love), as is
often thought and as is suggested by some of the language in Butler's
first sermon. I am not convinced but shall not debate this point, agreeing
for now that there are but two authorities in Butler's "polity of the
soul." Sidgwick goes on to maintain that "Butler's real view is not (as
is widely supposed) that self-love is naturally subordinate to conscience
– at least if we consider the theoretical rather than the practical relation
between the two" (*OHE*, 194 f.). I think that on this point he does not
adequately consider the passages in which Butler seems expressly to
state that conscience is naturally supreme, in authority if not in power,
over all the other principles in our nature, but again I shall let this pass.
Next, Sidgwick says that Butler treats conscience and self-love "as independent principles," which is true. However Butler thinks their authority, obligation, or reasonableness may be established, he does hold
that that of conscience is not derived from that of self-love or vice versa;
for him each faculty is authoritative, obligatory, and reasonable as such
or by its own nature. What this means and how it may be shown I shall
not discuss, since our question is only whether Butler was an ethical
dualist and, if so, in what sense.[12]

   Now comes the crucial point: Sidgwick goes on to write that, for
Butler, conscience and self-love are "so far coordinate in authority that
it is not 'according to nature' that either should be overruled." It is not
clear, however, that Butler means to hold that neither may ever be
overruled by the other, either in theory or in practice, to introduce the
distinction Sidgwick uses in an earlier quotation. In fact, using this
distinction, I think we can fairly say that Sidgwick believes Butler's real
view to be (1) that in *theory*, if conscience and reasonable self-love ever
did conflict (which Butler holds to be impossible in God's universe),
then the latter should prevail, and (2) that in *practice*, when they seem
to conflict, the former should *always* prevail or be permitted to prevail.
I say that Sidgwick ascribes view (1) to Butler, because in arguing that
Butler does *not* regard self-love as naturally subordinate to conscience,
Sidgwick writes as follows, quoting words from Butler:

[Butler] even goes so far as to "let it be allowed" that "if there ever should be,
as it is impossible there ever should be, any inconsistence between them,"
conscience would have to give way; since "our ideas of happiness and misery
are of all our ideas the nearest and most important to us . . . [so that] though
virtue or moral rectitude does indeed consist in affection to and pursuit of what

is right and good as such [i.e., in following conscience]; yet, when we sit down in a cool hour, we can neither justify to ourselves this or any other pursuit, till we are convinced that it will be for our happiness, or at least not contrary to it." (*OHE*, 196)

The passage in Butler that Sidgwick is quoting from is both startling and controversial, startling because its author has been proclaiming the supremacy of conscience, controversial because he uses the words "let it be allowed," which have been taken to mean that he does not himself subscribe to the rest of what he says in that passage. But Sidgwick reads it as meaning that Butler does in fact subscribe to what he is allowing here. This is shown by the fact that Sidgwick's next sentence is, "That the ultimate appeal must be to the individual's interest was *similarly* assumed in Shaftesbury's argument [to show that we should be virtuous]," and also by the fact that in *The Methods of Ethics* (119 f.) he quotes the same passage without the words "let it be allowed" as showing that Butler is "prepared to grant" what it says.

Now, I happen to believe that Sidgwick's reading of Butler is correct, though I cannot discuss the matter here. Butler does, I think, hold that, in the *abstract* or in *theory*, self-love is supreme even over conscience, or would and should be if it ever came to a showdown, which he firmly believes God cannot allow to happen. But he does also hold, as Sidgwick points out, that in *practice*, though conscience and reasonable self-love both *have* authority as such, that of conscience must always be obeyed, because in human experience the dictates of conscience are clear and certain, whereas those of self-love or egoistic reason, however certain they may seem, are always merely probable at best. And, says Butler, "the more certain obligation must entirely supersede . . . the less certain." He also says, in the words omitted, that it "destroy[s]" the less certain, so that the obligation of self-interest no longer exists, but in this I think he goes too far (*OHE*, 197).

In just what way, then, is Butler a dualist? He certainly is one in the sense of holding that there are (at least) two faculties or principles in human nature, one egoistic and the other not, each of which has some regulative power and authority as such and independently of the other. As far as I can see, however, he is not one in the further sense of thinking that they are fully coordinate in authority, obligation, and reasonableness, though Sidgwick seems to think he is. Their dictates are not *in principle* equally authoritative, obligatory, or reasonable for Butler; in principle, for him reasonable self-love is supreme. Sidgwick seems to think that a dualist will hold that his two faculties are coordinate in theory, in practice, or in both; but Butler does not hold them to be coordinate in either sense. Thus, by Sidgwick's own account, which I take to be correct, Butler is not as much of a dualist as he appears to think. Butler is an ethical dualist, but only in a rather qualified way. Sidgwick's early modern dualists are not as much on the same beam he is as he judges them to be.

3

I shall not look back at the earlier modern writers discussed by Sidgwick – Grotius, Hobbes, Cudworth, More, Cumberland, and Locke – to see if perchance they came closer to ethical dualism than he thought; nor at Balguy, whom he omits to mention but might have found interesting.[13] Of writers contemporary with or later than those we have reviewed, he first deals with Hutcheson, Hume, and Smith but makes no explicit mention of dualism in connection with them, though they are surely relevant to his generalization about "the most fundamental difference" between the ethical thought of the moderns and that of the Greeks. He thinks of these proponents of what is sometimes called "the ethics of sentiment" as continuing and developing the line of thought first taken by Shaftesbury. Hutcheson he seems to see as recognizing three regulative faculties, the "moral sense," "calm" self-love, and "calm" benevolence, but as linking the first and third and regarding them as "coordinate" and not conflicting, and then arguing that "a true regard for private interest always coincides with the moral sense and benevolence." Given this picture, Sidgwick might well regard Hutcheson as a dualist of some sort.[14]

According to Sidgwick, Hume denies the existence of the sort of general benevolence Hutcheson believes in, and effectively identifies the moral sense with sympathy; for Hume, sympathy is directly or indirectly the "principle of morals" in the sense of being the source of our moral feelings and judgments. But Hume regards it as "contemplative rather than active," as a faculty or principle in us, all right, but hardly a regulative one; he does not ascribe any authority to it: "he does not definitely recognise . . . any 'obligation' to virtue, except that of the agent's interest or happiness" (*OHE*, 211 f.). He does, however, attempt to show that the duties his theory of morals recommends are in the true interest of the individual. In a kind of way, then, Sidgwick seems to see Hume as recognizing two faculties in us, moral sense and self-love, and as regarding at least the latter as authoritative and regulative, much as Shaftesbury did. Something similar is, for him, true of Smith; Smith too is opposed to regarding reason, whether egoistic or universal, as the principle of morals, and again emphasizes sympathy as the source of moral feelings and judgments, though in a different way from Hume – especially feelings and judgments about others, but also, via a "complication" involving the idea of an impartial spectator, those about one's own conduct.

There are also the theological utilitarians, whom Sidgwick treats as forerunners of Bentham and Mill. He barely mentions Berkeley, which I think unfortunate, but says rather more about Gay, Hartley, Tucker, and Paley. Their basic psychology is egoistic and hedonistic, but, with the help of the theory of the association of ideas, they try to show that a moral sense, sympathy, and benevolence, though not innate, as Shaftesbury, Hutcheson, Hume, and Smith held them to be, may all develop and even come to be very strong in us; and with the help of a theological premise or two, they try to establish the principle of utility as the criterion of right and wrong, virtue and vice. Thus, in *The Methods of Ethics* (121) Sidgwick describes Paley as combining "the Universalistic Hedonism that he adopts as a method for determining duties" and "the Egoism which seems to him self-evident as a fundamental principle of rational conduct." We may suppose then that he would have to regard the theological utilitarians, not as dualists, but rather as recognizing only one basic regulative faculty, egoistic reason, much as he thought the ancients did in very different ways.

Sidgwick thinks of intuitionism and utilitarianism as the two new "methods of ethics" emerging in early modern times; of Cudworth, More, Clarke, and Butler as "the Earlier Rational Intuitionists," and Price, Reid, Stewart, Whewell, and others as the "later" ones, coming, as he sees things, after Butler had brought the opposition between intuitionism and utilitarianism into the open in his "Dissertation of the Nature of Virtue" (1736);[15] and of Bentham and Mill as later and non-theological utilitarians. And in *The Methods of Ethics* he is concerned to make out that at least some intuitionists and some utilitarians alike accepted "the principle that it is reasonable for a man to act in the manner most conducive to his own happiness," citing Clarke and Butler on the one side, Berkeley and Bentham on the other. Though he does not say so there, we may assume he would take this to show that members of both of these modern schools were dualists in his sense, recognizing two regulative faculties under the name of reason, conscience and reasonable self-love in the one case, utilitarian reason and egoistic reason in the other. Now, however, we must reemphasize that the principle he mentions – that of rational self-love – can be accepted and used in two rather different ways, which he does not clearly distinguish.

One is to regard promoting or at least not doing what is contrary to one's own good or happiness as one of our (moral) duties, along with being just, telling the truth, doing good to others, and so on, all of them alike being attested to by the same faculty of conscience or non-egoistic reason; or, alternatively, to regard self-interested prudence as one (moral) virtue among others, all approved by the same faculty. The other is to use the principle of rational self-love in answering the question why we should fulfill these duties or pursue and act out these virtues, in other words, to use the principle, not as a way of determining what is duty or what is virtue, or as constituting one duty or one virtue, not as a principle of *morality*, but as a principle of the *rationality* of conduct and character and as the way of showing that we should be moral, that is, do or be what is otherwise determined to be right or virtuous. The latter seems to be the view that Sidgwick ascribes to Butler, Clarke, and Bentham, and it does involve a kind of dualism in his sense of recognizing two regulative faculties, one egoistic and one non-egoistic, whether under the name of reason or not. The former seems to be the view of Price and, as we shall see, of Sidgwick himself. It should be added that one might accept and use the principle in question in *both* of the ways here described; it may be that this was in fact how Butler regarded it.

Coming now to the later intuitionists, it is clear that conscience or intuitive reason (one kind of "universal reason") is for them one of our regulative and governing faculties; the question is whether they recognize another, and my point just now was that their regarding a prudent concern for one's own good or happiness as a duty, obligation, or virtue, if they do, does not show that they do recognize another such faculty. For, as I said earlier, its being a duty or a virtue may itself be a deliverance of conscience or intuitive reason, the faculty they already recognize. Of course, if they think this faculty does declare such prudence to be a duty or virtue, along with others, then they will not be monists about how many duties or virtues there are, not even about basic, primary, or cardinal ones, but they do not thereby recognize a second regulative faculty. This they do only if they regard the question of whether it is rational to be moral as an open question *and* think that it is to be answered, as Shaftesbury, Butler, and Hume do, by showing that being moral is "for our happiness, or at least not contrary to it." And they need not think either of these things.

They do not all even regard "interest, one's own happiness, [as] a manifest obligation," as Sidgwick likes to say Butler does, using the latter's own words; Clarke does not, as we saw, and, as we shall see, others also do not. Price, however, does, as Sidgwick notes, quoting him as writing: "There is not anything of which we have more undeniably an intuitive perception, than that it is 'right to pursue and promote happiness,' whether for ourselves or for others" (*OHE*, 225).[16] Price here recognizes the obligation both of the principle of universal benevolence and of that of rational self-love, but he also acknowledges other duties as intuitive and independent of either of these principles: gratitude, veracity, fulfillment of promises, and justice. But none of this entails his finding two (or more) regulative faculties in us. The question is whether Price thinks that, for it to be rational or reasonable or "obligatory" to do our duty or be virtuous, this must be for our happiness or not contrary to it, and, though Sidgwick does not mention this, Price resolutely insists that that is not so; for him doing what is right is obligatory and rational as such – just because it is self-evident to reason that such and such is right or virtuous it must by the same token be obligatory and rational. For him the question why we *should* be moral is not an open one, as it was for so many of his predecessors, intuitionist or not. He is not recognizing self-love as a principle of rationality apart from conscience and is not a dualist in this sense, though he is a dualist, or rather a pluralist, in believing there are a number of basic duties and that "interest, our own happiness," is one of them. Of course, there is the question of a possible conflict between this duty and the others, but Price does not concern himself about *this* duality; perhaps he just assumes that all basic duties, being self-evidently rational, are also harmonious. In any case, their being in our interest is for him a condition neither of their being duties nor of its being rational always to act on them.

As for Reid, Sidgwick rightly ascribes to him "that duality of governing principles which we have noticed [in Butler]. . . . he considers 'regard for one's good on the whole' . . . and 'sense of duty' . . . as two essentially distinct and coordinate rational principles" (*OHE*, 228). He seems to think that for Reid the relation of the two is the same as it is for Butler but is especially concerned to show that Reid holds that the former principle "cannot reasonably be subordinated even to the moral faculty; in fact, a man who believes that virtue is contrary to his happiness on the whole – which cannot really be the case in a morally governed world – is reduced to the 'miserable dilemma whether it is better to be a fool or a knave' " (*OHE*, 228–9). Actually, the passage Sidgwick is paraphrasing in these two quotations occurs near the end of essay 3 of Reid's *Essays on the Active Powers of the Human Mind* and, with some omissions, runs as follows:

As there are, therefore, two regulating or leading principles in the constitution of man, a regard to what is best for us upon the whole, and a regard to duty, it may be asked, which of these ought to yield if they happen to interfere? . . .

the disinterested love of virtue . . . ought never to stoop to any other [principle]. . . . as to the supposition of an opposition between the two governing principles [there] can be no such opposition [while] the world is under a wise and benevolent [God]. . . . Indeed, if we suppose a man to be an atheist in his belief, and, at the same time, by a wrong judgment, to believe that virtue is contrary to his happiness upon the whole, this case, as Lord Shaftesbury justly observes, is without remedy. It will be impossible for the man to act, so as not to contradict a leading principle of his nature. He must either sacrifice his happiness to virtue, or virtue to happiness; and is reduced to this miserable dilemma, whether it be best to be a fool or a knave.

I take this passage to show, either by express statement or by implication, that for Reid neither of the two principles ought ever to stoop to the other – they are strictly coordinate – so that, if they ever did clearly conflict, then the agent involved could not know what to do and would be faced with a dilemma without any remedy. Reid goes on to remark, "This shows the strong connection between morality and the principles of natural religion." However, if *this* is Reid's view, then he not only is a dualist in Sidgwick's sense but is more of a dualist than Butler is, since, as we saw, Butler does not really hold that the two governing principles referred to are strictly coordinate in this way. Reid's dualism is more like Sidgwick's than Butler's.

Is Reid also holding self-love to be a moral duty? It seems that he is, for, as Sidgwick notes, Reid lists the principle of rational self-love as one of his axioms of duty. Sidgwick comments that Reid's doing this "seems rather inconsistent with [his] distinct separation of the 'moral faculty' from 'self-love' " (*OHE*, 230). But there really is no inconsistency here, for, as I pointed out, one may hold that prudent self-love is itself one of the duties witnessed to by the moral faculty of conscience, as Reid seems to be doing. Then he is accepting rational self-love *both* as a duty recognized by conscience and as a principle of rationality coordinate with conscience, which is possible, but he is not implying that self-love is somehow a *moral* faculty too, even though he regards it as also a *regulative* one. I should also note that, as far as I am aware, Reid does not suggest that we should obey conscience because doing so is for our own good, though he does think we should pursue our own good because conscience tells us to. In this sense, although he holds that his two governing faculties are equal, he seems to believe that the moral faculty is "more equal" than self-love. Even so, he does insist that they "are very strictly connected, lead to the same course of conduct [under God's administration], and cooperate with each other" (end of essay 3, chap. 1).

Sidgwick speaks well of Stewart but could have done better by him, for Stewart insists more than Sidgwick recognizes that there are two "rational and governing principles of action" in us, self-love (or regard to interest or one's own happiness) and "the moral faculty" or conscience, both under the name of reason. Also like Reid, when he comes to listing our moral duties to ourselves, he includes as one "*a steady regard . . . to the happiness and perfection of our own nature, and a diligent study of the means by which these ends may be attained*"[17] – a point Sidgwick fails to notice. More clearly than his predecessors, he states that "The various duties which have been considered [including a steady regard to our own good] all [are] *obligatory* on rational and voluntary agents; and they are all enjoined by the same authority, – the *authority of conscience.*" As one would expect, then, he not only regards the principle of rational self-love as a part of the moral law but also uses it to answer the question why we should live by that law, writing for instance that "these two principles [sense of duty and rational self-love], in general, lead to the same course of action, and we have every reason to believe, that if our knowledge of the universe were more extensive, they would be found to do so, in all instances whatever." And again that "I never could conceive that an all-wise, just, and benevolent Being would . . . make that to be our duty which is not, upon the whole, and generally speaking, (even without the consideration of a future state) our interest likewise." He does, however, also observe that different duties may appear to us to conflict and that the duty to be prudent may seem sometimes to conflict with our other duties, though he comments only that then it is difficult to tell what we should do – and that "it may not be easy to say, whether *all* of these obligations may not sometimes be superseded by paramount considerations of *utility.*" At least he does not think that all of the others, including that of a regard for the general welfare, may always be superseded by that of a regard for one's own good, even though he does imply that living by the moral law could not be rational if it were contrary to our happiness.

Sidgwick interprets Whewell's general moral view as differing "from that of his Scotch predecessors chiefly in a point where we may trace the influence of Kant – viz., in his rejection of self-love as an independent rational and governing principle, and his consequent refusal to admit happiness, apart from duty, as a reasonable end for the individual" (*OHE*, 233), and so as leaving "the moral reason . . . in sole supremacy," as we saw Price did (*OHE*, 233). Here Sidgwick contradicts his own later account of Kant and perhaps also misrepresents Whewell. The trouble, again, is that Sidgwick does not distinguish clearly between saying that seeking one's own happiness is a duty and saying that it is a reasonable end for one to have. Actually, as will be indicated later, for him these two statements come to the same thing; but it does not follow that this is true for others. Kant and Whewell do deny that one has a duty or obligation to seek one's own happiness, but it does not follow they deny that it is reasonable for one to pursue one's own happiness, or even that it would be unreasonable for one to be moral if that were contrary to one's happiness. Kant did not make the latter denials, as Sidgwick later notes (and as we shall soon see), and, so far as I can tell, neither did Whewell. Sidgwick shows only that Whewell did not regard a prudent concern for one's own happiness as a duty. But it is possible to hold that what is morally a duty and what it is rational to do or be are two different things; Sidgwick did not think so, nor did Price, but Clarke, Shaftesbury, Butler, and Kant did, and Reid may have.

Sidgwick goes on to deal with the later utilitarians, Bentham and J. S. Mill, before he takes up the Continental moral philosophers. As we saw, he cites Bentham as accepting the principle that it is reasonable to seek one's own happiness. As a utilitarian, however, Bentham insists that the principle of general utility should be our sole criterion of moral right and wrong, virtue and vice. But, though Sidgwick does not discuss this question, it does not follow that Bentham recognizes two regulative faculties in human nature. This depends on what faculty besides egoistic reason Bentham believes to be involved in our assenting to and acting on the principle of utility, and, given his egoistic and hedonist psychology, it is not clear that any other faculty, say "conscience" or "universal reason," is basically involved. Indeed, Sidgwick thinks that in the end Bentham's real doctrine was that "the constantly proper end of action" for any individual must be his or her "real greatest happiness," even though he also held that the greatest happiness of the greatest number is the "standard" of what is right or wrong in morals, so that he had to assume, as an empirical truth, that the conduct most conducive to general happiness *always* coincides with that which conduces most to the happiness of the agent, since he refused to rely on any theological premise (*OHE*, 244). Bentham is not an egoist in his method of ethics, as Sidgwick thinks the Greeks were, but he is not a dualist in his psychology either, as Sidgwick *says* the moderns are; he is a modern in one way but not in the other. And, of course, his psychology is largely a modern development.

Presumably to contrast Mill with Bentham, Sidgwick writes that Mill advocated "an unqualified subordination of private to general happiness" (*OHE*, 245). This is true of Mill's view about what is *moral*, but it need not therefore represent his view about what is rational in conduct. In fact, however, Mill does not advance self-interest as one of his considerations influencing our intellects to give their assent to the principle of utility in the way Bentham implicitly does, though he presumably does regard self-love as a "regulative faculty" in some sense. He certainly does not hold, as Sidgwick does, that self-love has a moral position comparable to that of a concern for the general happiness. In fact, rather than contending that the latter concern is as such authoritative, obligatory, or reasonable, he only tries to show that there are or may be sanctions or motives supporting it – external sanctions like praise and blame and especially internal ones like our social feelings and the feelings of conscience. These feelings for him are not innate, given his basic hedonistic and egoistic psychology, but they may be developed in us by conditioning, the association of ideas, and education in such a way as to lead us to become good utilitarians. They may even come to predominate over self-love in our lives. There is for Mill no *basic* duality in our psychology – basically a kind of egoism is supreme – but nonegoistic "faculties" do arise in us and may by education be made so strong that it is not necessary to convince us that living by the principle of utility is for our happiness or at least not contrary to it in order to justify that pursuit to us, cool hour or not. In a kind of way, we may thus end up having two regulative faculties in us after all, one egoistic and one not, with the latter being the stronger – though Mill would not want to call them "faculties." If this be dualism, Mill might like to make the most of it!

Of the remaining British and Continental authors treated by Sidgwick, I shall deal only with Kant, mainly because of his influence on Sidgwick's own ethical dualism, to which we shall come in Section 4. As we saw in connection with Whewell, Kant does not accept the principle of pursuing one's own happiness as a principle of duty; for him the only self-respecting duties one has are to respect one's humanity and to perfect oneself morally and otherwise.[18] Like so many of our previous writers, he also denies that self-love could *be* the moral faculty, for then moral imperatives would all be "hypothetical"; for Kant the moral faculty is a faculty of "categorical" imperatives, namely, pure practical reason, which is not egoistic but universalizing. Thus, in a sense, he recognizes two faculties in us relating to conduct and is a dualist. Yet he does not actually think that the desire for one's own happiness should in any way regulate or govern one's conduct; the moral faculty alone should do that. In this sense Kant is not a dualist. Moreover, like Clarke, Butler, Price, and Reid, he insists that doing one's duty is obligatory and rational as such, his ground being that our duties follow from the concept of a free rational being. This makes it look as if, like Price, Kant in no way recognizes self-interest as a principle of the rationality of conduct, as the others mentioned do, which also suggests that Kant is not a dualist in Sidgwick's sense. But this look is deceiving. As Sidgwick points out,

Kant recognizes by implication the reasonableness of the individual's regard for his private happiness. . . . Though duty is to be done for duty's sake, and not as a means to the agent's happiness, still, Kant holds, we could not rationally do it if we did not hope thereby to attain happiness [because we will have made ourselves worthy of it]. And Kant holds that we are bound by reason to conceive ourselves as necessarily belonging to [a moral world in which happiness is duly proportioned to merit]. . . . We must therefore postulate [such a world]: and this involves a belief in God and a hereafter. . . . I cannot theoretically know these beliefs to be true, but I must postulate them for practice, in order to fulfill rationally what I recognise as "categorically" commanded by the Practical Reason. (*OHE*, 276)

My duty is still categorical, and I am to do it as such, but I may hope and, to be rational in doing it, must believe that happiness will be its reward. In this way, Kant is after all recognizing two principles of rationality, though not quite in the way that Clarke, Butler, and Reid had, or that Sidgwick does. There is no suggestion in Kant that self-interest is a principle of morality or that it is the supreme principle of rationality; also, he does not appeal to it by trying to show that being moral *is* in our interest. For him being moral is rational as such and therefore must be rewarded with the happiness it deserves, and we are rational (in a further sense) if and only if, besides being moral, we act with the expectation that it will actually be so rewarded *because* it *deserves* to be. He does bring one's own happiness in again through the back door after ejecting it through the front, as the poet Heine remarked, but only by way of the principle that the morally good will deserves to be happy, not by way of arguing that it *will* be happy.

4

So much for Sidgwick *on* the history of ethical dualism. What of his own place *in* that history? To answer we must look at *The Methods of Ethics* rather than the *Outlines of the History of Ethics*, though we need not expound his own ethical theory as a whole. I shall be as brief as possible, sticking to what is relevant here, and also somewhat dogmatic. We have seen that there are rather different kinds of ethical dualism, more than are dreamed of in Sidgwick's history of modern ethics, and also that his predecessors, including even Butler, were less dualistic than he thought. I have a feeling Sidgwick thought not only that there had been progress from ancient to modern ethical theory, in the rise of non-egoism and dualism, and within modern theory up to Butler and Kant, but also that the modern view did not really work itself clear until he wrote *The Methods of Ethics*. What, then, was his own dualism like? Let us look first at his autobiographical account of its development. In it he writes as follows:

> it is surely the business of Ethical Philosophy to find and make explicit the rational ground of such action [the subordination of self-interest to duty]. I therefore set myself to examine methodically the relation of Interest to Duty. ... This investigation led me to feel very strongly *this* opposition, rather than that ... between so-called Intuitions ... and Hedonism. ... Hence the arrangement of my book. ... I put to [Mill] in my mind the dilemma: – Either it is for my own happiness or it is not. If not, why [should I do it]? ... I must somehow *see* that it was right for me to sacrifice my happiness for the good of the whole of which I am a part. ... [I] concluded that no complete solution of the conflict between my happiness and the general happiness was possible on the basis of mundane experience. (*ME*, xvi)

In this state of mind, he says, he reread Kant and Butler, deciding that Kant "did not settle finally the subordination of Self-Interest to Duty," and that Butler had come closer than he had thought to recognizing "a 'Dualism of the Governing Faculty' – or as I prefer to say 'Dualism of the Practical Reason.' " Then he ends the relevant part of his story by indicating that he found both ethical egoism and utilitarianism to have "an Intuitional basis" of self-evidence and adding,

> There was indeed a fundamental opposition between the individual's interest and either morality [intuitionism and utilitarianism] which I could not solve by any method I had yet found trustworthy, without the assumption of the moral government of the world: so far I agreed with both Butler and Kant. (*ME*, xx)

Notice that in these passages Sidgwick characterizes the opposition that troubled him in two ways: as an opposition between duty and self-interest and as a conflict between my happiness and the general happiness – about this, more later. In any case, it is not correct to say, using the terms employed in most of this chapter, that in *The Methods of Ethics* Sidgwick is a dualist in the sense of being one who finds that there are two basic governing faculties (or "principles" in the Butler – Hume sense) in the nature of man, as he suggests here and also in the preface to his second edition (*ME2*, xi). His view is "materially" less like Butler's than he represents it as being. Rather, he is a dualist only in that he finds there to be two ethical first principles in a *second* sense of "principle." In this sense, a basic principle is a general statement to the effect that a certain kind of consideration is an "ultimate reason" for acting or abstaining, or, alternatively, that a certain property of actions is an ultimate right-or-wrong-*making* one.[19] Once again, for Sidgwick, what is (ethically or morally) right equals what is ultimately rational to do equals what is ultimately the practically right thing to do. He holds then that there are two basic principles of ethics, morality, rationality, or practice, two ultimate reasons for action – the principle of utility or rational benevolence and that of rational egoism, both stated in hedonistic terms, that is, that both conduciveness to one's own happiness on the whole and conduciveness to the greatest general happiness are ultimate right-making or rational-making properties. Moreover, for him, the two principles are coordinate; they are not coordinate in *practice* – in practice Sidgwick opts for the "method" of utilitarianism rather than that of egoism – but they are coordinate in *theory* or, in a third sense of "principle," in *principle*, as the two "faculties" of previous dualists were not, excepting maybe Price and Kant but *not* Butler (as we have seen). For Sidgwick, the two principles are both authoritative, obligatory, and rational as such, independently of one another, and equally so; though he does not put it thus, each of them is a *sufficient condition* of a piece of conduct's or a life's being right or rational – at least until the other arrives on the scene. This is so because, according to Sidgwick, both are either self-evident or based on a "self-evident element," that is, seen by practical reason or conscience to be necessarily true and hence attested to by the same faculty of intuitive reason. In this sense, his ethical system is dualistic as to basic ethical principles rather than as to basic psychological faculties; there are for him two principles that should regulate and govern our conduct, at least in theory, though there is only one authoritative faculty. One can, of course, still say that it follows there are two uses of (nonintuitive) reason for Sidgwick, one in the application of the principle of hedonistic egoism and another in the application of that of hedonistic utilitarianism – or, respectively, "Egoistic Reason" and "Utilitarian Reason," only without capital letters.

Is there a "contradiction" in Sidgwick's system, as he alleges there is in Clarke's?[20] I think the answer (and a similar answer can be given for Clarke) is that there is a contradiction only if Sidgwick's two principles may and do conflict in practice. There is no problem if they never call for different courses of conduct. What makes Sidgwick's dualism so worrying for him, as those of his predecessors were not for them, is the fact that his two principles might conflict in practice, and *if* they did so in the final analysis (i.e., if they could be *known* to conflict), then *neither* of them could take priority over the other – we simply could not tell what we should do – plus, of course, the further fact that Sidgwick does not have Butler's assurance on other grounds of God's moral government of the world and cannot accept Kant's way of justifying postulating such a world. For Sidgwick the *only* grounds for any such belief are (1) his being simply unable to see any other way of answering the question, "What if we knew the two principles actually conflict?" and (2) his conviction that we cannot know on other grounds either that there is no such God or that the two principles do or will ever actually call for different ways of acting.

Sidgwick sometimes talks as if his two principles are reasonable from different points of view. If this were so, there could be no contradiction between them as such. Then the issue would be over which point of view we should take, and the trouble would be that there would be no way of answering *this* question. Actually, however, his speaking in this way shows up another rare unclarity in his usually clear mind. For his real view, as I understand it, is that the two principles are equally reasonable and valid from the same point of view – that of reason intuiting "self-evident elements." That is the crucial point that sends Sidgwick up the wall. Note, however, that the dilemma is not between duty and interest, as he and his interpreters sometimes represent it, since for Sidgwick both principles are at once principles of duty and of rationality. Hence the question "Why be moral or do what is right or duty?" cannot make sense for him; it is the same thing as asking "Is it rational to be rational?"[21] On his own view of ethics, Sidgwick logically cannot, and need not, argue that we should be virtuous or do our duty because this is for our own happiness or at least not contrary to it, for he does not distinguish between morality or virtue and what is rational, as Butler and others did.

This fact reflects the further point that there are, at least in modern times, two ways of conceiving of ethics. I do not mean the two ways distinguished by Sidgwick in *The Methods of Ethics* (2–4) when he writes, "Ethics is sometimes considered as an investigation of the true moral laws or rational precepts of conduct; sometimes as an inquiry into the nature of the Ultimate End of reasonable human action – the Good or 'True Good' of man – and the method of attaining it."[22] The first of these conceptions fits modern ethical systems pretty well, he thinks, but the second, though it fits ancient ones nicely, cannot be applied, "without straining," to modern intuitionist systems; hence, he proposes his own definition as covering both ancient and modern views of ethics, namely, "as the science or study of what is right or ought to be, as far as this depends upon the voluntary action of individuals" (*ME*, 4). As I said, he is thinking here in terms of an equation of the ethically or morally right or good with that which it is ultimately rational to do or be. However, in a deeper sense, *this* is itself only one way of conceiving of ethics, one which I think Sidgwick took over from the Greeks, and in modern times, both before and after Sidgwick, there has been a contrasting conception of which Sidgwick is not sufficiently aware,[23] one illustrated by Shaftesbury, Clarke, Butler, Hume, Reid, and others, perhaps by Kant, though perhaps not by Price. This other modern way of conceiving of ethics distinguishes between the ethical or moral *and* the ultimately practical or rational, even if it regards being ethical or moral as in fact ultimately practical or rational; and it insists that the questions "Why be moral?" and "Is it rational to be moral?" are open and sensible, even if the answer is "Yes." Its proponents may then identify the rational with what is ultimately for one's own good, happiness, or self-interest, as Shaftesbury, Butler, and others did; or they may argue that being rational need not and should not be conceived in such egoistic terms, since psychological egoism is false. For example, they might contend that the good or rational life is not the life that gives one the greatest balance of goods over evils but the life one would desire if one were clearheaded and logical and knew all of what is relevant; Sidgwick himself suggests such a view in *The Methods of Ethics*, book 1, chapter 9. The life one would desire under these conditions might not be the one that gives oneself the best score in terms of experienced good and evil, happiness and unhappiness. We may not be as egoistic as all that.

In different ways, the second line of thought seems to have been taken, after Sidgwick, by, for example, Hare, Brandt, Warnock, and Williams. I have defended it myself. This view would still involve a kind of dualism of practical reason, between the ethical or moral and the rational or nonmorally practical, a dualism not between two basic ethical principles or principles of rationality, as Sidgwick's is, but between the principle(s) of ethics (perhaps including one enjoining a prudential concern for one's own happiness, but perhaps not) and the principle(s) of rationality. Its proponents too must therefore deal somehow with the question of actual or possible conflicts between the two principles or sets of principles, as Susan Wolf has recently insisted and as Nagel has attempted to do. And one way of dealing with it, if one doubts the possibility of establishing a harmony of what is moral and what is rational, as well as the possibility of proving an ultimate disharmony between them, is to postulate such a harmony, whether this involves a theological belief or not.[24]

The distinction just made between two modern conceptions of ethics or moral philosophy crosses with that made by Sidgwick in the sentence last quoted (*ME*, 2–4), for proponents of either of the ways of viewing ethics that I distinguish may adopt either of his. Also, those adopting my first way may either be egoists and monists, as Sidgwick thinks the ancients were, or non-egoists and dualists, as Sidgwick is. Those espousing the second will be dualists at least in the sense indicated. Here my discussion of Sidgwick's ethical dualism and its place in the history of ethics must end, cryptic as it is. Perhaps, however, the preceding paragraphs may suffice to show that Sidgwick's type of dualism is not actually that which prevailed in earlier modern moral philosophy or that which prevails now, and also that while his way of posing his dilemma is not as final as he thought, resting as it does on a belief that both horns involve self-evident elements, something like that dilemma is still before us, as it was not before the Greeks. Sidgwick's grasp of the history of ethics was not faultless, as we have seen, but it was nevertheless remarkable, and one cannot help but wish that, like Moses, he could have carried his story beyond his own lifetime.

Notes

1 See "Sidgwick and the Dualism of Practical Reason," in *Perspectives on Morality*, ed. K. E. Goodpaster (Notre Dame: University of Notre Dame Press, 1976), pp. 193–207.

2 For my earliest interpretation, see my article on Sidgwick in *The Encyclopedia of Morals*, ed. Vergilius Ferm (New York: Philosophical Library, 1956), pp. 539–44.

3 In *Social Theory and Practice* 9 (1983): 165–97.

4 On this footnote, see Frankena, "*The Methods of Ethics*, Edition 7, Page 92, Note 1," unpublished manuscript.

5 Perfectionism is the view that one's end should be one's own perfection, excellence, or virtue, moral and/or nonmoral.

6 See *OHE*, 184, 201–18.

7 My review of his discussions of authors in sections 2 and 3 is an amalgam of what Sidgwick says in *OHE* and of material of my own.

8 Quoted from *British Moralists, 1650–1800*, ed. D. D. Raphael (Oxford: Oxford University Press [Clarendon Press], 1969), 1:192, 196, 202.

9 For Clarke, see ibid., 1:216; for Sidgwick, see *OHE*, 183.

10 Clarke does, however, seem to think a kind of obligation is connected with the latter, but not one of the "truest and formallest" kind (Raphael, *British Moralists*, 1:202).

11 Ibid., 1:257.

12 But see *OHE*, 198 f. For crucial passages from Butler used by Sidgwick in what follows, see Raphael, *British Moralists*, 1:331, 373.

13 For Balguy, see Raphael, *British Moralists*, 1:436–61.

14 Here in *OHE* Sidgwick seems to rely on Hutcheson's later *System of Moral Philosophy*. In the earlier *Illustrations upon the Moral Sense* Hutcheson does

not seem to regard the moral sense as regulative. See Raphael, *British Moralists*, 1:305 f.

15 See Raphael, *British Moralists*, 1:378–86.

16 Cf. ibid., 2:179.

17 Dugald Stewart, *The Philosophy of the Active and Moral Powers of Man*, 8th ed. (Boston: Phillips, Sampson, 1859). My quotations come from pp. 384, 424, 123, 433 f., and one from his *Outlines of Moral Philosophy* (Edinburgh: Constable, 1818), pp. 177 f.

18 He also holds that these self-respecting duties are determined in the same way (or by the same faculty) as our other-regarding duties are.

19 Here and in what follows I am influenced by J. B. Schneewind, *Sidgwick's Ethics and Victorian Moral Philosophy* (Oxford: Oxford University Press [Clarendon Press], 1977), esp. pp. 196, 305.

20 C. D. Broad thinks there is; see *Five Types of Ethical Theory* (New York: Harcourt, Brace, 1930), pp. 245, 253.

21 See Frankena, "Sidgwick and the Dualism of Practical Reason."

22 Cf. *OHE*, chap. 1.

23 But cf. Schneewind, *Sidgwick's Ethics*, p. 228.

24 In connection with this paragraph, see, e.g., Bernard Williams, *Ethics and the Limits of Philosophy* (Cambridge, MA: Harvard University Press, 1985), chap. 1; Thomas Nagel, *The View from Nowhere* (New York: Oxford University Press, 1986), chap. 10; Frankena, *Thinking about Morality* (Ann Arbor: University of Michigan Press, 1980), lectures 1 and 3. Nagel refers to Susan Wolf's articles, "Moral Saints," *Journal of Philosophy* 79 (1982), and "The Superficiality of Duty," unpublished manuscript.

7

Sidgwick and the rationale for rational egoism

DAVID O. BRINK

One of Sidgwick's concerns in *The Methods of Ethics* is with the structure of individual rationality. Theories of rationality are concerned with the way in which benefits and harms rationally ought to be allocated *among persons* and *across time*.

Theories might be classified by what they say about *whose* welfare matters. *Person-neutral* theories say that it is of no rational significance on whom a benefit or harm falls; an agent has reason to promote value, whether this value accrues to the agent or others. By contrast, a *Person-relative* theory insists that whom a benefit or harm befalls is of great rational significance to the agent. The most common form of person relativity is *agent relativity*; a theory is agent-relative if it insists that a benefit or harm must befall the agent to be of rational significance to her.

Theories of rationality might also be classified by their attitudes toward the *temporal location* of benefits and harms. A theory is *temporally neutral* if it is indifferent when benefits and harms occur; it is *temporally relative* if the temporal location of a benefit or harm affects its rational significance.

Sidgwick is a friend of *rational egoism*, although, as we shall see

I read some version of this material at Case Western Reserve University, Stanford University, University of California at Irvine, Massachusetts Institute of Technology, University of Iowa, Middlebury College, and the Sidgwick conference at the University of Chicago. I would like to thank audiences on those occasions for helpful discussion of these issues and especially my commentators at the Sidgwick conference, Stephen Darwall and John Deigh, for their probing comments. I would also like to thank Ann Bumpus, Philip Gasper, Diane Jeske, Julius Moravcsik, Georges Rey, Jack Sayers, Jerome Schneewind, Bart Schultz, Judy Thomson, and my colleagues in a Cambridge-area moral psychology study group for their comments on this material. Special thanks go to Terry Irwin, Derek Parfit, Sydney Shoemaker, Alan Sidelle, and Jennifer Whiting. Final revisions were made during a fellowship at the Center for Advanced Study in the Behavioral Sciences that was funded by an Old Dominion Fellowship from the Massachusetts Institute of Technology and by grants from the National Endowment for the Humanities (#RA–20037–88) and the Andrew W. Mellon Foundation. I would like to thank these institutions for their support.

(Section 1), there are different interpretations of the constancy of his friendship. Rational egoism claims that an agent has reason to do x just in case, and insofar as, x is in *her own* interest, welfare, or happiness. As such, rational egoism is agent-relative; a benefit or harm must affect the agent in some way to be of rational significance to her. Egoism's agent relativity represents a natural way of articulating the common thought that I have special reason to be concerned about my own life and welfare. Rational egoism is also temporally neutral; it says that the temporal location of a benefit or harm is, by itself, of no rational significance. Temporal neutrality represents a natural articulation of the common belief that I rationally ought to be just as concerned about future goods and harms as about present ones (of equal magnitude) and that preference for a smaller present good at the cost of a greater future good is a sign of irrationality. Rational egoism is, therefore, a *hybrid* theory of rationality: It is temporally neutral but agent-relative.

Egoism can be contrasted with two *purebred* theories of rationality: a fully neutral theory and a fully relative theory. We might call the fully neutral theory *rational altruism* or, following Sidgwick, *rational benevolence*; though he does not name the fully relative theory, we might naturally call it *presentism*. Rational benevolence is both temporally neutral and person-neutral; it holds that an agent has reason to do x just in case, and insofar as, x is valuable, regardless of whom the value accrues to or when it occurs. Presentism, on the other hand, is both temporally relative and agent-relative; it holds that an agent has reason to do x just in case, and insofar as, x is in his own present interest.

Rational egoism and its rivals are defined *structurally*; they are defined by their attitudes to the distribution of benefits and harms across time and among persons. These theories do not themselves say what constitutes a benefit or harm; this is the task of a theory of value or welfare. Different versions of egoism, altruism, and presentism result from different substantive theories of value or welfare.

Subjective theories of welfare claim that an individual's good consists in or depends importantly upon certain of her psychological states. *Hedonism* and *desire-satisfaction* theories are the most familiar forms of subjectivism.

Hedonism says that the good *is* a psychological state; it identifies a person's interest with her having pleasurable mental states or sensations. We might distinguish two different versions of hedonism, corresponding to two different theories of pleasure and pain: *simple* hedonism and *preference* hedonism. According to simple hedonism, pleasure is a simple qualitative mental state or sensation that varies only in duration and intensity, and the same is true of pain. According to preference hedonism, pleasure and pain are *functional* states: Pleasure is a mental state or sensation such that the person having it wants it to continue and will, ceteris paribus, undertake actions so as to prolong it, whereas pain is a mental state or sensation such that the person having it wants it to cease and will, ceteris paribus, take action to make it stop. There is no apparent reason why mental states having one of these functional profiles need be qualitatively similar or have the same feel.

Desire-satisfaction theories make the individual's good *depend upon* her psychological states; they claim that something is in an individual's interest just in case it would satisfy her actual desires or her counter-factual desires (i.e., the desires that she would have in some preferred epistemic state).

By contrast, *objective* theories of welfare identify a person's interests with certain character traits, the exercise of certain capacities, and the possession of certain relationships to others and the world and claim that these things are good for the agent independently of their producing pleasure for her or being the object of her desire.

Sidgwick, of course, rather brusquely dismisses objective theories of value or happiness as too indefinite to be part of a systematic ethical theory (*ME*, 90–3, 95). Instead, he embraces hedonism, in particular, preference hedonism (*ME*, 42–3, 46, 127, 131, 402); hedonism informs both his views about rationality and his views about morality.[1] But, though I shall at some points notice the difference his hedonism makes to his account of rational egoism, I shall concentrate on the issues Sidgwick raises about egoism itself; I shall not restrict discussion, as he does, to hedonistic versions of egoism or its rivals.

Egoism is a hybrid theory; it is neutral with respect to time but relative with respect to persons. As we shall see, this hybrid aspect of egoism may seem arbitrary. It may seem that we should distribute goods and harms by the same principles both within lives and across lives. Sidgwick raises this parity theme as a possible difficulty for egoism (*ME*, 418–19). More recently, Thomas Nagel and Derek Parfit have raised similar parity objections to egoism.[2] In *The Possibility of Altruism* (*PA*) Nagel argues from rationality's temporal neutrality to its person neutrality; he rejects egoism as part of a defense of full neutrality. In *Reasons and Persons* (*RP*) Parfit's preferred strategy is to argue from rationality's agent relativity to its temporal relativity; he rejects egoism as part of a defense of full relativity. Both Nagel and Parfit think we are entitled to reject egoism, because the egoist cannot sensibly deny the parity of time and person in a theory of rationality.

Though Sidgwick was aware of the parity argument, I think he sees the limits of the parity argument and suggests an egoist rationale for denying the parity of time and person. That rationale needs to be developed further than Sidgwick explicitly develops it, but its pedigree is certainly Sidgwickian.

1. The dualism of practical reason

Before discussing the parity issue, I need to situate my focus on rational egoism and its rivals within Sidgwick's larger aims. Egoism, of course, is one of Sidgwick's three methods of ethics. And as is well known, Sidgwick concludes *The Methods of Ethics*, somewhat reluctantly, by accepting the "dualism of practical reason." The dualism of practical reason results from the fact that two of Sidgwick's methods – an agent-relative theory that he calls, alternately, "rational egoism," "ethical egoism," or "prudence" and a person-neutral theory that he calls, alternately, "utilitarianism" or "rational benevolence" – are supposed to be equally defensible. As we have seen, the agent-relative method holds that an agent should promote *her own* happiness, whereas the person-neutral method holds that she should promote *total human* (or sentient) happiness. Sidgwick, following Butler, thinks that the dictates of disinterested benevolence and enlightened self-interest coincide to a great extent (*ME*, 9–10, 84–5, 162–75, 499–509).[3] Nonetheless, the coincidence of the two methods is imperfect, and they justify actions in terms of different properties of those actions. The incompatibility of the two methods, each of which Sidgwick takes to be self-evident, is what produces the dualism of practical reason.

The fact that Sidgwick freely alternates among different labels for the agent-relative and person-neutral methods and does not explicitly distinguish between theories of moral obligation and theories of rationality or reasons for action reflects his *internalist* sympathies. These facts and his explicit remarks about what a method of ethics is reflect the internalist assumption that moral theories just are theories about what an agent has reason to do (*ME*, 6, 23, 78, 83, 174). One consequence of this internalist assumption is that the rational justification of moral considerations is not an open question. It is not possible to think that a method of ethics is true and still ask whether there is reason to be moral, for the true method of ethics just states what it is ultimately reasonable to do. On this internalist reading, Sidgwick *identifies* rational egoism with ethical egoism and utilitarianism with rational benevolence and construes the dualism of practical reason as conflict between *competing* moral theories or theories of reasons for action.

An *externalist*, by contrast, denies this internal or conceptual connection between morality and rationality; externalism distinguishes between moral theories and theories of rationality or reasons for action and insists that the rational justification of moral demands depends upon the nature and content of moral norms, the nature and content of the norms of rationality, and various natural facts about the agent whose conduct is in question. An externalist will naturally think of moral theories as attempts to systematize and make coherent our considered beliefs, especially our considered moral beliefs, and will naturally think of theories of rationality as attempts to state the conditions under which an agent's conduct is rationally justified or reasonable. The norms of rationality, for the externalist, typically have a kind of primacy in practical reasoning; they are the norms that regulate practical reasoning and with which other norms (e.g., moral norms) must agree if these other norms are to deserve an important role in practical reasoning. Thus, externalism implies that we could first (defeasibly) identify the correct moral theory (e.g., the theory that best systematizes our considered moral beliefs) and then ask whether an agent has reason to comply with the moral obligations recognized by that theory.

An externalist, therefore, would want to distinguish fairly sharply between theories of morality and theories of rationality. In particular, the externalist would not identify rational egoism with ethical egoism or rational benevolence with utilitarianism; though the members of each pair are structurally isomorphic, they apply to different subjects. The first member in each pair represents a claim about the nature of reasons for action, whereas the second member of each pair represents a claim about the nature of moral obligation; and it is not the case that a member of one pair entails the other member of that pair. This means that an account of the structure of rationality does not require the same structure for morality. So, for instance, an agent-relative account of rationality is compatible with a person-neutral account of morality; one can think that utilitarianism is the right account of moral obligation while thinking that rational egoism is the right account of the conditions under which an agent has reasons for action. One would then think that the issue about the rational authority of morality is resolved by seeing the extent to which utilitarian moral demands can be shown to be defensible to a rational egoist, and this would require further articulation of the demands of both utilitarianism and enlightened self-interest.

These claims make possible an externalist reading of the dualism of practical reason. On this reading, Sidgwick implicitly considers both rationality and morality and defends structurally different theories for the two domains. In particular, he defends the agent-relative rational egoism in preference to the person-neutral rational benevolence; but he also defends a person-neutral moral theory – utilitarianism – in preference to the agent-relative ethical egoism. The dualism of practical reason, on this reading, represents the conflict between an agent-relative theory of rationality and a person-neutral theory of morality, in particular, the problem of whether and, if so, how utilitarian moral demands can be shown to be rationally authoritative on rational egoist grounds. The externalist reading requires us to think of the agent-relative component of the dualism as rational egoism, rather than ethical egoism, and of the person-neutral component of the dualism as utilitarianism, rather than rational benevolence. It asks us to see the dualism, therefore, not as a conflict between competing conceptions of the same subject matter but as raising the issue about the rational authority of morality.

Sidgwick is ambivalent between the internalist and externalist interpretations of the dualism of practical reasoning. The facts that he freely alternates between these different labels for the agent-relative and person-neutral theories, that he regards them both as methods of ethics, and that he often characterizes a method of ethics as an account of what is ultimately reasonable to do are evidence for the internalist reading (cf. *ME*, 6, 23, 78, 83, 174). However, there is what I regard as philosophically more significant evidence for the externalist reading. Very briefly, the main evidence is this.[4]

First, the structure of much of the argument of *The Methods of Ethics* – in particular, Sidgwick's argument that common-sense morality is unconsciously and inchoately utilitarian – reflects the externalist conception of a method of ethics as an attempt to provide an account of morality that will systematize our considered moral beliefs (*ME*, 14, 77). More specifically, Sidgwick's epistemological commitment to *philosophical intuitionism* requires him to hold that first principles that systematize our moral beliefs are justified if and only if they meet four tests of self-evidence: They must be (1) clear and precise, (2) evident upon reflection, (3) mutually consistent, and (4) generally acceptable (*ME* 338–42).[5] This conception of a method of ethics need not imply that moral obligations, as recognized by the theory that meets these conditions, always supply agents with reasons for action.[6]

Second, Sidgwick does often think of the dualism as raising the issue of the rational authority of morality (cf. *ME*, xv–xxi, 162–75, 496–509). Here he is thinking of the dualism as reflecting the tension between a utilitarian account of *duty* and an egoist account of *interest* or rationality, not as a conflict between competing conceptions of duty (or rationality). This reading is reflected in a passage in Sidgwick's short intellectual autobiography contained in the preface to the sixth edition of *The Methods of Ethics*.

I therefore set myself to examine methodically the relation between Interest and Duty.... Let us suppose that my own Interest is paramount. What really is my Interest, how far can acts conducive to it be known, how far does the result correspond with Duty (or Wellbeing of Mankind)? (*ME*6, xvi)

Only the externalist reading of the dualism allows us to understand it as discussing the rational authority of moral requirements.[7]

Third, Sidgwick's epistemological claims support the externalist reading of the dualism of practical reason. He claims that the agent-relative and person-neutral methods are each the object of a fundamental intuition; that is, each is self-evident (*ME*, 382, 391). And, as we have seen, one of the conditions of self-evident propositions is that they be mutually consistent (*ME*, 341). But, on the internalist reading, the two methods seem not to be mutually consistent; they make incompatible claims about the same subject matter. This is clearly true if, as Sidgwick believes, the two methods are extensionally inequivalent (*ME*, 175, 503). But it would also be true even if the two methods were extensionally equivalent (i.e., even if their coincidence was perfect), because, on the internalist reading, they cite different properties of actions as the on-balance right-making property.[8] These are not consequences of the externalist reading. For on that reading, the two methods are not competing theories of the same subject matter; rather, the person-neutral theory represents a utilitarian account of morality, and the agent-relative theory represents an egoist account of rationality. Because morality and rationality are different domains, both utilitarianism and egoism can be true. Hence, only on the externalist reading can both be objects of intuition.

Of course, it is important that the externalist reading embody some sort of dualism or tension in practical reason, and it does. Though rational egoism and utilitarianism are theoretically consistent, the rational authority of moral considerations, on this reading, depends on the extent of the coincidence of duty and interest. And because Sidgwick believes that this coincidence is imperfect, there is a tension or practical inconsistency between egoism and utilitarianism; we cannot always act so as to satisfy both egoism and utilitarianism.

Finally, as these last two points illustrate, the externalist reading allows us to explain the common view that, despite his disclaimers to be defending any one of the methods (*ME*, x), Sidgwick endorses both rational egoism and utilitarianism. He can embrace both compatibly on the externalist reading of the dualism of practical reason, because, on this reading, they defend different structures for different domains. On the internalist reading, by contrast, his commitment to neither utilitarianism nor rational egoism can be wholehearted, because his commitment to either must be qualified by his commitment to the other.

I think that the philosophical aspects of the externalist reading that I have just sketched can be elaborated so as to provide a very strong case for the externalist reading. For this reason, I shall assume this reading of the dualism of practical reason in most of what follows. I want to focus on Sidgwick's claims about rationality or reasons for action, in particular, his reasons for defending the agent-relative rational egoism against its person-neutral rival – rational benevolence. This means construing the agent-relative theory as rational egoism, *rather than* ethical egoism,[9] and construing the person-neutral theory as rational benevolence, *rather than* utilitarianism.

The friend of the internalist reading can reinterpret most of my claims mutatis mutandis, construing my discussion as applying to morality as well as rationality (e.g., to ethical egoism as well as rational egoism and to utilitarianism as well as rational benevolence). But I shall leave the internalist reinterpretation of my claims to others.

2. The parity of time and person?

Unlike the fully neutral rational altruism or rational benevolence or the fully relative presentism, rational egoism is a hybrid theory of rationality; it is temporally neutral and agent-relative. Can this hybrid character be justified? Is it reasonable to treat time and person differently, as egoism does, or is egoism an unhappy compromise between the two purebreds? Egoism is committed to saying that it makes all the difference *on whom* a benefit or burden falls and none whatsoever *when* it falls. On reflection, this may seem arbitrary. As Sidgwick notes, in discussing the "proof of utilitarianism":

From the point of view, indeed, of abstract philosophy, I do not see why the axiom of Prudence [rational egoism] should not be questioned, when it conflicts with present inclination, on a ground similar to that on which Egoists refuse to admit the axiom of Rational Benevolence. If the Utilitarian [rational altruist] has to answer the question, "Why should I sacrifice my own happiness for the greater happiness of another?" it must surely be admissible to ask the Egoist, "Why should I sacrifice a present pleasure for a greater one in the future? Why should I concern myself about my own future feelings any more than about the feelings of other persons?" (*ME*, 418)

The egoist must ask the altruist, "Why should I sacrifice my own good for the good of another?" But the presentist can ask the egoist, "Why should I sacrifice a present good for myself for the sake of a future good for myself?" These questions may seem parallel. We must decide where among lives and when within lives to locate goods and harms. Because both are matters of position or location, shouldn't they be treated the same? If present sacrifice for future benefit is rational, why isn't sacrifice of one person's good for the sake of another's? Alternatively, if sacrifice for another is not rationally required, why is a present sacrifice for a future benefit rationally required? In this way, egoism may seem to be an unstable hybrid; either we should be fully neutral and accept altruism, or we should be fully relative and accept presentism.

Before discussing Sidgwick's attitude toward this parity claim, we might note how recent writers have made use of similar parity claims in arguing against egoism.

Nagel assumes that time and person are parallel and argues from the temporal neutrality that egoism concedes to person neutrality. Just as the interests of an agent's future self provide him with reasons for action now, so too, Nagel argues, others' interests can provide an agent with reason for action. Failure to recognize temporal neutrality involves temporal dissociation – failure to see the present as just one time among others – and failure to recognize person neutrality or impersonality involves personal dissociation – failure to recognize oneself as just one person among others. Therefore, an agent has a reason to do x just insofar as x is in someone's interest, regardless of whom the value accrues to or when it occurs. Rational egoism is false, and rational altruism or benevolence is true (*PA*, 16, 19, 99–100).[10]

Alternatively, we might treat time and person as parallel and argue from the agent relativity that egoism concedes to temporal relativity. If my sacrifice for another is not rationally required, it may seem that we cannot demand a sacrifice of my current interests for the sake of distant future ones. If so, we will think that it is only the present interests of the agent that provide her with reason for action. This is the strategy that Parfit develops, which he thinks Sidgwick anticipated (*RP*, 137–44).[11]

As a hybrid *S* [rational egoism] can be attacked from both directions. And what *S* claims against one rival may be turned against it by the other. In rejecting Neutralism [person neutrality], a Self-interest Theorist [rational egoist] must claim that a reason may have force only for the agent. But the grounds for this claim support a further claim. If a reason can have force only for the agent, it can have force for the agent only at the time of acting. (*RP*, 144)[12]

3. A Sidgwickian rationale

Sidgwick agrees that a presentist can challenge rational egoism in this way. But, whereas Parfit thinks that the egoist cannot meet this challenge, Sidgwick thinks this challenge is unanswerable only on a very extreme kind of skepticism about personal identity. The passage in which Sidgwick raises the parity theme continues this way.

It undoubtedly seems to Common Sense paradoxical to ask for a reason why one should seek one's own happiness on the whole; but I do not see how the demand can be repudiated as absurd by those who adopt the views of the extreme empirical school of psychologists. . . . Grant that the Ego is merely a system of coherent phenomena, that the permanent identical "I" is not a fact but a fiction, as Hume and his followers maintain; why, then, should one part of the series of feelings into which the Ego is resolved be concerned with another part of the same series, any more than with any other series? (*ME*, 418–19)

So Sidgwick sees the presentist's challenge to rational egoism but thinks we can meet this challenge, because it depends upon denying that persons are numerically distinct and temporally extended. Later, he suggests that the *separateness of persons* is what underlies rational egoism.

It would be contrary to Common Sense to deny that the distinction between any one individual and any other is real and fundamental, and that consequently "I" am concerned with the quality of my existence as an individual in a sense, fundamentally important, in which I am not concerned with the quality of existence of other individuals: and this being so, I do not see how it can be proved that this distinction is not to be taken as fundamental in determining the ultimate end of rational action for an individual. (*ME*, 498)

In these two passages Sidgwick clearly appeals to the *metaphysical* separateness of persons, in particular, to the numerical distinctness of persons and the fact that persons are temporally extended entities as part of a justification for egoism. Sidgwick seems to claim that the numerical distinctness of persons somehow justifies agent relativity and the fact that persons are temporally extended somehow justifies temporal neutrality.

Though I think that these facts about the metaphysical separateness of persons are important, the egoist's rationale cannot rely on them exclusively. This is clear from the context of this passage; it occurs as part of Sidgwick's discussion of the "proof" of rational benevolence. The proof goes something like this (*ME*, 382, 403, 420–1, 497–8):

1. I have reason to promote happiness in my life.
2. I can promote happiness in other lives.
3. Hence, I have reason to promote happiness generally.

As Sidgwick points out, the cogency of this argument turns on the interpretation of (1) (*ME*, 420, 497–8). (1) is ambiguous between two claims: (1*a*) I have reason to promote my happiness qua *happiness*, and

(1*b*) I have reason to promote my happiness qua *my* happiness. As Sidgwick notes, the argument is valid if and only if (1) is read as (1*a*), but the egoist will reject (1*a*) in favor of (1*b*). Sidgwick tries to explain *why* the egoist insists on (1*b*) in this passage that appeals to the separateness of persons (*ME*, 498). This passage provides such an explanation only if it is taken to assert or suggest a *normative* claim that goes beyond the metaphysical separateness of persons. Sidgwick supposes that because we are separate persons, with different lives to lead, it is unreasonable to demand *uncompensated sacrifices* of agents. Because we are separate persons, I am not compensated when I undergo a sacrifice for a greater benefit to you; your gains cannot make up to me for my losses. Sidgwick's appeal to the separateness of persons implicitly invokes this principle that the *rationality* of sacrifice requires compensation (SRC). In particular, SRC claims that an agent has reason to make a sacrifice if and only if the agent receives sufficient compensation in return.[13] SRC would explain why we should read (1) as (1*b*), rather than (1*a*).

Something like SRC is also reflected in Sidgwick's discussion of the relationship between an agent's happiness and duty.

And a similar conclusion seems irresistible even in more ordinary cases, where a man is called on to give up, for virtue's sake, not life, but a considerable share of the ordinary sources of human happiness. Can we say that all, or even most, men are so constituted that the satisfactions of a good conscience are certain to *repay them for such sacrifices*, or that the pain and *loss* involved in them would certainly be *outweighed* by the remorse that would follow the refusal to make them? (*ME*, 171; emphasis added)

This passage is fairly typical of his use of the language of "sacrifice" in various discussions of the relation between rational egoism and other-regarding moral conduct and concern (cf. *ME*, 174, 404, 498, 499, 501, 502).

If we read Sidgwick's appeal to the separateness of persons to embody an appeal to SRC as well as to the claim that persons are distinct, temporally extended entities, then we can see his rationale for egoism's hybrid character.

SRC and common-sense claims about personal identity over time allow the egoist to deny the parallel between time and person. The egoist claims that uncompensated sacrifices are not rationally required and insists that there is automatic *intra*personal compensation but no automatic *inter*personal compensation. Compensation requires that benefactors also be beneficiaries, and for compensation to be automatic benefactor and beneficiary must be one and the same. In the diachronic, intrapersonal case one's sacrifice of a present good for a (greater) future good is rational, because there is compensation later for the earlier sacrifice; benefactor and beneficiary are the same. This explains temporal neutrality. But in the interpersonal case, benefactor and beneficiary are different people; unless the beneficiary reciprocates in some way, the agent's sacrifice will be uncompensated. This explains agent relativity. This is the basic structure of the egoist's rationale for the hybrid treatment of time and person, but it calls for various further comments.

4. The separateness of persons

SRC reflects the normative separateness of persons. As I've interpreted him, Sidgwick finds SRC implicated in common-sense views about the separateness of persons: It's unreasonable to expect me to make sacrifices for another, because the benefits to another do not compensate me for the sacrifice that I incur. If Sidgwick is right, we should expect to find SRC reflected in some common intuitions about the rationality of sacrifice.

First, SRC provides an explanation of the common view that we have special reason to be concerned about our own lives and welfares that we don't have to be concerned about others. An agent's reasons seem not in general to be proportional to the good that she can do. For example, the fact that Bonny could confer a benefit upon an applicant to her firm by resigning her position does not seem to give her reason to resign her position. Nor does it seem to be true, as a person-neutral theory would imply, that our decision about whether Bonny has (sufficient) reason to resign her post to benefit the applicant to her firm awaits some showing that the job is more important to her than it is to the applicant.

Moreover, SRC provides a natural explanation of traditional worries about the rational authority of morality that, on the externalist reading, underlie Sidgwick's views about the dualism of practical reason. Sidgwick does often think of the dualism as raising a worry about the rational authority of morality (cf. *ME*, xv–xxi, 162–75, 496–509). The basis of this worry is the claim that morality requires agents to benefit or respect others in ways that seem to constrain the pursuit of their own interest or happiness. But this worry seems to rely ultimately on the assumption that the rationality of sacrifice presupposes compensation. For there is difficulty in defending the rational authority of other-regarding moral demands only if we assume that the rationality of sacrifice requires compensation, as the agent-relative theory claims.

Now it might be claimed that these intuitions do not require anything as strong as SRC or egoism's agent relativity but require only the claim that the agent's welfare has *greater* weight than the welfare of others in determining her reasons for action. This *agent-weighted theory* would represent the interests of others as providing the agent with reasons for action but with weaker reasons than the agent's own interest would provide. By denying that an agent's reasons for action are directly proportional to the value she can produce, the agent-weighted theory can perhaps accommodate our intuitions that seem inconsistent with person neutrality without embracing agent relativity or SRC.

But the egoist has reason to resist the agent-weighted explanation of our intuitions. First, the agent-weighted theory doesn't address our intuitions that tell against demanding uncompensated sacrifices. Because it gives greater rational significance to a good or harm of a given magnitude that befalls the agent than it does to a good or harm of the same magnitude that befalls another, the agent-weighted theory will only demand sacrifices of agents when the sacrifice secures a much larger good or prevents a much larger harm to some other individual or group. But it is still true that this seems to be an uncompensated sacrifice. The good to others does not provide the agent with a counterbalancing good; his interests are still sacrificed to those of others. And it may seem, therefore, that this sort of self-sacrifice cannot be rationally required.

Second, it must be remembered that SRC is a premise in a rationale for egoism that is intended as a response to the charge that egoism's hybrid character is arbitrary and unmotivated. This charge is based on an assumption of the parity of time and person in rationality, and this parity assumption is supposed to support a purebred conception of rationality that is either fully neutral or fully relative. But the agent-weighted theory is neither fully agent-relative nor fully person-neutral, much less fully relative or fully neutral; it is itself hybrid (with a vengeance) and so can provide no comfort to the friends of full neutrality or full relativity.

Third, though I cannot defend the claim here, some versions of rational egoism can help themselves to whatever appeal the agent-weighted theory might have. For instance, I think that rational egoism has the resources to justify concern for others, on the agent's part, proportional to the strength of the causal and, in particular, psychological connections that they bear to him, by representing such psychological relations as extending the agent's own interests (cf. Section 18).[14] If so, we may be able to represent the central claims of the agent-weighted theory as theorems of rational egoism. I doubt that the conception of the agent's interests that this form of egoism requires is compatible with Sidgwick's hedonism, and so Sidgwick may have to reject the appeal of the agent-weighted theory outright (e.g., on one of the two grounds mentioned above). But some versions of rational egoism may be able to represent the structure of the agent-weighted theory compatibly with SRC.

Finally, it is important to notice that the rational egoist's opponent in the parity argument assumes SRC. The parity argument purports to refute egoism by relying only on assumptions that the egoist already admits; it claims that the egoist is hoist with his own petard (cf. *PA*, 87). Recall that the parity argument treats the egoist's demand "Why should I sacrifice my interests for another?" and the presentist's demand "Why should I now sacrifice my present interest for my future interests?" as parallel. So Parfit's attempt to argue from egoism's agent relativity to presentism's full relativity necessarily relies on something like SRC. Moreover, Nagel seems to assume something like SRC when he rejects the interpersonal balancing, which a person-neutral theory allows, by appeal to "the extremely strict position that there can be no *inter*personal compensation of sacrifice" (*PA*, 142; emphasis added). SRC is a controversial claim, but it is not the issue in this structural debate.

The egoist rationale also rests on the metaphysical separateness of persons. Sidgwick thinks that these metaphysical assumptions about personal identity are seriously challenged only by Humean views about personal identity. Later (Sections 9–18), I will discuss whether and, if so, how this egoist rationale is compromised by Humean and other views of personal identity. But these issues are not our present concern. As long as agents are metaphysically distinct, interpersonal compensation is problematic; and as long as agents are temporally extended, diachronic, intrapersonal compensation is automatic.

5. Temporal neutrality

Because diachronic, intrapersonal compensation is automatic, it is the importance of the agent's interests and not their temporal location that determines what an agent has most reason to do. Sidgwick expresses this commitment to temporal neutrality as follows:

Hereafter *as such* is to be regarded neither less nor more than Now. It is not, of course, meant, that the good of the present may not reasonably be preferred to that of the future on account of its greater certainty: or again, that a week ten years hence may not be more important to us than a week now, through an increase in our means or capacities of happiness. All that the principle affirms is that mere difference of priority and posteriority in time is not a reasonable ground for having more regard to the consciousness of one moment than to that of another. (*ME*, 381; cf. 111–12, 124 n.)

As Sidgwick notes in this passage, this kind of temporal neutrality is perfectly compatible with the claim that rational *planning* should take into account the uncertainty of my continued existence. We can explain this point by drawing a useful distinction between *subjective* and *objective* rationality (cf. *ME*, 207–8, 394–5). Claims of objective rationality are claims about what an agent has reason to do given the facts of the situation, whether or not he is aware of these facts or in a position to recognize the reasons that they support. Claims of subjective rationality are claims about what the agent has reason to do given his beliefs about his situation or what it would be reasonable for him to believe about his situation. The egoist can admit that the existence of my near future is more certain than the existence of my distant future and that this epistemic fact should affect what it is subjectively rational for me to do; he claims only that, insofar as I have both present and future interests, they provide me with equally strong objective reasons for action.[15]

6. Agent relativity

Because I am a separate entity, I am not automatically compensated by benefits to another, and this makes interpersonal sacrifice problematic. But SRC does not imply that others cannot be beneficiaries of the agent's actions; it requires only that the agent be an appropriate beneficiary. Others will often be beneficiaries of actions that benefit the agent. Sometimes benefits to others will be by-products of benefits the agent pursues and secures for herself. In other cases the agent will benefit *from* or *by* benefiting others. For instance, agents will often receive benefits in return for those they confer, as in most systems of cooperation for mutual advantage. In this way the egoist can often justify being a reliable benefactor (cf. *ME*, 164–70, 499–503).

The egoist may also be able to justify other-regarding action and concern as a kind of "false target" for promoting the agent's own good. Sidgwick insists on the so-called paradox of egoism, according to which an agent may best promote her own interest not by doing things with the aim of maximizing her own welfare but by developing concerns for people and activities for their own sakes (cf. *ME*, 48, 136, 403). The paradox of egoism explains why even hedonistic egoists should care for others for their own sakes.

Finally, versions of rational egoism that employ an objective conception of welfare or happiness have resources for justifying other-regarding conduct and concern that are not available to subjective (e.g., hedonistic) versions of egoism. Many objective conceptions of welfare recognize a variety of social or other-regarding components in a person's good. They claim that family relations, friendships, and social relations involving mutual concern and respect make our lives more valuable than they would otherwise be. By having friends and cooperating with others on a footing of mutual concern and commitment, we are able to exercise new capacities, secure ourselves against a variety of misfortunes, and generally extend our interests in new ways. On such views, the good of others is *part of* my good, and so I will benefit directly and necessarily by benefiting them. If such a view about value can be defended, it will allow for the possibility of interpersonal compensation and so provide the basis for a robust defense of other-regarding conduct and concern on egoist grounds.

Of course, it is an open question exactly how far such strategies can be used to provide agent-relative justification of other-regarding conduct and concern. I do not wish to assess the success of these strategies here; my present purpose is only to forestall possible misunderstandings of the commitments of agent relativity and to insist that the success of such justifications of other-regarding action and concern *is* a genuinely open question.[16]

7. A rationale for egoism's hybrid character

So the metaphysical and normative appeals to the separateness of persons represent the egoist's reasons for holding a hybrid theory of rationality consisting of agent relativity and temporal neutrality. These premises, though not indisputable, are, Sidgwick claims, reflected in much common-sense thinking about rationality and personal identity.

Sidgwick's egoist will rightly resist the parity argument. She will see no reason to follow the altruist, who infers person neutrality from temporal neutrality: Stages of other people are not stages of me, present or future, and, as a result, I may not be compensated for my sacrifices to others. She will see no reason to follow the presentist, who infers temporal relativity from agent relativity: Unlike the stages of other people, my future self is a stage of me, and, as such, I do receive compensation when I make present sacrifices for my own future benefit. Diachronic, intrapersonal compensation is automatic; interpersonal compensation is not.

Because the egoist offers a *rationale* for rejecting parity, egoism's hybrid character cannot be represented as arbitrary or unmotivated, and arguments against egoism cannot simply appeal to the parity of time and person and the hybrid character of egoism. My aim is not to provide a full-blown defense of rational egoism or to argue that egoism's purebred rivals are untenable. In particular, I am not suggesting that there are no serious questions to raise about Sidgwick's requirement that sacrifice be compensated, his assumptions about personal identity, or the implications of agent relativity and temporal neutrality.[17] Rather, the rationale implies that the parity argument itself cannot be used to defeat egoism or motivate its purebred rivals and shows where the assessment of egoism should focus.

8. Temporal neutrality and the bearers of reasons

The presentist might claim that the egoist rationale does not respond adequately to his appeal to full relativity. The egoist insists that *intra*personal compensation is automatic, because benefactor and beneficiary are the same. This assumes that it is the temporally extended being – the person – who is the agent and bearer of reasons for action. But the presentist might think that the appeal to full relativity undermines this natural assumption. The egoist is being asked to explain why my present self should be sacrificed for the benefit of my future self. This may make it look as if it is a person stage, *me-now*, rather than me, who is the bearer of reasons. If so, the egoist's rationale would seem to fail. Me-now can fairly complain that it's being asked to make an uncompensated sacrifice. After all, the benefits of me-now's sacrifice accrue not to me-now but to me-later. Me-now seems no more automatically compensated for its sacrifice to me-later than I am by my sacrifice to you. Perhaps diachronic, intrapersonal compensation is not automatic; SRC may seem to force us to reject egoism in favor of presentism.[18]

There is automatic intrapersonal compensation, but interstage compensation is problematic. Thus, whether the challenge of temporal relativity can be met depends upon how that challenge is formulated. We may ask the egoist whether *my present self* (me-now) has reason to sacrifice its interests for those of my future self (me-later). But we may ask instead – as Sidgwick does – whether *I* have reason to sacrifice my current interests for the sake of my future interests.[19] The egoist can answer the second question: I am compensated by a present sacrifice for a (greater) future gain, because that future self is a part of me. Egoism's temporal neutrality seems threatened if and only if we formulate the challenge the first way. Are the bearers of reasons persons or person stages?[20]

Our answer may depend upon the "life span" of a person stage. If the appeal to temporal relativity is to be part of an appeal to full relativity, and if this appeal is supposed to show that person stages are the agents, then person stages should be understood here as instantaneous time slices or temporally minimal cross-sections of a person's life. Otherwise, it would seem, the appeal to relativity could not be full or complete. Call such a temporally minimal person stage a *person slice*.

The normal assumption is that it is persons, rather than person slices, who are agents. Is there any positive reason for thinking otherwise? Perhaps the presentist thinks that everyone – including the egoist – must recognize the existence of temporally indexed reasons for action and that their existence requires us to view person slices, rather than persons, as the bearers of reasons. My deliberations are always about what I should do, plan, omit, or postpone *now*, and I must deliberate on the basis of my *current* beliefs, aims, and values. Does this show that the real units of practical deliberation are person slices?[21]

Perhaps we could represent temporally indexed reasons for action as the reasons held by person slices. On this view, we treat temporally indexed reasons for action as an agent-at-a-particular-time's reasons to do something. But surely it is more natural to treat them as an agent's reasons to do something at a particular time.

So far, the conception of agents as person slices is without positive motivation. Moreover, it seems indefensible. For the defense that this conception affords presentism requires that person slices have interests. For me-now to be the bearer of reasons, me-now must have interests. And it is not clear that person slices do have interests.[22] Whether the entity me-now can have interests may depend upon which theory of interest or welfare is correct.

If pleasure is a simple, qualitative sensation or mental state and a hedonistic theory of welfare is correct, then perhaps me-now has interests. Person slices may contain qualitative mental states, such as pleasure.

But, first, Sidgwick is a preference hedonist, not a simple hedonist. A person's mental state is a pleasure only if it is one that she wants to continue and that she will, ceteris paribus, take steps to make continue. But then a preference pleasure is already a state that is essentially the state of a temporally extended entity. If so, the bearer of preference pleasures would seem to be a person, rather than a person slice.

Moreover, despite Sidgwick's allegiance to hedonism, hedonism seems an implausible theory of welfare, because a large part of an agent's interest seems to consist in his *being a certain sort of person*, that is, a person with a certain sort of character who exercises certain capacities and develops certain kinds of personal and social relationships. This is true not only on objective theories of value or welfare, which take welfare to consist in being a certain sort of person, but also on desire-satisfaction theories of welfare. Furthermore, our desires are the desires of temporally extended beings, and the content of most of our desires is conditioned by this fact. If so, our conception of interests and welfare (i.e., of what makes a life go well) is fundamentally *diachronic*. And this seems to imply that it is temporally extended beings, as the egoist assumes, rather than person slices, who are the bearers of interests.

Moreover, not only is it doubtful whether person slices have interests, but also it is questionable whether having interests is sufficient for having reasons for action. A person slice will not persist long enough to perform actions or receive the benefits of actions. If so, then person slices cannot have reasons for action even if it is possible for them to have interests, that is, even if it is possible for their short existences to go better or worse.

What if we construe person stages not as person slices but as temporally extended cross-sections of a person's life? Call this the conception of person stages as *person segments*. Person segments, unlike person slices, can have some interests and can live long enough to perform and receive some of the benefits of actions. The appeal to full relativity, so construed, would also seem to challenge rational egoism's temporal neutrality, because me-now, conceived here as a person segment, may not be compensated for its sacrifice to me-later, conceived of as a later segment of the same person.

However, appeal to person segments as the bearers of reasons leads to a proliferation of agents and consequent indeterminacies in questions about practical deliberation that are troubling and unnecessary. Person segments are made up of temporally related series of shorter person stages (e.g., slices) and so contain parts that also belong to other person segments; that is, person segments overlap. Consider a person consisting of person stages $p2$ through $p10$. (Fig. 7.1) The person segment $PS1$ consisting of person stages $p3$ through $p7$ contains within it, for example, part of the person segment $PS2$ consisting of $p4$ through $p8$ and part of the person segment $PS3$ consisting of $p5$ through $p9$. Suppose the time is $t6$. If, as we normally assume, it is the person P that is the subject of practical deliberation, the egoist rationale allows us to identify her reasons for action. If person segments are agents, whose reasons for action should we be concerned about now: those of $PS1$, those of $PS2$, or those of $PS3$? (This names only three of continuum many possibilities.) Of course, we can identify the reasons for action of each of these entities. But reasons for action are supposed to be related in some way to practical deliberation. Whose practical deliberation is in question?

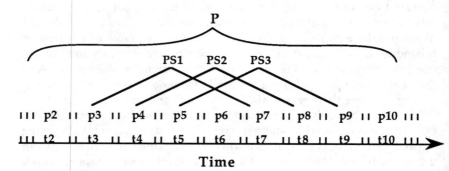

Figure 7.1

The friend of person segments might reply by arguing that some person segments are more *salient* than others. Person segments are individuated temporally, but some person segments display more internal psychological coherence and integrity than others. Some cross-sections of a person's life cut that life at its psychological joints, whereas others do not. So, it might be argued, at any point in time the subject of practical deliberation should be identified not with just any person segment but with the salient person segment existing at that time.

Though this suggestion no doubt reduces the proliferation of agents, I don't see that it will eliminate indeterminacy. This is because salient segments will themselves surely overlap. Psychological change is generally fairly continuous but proceeds at different rates along different dimensions of the person's personality. Even if there were mutual interaction among all aspects of a person's psychological makeup, there would still be distinguishable cognitive and affective aspects of a person's mental life whose development and careers would be staggered (cf. linguistic skills, mathematical skills, athletic skills, political beliefs, tastes in food, friendships, and career goals and expectations). This is just to say there are a great many different psychological joints at which to cut for salience. If so, there will be overlapping salient segments, producing significant, even if less extreme, proliferation and indeterminacy. Indeed, so long as the person is herself a salient segment, there will always be at least two possible agents on the person-segment view.

Moreover, these person segments, salient or otherwise, do and must interact and cooperate. They do interact and cooperate, much as distinct individuals interact and cooperate in groups, in order to plan and execute long-term projects and goals. They must interact and cooperate if only because they have to share a body and its capacities in order to execute their individual and collective goals, much in the way that individuals must sometimes interact and cooperate if they are to use scarce resources to mutual advantage.[23] Indeed, both the ease and necessity of interaction among person segments will be greater than that among persons, because the physical constraints and the reliability of fellow cooperators are greater in the intrapersonal case. But this means that person segments will overlap with each other; they will stand to each other and the person much as strands of a rope stand to each other and the rope. Though we can recognize the overlapping strands as entities, the most salient entity is the rope itself. So too, the most salient entity is the person, even if we can recognize the overlapping person segments that make up the person.

In this way, person segments also represent a rather arbitrary stopping place. Someone might think that the appeal to full relativity argues for agents with shorter life spans than persons. If so, then an appeal to *full* relativity would seem to argue for person slices as agents. But if, as I have argued, that conception cannot be maintained, then it seems arbitrary to settle on person segments. Once we extend the life span of the agent beyond the temporally minimal conception that the appeal to full relativity might have seemed to support, it seems we should keep going until we reach an entity with the most natural borders, namely, the person.

These, I think, are good reasons to preserve the normal assumption that it is temporally extended beings – specifically, persons – who are agents. But it might seem that, for all this, this assumption is really incoherent. I have identified the person with the temporally extended object, some of whose parts lie in the future. But then the person is in one sense "not all there" at the time of deliberation and action. But how then could the person be the agent who deliberates and acts, and if it cannot be the agent, how can the person be the bearer of reasons?

I find these issues difficult and obscure. But I doubt that they threaten the assumption that it is persons who are agents. Notice, first, that person slices seem to be the only candidates for agency that avoid some form of this objection. For person segments extend from the instant of deliberation or action into either the future or the past (or both); so person segments are also entities with parts that are "not all there" at the time of deliberation or action. Only one person slice is "all there" at this time. But we've already seen that that conception of agency is indefensible. We might, therefore, wonder whether the agent, or the entity (or entities) whose interests determine what rationally ought to be done, need be "all there" at the time of action.

Consider an analogy with nations. We speak of nations as actors that enact legislation, start wars, and so on. We also think of nations as having interests and acting in their interests. But a nation is composed, at least in part, by its entire current population. And there is certainly some sense in which the entire population does not enact legislation or start wars. Instead, certain individuals or groups act as representatives of a larger, spatially dispersed group of which they are members. We don't conclude that nations cannot be actors or the bearers of interests. Instead, we conclude that a nation can act when its deputies act on behalf of the national interest, that is, the interest of the spatially dispersed group. Similarly, the present self can act as representative of the temporally dispersed entity, the person, by acting in the interest of this being. If so, then the fact that the temporally extended person is "not all there" at the time of action is not a reason to deny that it is nonetheless the remote actor, the agent, or the entity whose interests determine what agents have reason to do.

I conclude from these considerations that the egoist's rationale for his hybrid treatment of time and person can rest securely on the assumption that it is the person that is the bearer of reasons. On this assumption, there is automatic diachronic, intrapersonal compensation, and so SRC does justify temporal neutrality.

9. Rational egoism and personal identity

As we have seen, Sidgwick thinks that rational egoism requires the common-sense belief in the separateness of persons and that it would be seriously challenged by a Humean account of personal identity (*ME*, 418–19). Nor is such linkage between assumptions about personal identity and our attitudes toward self-concern and future concern uncommon. As Sidgwick was certainly aware, Butler had claimed that concern for one's future and moral responsibility would be undermined by Locke's account of personal identity in terms of memory connectedness. Butler claimed that it followed from Locke's view that "it is a fallacy . . . to charge our present selves with anything we did, or to imagine ourselves interested in anything which befell us yesterday, or that our present self will be interested in what will befall us tomorrow."[24] And recently Parfit has likened his own "reductionist" account of personal identity to the views of Locke and Hume and argued that reductionism undermines egoism's temporal neutrality (*RP*, 139, 307–20). In what way, if any, does the egoist rationale depend upon particular assumptions about personal identity, and is it undermined by Humean or reductionist views?

10. The Humean challenge

Consider Sidgwick's reference to Hume. He does not actually say that egoism is undermined by Humean views; he says only that the presentist challenge cannot be "repudiated as absurd" by the Humean. Nor is Sidgwick clear about precisely what aspect of the Humean view poses the challenge. He refers to two distinct features of Hume's view: (1) the fact that Hume says that personal identity through time is "not a fact, but a fiction," and (2) the fact that Hume "resolves" the Ego into a series of experiences. (1) and (2) reflect two different aspects of Hume's views about personal identity.[25]

(1) Hume is a skeptic about personal identity, as he is about other matters of fact, and claims that the idea of personal identity is a fiction. (2) He also offers a constructive account of personal identity, analogous to his constructive account of causation, according to which personal identity resolves itself into (*a*) objective facts about the resemblance, contiguity, and causation among perceptions and (*b*) the subjective fact that we come, by a process of association, to construe the perceptions which are so related as belonging to a single enduring object. We might designate (1) as Hume's *skeptical* thesis and (2) as his *reductionist* thesis.

Is the egoist rationale undermined by skepticism about personal identity? If there is no such thing as personal identity through time, then selves are not temporally extended. If no future self will be me, then SRC seems to give me no reason to be concerned about any future self; it would seem that no benefits to any future self could compensate for a sacrifice of my interests. In one sense, then, skepticism about personal identity through time seems to undermine temporal neutrality; it seems to undermine future concern.[26] However, in another sense it does not; it does not undermine concern for my future self. It is not that skepticism robs me of special concern for my future self; it robs me of a future with which to be concerned. While the implications of skepticism about personal identity through time for temporal neutrality are mixed in this way, such skepticism would presumably leave the rationale for agent relativity intact. Indeed, it would in a way expand the implications of agent relativity, because it would force us to recognize more distinct selves and so more problems of interpersonal compensation.

But insofar as Hume is a skeptic, he seems to think that there is no such thing as synchronic identity either; there is no fact about the members of any set of experiences that makes them all mine. If so, there are no distinct agents, and so no grounds for insisting on compensation. This may seem like a threat to egoism's agent relativity. Perhaps it is, but not in a way that supports person neutrality, for it simply dissolves the question of how to distribute goods and harms among persons as misconceived. Thus, skepticism about synchronic personal identity does not so much reject SRC as suggest that it rests on a false presupposition, namely, that there are benefactors and beneficiaries.

It seems, therefore, that complete skepticism about personal identity dissolves the debates between egoism and its rivals and does not so much defeat egoism or its rationale. Skepticism about personal identity through time without skepticism about synchronic identity threatens egoism only if we construe temporal neutrality as requiring future concern, rather than concern for one's own future self.

But skepticism about personal identity is, as Sidgwick notes, an extreme position. Even Hume cannot confine himself to the skeptical conclusion but must offer a constructive, reductionist account of personal identity. Is egoism or the egoist rationale undermined by reductionist accounts of personal identity?

11. Parfit's reductionist objection

I propose to pursue this issue by examining Parfit's claim that a reductionist account of personal identity of the sort that he defends in part 3 of *Reasons and Persons* provides (new) arguments against rational egoism and temporal neutrality. Because our concern is whether reductionist accounts of personal identity undermine egoism's hybrid rationale, I shall simply assume that Parfit's main arguments for reductionism are successful and ask whether his conclusions about egoism follow.

Reductionism and nonreductionism begin as accounts of when two person stages are stages of the same person; that is, both offer accounts of the relation of co-personality. Though Parfit offers a number of different characterizations of the dispute between reductionism and nonreductionism, an important difference, for our purposes, is that, whereas reductionists think that co-personality just consists in the holding of certain other (e.g., physical or psychological) relations among these person stages, nonreductionists claim that co-personality cannot be analyzed in terms of other, more basic relations but must remain a "simple and unanalyzable," "further" fact (*RP*, 210 f.).

Parfit also thinks that the reductionist will claim that it is the holding of the right relations – call the right set of relations "relation R" – among person stages, rather than personal identity per se, that is what matters (this is supposed to be demonstrated by fission cases, of the sort discussed in section 16). Parfit defends a version of *psychological* reductionism, according to which relation R is a function of both "psychological continuity and connectedness." Of these two conditions, psychological connectedness is explanatorily prior (cf. *RP*, 204–9). The psychological states of two person stages $p1$ and $p2$ at times $t1$ and $t2$ are psychologically *connected* just in case they are causally related in the appropriate way and are significantly similar (e.g., in terms of beliefs, desires, and intentions). Because the similarity relation is not exact similarity, psychological connectedness can vary and, in particular, can depreciate over time. Thus, $p1$ can be psychologically connected to $p2$, and $p2$ can be psychologically connected to $p3$, but $p3$ need not be, and is unlikely to be, as closely connected with $p1$ as $p2$ is. A series of person stages $p1$ through pn at times $t1$ through tn is psychologically *continuous* just in case the members of every pair of temporally contiguous stages in this series are psychologically connected. It follows that $p1$ and pn can be psychologically continuous even if they are not psychologically well connected or connected at all.

Parfit thinks that we often realize this possibility and that, because our continued existence is a function of psychological connectedness as well as continuity, this fact about our lives undermines the temporal neutrality of rational egoism (the view he calls the "self-interest theory" or "S"). This fact about our lives is supposed to show that it is rational (independently of the greater uncertainty of our continued existence) for us to be less concerned about our distant future than about our near future.[27]

12. Metaphysical depth?

At a number of points Parfit claims that co-personality is metaphysically "less deep" according to reductionism than it is according to nonreductionism. Once we become convinced of reductionism, he thinks, we should reject egoism's temporal neutrality (*RP*, 309–12). The idea seems to be that if personal identity over time is less deep, intrapersonal compensation is compromised.

We can concede that co-personality is less metaphysically deep according to reductionism precisely because reductionism claims that co-personality has familiar, unproblematic metaphysical analysans. But there is no general reason to suppose that this kind of metaphysical depth affects the justification of concern. This is because our concern about some entity or property may attach to its *functional role*, rather than to its metaphysical or compositional analysans. For instance, a materialist should be no less concerned to prevent pain (her own pain or that of another) than a dualist,[28] and, ceteris paribus, I should care just as much for mint chocolate chip ice cream upon learning its chemical composition. Similarly, I don't see why becoming convinced that a future self's being part of me consists in its being part of an R-related series of selves or person stages should make me any less concerned about that self. The relevant premise in the egoist rationale asserts the metaphysical separateness of persons. But, though Sidgwick's claim that common sense believes that the distinction among persons is both "real and fundamental" (ME, 498) may suggest an issue of metaphysical depth, the relevant claim in the rationale is simply that persons are metaphysically distinct and temporally extended. The rationale requires only this fact about the separateness of persons, not any particular metaphysical account of this fact.

Now, of course, sometimes our beliefs about the metaphysical analysans of some entity or property will or should affect its role in our conceptual network in certain ways. For instance, we may learn that some gustatory properties of mint chocolate chip ice cream supervene on its saturated-fat content, and this may affect its desirability. But then this is what needs to be argued in the case of a reductionist account of personal identity. We need an account of how the particular analysans to which the psychological reductionist appeals justify a change in our attitudes. Metaphysical *depth* does not establish this.

However, there are other ways in which Parfit does or might think reductionism undermines egoism's temporal neutrality. One argument appeals to the normal cases in which relation R and personal identity coincide; the other argument appeals to fission cases in which relation R and personal identity diverge.

13. A discount rate for the normal, nonbranching case?

Parfit's principal argument that reductionism undermines egoism's temporal neutrality applies to the normal, nonbranching cases where relation R and personal identity coincide. Relation R is what matters. According to Parfit, relation R consists of psychological continuity and connectedness. But psychological connectedness is a matter of degree and, in particular, can and does depreciate over time. Because relation R is what matters and it consists of psychological connectedness as well as continuity, Parfit claims, I should (other things being equal) care more about my near future than about my more distant future. In fact, he accepts a kind of discount rate that proportions concern to psychological connectedness.

My concern for my future may correspond to the degree of connectedness between me-now and myself in the future. Connectedness is one of the two relations that give me reasons to be specially concerned about my own future. It can be rational to care less, when one of the grounds for caring will hold to a lesser degree. Since connectedness is nearly always weaker over long periods, I can rationally care less about my further future. (*RP*, 313)

As Parfit notes, this is a discount rate with respect to connectedness and not with respect to time itself (*RP*, 314). His discount rate should, therefore, be distinguished from the discount rate with respect to time that C. I. Lewis calls "fractional prudence."[29] Egoism is neutral with respect to time itself and so must deny fractional prudence. But egoism's temporal neutrality is also inconsistent with Parfit's discount rate, because temporal neutrality requires a kind of equal concern among parts of one's life that is inconsistent with a discount rate. The magnitude of a good or harm should affect its rational significance. But temporal neutrality implies that the temporal location of a good or harm within a life should be of no rational significance. If so, then an agent should be equally concerned about goods and harms (of equal magnitude) at any point in his life. In particular, if near and more distant future selves are both stages in his life, then, other things being equal, an agent should have equal concern for each, even if the nearer future self is more closely connected with his present self.

Parfit's discount rate is, therefore, incompatible with egoism's temporal neutrality. But reductionism does not imply a discount rate, and we should not accept one. There are two main grounds for rejecting a discount rate.

14. Two forms of psychological reductionism

Parfit's argument here requires that relation R consists in psychological connectedness as well as psychological continuity (*C&C*), for it is only psychological connectedness that will normally depreciate over time (my distant and near future selves are both continuous with my present self). Now one form of reductionism would claim that relation R consists *only* in psychological continuity (*C*).[30] If it is only *C* that matters, then I have no less reason to be concerned about my distant future than about my near future, because each is equally continuous with my present and past selves, even if each is not equally well connected with my present self. Hence, it is not reductionism per se but only Parfit's version of reductionism (*C&C*) that threatens egoism's temporal neutrality.

Throughout much of Parfit's discussion of personal identity, he is agnostic about whether relation R consists in *C* or *C&C* (*RP*, 207, 262, 271, 279, 283). His only explicit argument for *C&C*, as against *C*, is that we are averse to many possible losses in psychological connectedness; thus, connectedness "matters to us" (*RP*, 301–2). But our aversion to losses in psychological connectedness does not require *C&C*.

The clearest cases of aversion to substantial psychological change involve cases that we regard as *corruption*, where I become a less attractive person. But a natural explanation of this aversion is to the *disvalue* of the psychological profile I would be acquiring and not to loss of connectedness per se. This alternative explanation of my aversion is reinforced by the fact that I presumably wouldn't be averse to loss of psychological connectedness involved in a psychological change that I have reason to regard as an *improvement*.

Indeed, *C&C* faces a problem explaining why we have reason to improve ourselves in ways that involve significant psychological changes. If *C&C* is true, then it becomes more difficult to explain how a person has agent-relative reason, as he surely seems to, to undergo a process of "improvement" – even though it is agreed that the person emerging from the process is better off than the person beginning the process.[31] Indeed, for *C&C*, the more significant the improvement, the less agent-relative reason there is to undertake it.

To undermine egoism's temporal neutrality, therefore, Parfit must not only defend psychological reductionism but must provide a more serious argument for construing *R* as *C&C*, rather than *C*.

15. Persons and their temporal parts, again

Moreover, Parfit's own form of reductionism (*C&C*) fails to support a discount rate or undermine temporal neutrality. The possibility that Parfit thinks undermines rational egoism is the case in which my distant future self, though continuous with my present self, is less well connected with my present self than is my near future self. This possibility does not threaten temporal neutrality even if, as Parfit assumes, connectedness as well as continuity is constitutive of relation *R*. This possibility demonstrates only a fact about the relation *among my stages*, not a fact about the relation *between my stages and me*. This possibility would undermine temporal neutrality only if *I* was identified with my present self or with a person segment ending with my present self. But, of course, I am neither my present self nor a mere person segment; I am a person, that is, a certain kind of temporally extended being.

We can put this point another way. Parfit claims to be discussing what people have reason to do, but his argument is plausible only if it is person slices or person segments, rather than persons, that are the bearers of reasons for action. Suppose I consist of a series of *R*-related

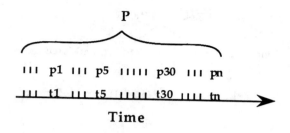

Figure 7.2

persons stages, including $p1$ through pn at times $t1$ through tn (Fig. 7.2). The time is $t1$. Though $p5$ and $p30$ are equally continuous with my present self, $p5$ is better connected with my present self than $p30$ is. *Only if* it is the person slice $p1$ or some person segment ending with $p1$, rather than the person P, that bears the reason for action does the depreciation of connectedness from $p1$ to $p30$ undermine temporal neutrality. For we can see how there is less of what matters between $p1$ and $p30$ than there is between $p1$ and, say, $p5$. This explains why $p1$ or *some person segment ending in $p1$* should be less concerned about the welfare of $p30$ than *it* should be about the welfare of $p5$. But P is not identical with $p1$ or any person segment ending in $p1$, and the welfare of $p30$ is every bit as much part of P's welfare as is the welfare of $p5$; so this fact about the degree of connectedness between $p1$ and $p30$ does not affect P's reasons for action. And, for the reasons already discussed (Section 8), it is persons, and not person slices or person segments, who are agents. Because all parts of a person's life are equally parts of her life, even if they are R-related to each other in varying degrees, benefits and harms are equally benefits and harms to her regardless of their temporal location in the R-related series that is her life. But then depreciation of connectedness does not threaten temporal neutrality.

At one point, Parfit considers and rejects the sufficiency of an egoist appeal to the claim that all parts of a person's life are equally parts of that life (*RP*, 315–16). He appeals to an analogy with relatives. He claims that although all members of an extended family are equally relatives, this doesn't justify equal concern among them; for instance, it wouldn't give my cousin as strong a claim to my estate as my children (*RP*, 316). Is this a good analogy? Consider the following case (Fig. 7.3). Grandpa Zeke and Grandma Zelda have two children, Zeke Jr. and Zelda Jr. With his wife, Zenobia, Zeke Jr. has one child, named Zeke III; with her husband, Zach, Zelda Jr. has two children, named Zach Jr. and Zelda III. Parfit wants to say that though it's true that

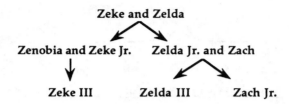

Figure 7.3

these people are all equally relatives it doesn't follow that, say, Zeke
Jr. should be as concerned about Zelda III (his niece) as he should be
about Zeke III (his son); for instance, Zelda III doesn't have the same
sort of claim on Zeke Jr.'s estate as Zeke III does. But to focus on the
concerns of Zeke Jr. or the disposition of his estate is precisely the
interpersonal, intrafamily analog of taking a person stage, rather than
the person, as the agent in the intrapersonal case. And I have argued
against doing this in the intrapersonal case. The intrafamily analog of
the person (in the intrapersonal case) is the family itself. Thus, the
correct intrafamily analog would be to focus on the distribution of some
asset that belongs to the entire family. Here neutrality seems appropriate
in light of the fact that all are equally parts of the family, even if some
are more closely related than others. Thus, if Zelda Jr. is acting as the
trustee of the family corporation, then, other things being equal, she
ought to allocate as large a share of dividends to Zeke III (her nephew)
as she does to Zach Jr. and Zelda III (her own children), even though
Zach Jr. and Zelda III are more closely related to each other and to
her than any of them is to Zeke III.

The moral is this: As long as we focus on the attitude appropriate for
a whole to take toward any one of its parts, the relations that its parts
bear to each other are, ceteris paribus, irrelevant.[32] And as long as
persons are the relevant whole, this vindicates egoism's temporal
neutrality.

16. Egoism and fission

Someone might think that fission cases provide an independent, even if
less general, argument against rational egoism (cf. *RP*, chap. 12). As
I've explained it, egoism relies on SRC. Automatic compensation seems
to require that the *very same person* who is benefactor be beneficiary.
This condition may not seem to be satisfied in the fission cases, even
though the products of fission are *R*-related to the subject of fission.
And, as Parfit effectively argues, it seems rational for the subject of

fission to be concerned about all fission products that are *R*-related to her. In this way, fission may seem to undermine egoism's agent relativity.

Consider the following case. Tom, Zeke, and Zach are identical triplets and get in a serious car accident. Zeke and Zach are brain-dead; Tom is not, but his body is hopelessly mangled. Assume that it is possible to transplant Tom's brain into Zeke's body and that this preserves Tom's psychological continuity. If we do this (case 1), we regard Tom as the surviving recipient and Zeke as the dead donor (Zach is simply dead). Assume that half the brain is sufficient to sustain psychological continuity. If half of Tom's brain is seriously damaged and we transplant the healthy half into Zeke's body (case 2), Tom again survives. If, however, Tom's entire brain is healthy and we transplant half of it into Zeke's body and half into Zach's (case 3), then the logic of identity prevents us from regarding either of the recuperating patients as Tom. This is the fission case (see Figure 7.4). Call the recuperating patient in Zeke's body Dick and the one in Zach's body Harry. There is just as much psychological continuity between Tom and Dick and between Tom and Harry as there was between Tom and the recuperating patient (i.e., Tom) in cases 1 and 2. Moreover, Dick and Harry have exactly equal claims to being Tom; so if Tom is identical to Dick, then Tom must also be identical to Harry. But identity is a transitive relation, and Dick is not the same person as Harry; therefore, neither can be Tom. (Sam and Fred are series of *R*-related person stages, each of which begins with Tom's stages.) The important features of case 3 can be represented as in Fig. 7.4. Because Tom survives transplants 1 and 2, he has good egoist reason to be concerned for the recuperating patient in both cases. Because Tom does not survive transplant 3, it looks as if he can have no egoist reason to be concerned about Dick or Harry; it looks as if he could not be compensated for any sacrifice that he might make to Dick or Harry. But he should be just as concerned about Dick and Harry as he is about his recuperating self in cases 1 and 2, because he bears exactly the same (intrinsic) relationships to Dick and Harry in case 3 as he does to his recuperating self in cases 1 and 2. What really seems to matter as far as the rationality of concern is psychological continuity, not personal identity per se. But then agents have reason to be directly concerned about other selves, and this seems inconsistent with egoism's agent relativity.

17. Egoism with intracontinuant compensation

If the egoist accepts reductionism, she may want to claim that maximal series of *R*-related person stages – call them *continuants* – are the bearers

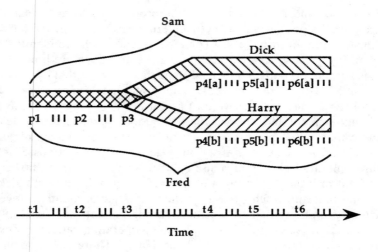

Figure 7.4

of reasons for action. Indeed, reductionism would seem to imply that continuants are the entities with the most natural borders and, hence, are the most suitable agents (cf. Section 8). The egoist could then reformulate SRC in terms of continuants, rather than persons (though psychological continuants will normally be single persons).[33] According to this proposal, it is the continuants Sam and Fred, rather than Tom, who have reasons for action. Because they each survive fission, each can be compensated for sacrifices that Tom might make; intracontinuant compensation is automatic. Sam and Fred will have some common reasons and some competing reasons corresponding to their common and competing interests. We could even construct a notion of Tom's reasons out of the reasons common to Sam and Fred and an equitable accommodation between their competing reasons. Thus, we might claim that Tom has reason to take care of his health and to divide his estate equitably between Dick and Harry.

This strategy does introduce a kind of ambiguity about the subject of practical deliberation at $t3$, somewhat akin to the sort of ambiguities generated by the proposal that it is person segments, rather than persons, that are agents (see Section 8). But that proposal generated continuum many possible subjects of practical deliberation in every case; the present strategy generates ambiguities only in fission cases and, even here, only as many alternatives as there are fission products.

I haven't addressed all the ramifications of this proposal, and I agree that some of these claims are complicated and may initially sound a little strange. But fission *is* strange, and I can't see anything obviously incoherent or implausible in this egoist proposal.[34]

18. Egoism with interpersonal compensation

Alternatively, we might retain the original formulation of SRC in terms of persons, rather than continuants, and reconcile the rationality of Tom's concern with Dick and Harry and SRC by claiming that Dick's good and Harry's good are *part of* Tom's good.

I think that it makes sense to claim that there can be people A and B who are related such that B's good is a *part* or *component* of A's good and that, in such cases, A benefits directly and necessarily by B's benefit. This sort of relationship is most commonly thought to obtain where A and B interact on an intimate basis and share important goals and interests, as is often the case between intimates (e.g., parents and children, spouses, and very close friends). If B's good is part of A's good, then A will be compensated for her sacrifice for B by B's benefit, even if she does not otherwise benefit, and this will give her reason to benefit B. And this is true even though A and B are distinct individuals (here I assume that we do not want to treat A and B as parts of some spatially dispersed person C). This does not violate SRC, because A is also a beneficiary by virtue of her relationship to B.

In the cases where A and B are intimates the ground for regarding B's good as part of A's good (and vice versa) seems to be that A and B share important goals and interests and interact with each other on an intimate basis. Indeed, in the normal case their psychological similarity will be in large part due to their interaction (e.g., to their common experiences and discussion). Of course, these are the sorts of conditions of psychological continuity and connectedness that are maximally realized in the *intra*personal case. Here they are realized to a very large extent in the *inter*personal case, and this is what grounds our claim that B's interests extend A's and that B's good is part of A's good (and vice versa). We might say that B stands to A as "another-self."[35] Now Dick and Harry represent the limiting interpersonal case; they share Tom's goals and other psychological traits to the maximal extent possible, and they acquired these traits by a direct causal process from Tom. Indeed, fission cases seem to present the clearest case for claiming that one person's good is part of another's. In these cases, A and B are distinct, yet A stands to B as A normally stands to herself; and this is the strongest possible relationship for finding A's welfare implicated in B's.

Of course, unlike intimates who have ongoing interactions, Tom doesn't have an ongoing relationship with either Dick or Harry; indeed, he doesn't temporally overlap with either of them. Tom passes on his traits to Dick and Harry and ceases to exist in the process. In this way, the relationship between Tom and Dick and Harry is highly *asymmetrical*; Dick and Harry owe their existence and nature to Tom, but not vice versa. For this reason, the parent–child relationship may present a better interpersonal model for the fission case than the relationship between spouses or friends. In many parent–child relationships the child's physical and psychological nature are to a significant degree a causal product of the parent's physical and psychological nature and activities, but not vice versa. This is how we can explain the common views that the parent's interests are extended to the child's welfare, that the child's welfare is part of the parent's good, and that the parent's interests extend beyond her own existence. The continuity between Tom and both Dick and Harry is even greater than that between parent and child; this is our ground for claiming that Dick and Harry extend Tom's interests and for claiming that Dick's good and Harry's good are part of Tom's.

And, of course, the asymmetrical character of the psychological relationship is clearest in the normal, intrapersonal case. In the normal, nonbranching case relation R both extends the agent's interests and extends the agent. Tom is a person who consists of a nonbranching series of psychologically continuous person stages $p1$ through $p3$. The psychological continuity from $p2$ to $p3$ extends Tom's interests in the sense that $p3$ inherits, carries on, and carries out $p2$'s projects and plans. In this nonbranching case, it also extends Tom's life. In the fission case, however, relation R does not literally extend Tom's life, because neither Dick nor Harry is Tom. But, by virtue of being fully psychologically continuous with Tom, Dick and Harry will each inherit, carry on, and carry out Tom's projects and plans (though presumably in somewhat different directions over time). This seems to be a good ground for claiming that Dick and Harry extend Tom's interests even if they do not literally extend his life. Tom can regard Dick and Harry as extending his interests in the very same way that his own future self would normally extend his interests.

If so, Tom can regard Dick's good and Harry's good as part of his own good, and we can explain how Tom could be compensated for benefits he might bestow on Dick or Harry. This means that the rational egoist can claim that an agent should be concerned about selves that are R-related to his present self, even when these selves are distinct people. Indeed, the existence of interpersonal psychological continuity makes possible an egoist justification of various forms of other-regarding conduct and concern.

In fact, this egoist justification of concern for others to whom one is *R*-related (i.e., other-selves) allows an egoist justification of temporal neutrality even on the assumption (rejected in Section 8) that person segments, rather than persons, are agents. Person segments have reason to care about future segments to whom they are *R*-related. Assume, contrary to fact, that person segments are agents. Temporally contiguous person segments will be strongly *R*-related, and so the earlier segment will have egoist reason to benefit the later segment, even when psychological connectedness as well as continuity matters, despite the non-identity of the person segments. In the case of temporally distant person segments that are psychologically continuous but not psychologically well connected, the earlier segment will have egoist reason to benefit the later segment just in case psychological continuity alone matters.[36]

19. Conclusion

Sidgwick believes that the rational egoist has a rationale for his hybrid treatment of time and person that relies on metaphysical and normative aspects of the separateness of persons. Intrapersonal compensation is automatic, whereas interpersonal compensation is not. Because the normative separateness of persons makes compensation a condition of rational sacrifice, it supports agent relativity and temporal neutrality. The egoist's opponent must confront these assumptions about the separateness of persons directly and cannot simply appeal to the parity of time and person as an objection to egoism's hybrid character. I have tried to defend this rationale against two challenges that Sidgwick's discussion naturally suggests. Someone might try to defend the fully relative, presentism, against egoism, by challenging the egoist assumption that it is temporally extended beings – specifically, persons – who are agents and subjects of compensation. But this challenge can be met; neither person slices nor person segments are suitable subjects of practical deliberation or reasons for action. Nor does this egoist rationale depend upon special assumptions about personal identity. Egoism is perhaps undermined, or the debate among egoism and its rivals dissolved, if we accept skepticism about personal identity. But such skepticism is, as Sidgwick notes, extreme. Egoism is not undermined by reductionist accounts of personal identity. A reductionist account in terms of psychological continuity is no threat to egoism's temporal neutrality. Nor does a reductionist account in terms of psychological continuity and connectedness threaten egoism. The egoist should be unimpressed by the reductionist's claim about the depreciation of psychological connectedness among person stages over time, because it is whole persons who are agents and whose welfare grounds reasons for action. Finally, the egoist can accommodate fission cases. She can formulate her principle about the rationality of sacrifice in terms of a reductionist notion of continuants, rather than persons, and claim that fission allows automatic intracontinuant compensation. Alternatively, she can argue that the person who is the subject of fission is compensated by her sacrifices on behalf of her fission products, because their good is part of her good; if so, she can defend egoism by recognizing some forms of interpersonal compensation. If so, Sidgwick is right that rational egoism's commitment to the separateness of persons explains its asymmetrical treatment of interpersonal and intertemporal distribution in a way that is metaphysically robust.

Notes

1 Sidgwick's position is somewhat more complicated than this suggests. Though he seems to embrace hedonism, and his versions of egoism and utilitarianism each takes hedonism as its theory of value, he also discusses sympathetically a counterfactual desire-satisfaction theory of the concept of goodness (*ME*, 109–12). One way of reconciling the two accounts is this: He distinguishes between the concept and content of goodness (*ME*, 109). The counterfactual desire-satisfaction theory is an account of the concept of goodness, whereas pleasure is the only object of counterfactual desire (*ME*, 113–14). The only problem with this interpretation is that Sidgwick actually suggests that pleasure *or* human excellence is the only object of counterfactual desire (*ME*, 114). But perhaps the interpretation is not at fault here. For Sidgwick does proceed, after this, simply to ignore the second disjunct. Perhaps he thinks that the indefiniteness of the second disjunct (*ME*, 90–3, 95) disqualifies it from figuring in a scientific treatment of value.
2 Thomas Nagel, *The Possibility of Altruism* (Princeton: Princeton University Press, 1970) (hereafter *PA*), esp. pp. 16, 19, 99–100. Nagel has revised his views in *The View from Nowhere* (New York: Oxford University Press, 1986), chaps. 8–9. In particular, he now denies that all reasons are person-neutral. I shall be concerned with *PA*'s defense of the fully neutral theory. Derek Parfit, *Reasons and Persons* (Oxford: Clarendon Press, 1984) (hereafter *RP*), esp. pp. 94–5, 126–7, 137–48, 156, 192–3.
3 Bishop Joseph Butler, *Five Sermons*, ed. S. Darwall (Indianapolis: Hackett, 1983), esp. preface, paras. 28, 35, 39; sermon 1, para. 6; sermon 3, 7–9.
4 For further argument, see David O. Brink, "Sidgwick's Dualism of Practical Reason," *Australasian Journal of Philosophy* 66 (1988): 291–307. My reading of the dualism of practical reason might be compared with the more internalist reading in William Frankena, "Sidgwick and the Dualism of Practical Reason," *Monist* 58 (1974): 449–67, and "Sidgwick and the History of Ethical Dualism," (Chapter 6, herein).

5 I think that Sidgwick supposes that the dialectical examination of common-sense morality is implicit in conditions (1), (2), and (4). I'm less sure that Sidgwick can reconcile the necessity of such a dialectical inquiry or the way in which this inquiry compares the implications of putative first principles with common-sense moral judgments with the foundationalist aspects of philosophical intuitionism. Unfortunately, I cannot pursue this matter here; I outline some of these worries in *Moral Realism and the Foundations of Ethics* (Cambridge: Cambridge University Press, 1989), pp. 107–13.

6 Of course, the externalist will concede that correct moral theories supply agents with moral reasons for action, for this is just to say that they articulate moral norms that do apply to agents (independently of their beliefs or attitudes). But this does not yet imply that agents who fail to act on such norms are pro tanto irrational.

7 It is worth noting in these passages (*ME6*, book 2, chap. 5; preface; concluding chapter) that Sidgwick normally refers to the person-neutral theory as utilitarianism, though he does sometimes refer to it as rational benevolence, and always refers to the agent-relative theory as egoism, rational egoism, or prudence, and never as ethical egoism.

8 On this point I agree with C. D. Broad, *Five Types of Ethical Theory* (London: Routledge and Kegan Paul, 1930), pp. 159, 253; see my "Sidgwick's Dualism of Practical Reason," pp. 304–5. Contrast J. B. Schneewind, *Sidgwick's Ethics and Victorian Moral Philosophy* (Oxford: Oxford University Press [Clarendon Press], 1977), pp. 372–4. There are really two distinct grounds for the incompatibility of the two methods on the internalist reading. First, Sidgwick standardly says that a method of ethics is an account of what is *ultimately* right or reasonable to do (*ME*, 6, 77 n., 78, 83, 84, 174). This makes ethical egoism and utilitarianism incompatible methods if "ultimately" means "on-balance" or "all things considered." However, this does not make them incompatible if we read "ultimately" as "nonderivatively" (cf. *ME*, 6, 8). But, however we interpret "ultimately," the two methods are incompatible if a method of ethics states *the* right-making characteristic, for two different properties cannot both be the right-making property. Now I should have thought this would be the normal way of understanding ethical egoism and utilitarianism, and it is the way Sidgwick usually describes a method of ethics (*ME*, 6, 83, 84, 174, 403; but see 77 n., 421). Even if I'm right about the incompatibility of the two methods on the internalist reading, the friend of that reading could admit this and claim only that egoism and utilitarianism are *equally evident*. The problem with this is that Sidgwick thinks not only that they are equally evident but also that each is evident (*ME*, 382, 391).

9 *Rational* egoism claims that an agent has reason to do x just insofar as x is in his own interest; *ethical* egoism claims that an agent's (one and only) moral obligation is to promote his own interest; and *psychological* egoism claims that agents act only so as to promote their own (real or perceived) interest. The externalist reading distinguishes rational egoism from ethical egoism, whereas the internalist reading identifies rational egoism and ethical egoism.

Both readings, however, distinguish these two forms of egoism from psychological egoism; Sidgwick clearly rejects psychological egoism (*ME*, book 1, chap. 4).

10 This is perhaps a little misleading. Rational altruism or benevolence, as Sidgwick and I understand it, is a person-neutral teleological theory (the theory that stands to rationality as utilitarianism stands to morality), whereas Nagel does not understand altruism this way. His remarks about the "combinatorial problem" (*PA*, chap. 13, esp. pp. 134–42) show that he intends something weaker by his doctrine of altruism. Though it is in this way misleading simply to identify Nagel's altruism with rational benevolence, his use of the parity argument commits him, as we shall see (Section 4), to a fairly strong interpretation of altruism (because many theories that merely deny egoism's agent relativity are themselves hybrid theories). Because I won't be concerned with the combinatorial (i.e., distributive) differences between rational benevolence and these strong interpretations of Nagel's altruism, nothing important I say should turn on the difference between Nagel's altruism and Sidgwick's rational benevolence.

11 Notice that Parfit's fully relative theory of reasons for action – the present-aim theory – claims that an agent has reason to do something insofar as doing so would fulfill his present aims or desires (*RP*, 95). This may seem rather different from my presentism, which claims that an agent has reason to do something insofar as doing so would contribute to his present interests or would supply him with present benefits. But the present-aim theory can be understood as a version of presentism that employs a desire-satisfaction theory of value or welfare. (Notice that there is no restriction on the content of an agent's desires – in particular, no demand that the desires be self-confined or self-referential – in the present-aim theory, but neither need nor should there be in desire-satisfaction versions of presentism or egoism.) Now perhaps the present-aim theory can be understood and motivated in other ways. For instance, someone might motivate its appeal to desires by claims about the instrumental nature of rationality and its appeal to present desires by appeal to the thought that reasons for action are connected with deliberation and deliberation must proceed from the agent's beliefs and desires at the time of acting (see Section 8). But, though the present-aim theory might be so understood and motivated in another context, it must be understood and motivated as a version of presentism in this context. The fully relative version of the parity argument argues from views that distribute benefits or welfare in certain ways among persons and across time; so, as presentism claims, the fully relative view must itself be a view about the interpersonal and intertemporal distribution of benefits or welfare. Moreover, this is clearly Sidgwick's focus; his fully relative view is one that denies that an agent should sacrifice a present good (pleasure) for a greater future good (pleasure). So he clearly treats the fully relative theory as a version of presentism. And Parfit claims that his appeal to full relativity is basically Sidgwick's challenge (*RP*, 138–42).

12 It is unclear whether Parfit's neutralism is equivalent to rational altruism or benevolence, as Sidgwick and I understand it, or whether it is the mere denial of egoism's agent relativity (cf. n. 10). This matter is further clouded by the fact that Parfit sometimes associates neutralism with morality or the moral point of view (*RP*, 95) and discusses both consequentialist and non-consequentialist accounts of morality's structure. But, as with Nagel (cf. n. 10), Parfit's use of the parity argument commits him, as we shall see (Section 4), to a fairly strong interpretation of neutralism (because many theories that merely deny egoism's agent relativity are themselves hybrid theories). Because I won't be concerned with the distributive differences between rational benevolence and these strong interpretations of neutralism, nothing important I say should turn on the difference, if any, between Parfit's neutralism and Sidgwick's rational benevolence.

13 A very similar claim linking the separateness of persons with a claim that the *morality* of sacrifice requires compensation is a familiar theme from recent moral philosophy. (Cf. *PA*, 138, 142; John Rawls, *A Theory of Justice* [Cambridge, MA: Harvard University Press, 1971], pp. 23–4, 26–7, 29, 187–8, 191; and Robert Nozick, *Anarchy, State, and Utopia* [New York: Basic, 1974], pp. 31–4.) It is important to notice that SRC forbids *all* balancing among people; this imposes severe distributional constraints. Although such constraints may be defensible as applied to the rationality of sacrifice, if the rational point of view is essentially the agent's point of view, they conflict with very well-entrenched claims about morality's impartiality; for instance, any moral theory that recognizes duties of mutual aid must apparently violate SRC. (Cf. Brink, "The Separateness of Persons, Distributive Norms, and Moral Theory," in *Value, Welfare, and Morality*, ed. R. Frey and C. Morris [Cambridge: Cambridge University Press, forthcoming]). If SRC is more plausible as an assumption about the rationality of sacrifice than about the morality of sacrifice, then this is further support for the externalist reading of Sidgwick, for Sidgwick does appeal to the separateness of persons to support egoism, and only the externalist reading allows us to represent egoism as a theory about rationality, rather than morality.

14 See my "Rational Egoism, Self, and Others" in *Identity, Character, and Morality*, ed. O. Flanagan and A. Rorty (Cambridge, MA: MIT Press, 1990).

15 Another misunderstanding about temporal neutrality may be worth avoiding. Temporal neutrality claims that what I now have most reason to do is what will most advance my overall good. This may require present sacrifices for my future benefit (now-for-then sacrifice). In one sense, this requires acting on interests that I do not now have, but this does not require me to act as if I now had those interests. For instance, it does not require me to eat or buy foodstuffs now in order to satisfy my future hunger. Where temporal neutrality requires now-for-then sacrifice, it requires only that I act now so as to be able to secure my future good at that time. For instance, it requires only that I set aside or employ my resources now so that I will then have the means available to satisfy the hunger that I will have then. Recognition

of this fact may tend to undermine the force of Parfit's criticisms of S (i.e., rational egoism) on the ground that its temporal neutrality requires us to act now (1) on past desires we no longer have and (2) on future desires we do not yet possess (cf. *RP*, chap. 8, esp. secs. 59–61). But to pursue these issues would require a fuller discussion than I have space for here.

16 I explore these egoist strategies for justifying other-regarding conduct and concern more fully in my "Rational Egoism, Self, and Others."

17 For example, Parfit raises some interesting questions about egoism's temporal neutrality (*RP*, pt. 2, chap. 8), which I cannot pursue here.

18 As we have seen, Parfit makes the appeal to full relativity (*RP*, chap. 7). Although this appeal to person stages is not his official view (*RP*, 95, 135, 139–45), it is suggested by some things he says (*RP*, 140, 164) and is a response worth exploring in any case.

19 Sidgwick says: "it must surely be admissible to ask the Egoist, 'Why should I sacrifice a present pleasure for a greater one in the future? Why should I concern myself about my own future feelings any more than about the feelings of other persons?' " (*ME*, 418). Cf. Parfit, who says: "A Present-aim theorist [i.e., presentist] can ask, 'Why should I give weight *now* to aims which are not mine *now*?' " (*RP*, 95).

20 Some reject a metaphysics of temporal parts; see, e.g., Judith Thomson, "Parthood and Identity across Time," *Journal of Philosophy* 80 (1983): 201–20, esp. 210–13. If the critics of temporal parts are right, it seems that temporal parts cannot be the bearers of reasons and that the egoist rationale is not threatened. However, I do not share these metaphysical scruples. In any case, I want to argue that the egoist can and should resist the suggestion that temporal parts of people are the bearers of reasons *even if* temporal parts are respectable entities.

21 This reasoning is perhaps suggested by Williams when he bases his reservations about temporal neutrality on the thought that "The correct perspective on one's life is *from now*." Bernard Williams, "Persons, Character, and Morality," reprinted in his *Moral Luck* (Cambridge: Cambridge University Press, 1981), p. 13.

22 Parfit himself questions the intelligibility of this claim (*RP*, 135). Question: Must this presentist attack on egoism assume not only that me-now has interests but also that its interests are not parasitic on or posterior to *my* interests?

23 Cf. Christine Korsgaard, "Personal Identity and the Unity of Agency: A Kantian Response to Parfit," *Philosophy & Public Affairs* 18 (1989): 101–32.

24 Joseph Butler, *The Analogy of Religion*, app. 1, reprinted in *Personal Identity*, ed. J. Perry (Los Angeles: University of California Press, 1975), p. 102.

25 See David Hume, *A Treatise of Human Nature*, ed. P. H. Nidditch (Oxford: Oxford University Press, 1978), book 1, pt. 4, sec. 6.

26 This appearance may be misleading if I can regard the good of those future, other selves that are connected to me by the appropriate ties as part of my

own good (cf. Section 18). This would allow for posthumous benefits and harms and for the possibility of interpersonal compensation.

27 There are two other possible views that I will not discuss separately. I will not discuss the less moderate, "extreme claim." which Butler accepts and Parfit discusses (*RP*, 307–12), according to which reductionism completely undermines any special concern for oneself and one's future. Because I think that egoism survives even the moderate claim, there's not much reason to discuss the extreme claim directly. I will also not discuss the more moderate claim that insists only that this discount rate of concern for one's future is not irrational but does not insist that it is rationally required. Though the friend of temporal neutrality must deny the more moderate claim as well, the reductionist argument, if successful, surely supports the moderate claim that a discount rate of concern is rationally appropriate where the relations that matter hold to a reduced degree.

28 Cf. Sydney Shoemaker, "Critical Notice of Derek Parfit, *Reasons and Persons*," *Mind* 94 (1985): 451.

29 See C. I. Lewis, *An Analysis of Knowledge and Valuation* (La Salle, IL: Open Court, 1946), p. 493.

30 This is compatible with my earlier claim that continuity is defined in terms of connectedness. Take a series of temporally contiguous or successive person stages $p1$ through $p3$: $p1$ and $p3$ are continuous, I said, just in case $p1$ is well connected with $p2$ and $p2$ is well connected with $p3$. This is why connectedness is explanatorily prior. Nonetheless, continuity could be all that mattered if the persistence of what matters from $p1$ through $p3$ requires only that $p3$ be continuous with $p1$ and not also that it be well connected with $p1$.

31 Compare Aristotle's discussion of the puzzle about whether to wish one's friend the good of divinity (*Nicomachean Ethics* [*EN*] 1159a5–11). Aristotle claims that one who cares about the friend for the friend's own sake would not wish this good on a friend, because the friend would not survive the transformation. Though Aristotle's claim seems plausible, *C&C*'s corresponding claims about the (ir)rationality of self-improvement seem implausible. Aristotle's claim is plausible, because it's plausible to think that the species or genus to which an individual belongs is an essential property of that individual, whereas it seem implausible to think that an individual's current psychological profile is essential to that individual's persistence in the way that *C&C* seems to require.

At one point, Parfit does suggest that my reasons to be concerned about the person who emerges when I undergo a psychological change depend upon both (1) the degree of connectedness between that person and myself prior to the change and (2) the value of the new psychological profile (*RP*, 299). But (2) is something the egoist can happily admit and requires no special claims about personal identity. Moreover, as I've suggested, (1) seems implausible, even when it's conjoined with (2), and may gain specious plausibility from its association with (2).

32 Of course, *ceteris* is not *paribus* if the relations among the parts of a whole are such that a given part is a less important part of the whole than others (e.g., as my fingernail is a less important part of my body than my heart). In such a case, treatment of the parts as equals may not support equal treatment of the parts. But notice that this will be a result of the relation between that part and the whole and not simply between that part and other parts. Notice also that this will be compatible with temporal neutrality.

33 This suggestion is somewhat similar to Lewis's view, though he seems to want to identify persons and continuants, as I do not. See David Lewis, "Survival and Identity," in *The Identities of Persons*, ed. A. Rorty (Los Angeles: University of California Press, 1976), esp. pp. 24–9.

34 One possible problem concerns *overpopulation*. Because some people (e.g., friends and spouses) share some psychological states (e.g., beliefs, aims, and values) as the result of their causal interaction, they will be weakly psychologically continuous with each other (see Section 18). If our notion of a continuant includes series of selves that are connected by any degree of continuity whatsover, then, unlike the fission case, there will be many more continuants than persons. I'm not sure if our notion of a continuant need be this liberal, and I'm not sure that there's anything unacceptable about the population boom that would result from such liberality. If there is a worry here, it may be reason to prefer the second egoist reply (Section 18).

35 This phrase comes from Aristotle's justification of friendship in *EN*, book 9 (1166a30–2, 1170b6–8). For further discussion of Aristotle's justification of friendship and its relevance to egoist justifications of morality, see T. H. Irwin, *Aristotle's First Principles* (New York: Oxford University Press, 1988), chap. 18, and my "Rational Egoism, Self, and Others."

36 If connectedness matters as well, then, on the contrary-to-fact assumption that it is person segments that are the bearers of reasons for action, the person segment bearing the reason for action will have less reason to regard the distant *R*-related person segment as another-self than it has to regard the near *R*-related segment as another-self. *This* would justify a discount rate of egoistic concern, but I don't think we need accept all of the premises on which this conclusion rests.

8

Sidgwick on ethical judgment

JOHN DEIGH

British moral philosophy has had two great traditions. Its empiricist tradition, which began with Hobbes and resurged with Hume and the classical utilitarians on whom Hume exercised so much influence, takes ethical judgments to be founded on or to originate in desire or feeling. Its intuitionist tradition, which formed in reaction to Hobbes and continued by way of debate with Hume and the classical utilitarians, takes ethical judgments to be deliverances of reason which subserve neither desire nor feeling and in which one recognizes and affirms morality's fundamental precepts. Within the empiricist tradition several works have supreme importance as alternative statements of its philosophy. Within the intuitionist tradition, by contrast, *The Methods of Ethics*, Sidgwick's masterwork, towers above the others.

The pedigree of Sidgwick's *Methods* is established early in the work when, in the third chapter of its first book, Sidgwick queried the nature of ethical judgment and gave in response a distinctively intuitionist account. He fashioned this account to settle the dispute between intuitionism and empiricism over the proper conception of ethical judgment, and the argument he advanced for his side appears to leave empiricism without a rejoinder. This argument is the subject of the present study. In the first two sections I shall set it out as I read it and argue for this reading as against an alternative. Then, in the third and last section, I shall critically examine the argument and assess its cogency. My conclusion will be that the argument fails to vindicate intuitionism. The reasons for its failure should prove instructive.

1

Sidgwick's argument proceeds from consideration of two issues: the sense of the words "right" and "ought" in expressions of ethical judg-

I am grateful to David Brink for several suggestions and points about his work and about the topic in general. This essay began as a set of comments on the version of his contribution to this volume that he read at the University of Chicago's conference on Sidgwick.

ment and the role of such judgment in motivating human action. Sidgwick saw an important connection between these issues, and he used this connection to ground the intuitionist conception of ethical judgment on observations of common human experience. His argument extends over the whole of chapter 3 of book 1. Its crux, however, occurs in the chapter's opening section, where the two issues are joined.

In this section Sidgwick speaks first to the issue concerning the role of ethical judgment in motivating human action. For him, the issue is defined sharply by Hume's thesis that no exercise of reason can alone influence the will. Hume, as we know, used this thesis to great effect in arguing against rationalist ethics. Morality is essentially practical, Hume declared, and this is to say that moral opinion can by itself influence the will. Hence, our moral opinions are not exercises of our reason. Morality, at bottom, is a matter of feeling and not judgment. Sidgwick starts from propositions that contradict this conclusion. Morality is basically a matter of judgment, and the judgments it particularly concerns are judgments of what it is right to do and what one ought to do. On the issue of whether such judgments can by themselves motivate action, then, Sidgwick argues affirmatively by first redefining the issue as that of whether such judgments are reducible to judgments of empirical fact or one's own mental state and, second, asserting that they are not, that to the contrary they involve a fundamental notion, which the words "right" and "ought" express and which is "essentially different from all notions representing facts of physical or psychical experience" (*ME*, 25).

The argument's crucial step, obviously, is Sidgwick's redefinition of the first issue. It is here that the two issues are joined. He bases this step, I believe, on the following observations. It is clear, he thinks, from reflection on experiences of the kind we commonly describe, whether correctly or not, as a conflict of reason and passion or reason and appetite that the deliverances of reason in these experiences have influence on the will. These deliverances are judgments of what it is right to do or what one ought to do, and the experiences are those of being strongly inclined by passion or appetite to act against these judgments and of needing to summon the strength of will to resist the inclination. It is also clear, Sidgwick thinks, that some judgments can and do influence the will indirectly in the way Hume supposed. That is, they can influence the will by altering the understanding the agent has of the objects of his already existing desires and the means and obstacles to their attainment. Such judgments, given this description of the indirect way in which they can influence the will, must be either judgments of empirical fact or judgments of one's own mental state; and when reason works in the service of already existing desire to influence the will, it does so by means of them alone. The issue therefore becomes that of whether judgments of what it is right to do or what one ought to do are reducible to judgments of empirical fact or one's own mental state. For if they are not, then when they influence the will, as they do, for instance, in the experiences of conflict on which Sidgwick bids us to reflect, they must do so directly.

Sidgwick's argument, as I have explained it so far, has three main premises: that morality is a matter of judgment as opposed to feeling; that its special notion is irreducible to physical or psychological notions; and, a central doctrine of Hume's argument, that morality is essentially practical. The first two are evident in my explanation, whereas the last is implicit in the lesson Sidgwick draws from his reflection on the experiences we commonly describe as a conflict between reason and passion. As a set, these three propositions contain the defining elements of Sidgwick's conception of ethical judgment. The first two reveal his commitment to intuitionism. Taken together, they distinguish this position in ethics from noncognitivism, on the one hand, which denies that morality is a matter of judgment, and naturalism, on the other, which denies that morality's special notions are irreducible to physical or psychological notions. The third, then, when conjoined with the other two, yields Sidgwick's singular formulation of intuitionism: An ethical judgment is an exercise of reason whose constitutive notion is not only simple, in Locke's sense, but also practical, in the sense that Hume's doctrine requires.

The singularity of this formulation will be apparent to any student of the metaethical wars that were waged within Anglo-American philosophy during the middle decades of this century. For Hume's doctrine was the chief weapon used against intuitionism by the noncognitivists. They were able to use this doctrine to attack intuitionism and to do so effectively because the leading intuitionists of this period accepted the other central doctrine of Hume's argument, that reason is inert. Specifically, the noncognitivists argued that intuitionism sprang from a mistake: Although its adherents correctly took the terms special to ethics, terms such as "right" and "ought," to be indefinable in terms that expressed physical and psychological notions, they mistakenly inferred from the indefinability of these terms that they expressed simple notions. What explained the indefinability of a term like "right," the noncognitivists maintained, was its essentially practical character, which they then variously specified as its emotive meaning, magnetic effect, prescriptivity, commendatory force, et cetera. By thus making the choice between their position and intuitionism a choice between competing explanations of what makes ethical terms indefinable in terms that express physical and psychological notions, they made their position appear to be a significant advance over intuitionism. After all, that the terms are essentially practical seems a more powerful explanation – richer and more easily verified – than that they express simple notions. Sidgwick, as we've seen, rejected Hume's doctrine of the inertness of reason, and this rejection was then reflected in the way he defined ethical judgment and characterized the fundamental notion it involved. As a result, his formulation of intuitionism avoids the issue of competing explanations that the noncognitivists pressed to such advantage. It falls, therefore, outside the range of their attack.

The distance between Sidgwick's formulation and that of the leading twentieth-century intuitionists Prichard and Ross can be seen in their different relations to Kant. For Prichard and Ross, unlike Sidgwick, broke with Kant on the question of moral motivation.[1] They attributed such motivation to a desire to do what is right that is independent of ethical judgment. Sidgwick, by contrast, agreed with Kant in taking ethical judgment to be the source of such motivation. Indeed, as the vocabulary and distinctions he borrowed from Kant indicate, he followed Kant's general views on the nature of ethical judgment. In particular, he characterized ethical judgments as imperatives or dictates of reason. "[W]hen I speak of the cognition or judgment that 'X ought to be done' – in the stricter ethical sense of the term ought – as a 'dictate' or 'precept' of reason to the person to whom it relates, I imply that in rational beings as such this cognition gives an impulse or motive to action" (*ME*, 34). In words relevant to current philosophical debate, for Sidgwick, as for Kant, a rational agent, in recognizing that it is right to do a certain action or that it ought to be done, recognizes a reason for doing it.

One question, however, that arises from this debate is whether the cognition that it is right to do a certain action or that it ought to be done of which Sidgwick speaks here is a cognition of a duty to do it. Put differently, the question is whether the notion of duty falls within the scope of the fundamental notion of ethics that Sidgwick intended his argument to capture and that he identified with the stricter ethical sense of the words "right" and "ought." And to fully understand Sidgwick's account of the nature of ethical judgment we must address this question.

2

The debate that gives rise to the question concerns the use of "ought" to express moral judgments, specifically, judgments of duty. On one side of the debate are the internalists, philosophers who hold that this moral use of "ought" implies a reason for action. On their view, to say that a certain action ought to be done, meaning that it is one's duty to do it, implies that one has a reason to do it. On the other side are the externalists, philosophers who deny internalism. On their view, one can say that a certain action ought to be done, meaning that it is one's duty to do it, without thereby implying that there is a reason to do it. Since Sidgwick's argument, as I have so far explained it, if sound, would show only that some judgments about what it is right to do or what ought to be done imply reasons for action irrespective of any desire or feeling, it remains pertinent to ask whether his argument places him on either side of this debate.

It would be surprising, of course, if the argument turned out to place him on the side of the externalists. Yet, recently, David Brink, in an essay on Sidgwick's famous quandary over the relation between egoism and utilitarianism, has proposed an interpretation that places Sidgwick squarely on this side.[2] Brink's principal interpretative interest is in explaining the dualism of practical reason to which Sidgwick was led by his conclusion about the equal and independent tenability of egoism and utilitarianism. On the received interpretation, the dualism represents Sidgwick's failure to reconcile completely the fundamental principles of morality, specifically, the axioms of prudence and rational benevolence on which egoism and utilitarianism, respectively, are founded. On the interpretation Brink proposes, which he appropriately dubs "the externalist reading," the dualism represents Sidgwick's failure to solve the traditional problem of finding compelling reasons to be moral. Accordingly, in view of Sidgwick's firm belief in utilitarianism as the correct theory of duty, Brink reasons that Sidgwick must at least implicitly have regarded egoism as the correct theory of reasons for action. And once it is assumed that Sidgwick, at least implicitly, distinguished between these two domains of study, that of duty, on the one hand, and rationality as regards action, on the other, and took egoism rather than utilitarianism to be the correct theory of the latter while taking utilitarianism rather than egoism to be the correct theory of the former, it follows that, on his view, judgments of duty do not necessarily imply reasons for action. In other words, on Brink's externalist reading, the notion of duty falls outside the scope of the fundamental notion of ethics that the argument of book 1, chapter 3, is intended to capture. Further consideration of the argument, however, shows that this result is not a happy one. It shows, that is, that Sidgwick, as we would expect and as far as this chapter goes, sided with those philosophers who think judgments of duty necessarily imply reasons for action.

That Sidgwick held this view is first signaled at the point in the argument where he reflects on experiences of the kind we commonly describe as a conflict between reason and passion. He offers there two examples: the experience of judging, while in the grip of anger, that the act one's emotion prompts would be unjust or unkind; and the experience of judging, while subject to some strong bodily appetite, that the act one's appetite inclines one to do would be imprudent. And he indicates that the judgment in the first example concerns duty whereas the judgment in the second concerns self-interest. Hence, in view of the former, it is clear that Sidgwick regarded judgments that one has a duty to do a certain act as belonging to the class of ethical judgments (i.e., those judgments that the words "right" and "ought" in their stricter ethical sense are used to express), since he meant the former to be an example of a judgment that can influence the will but is irreducible to judgments of empirical fact or one's own mental state.

Subsequently, for the purpose of further examining this question of the irreducibility of ethical judgments, Sidgwick explicitly distinguished two kinds of ethical judgment, moral and prudential, according as the judgment concerns duty or self-interest. The passage in which he made this distinction is worth quoting, since the distinction is not unproblematic.

In considering this question it is important to take separately the two species of judgment which I have distinguished as "moral" and "prudential." Both kinds might, indeed, be termed "moral" in a wider sense. . . . But in ordinary thought we clearly distinguish cognitions or judgments of duty from cognitions or judgments as to what is "right" or "ought to be done" in view of the agent's private interests or happiness: and the depth of the distinction will not, I think, be diminished by the closer examination of these judgments we are now to enter. (*ME*, 25–6)

The problem the distinction creates is one of uncertainty. Does it import into Sidgwick's account of the nature of ethical judgment a different sense of the terms "right" and "ought" from the one he called the stricter ethical sense and identified with the fundamental notion of ethics? This problem is particularly urgent because if the distinction did import into Sidgwick's account two different senses of these terms, a moral sense and a prudential one, and if the moral sense differed from Sidgwick's stricter ethical sense, then the notion of duty that the terms "right" and "ought" expressed when used in this moral sense would fall outside the scope of the fundamental notion and Sidgwick's argument would thus be thrown into confusion. This possibility may then give some hope to the externalist reading, inasmuch as that reading offers a way out of the confusion. But consideration of how Sidgwick used the distinction to advance his argument for the irreducibility of ethical judgments and how that argument proceeds argues against the possibility and so dampens this hope.

Briefly, as he implied in the passage quoted above, he thought the best way to see the irreducibility of ethical judgments was to examine separately specific types of such judgment, and the distinction thus served to separate the relevant types. He then proceeded to examine and make the case for the irreducibility of moral judgments before examining and making the case for the irreducibility of prudential judgments. Finally, in making the latter case, he divided it into two parts and based one of them on the results of the former. Both this ordering of the two cases and his basing part of the latter on the former indicate that Sidgwick regarded the former as the principal or at least the clearer case. Hence, they indicate that Sidgwick took moral judgments to be the primary or clearest examples of what he meant by an ethical judgment and, correspondingly, that he took the notion of duty to be the primary or clearest representative of what he meant by the fundamental notion of ethics. The way the argument proceeds, therefore, rules out the idea that the distinction he drew between the two types of judgment imports into his account a notion of duty that falls outside the scope of the fundamental notion. The idea, then, cannot be the start of an externalist reading. Indeed, the externalist reading seems at this point at greatest odds with Sidgwick's argument. For, given what the irreducibility of an ethical judgment signifies in this argument, we can say that, for Sidgwick, moral judgments represented the primary or clearest examples of inherently motivational judgments or, in other words, they represented the primary or clearest examples of when in recognizing that it is right to do a certain action or that it ought to be done one recognizes a reason to do it.

All of this notwithstanding, the distinction Sidgwick drew between moral and prudential judgments remains a problem, and until we get to the bottom of it the externalist reading will continue, I think, to have some hold on our imagination. The source of the problem becomes apparent in the last section of chapter 3, where Sidgwick made the case for the irreducibility of prudential judgments. This case, as I mentioned, is divided into two parts. In the first part, prudential judgments are understood to be judgments about what it is right to do or what one ought to do in view of one's interest in one's own happiness, and the end in view of which these judgments are made, one's own happiness, is then assumed to be unconditionally prescribed by reason. In the second part, the same understanding of prudential judgments holds, but the end in view of which they are made is assumed to be given by a desire that is not itself the product of reason. Taking our cue from Sidgwick, we can say that the first part proceeds on the assumption that prudential judgments presuppose an unconditional dictate of reason, a categorical imperative, to adopt as one's end one's own happiness. They are thus analogous to moral judgments that presuppose a categorical imperative to adopt as one's end some such universal end as the general happiness, and the argument of this part consists in an appeal to this analogy. By contrast, the second part proceeds on the assumption that no categorical imperative lies behind prudential judgments but rather that their validity is determined relative to an end that one has adopted but that reason has not prescribed. They are thus all mere hypothetical imperatives, and the argument of this part consists in an attempt to show that even a mere hypothetical imperative is irreducible to judgments of empirical fact or one's own mental state. What emerges, then, in effect, is a distinction between alternative accounts of the validity conditions of prudential judgments, and it is this distinction that creates the problem. The ambiguity it fosters makes it uncertain whether Sidgwick's earlier distinction between moral and prudential judgments imports into his account a different sense of "right" and "ought" from their stricter ethical sense. For the answer arguably depends on which account of the validity conditions one follows.[3]

On the first, the account according to which prudential judgments presuppose a categorical imperative, the sense of the terms "right" and "ought" when they are used to express prudential judgments is the same sense as the one they have when they are used to express moral judgments. So the distinction between the two types of judgment does not introduce any new sense of these terms. Indeed, to distinguish between the two types as Sidgwick did is, on this account, misleading since prudential judgments form only a subclass of moral judgments. They concern self-regarding duty, the duty to promote one's happiness, and consequently the opposition between duty and what is "right" or "ought to be done" in view of one's private interests or happiness, on which Sidgwick's distinction between the two types of judgment turns, is illusory. On the second account, the account according to which prudential judgments are mere hypothetical imperatives, the sense of "right" and "ought" when used to express prudential judgments is arguably different from the sense they have when used to express moral judgments. So the distinction between the two types of judgment, one could argue, introduces a new sense. At the same time, because this new sense, assuming the distinction introduces one, attaches to "right" and "ought" when they are used to express *prudential* judgments, its introduction does not affect our earlier conclusions about moral judgments or their constitutive notion of duty. It does not, in other words, give renewed hope to an externalist reading.

What is more, Sidgwick's distinction between the two types of judgment is, on this account too, misleading. For unless psychological egoism holds – and Sidgwick went on to demolish it in the next chapter – prudential judgments form only a proper subclass of mere hypothetical imperatives, and there is nothing about the members of this subclass to warrant distinguishing them and not other mere hypothetical imperatives from moral judgments. Thus, contrary to what Sidgwick said in the passage in which he explicitly distinguished between moral and prudential judgments, the distinction loses its depth upon closer examination. It does not, despite what one might easily suppose, represent a deep fissure in Sidgwick's thought that divides morality from practical reason. And the absence of such a fissure in Sidgwick's thought tells against the externalist reading.

A quick review should make this last point clear. The heart of the reading, as Brink presents it, is the thesis that Sidgwick's conclusion about the dualism of practical reason represents an admission of failure to solve the traditional problem of finding compelling reasons to be moral, and to render Sidgwick's interest in reconciling utilitarianism and egoism as an interest in solving this traditional problem requires supposing that Sidgwick divided the field of his study into two domains, morality and rationality as regards action, and took egoism rather than utilitarianism to be the correct theory of the latter and utilitarianism rather than egoism to be the correct theory of the former. Accordingly, it requires supposing that the distinction between morality and prudence is deeply embedded in Sidgwick's thought, since egoism, in being the theory of rational self-interest, is a theory of prudence.[4] Yet, as we've seen, closer examination of Sidgwick's distinction between moral and prudential judgment proves otherwise. Specifically, reflection on the ambiguity in Sidgwick's understanding of prudential judgment shows that either the distinction corresponds to a distinction of one species of moral judgment from the entire genus, in which case it would make no sense to distinguish egoism as a theory of morality from egoism as a theory of rationality as regards action, or it corresponds to a distinction between a species of mere hypothetical imperatives and the entire genus of moral judgments, in which case it would make no sense to single out egoism from all other coherent systems of mere hypothetical imperatives as the more rationally justified. Hence, either case opposes the externalist reading.

Sidgwick, of course, did not treat egoism as a system of mere hypothetical imperatives. He did, however, recognize the possibility. Thus, corresponding to his distinction between alternative accounts of the validity conditions of prudential judgments is a distinction he made between alternative views of egoism regarded as a system of ethics. On one view, egoism is a system founded on a categorical imperative. Its foundational imperative is that one ought to adopt one's own greatest happiness as the ultimate end of one's actions. On the other view, egoism is a system of mere hypothetical imperatives and, to quote Sidgwick, "does not properly regard the agent's own greatest happiness as what he 'ought' to aim at: but only as the ultimate end for the realization of which he has, on the whole, a predominant desire" (*ME*, 36). The first view is the one Sidgwick took in the bulk of his treatise, but the second, as he remarked in a subsequent footnote, "is admissible" (*ME*, 98 n.1). And he further implied that one could similarly distinguish alternative views of utilitarianism. These distinctions between alternative views of egoism and utilitarianism suggest a division of ethics into two domains, the domain of systems founded on categorical imperatives and the domain of systems of mere hypothetical imperatives. This division, to be sure, is not the same as the one the externalist reading implies. But the latter, it is plausible to suppose, is the misconstruction of the former that results from seeing the distinction between morality and prudence as deeply embedded in Sidgwick's thought, and the naturalness of this misconstruction would then explain the attraction of the externalist reading.

At the same time, correcting the error would not revive the reading's prospects. For with regard to neither of the domains that the former division defines can one interpret Sidgwick as taking egoism to be the correct theory of that domain. Thus, one cannot interpret Sidgwick as having taken egoism as the correct system of mere hypothetical imperatives, because such a view would entail holding that reason required one to adopt one's own happiness as the ultimate end of one's actions, and in taking egoism to be a system of mere hypothetical imperatives, one assumes that the ultimate end is not an end that reason prescribes. Nor can one interpret Sidgwick as having taken egoism as the correct system among those founded on categorical imperatives, because such a view would be the same as taking egoism as the correct theory of duty. In sum, the division of domains that the externalist reading implies corresponds to a misconception of how the distinction between morality and prudence figures in Sidgwick's thought, and the division that corresponds to the correct conception of how the distinction figures in Sidgwick's thought does not fit the externalist reading.

Having affirmed an internalist reading of Sidgwick's argument, we may now turn to its assessment.

3

Let us begin our assessment by gently probing the oddity of Sidgwick's willingness to consider systems of mere hypothetical imperatives as among the methods of ethics. Such willingness is sure to seem out of place in an intuitionist account of the nature of ethical judgment. Systems of mere hypothetical imperatives, after all, are a standard product of empiricist moral philosophy – Hobbes's ethics being the most obvious example. So, presumably, the conception of ethical judgment they presuppose conflicts with the intuitionist conception. This oddity, however, can be resolved. The key to its resolution lies in the second part of Sidgwick's case for the irreducibility of prudential judgments.

Recall that for this part of the case Sidgwick assumes that prudential judgments are mere hypothetical imperatives. He then argues that the "ought" that is used to express such judgments has the same sense as when it is used to express categorical imperatives. That is, he holds and defends the thesis that the fundamental notion of ethics is a constituent of mere hypothetical imperatives as well as categorical ones, the difference in their validity conditions notwithstanding. Yet, clearly, he could not hold this thesis unless he was willing to consider systems of mere hypothetical imperatives as among the methods of ethics. At the same time, though, the thesis counters the presumption that the conception of ethical judgment such systems presuppose conflicts with the intuitionist conception. Hence, considering such systems as among the methods of ethics does not spoil the uniformity of his account. A method of ethics, according to Sidgwick, is a rational procedure whose application yields dictates of reason that qualify as ethical judgments, and on Sidgwick's account these dictates include both hypothetical and categorical imperatives.

Although Sidgwick is thus able to maintain his view of hypothetical imperatives despite the proprietary claims of empiricism, in doing so he deviates significantly from Kant. As we noted earlier, Sidgwick took a dictate of reason that qualifies as an ethical judgment to be a "cognition [that] gives an impulse or motive to action" (*ME*, 34), and it follows then that he regarded hypothetical as well as categorical imperatives as inherently motivational. Both, on his account, are sources of purely rational motives. Kant, by contrast, held that only categorical imperatives are a source of such motives. Indeed, in Kant's ethics, the only purely rational motive, the only one that originates in the operations of reason alone, is the motive of duty. Consequently, for Kant, judgments of duty, which is to say, categorical imperatives, exhaust the class of inherently motivational judgments. The difference between Sidgwick's account and Kant's comes therefore to this: On Sidgwick's account purely rational motivation comprehends more than moral motivation (narrowly defined by the motive of duty), whereas on Kant's account the two are identical.

Sidgwick's view of hypothetical imperatives thus puts him at odds with both the empiricists and the followers of Kant. Both, that is, would object to his construing all hypothetical imperatives as, in his sense, dictates of reason, though of course their objections would take different forms. Still, their common opposition suggests this view as the place to look if one suspects weaknesses in Sidgwick's account. The view represents middle ground, so to speak, between these two camps, and as such it is an inviting target for suspicions of weakness. What is more, additional probing of Sidgwick's argument confirms these suspicions.

The argument's main point is that prudential judgments, even when conceived of as mere hypothetical imperatives, are irreducible to judgments of empirical fact or one's own mental state. For Sidgwick, following the argument of the opening section of chapter 3, takes this point as sufficient for showing that the word "ought" has the same sense whether it is used to express a hypothetical or a categorical imperative. That is, he takes it as sufficient for showing that the fundamental notion of ethics is a constituent of prudential judgment even when such judgment is conceived of as a mere hypothetical imperative. The brunt of the argument then is to substantiate its main point, and to accomplish this Sidgwick turns to an example:

When (e.g.) a physician says, "If you wish to be healthy you ought to rise early," this is not the same thing as saying "early rising is an indispensable condition of the attainment of health." This latter proposition expresses the relation of physiological facts on which the former is founded; but it is not merely the relation of facts that the word "ought" imports: it also implies the unreasonableness of adopting an end and refusing to adopt the means indispensable to its attainment. (*ME*, 37)

Yet Sidgwick's concentration on substantiating this point is misplaced. A prior question, which he does not address, is much more troublesome. Specifically, one could first challenge Sidgwick's argument by asking whether the argument of the opening section even applies to prudential judgments conceived of as mere hypothetical imperatives, and Sidgwick, I think, would be hard pressed to come up with a satisfactory answer. The reason for the difficulty is that the earlier argument proceeds from reflection on experiences we commonly describe as a conflict of reason and passion or reason and appetite, and no such conflict seems to arise when reason is only issuing hypothetical imperatives in the service of what Sidgwick calls nonrational desires, by which he means desires that originate independently of any dictate of reason.

As we noted before, Sidgwick divides the experiences from reflection on which the argument of the opening section proceeds into two classes, which he then treats as separate cases. On the one hand, there is the experience of conflict in which a moral judgment represents what the common description denotes as the side of reason. On the other, there is the experience of conflict in which a prudential judgment represents what the common description denotes as the side of reason. One could then say that the thrust of the entire chapter was to confirm the correctness of the common description of these experiences in either case and that, in the opening section, Sidgwick argued for the controlling thesis that the description would be correct if the moral or prudential judgment in question were irreducible to judgments of empirical fact or one's own mental state. It would seem, though, that the irreducibility of a prudential judgment could not have this implication if the judgment were a mere hypothetical imperative. For such an imperative, by our very understanding of it, is the product not of reason alone but rather of reason operating in the service of some nonrational desire, and consequently any conflict between the impulse to act as it directs and some passion or appetite would seem to be correctly described as a conflict between two nonrational desires and not as a conflict between reason and passion or reason and appetite. Hence, it would seem that prudential judgments, when conceived of as mere hypothetical imperatives, lie beyond the reach of the argument of the opening section.

Evidently, then, this argument proves too much. A mere hypothetical imperative seems more aptly construed as a counsel of reason than a precept or dictate, and the role of reason in the issuance of such imperatives is more aptly explained as that of a guide than that of a mover. In this refrain empiricism would reassert its proprietary claim on systems of mere hypothetical imperatives. The question, then, is where the argument goes wrong; and the answer must lie in its crucial step, the step at which Sidgwick redefines the issue of whether an ethical judgment can by itself motivate action as that of whether it is irreducible to judgments of empirical fact or one's own mental state. Empiricists need not regard mere hypothetical imperatives as reducible to such judgments.

When Sidgwick takes this step, he carefully describes how some judgments motivate action indirectly in the way Hume supposed. He states, in effect, that every judgment of this sort is either a judgment about the means to attaining the object of an already existing, nonrational desire or a judgment that further or more specifically characterizes the object of such a desire. The judgment, then, is either identical or reducible to a judgment of empirical fact or one's own mental state since it amounts to either a judgment about causal relations or a judgment about the character of certain experiences. In addition, Sidgwick takes the time to point out that, although he calls the desires these judgments serve nonrational and even irrational – the latter term being reserved for times when they appear to conflict with reason – their impulses are commonly modified and directed by these judgments and so commonly prompt intelligent action. And as he describes the process by which such action typically comes about, it occurs without the intervention of any judgment that it is right to do that action or that it ought to be done.

Where then do hypothetical imperatives fit in? Let us consider Sidgwick's example of the judgment that one ought to rise early. This would be a hypothetical imperative if its validity required that the action it prescribed be an indispensable means or the fittest means to some end the agent had in fact adopted. In Sidgwick's example this end is one's own health. Moreover, since he intends this to be an example of a mere hypothetical imperative, we are to assume that the adoption of this end is not something reason has prescribed. Rather, so we are to assume, it follows from some nonrational desire, the love of life, say, or the desire for the pleasures of vigorous activity. He also, obviously, intends it to be an example of a judgment that can motivate action, and consequently we must regard it as a judgment that the agent addresses to himself. We must regard it, that is, as the judgment "I ought to rise early." The key point to note, then, is that the consideration on which the agent bases this judgment is the same as the consideration on which he would be acting if he got up early from a desire to retain or improve his health and without the intervention of any hypothetical imperative in the process that leads from the desire to the action. In either case, the relevant consideration is that early rising is essential to good health, and in the latter case this thought brings him to focus his desire for good health on getting up early without his first passing through the hypothetical imperative that prescribes such actions. Consequently, the occasions when he would make the judgment "I ought to rise early" must be occasions when the action is not immediately forthcoming, either because it cannot be done in the circumstances he faces or because some conflicting desire causes him to vacillate. And indeed, even when he makes the judgment in circumstances in which the action cannot be done, he must be somewhat unsure about whether he will in fact do it when the right circumstances arise, for otherwise he would simply decide to do it. That is, he would simply conclude "I will do it" rather than "I ought to do it." A hypothetical imperative, therefore, represents to the agent the act it would be rational for him to do relative to some end he has adopted, follows from the same consideration on which he would do the act or decide to do it if nothing deterred or distracted him, and is issued when the agent is to some extent disengaged from taking immediate action or making a firm decision.

Clearly, on this account, the motivational force we attribute to a hypothetical imperative has the same genesis and explanation as the motive we would attribute to an agent who acted on the same consideration as the one from which the imperative follows or who decided so to act on the strength of that consideration. Hence, if the motive behind the action or decision could be traced to some nonrational desire, then the imperative's motivational force originates in that desire; and if the action or decision would have sprung from some nonrational desire because of a judgment that taking the action is the only or best way to attain that desire's object, then the imperative derives its motivational force from this desire by virtue of that judgment. In short, the same type of explanation applies to mere hypothetical imperatives as applies to certain actions and decisions.

Accordingly, mere hypothetical imperatives no more represent reason's conative power than do the actions and decisions that have the same type of explanation. This type of explanation fits Hume's account of the way some judgments motivate action indirectly and thus illustrates how reason sometimes influences the will by subserving desire. Mere hypothetical imperatives, then, likewise result from reason's subservience to desire. Consequently, one can affirm that such imperatives are irreducible to the considerations on which they are based, or any other judgments of empirical fact or one's own mental state for that matter, and at the same time deny that their motivational force originates even in part independently of any nonrational desire.

Sidgwick's error in thinking otherwise should now be apparent. It is due to a faulty assumption on which the crucial step of his argument in the opening section depends, the assumption that when reason influences the will by subserving desire it does so *solely* by altering the understanding the agent has of desire's objects and of the means and obstacles to their attainment. In other words, the step depends on the assumption that when a judgment, a deliverance of reason, has influence on the will in virtue of its relation to some preexisting desire it derives that influence solely through a partnership with that desire. This assumption, however, as the foregoing discussion reveals, does not hold of mere hypothetical imperatives. Their influence on the will comes from being the products of such partnerships rather than being partners themselves. Hence, though their irreducibility to judgments of empirical fact or one's own mental state implies that they are unsuitable for the kind of partnership Sidgwick had in mind, their being unsuitable for partnerships of this kind does not imply that their influence on the will originates independently of any nonrational desire. Sidgwick's error consists, then, in his thinking, mistakenly, that such unsuitability carries this implication.

Sidgwick's error may, nevertheless, seem to pertain only to his treatment of prudential judgments conceived of as mere hypothetical imperatives. It may therefore seem removable. In fact, though, his failure to fit these judgments when they are so conceived to his account of the nature of ethical judgment spells defeat for the entire argument of chapter 3. For it shows that a judgment's irreducibility to judgments of empirical fact or one's own mental state does not have the significance Sidgwick ascribed to it. The words "right" and "ought" when used in expressions of ethical judgment may indeed express a unique and fundamental notion, but its being unique and fundamental does not mean that the judgments of which it is a constituent can influence the will independently of any nonrational desire. It does not mean that these judgments are dictates of reason in Sidgwick's sense. Hence, the force that the notion has when applied in ethical judgment may not originate in the operations of reason. It may, instead, originate in the impulses of appetite and passion. Contrary to intuitionism, then, the fundamental notion of ethics may not be entirely a creature of reason, and ethical judgments may not be deliverances of reason that subserve neither desire nor feeling.

Of course, the defeat of Sidgwick's argument in chapter 3 does not entail the demise of his intuitionist conception of ethical judgment. It only leaves the latter ungrounded. And it might then be said in Sidgwick's defense that, the error of the argument's crucial step notwithstanding, the argument does succeed in refuting any empiricist program of reducing ethical judgments to judgments of physical and psychical fact, and this refutation is sufficient for Sidgwick's purposes. For it narrows the question to one of deciding between Sidgwick's intuitionist conception and a conception according to which ethical judgments are mere hypothetical imperatives, and the decision is sure to go in Sidgwick's favor once attention is turned from prudential judgments to moral judgments. The latter, after all, are for Sidgwick the clearest if not the primary case of ethical judgment, and careful and well-focused reflection on transparent examples of them, like the common example of judging, in circumstances in which it would be highly advantageous to lie, that one ought to tell the truth, will confirm their categorical character and so confound any conception of them as mere hypothetical imperatives. Sidgwick, admittedly, read too much into the irreducibility of judgments of what it is right to do or what one ought to do, and he erred in failing to distinguish between the sense that the words "right" and "ought" have when used to express categorical imperatives and the sense they have when used to express mere hypothetical imperatives. But starting with the more restricted implication of an ethical judgment's irreducibility to judgments of physical or psychical fact and then, with respect to this distinction between the two senses of "right" and "ought," reflecting carefully on which of the two senses applies to transparent examples of moral judgment will bring one to the same result as the argument Sidgwick gave. These considerations, so this defense of Sidgwick would conclude, will serve to vindicate intuitionism as he formulated it.

This defense plainly depends on the probative force of careful and well-focused reflection on transparent examples of moral judgment. It assumes that we can be confident in the conclusions of such reflection. Yet this assumption is unwarranted. Reflection on such examples for the purpose of discerning the nature of moral judgment is liable to two mistakes, and there is no way to prove that one has avoided both. In particular, no one who concludes from reflection on these examples alone that moral judgments are categorical imperatives can acquit himself of the charge of having made one or the other of these two mistakes. Thus, on the one hand, one might mistake for a moral judgment a mere affirmation of some standard of conventional morality. Such an affirmation is categorical, to be sure, but it need not have any influence on the will. Sidgwick himself cautions against making this mistake when he distinguishes moral judgments that are ethical judgments, strictly speaking (i.e., that contain the fundamental notion of ethics), from "judgments resembling moral judgments in form, and not distinguished from them in ordinary thought, in cases where the obligation affirmed is found, on reflection, to depend on the existence of current opinions and sentiments as such" (*ME*, 30).[5] On the other hand, having guarded against making this first mistake by fixing one's attention on judgments of whose influence on the will one was certain, one might then mistake reason for the source of this influence. Hume cautions against making this mistake when he famously diagnoses the fallacy of rationalist moral philosophy, both ancient and modern, as the confusion of reason with calm passion. We cannot, solely from reflection on our experiences of moral judgment, however clarifying and sharp our introspective powers, know the true source of its influence on the will. To insist, to the contrary, that we can, that our powers of reflection on such matters are fundamentally probative, and that their testimony is self-evident, is to make an appeal of the sort characteristic of intuitionism and largely responsible for its eclipse.

Sidgwick, to his credit, offered an argument instead.

Notes

1 See H. A. Prichard, "Duty and Interest," in Prichard, *Moral Obligation and Duty and Interest: Essays and Lectures* (Oxford: Oxford University Press, 1968), pp. 223–5; and W. D. Ross, *The Right and the Good* (Oxford: Oxford University Press [Clarendon Press], 1930), pp. 157–8.

2 David O. Brink, "Sidgwick's Dualism of Practical Reason," *Australasian Journal of Philosophy* 66 (1988): 291–307. Brink's complete view, I should note, is more complicated than I have indicated. He thinks Sidgwick's text admits of both an internalist and an externalist reading, but he favors the latter over the former as the reading that best captures the text's philosophical import. See Brink's "Sidgwick and the Rationale for Rational Egoism" (Chapter 7, herein) for a concise statement of his view.

3 Sidgwick himself thinks that same sense is expressed in either case. The difficulty into which this view leads him is discussed below in Section 3.

4 Brink, for instance, makes this supposition when he takes Sidgwick to be seriously concerned with answering the questions of whether and to what extent duty opposes self-interest and advances this concern as one of the main grounds for an externalist reading. See Brink, "Sidgwick's Dualism of Practical Reason," pp. 303–4. Brink cites several parts of the text as evidence of this concern, but none of them is decisive. The most important is chapter 5 of book 2, where Sidgwick considers whether egoism could look to the common rules of morality as the proper guides for achieving happiness. This chapter appears to contain discussion of conflicts between duty and self-interest that would entail a basic distinction between moral and prudential judgment, but a close reading shows that Sidgwick is careful to qualify his use of the term "duty" so that it does not express a notion that falls within the scope of the fundamental notion of ethics. Thus, he says at the outset that examining the question that the chapter concerns necessitates using the received notions of duty, and he indicates in his subsequent argument that the duties in question are the duties of conventional morality. Hence, no conflict between duty and self-interest of the kind that would support an externalist reading is under consideration in this chapter.

5 See also Philippa Foot, "Morality as a System of Hypothetical Imperatives," *Philosophical Review* 81 (1972): 305–16, for a discussion of this distinction.

Part III

Hedonism, good, perfection

9

Sidgwick on desire, pleasure, and the good

THOMAS CHRISTIANO

In this essay, I shall discuss Sidgwick's argument for the claim that pleasure is the good. Along the way I shall point to various problematic points in his argument. And in the end I shall try to show what kinds of amendments might solve the difficulties that I see. The basic problem that arises in Sidgwick's view concerns the motivation for introducing desire as the material element in his theory of the good. Sidgwick never tells us why he entertains a desire-based conception of goodness. This difficulty is related to the question of why Sidgwick thinks that we must concern ourselves with the *sorts* of objects that are desired, or so I shall show. Finally, one wonders why Sidgwick thinks that he has even come close to solving the problem of the ultimate good when he has conceded that he cannot reduce, to his opponents' satisfaction, the value of some instances of "ideal goods" (such as knowledge, virtue, or aesthetic appreciation) to some function of pleasure. The difficulties that Sidgwick's account encounters are, I think, problems for any view of the good that is desire-based and that imposes formal requirements of rationality on conceptions of goodness. Thus, though I shall focus my attention on Sidgwick's theory, I believe that the problems raised in this essay are significant for many desire-based theories of value.[1]

There are three layers to Sidgwick's account of the good. The first identifies various formal constraints that any concept of good must satisfy; the second gives Sidgwick's analysis of the notion of good by imposing the formal constraints on a material element, desire; and the third layer is the argument that the only sort of object that fits the analysis of good given in the second layer is pleasure. And there are two basic components in Sidgwick's argument: the formal constraints on goodness and the intrinsic relation between goodness and desire.

I have benefited from the critical comments of Stephen Darwall, Jerome Schneewind, and Bart Schultz in preparing the final version of this essay.

I shall proceed by presenting the formal constraints on goodness, then I shall discuss Sidgwick's two definitions of "good on the whole," and then I shall present his arguments for why pleasure and only pleasure is the good. Along the way I will show the difficulties with the argument, and finally I shall attempt to give a partial solution to some of these problems.

1. The concept of the good

We need to distinguish three different notions first: the concept of the good, the concept of the good on the whole, and the idea of our greatest good. Sidgwick's principal concern in chapters 9 in book 1 and 14 in book 3 on the good is to define "good on the whole." The notion of "good" applies to parts of this good on the whole. And I understand Sidgwick to be saying that one's good on the whole is one's greatest good.

Sidgwick limits his discussion to things that are good in themselves and not good as means to other things. And most of his argument is concerned with elaborating the notion of the good of one person. While Sidgwick gives his definition of the Good, he spells out certain formal conditions on the idea of good. In particular, he says that one's good on the whole is an authoritative notion (ME, 112). Hence, the idea of good on the whole must be action-guiding in some sense. And it implies a rational dictate. For Sidgwick, rational dictates are imperatives for action (ME, 34). Hence, if something is good on the whole for me, it follows that there is a dictate that says that I must pursue it if I can. Furthermore, Sidgwick says of a dictate that a "possible conflict of motives seems to be connoted by the term 'dictate' or 'imperative' which describes the relation of Reason to mere inclinations or non-rational impulses by comparing it to the relation between the will of a superior and the will of his subordinates" (ME, 34–5). Finally, given Sidgwick's conception of "ought," if I ought to pursue some end now, then in any similar circumstances I must do the same thing (ME, 33). Hence, we can infer a requirement of generality on the notion of good on the whole.

Furthermore, Sidgwick imposes another constraint on the notion of good on the whole, which is that it can make sense to claim that something is a greater or lesser good. This is a general requirement of comparison. He says that this entails the claim that the Ultimate Good can be divided into constituents that are quantitatively comparable (ME, 110). This constraint appears to be independently grounded, but it is also partly grounded in the authoritativeness requirement. I shall explore this connection later.

2. The definition of good

Sidgwick defines the good on the whole in terms of desirability. His first definition is as follows: "A person's future good on the whole is 'what he would now desire and seek on the whole if all the consequences of all the different lines of conduct open to him were accurately foreseen and adequately realized in imagination at the present point of time' " (*ME*, 111–12).[2] Following Broad, I shall call this the ideal desirability account of good on the whole.[3] The first notion we have to inquire into is the notion of desire. Sidgwick defines "desire" as a "felt impulse or stimulus tending to the realization of what is desired" (*ME*, 43, n. 2), and he frequently substitutes this word with "impulse" or "impulsive force." He also describes the ideal desirability account as involving a "hypothetical composition of impulsive forces."[4] Hence, Sidgwick appears to be defining the notion of the good with a notion of desire which does not distinguish between rational or irrational desire. And what I desire, I desire not because I think it is good; rather, it is good because I desire it. But this definition does introduce two constraints on the desire that is to provide the basis of value: The desire must be fully informed, and it must involve "an equal regard for all the moments of our conscious experience" (*ME*, 111).[5] This constraint is imposed since it is "an essential characteristic of rational conduct."

This definition appears to give us a conception of what is our greatest good since it says not only what a person would desire but also what one would seek. Presumably, this suggests that the person would desire the thing the most. Furthermore, it should be noted that this definition includes a temporal index, which should be omitted from a completely satisfactory account.

The vexing question here is, Why desire? What is the justification for claiming that the good is what is desirable? We might entertain a few hypotheses here. One that we can rule out fairly quickly, I think, is that Sidgwick believes that what is good must motivate a person and that only desire can motivate. We should be able to rule this out on the grounds that, for Sidgwick, "good on the whole" entails a rational dictate that contains its own motivational force distinct from desire. Sidgwick quite explicitly states that good on the whole is that at which it is ultimately rational to aim and that "the adoption of an end as paramount . . . is quite a distinct psychical phenomenon from desire, it is a volition" (*ME*, 37).

An interesting possibility is suggested by Schneewind when he says that "the concept of 'good' seems to be linked to the sentient and desiring side of our nature as 'ought' and 'right' are to its active aspect."[6] He defends this contrast by referring to Sidgwick's view that "ought" implies "can" and the opposing claim that "good on the whole" does not always imply that one can bring it about. Furthermore, Schneewind shows that, for Sidgwick, "a judgment that an act ought to be done or is right implies 'an authoritative prescription to do it.' A judgment that an act is good does not imply such a directive." Although both of these observations are correct, they are not conclusive. First of all, whatever good on the whole I can achieve by voluntary action I am required by reason to aim at and, second, Sidgwick says that my good on the whole implies a rational dictate. Also Sidgwick claims that perfection, which in some cases involves the perfection of the active aspect of our nature, is a potential candidate for the good even though it is not connected with sentience (*ME*, 78). Finally, even if the good is somehow connected with the sentient part of our nature inasmuch as the good is a property of sentience, this does not explain why the objects of desire (which may or may not be connected with sentience) are what is good. Sidgwick's view does not tell us that desire is good in itself; it is the objects which are good in themselves. And the good does not tell us what to desire; the ultimate good is defined as the object of desire (suitably qualified). Hence, it appears that the problem remains.

One more possible hypothesis is that Sidgwick thought that desire under certain circumstances was the only possible source of evidence for what is good. This hypothesis suffers from the same defect as the others, that is, of never having been hinted at by Sidgwick. I shall not pursue it further here. But I shall explore the possibility later as a possible way of understanding some of Sidgwick's arguments about the good and pleasure.

3. Desires in harmony with reason

Sidgwick is unsatisfied with his definition in terms of ideal desirability because it does not show how my good on the whole can be authoritative for me. It does not imply any rational dictate. It merely describes a hypothetical desire in terms of fact. Sidgwick revises the definition: "A person's good on the whole is what that person would desire were that person's desires in harmony with reason assuming that person's own existence alone to be considered" (*ME*, 112). I shall call this the rational desirability account.[7] It is the one Sidgwick ends up with, but it is hard to see what it brings to our understanding of the good. He claims that a rational dictate is implicit. We will want to see why Sidgwick thinks this.

The reason why Sidgwick introduces this rationality constraint is that the notion of one's ultimate good on the whole must be authoritative, and hence it must imply a rational dictate to pursue it (*ME*, 35, 93, 112).[8] For Sidgwick, "good on the whole" is a rational concept which implies an "ought." Since desires for Sidgwick are "impulses," it is not clear how under any condition they could imply a rational dictate. The new definition is supposed to remedy this problem. This will depend on what "rational desire" means.

One way to understand the idea of a rational desire is that it is a desire for what I ought to desire. This makes some sense except it does not tell us much. We already know that the good on the whole is what we ought to aim at. To say that it is what we ought to desire does not get us much further. Also, the purpose of introducing desire into the account of the good is to provide a material element that will help us determine what is good. To analyze rational desire in terms of what I ought to desire undermines that purpose.[9]

Perhaps we should take our cue from what Sidgwick says earlier regarding the relation between self-love and reason.[10] He explains that it is the generality and comprehensiveness of the desire that give it its authority when other impulses conflict (*ME*, 93). We will explore these two requirements later when we see how they function to produce the argument for the goodness of pleasure. For the moment, we should note how Sidgwick applies these two requirements to the notion of self-love.

Self-love seems to be understood by Butler ... as a desire of one's own pleasure generally, and of the greatest amount of it obtainable, from whatever source it may be obtained. ... it is upon this generality and comprehensiveness that the "authority" and "reasonableness" attributed to Self-love in Butler's system are founded. ... pleasure of some kind results from gratifying any impulse; thus when antagonistic impulses compete for the determination of the will we are prompted by the desire for pleasure in general to compare the pleasures which we foresee will respectively attend the gratification of either impulse, and when we have ascertained which set of pleasures is the greatest ... the desire for pleasure in general reinforces the corresponding impulse. (*ME*, 93–4)

In this account, the desire for pleasure in general rules out considerations of the quality, time, and sources of the pleasures in estimating their worth, and the comprehensiveness of the desire enjoins us to maximize the surplus of pleasure over pain.

I suggest that we use these criteria (in addition to that of full information) to elaborate what Sidgwick has in mind by rational desire in the definition above and without any specification of the object of desire. A desire I have is reasonable and authoritative if it is what I would desire were I to require that my desire be informed, comprehensive, and generalizable. It is generalizable if what satisfies the desire at one point must be an element of a general class, any member of which satisfies the desire. It is comprehensive in that it is a desire that covers a whole life, and for every possible course of action the desire can be said to be more or less satisfied. Those desires that conflict with this overall desire are deemed irrational. Hence, if we see two conflicting desires, we should determine which one will lead to the greatest satisfaction, which is measured in terms of the strength of desire.

This definition retains what is needed from the notion of desire. But it differs from the ideal desirability conception insofar as it eliminates any reference to time and hence is not merely about a person's future good. Sidgwick's conception of a person's good on the whole is one which permits a variety of things to be good. The question to be asked is, What would a person desire given these constraints? Would a person always have the same desire under these conditions, and would all human beings have the same desires insofar as they were rational?

It is still not clear that this definition of rational desires shows how the desire can be authoritative. Sidgwick claims that this calm desire implies a rational dictate. It does provide a unique impulse to action that should prevail whenever there is a conflict with other impulses. That is, a comprehensive and general desire should provide something like the will of a superior when it occurs together with conflicting desires. Hence, it seems to do the job that an imperative is supposed to do. Still, it is merely a desire, although it satisfies a few more constraints. It is hard to see how this impulse can "imply" anything, let alone a rational dictate: (1) Since it is an impulse, it does not have any logical structure, and hence it cannot imply things any more than a stone can imply something; (2) also, it is merely a fact. How can we derive an ought from a fact?

I shall leave this topic for the moment and proceed to the next step in Sidgwick's argument, which is to show that pleasure is the ultimate object of rational desire.

4. Why pleasure?

One might wonder why Sidgwick is not content to stop here. He has given us a definition of "good on the whole" that ostensibly gives us a rational dictate to aim at it. And he has supplied us with a fully quantitative conception of goodness that allows for comparisons of goodness.

Sidgwick does not stop here, however, but asks what might be the objects of rational desire. And he seems to have a requirement that these objects be describable at least in terms that are independent of desire or in such a way that it does not follow from the definition of good. Hence, the candidates for the good are types of possible objects of desire: knowledge, contemplation of beauty, virtue, and pleasure. Sidgwick, in other words, seems to move from a relational specification of the good to an inherent specification of the good. He wants to have a theory of the good that allows it to be specified by some property inhering in the object. The structure of the argument will be to proceed from the definition of the good on the whole in terms of the rationally desirable to an identification of some types of rationally desirable objects. Hence, if we say that this pleasure is rationally desirable it will follow that all pleasures are rationally desirable. Furthermore, this move is not made as a result of an observation that, as a matter of fact, all objects of a certain type are the objects of a rational desire. It is rather the other way around; namely, from the fact that we can establish that this thing is desirable, we are committed to regarding all things of the same sort as desirable, and if we find an instance in which one of the things of this sort is not desirable, then it follows that objects of this sort are not desirable. This form of argument is crucial to Sidgwick's subsequent arguments against other potential candidates for goodness, as I will show later.

Notice that this gets us beyond the idea that desirability itself is the good-making feature of goods. On the desirability account by itself it appears perfectly acceptable to say that, though a pleasure may be desirable now in current circumstances, the very same pleasure in similar circumstances may not be desirable to me later. And the reason for this is merely a change in what I desire. From the fact that I desire a particular thing now it does not follow that I will desire the same thing later. Hence, if desirability is a good-making feature, there may not be a way to generalize from what one desires now to what one will desire later, and therefore there may be no way to classify goods into sorts (other than desirability), and even if there were such a way, this would have to be a purely empirical discovery.

It might be thought that the generality requirement which is imposed on oughts and which we have noted is part of what Sidgwick has in mind by rational desirability explains why Sidgwick immediately passes from his definition of good on the whole to inquiry into the sorts of goods there are. But this does not explain it. The generality requirement does not entail that we need to have inherent good-making features. The requirement should be satisfiable merely by invoking the condition that the object is good by virtue of its relation to desire. The generality requirement on goods might tell us that, if we think this object is good, then all objects similarly situated must also be good. But the similarity could be specified by means of determining the relation of desire to the object.

Nevertheless, the requirement that the good-making property be inherent in the good object and that generalization should proceed over the inherent features of the desired objects is of basic importance to Sidgwick's argument that pleasure and only pleasure is good.

I shall quickly canvass the argument that pleasure is a good. Sidgwick has defined pleasure in the following way:

> Let pleasure be defined as feeling which the sentient individual at the time of feeling it implicitly or explicitly apprehends to be desirable; desirable, that is when considered merely as feeling, and not in respect of its objective conditions or consequences, or any of the facts that come directly within the cognisance and judgments of others besides the sentient individual. (*ME*, 131)

Sidgwick defines pleasure in this way for two basic reasons: to avoid commitment to a qualitative characterization of pleasure and pain; and to make it possible to measure pleasure and pain each on its own and together on a single quantitative scale. From this definition Sidgwick's argument for the goodness of pleasure is fairly simple.

Sidgwick argues that the apprehension by an individual of the desirability of a current feeling qua feeling must be taken to be final. And he appears to mean incorrigible when he says that it is final (*ME*, 398, n. 2). Thus, the fact that a person judges that a current feeling is desirable is incorrigible evidence that the feeling is desirable. Hence, every pleasure is desirable. Therefore, pleasure is a good.

There is a difficulty with this argument that Sidgwick and his commentators seem not to have noticed. The judgment of the desirability of a thing is a counterfactual judgment; it states that a person would desire the thing were that person fully aware of the state of attainment. And in the case of a feeling, to say that it is desirable is to say that a person would desire it when that person is fully aware of what it feels like. A feeling is apprehended to be desirable by an agent when either (1) the agent apprehends that he would desire the feeling were he to be fully aware of it and the agent does not now desire it, or (2) the agent apprehends that he would desire the feeling with full awareness and he does desire the feeling with full awareness. I say that if the apprehension is taken to be certain, then it can only be so on the second interpretation. This is because the first interpretation requires that one not have a full awareness of the feeling since such a full awareness would lead to the desire for it. And if one does not now have a full awareness of the feeling, the claim that if one did one would desire it cannot be a matter of self-evidence. This would be because the desire and the feeling would be represented merely in idea, and such a representation, according to Sidgwick, might be erroneous (*ME*, 129).

This shows that the evidence a person has when she apprehends the feeling to be desirable is that she has a full awareness of the feeling and she has a desire for that feeling. But the counterfactual judgment implied in Sidgwick's definition of pleasure requires a stronger relation between the desire and the feeling. It not only requires that the feeling be the object of the desire; it also requires that the desire for that feeling would have been experienced had the objective conditions and the other elements of the mental states the person was in been different. At least this seems to be the most plausible interpretation of the clause "considered merely as feeling."[11] Hence, to show that my feeling is desirable considered merely as feeling I would have to know whether I would desire the feeling under different objective conditions and circumstances or when it is accompanied by different mental states.

To know this I would have to experiment and represent the feeling to myself when I am concerned with assessing the desirability of the current feeling qua feeling. Hence, one would need in this context a method of variation in order to make sure of this. Otherwise, the desire may actually be for the whole mental state, including elements that are not feelings. If I experience pleasure while reading a novel, clearly the novel is causing my feeling, but might not the fact that I am reading a novel also be part of what makes the feeling desirable? That is, were I to have that same feeling produced in me without reading the novel, would it still be experienced as desirable? And if not, would we say that the feeling was desirable "considered merely as feeling"? One might say it is really the whole mental state that was desired here.

But if I need to represent to myself in imagination the hypothetical feeling along with a desire given different objective circumstances, and different unfelt elements of consciousness, my representation might be erroneous. Therefore, I can be wrong in my judgment concerning the desirability of the current feeling considered merely as feeling. If I am wrong in some cases, then not all pleasures, that is, feelings that are apprehended to be desirable, are desirable qua feeling. Therefore, not all pleasures are good. From this it follows that pleasure is not a good.[12]

5. Why only pleasure?

Sidgwick limits his discussion of goods to qualities of human existence. And he includes among these pleasure and perfection, including "ideal goods" such as knowledge, contemplation of the beautiful, and virtue.[13] Finally, he argues that it is only consciousness that can be good, and from that point he argues that only feelings fall within the domain of the good. How does he succeed in narrowing down the possible object of desirability?

The trouble with other goods such as knowledge and virtue or the contemplation of beauty is that they cannot be counted as the object of rational desires because (1) they are composed of mental states that are desired only if they are pleasurable or if the mental state corresponds to some external fact, for example, truth, beauty, or virtue; otherwise the mental states are "neutral in respect of desirability" (*ME*, 398). (2) The objects to which the mental states correspond are merely external facts that are not in themselves desirable. (3) The composites are not desirable either. Also, (4) inasmuch as they have value, it can be explained by virtue of their relation to pleasure either in that they give pleasure as a by-product or they are productive of pleasure in the long run. Furthermore, (5) they can be inconsistent with the value of pleasure; for example, the life of the virtuous martyr is desirable on the whole in respect of its virtue but undesirable on the whole in respect of its pain. (6) They cannot be compared in terms of value to pleasure by means of a higher principle. Hence, they cannot be the object of rational desires.

I would like to focus on arguments (5) and (6). Suppose, as Sidgwick imagines an opponent doing, we reject the first four claims and insist on a clear, precise, underived, and irreducible desirability for knowledge, and virtue, and the contemplation of beauty (*ME*, 401). We must still accept the fact of conflict between these and pleasure on occasion and we must still accept the claim that they are not comparable. What do we do then? Here, I quote Sidgwick in full:

> If we are not to systematize Universal Happiness as their common end, on what other principles are we to systematize them? It should be observed that these principles must not only enable us to compare among themselves the values of the different non-hedonistic ends which we have been considering, but must also provide a common standard for comparing these values with that of Happiness; unless we are prepared to adopt the paradoxical position of rejecting happiness as absolutely valueless. For we have a practical need of determining not only whether we should pursue Truth rather than Beauty, or Freedom or some ideal constitution of society rather than either, or perhaps desert all of these for the life of worship and religious contemplation; but also how far we should follow any of these lines of endeavor, when we foresee among the consequences the pains of human or other sentient beings, or even the loss of pleasures that might otherwise have been enjoyed by them.

I have failed to find – and am unable to construct – any systematic answer to this question that appears to me deserving of serious consideration: and hence

I am finally led to the conclusion . . . that the Intuitional method . . . yields . . . pure Universalistic Hedonism. (*ME*, 406–7)

This passage states the arguments (5) and (6) that I have described. I will show how (5) is connected to the inherence and generality requirements. For argument (5), I shall concentrate on Sidgwick's example of the virtuous martyr. He claims that there are cases where the assessment of the value of a life (or a part of a life) based on the value of pleasure conflicts with the assessment of the value of a life based on virtue. An example of this is the life of a virtuous martyr. He asks us to consider whether "Virtuous life would remain on the whole good for the virtuous agent, if we suppose it combined with extreme pain. The affirmative answer to this question . . . is a paradox from which the modern thinker would recoil. . . . he would hardly venture to assert that the portion of life spent by the martyr . . . was in itself desirable." And this argument is used to defend the conclusion that "so far as we judge virtuous activity to be a part of Ultimate Good, it is . . . because the consciousness attending it is judged to be in itself desirable for the virtuous agent" (*ME*, 397).

The life of the martyr is good on the whole from the standpoint of virtue but bad on the whole from the standpoint of pleasure. From the argument mentioned above, pleasure is clearly a good. Therefore, insofar as the standpoint of virtue says that this life is good on the whole and it is clear that it is not good on the whole, virtue cannot be a good. For both pleasure and virtue, there are two steps in this conflict. First, the generality requirement: If some property x is good, then this instance of that property x is good. The second step is if these instances of x are good, then this $x$ness on the whole is good on the whole. Sidgwick appeals to our modern judgment that the life of the virtuous martyr is not on the whole good, and from that he infers that virtue is not a good (except insofar as it is attended with or is a means to pleasure). This invokes the contrapositives of the previous judgments. Since there is a life that is virtuous on the whole that is not good on the whole, then the virtues that make up this virtuousness cannot be goods, and if these virtues are not good then virtue is not a sort of good.

The second premise in this argument is a statement of the comprehensiveness requirement I mentioned earlier. Notice that even if this requirement is correct one needs the generality requirement as well to make the argument about the virtuous martyr go through. This is because it would not follow from the claim that these virtues are not goods that virtue is never an irreducibly, and intrinsically, good thing unless the generality and inherence requirements held.

One might think that the comprehensiveness requirement is implausible, but this is what Sidgwick is arguing for in the above passage. Here Sidgwick argues that there can be only one single value and that value must be such that it makes sense to speak of greater and lesser amounts of it. And the greatest amount must be what is good on the whole. The argument that he gives for this is connected to the formal constraints on goodness. Goodness on the whole implies a rational dictate. He argues that a coherent account of ultimate good must issue in unique and determinate dictates in every case. This entails, first, that in order to fulfill this "practical need" we need to be able to compare the values of different courses of action. This seems clear in that we have to be able to determine which action will lead to the best outcome. Second, he claims that in order to compare these different values we need a common standard of comparison. Hence, in order to compare the values of different courses of action our valuations must be commensurable. And, third, from this Sidgwick seems to infer that we need a common value with which to assess greater and lesser value. We must be able to reduce the values of other things to some function of this one value. Hence, if virtue is a value, it must be the only value, and it must be the common standard by which to judge all other things. And then we would have to be able to add up virtue to virtuousness on the whole and say that that is good on the whole.

We have a concept of good which is rational and hence must give us determinate dictates. Either pleasure or some other value must constitute the way in which we resolve conflicts between these. This further value must reduce the others and be something that can be added up. Or we may choose pleasure as the ultimate good because it is the most obvious case of a desirable object. There are also some cases where it is plausible to claim that the value of the other things can be reduced to the quantity of pleasure while instances of the contrary claim are very much implausible.[14] Also, pleasure is generally agreed to be good whereas there is disagreement about the other goods. Hence, pleasure is the good.

Notice, however, that Sidgwick argues here that if there is a common value then pleasure seems to be the most likely candidate. But he has not shown that pleasure is the common value. Indeed, he has conceded that some may not accept his attempted reduction of the goodness of ideal goods to pleasure. Surely, those who refuse to accept arguments (1) through (4) can provide an example similar in structure to Sidgwick's example of the virtuous martyr but to the opposite effect. They may point to the life of the satisfied pig and argue from the comprehensiveness and generality requirements that pleasure is not the good since the pleasurableness on the whole of the satisfied pig does not imply the goodness on the whole of that life. Therefore, if commensurability requires a common value, then we can insure that our values are commensurable only by arbitrarily ruling out those goods which are as a matter of fact desired in an informed and general way and independent of their relation to pleasure. But this seems an arbitrary way of insuring the rationality of our notion of ultimate good. Hence, it appears that Sidgwick's argument cannot go through.

6. The central difficulty

The question that all of this raises about Sidgwick's view is, What if we cannot find a desirable object that satisfies all the formal constraints Sidgwick places on the conception of the good? Does this mean that, though there are desirable objects, there are no good objects? This would follow from the rationality requirements on the conception of the good. Furthermore, once we look at the issue this way, it would appear to be an utterly fortuitous psychological fact if it turned out that only pleasures proved to be desirable. The far more likely situation is one where individuals have a plurality of informed general desires.

With regard to the good, we appear to be in a similar situation to that which Sidgwick finds in the dualism of practical reason. The arguments might be parallel. Practical reason, in order to be rational, must issue in unique and determinate dictates; the dualism of practical reason shows that it does not issue in unique and determinate dictates; therefore, there is no practical reason or the operation of practical reason would be "illusory" (*ME*, 508). By parity of reasoning, the ultimate good is a rational notion; in order for it to be rational, it must issue in unique and determinate dictates; the plurality of desirable objects shows that it does not issue in unique and determinate dictates; therefore, there is no good.

The problem here is that in order to have a coherent account of good, Sidgwick must argue for a value monism. But it seems unlikely that he can succeed in establishing monism by arguing for a unique sort of rationally desirable object. The material and formal elements of his conception of the good pull in opposite directions.

7. Alternative accounts

There are three other possibilities still available to Sidgwick here. (1) He can reject the idea that the good is what is rationally desirable. (2) He can reject the claim that in order to have a common standard

one needs to have a single value and just argue that desirability is th
common standard of goodness. He would be rejecting the inherenc
requirement I identified earlier. Finally, (3) he could argue that, thoug
pleasure does not provide us as yet with a completely satisfactory cor
ception of good, it is the one for which we have the most evidence.

The previous version of Sidgwick's argument seemed to insure th
rationality of the concept of goodness by eliminating some candidate
for goodness by arbitrary means. The argument fails since it relies o
an arbitrary way of making sure that "good" is a rational concept. W
could avoid the problem altogether by defining the good as what i
desirable and not attempting to discover any object of desire that i
general and comprehensive. After all, there can also be conflicts betwee
different types of pleasure, and we resolve that conflict by reference t
the claim that some are more desirable than others. If this means ca
be used for resolving conflicts between pleasures, why can't the notio
of desirability be used in general as the measure of ultimate good? I
appears to give us a common standard without giving us a commo
value. Hence, we might say that my desires are in harmony with reaso
if they are for objects that fit into a life that is desirable on the whol
for me.

Though I will not argue for this claim here, I do not think that a
informed desire account will give us an account of the good that ca
issue in determinate dictates any more than the account we have bee
discussing.[15] Hence, I shall move to a discussion of the third possibilit
that I have suggested.

8. The evidentiary view of desire

Given the difficulties with using desirability as the common standard fo
determining goodness, it appears that either desirability must be rejecte
as part of our conception of the good or we can retain desirability as
kind of source of evidence for what is good. I would like to make
number of claims on behalf of this alternative. It is a way of under
standing many of the elements of Sidgwick's argument that have so fa
appeared obscure or unmotivated. And it makes sense of them by mak
ing the argument work for the most part. The defect with the claim i
that it is never mentioned as a possibility by Sidgwick. But no othe
justification of the role of desire is given by Sidgwick either. I do nc
claim that it is what Sidgwick had in mind; I only wish to suggest it a
a plausible account of the role of desire which might save most of h
argument for pleasure and is consistent with the rest of the theory tha
Sidgwick gives.

The merits of this approach are: (1) It says something about why we are concerned with desire in the first place; and this motive is consistent with the rest of the theory. (2) It tells us why Sidgwick automatically moves from the "definition" of good in terms of rational desirability to a discussion of the possible sorts of objects of desire. (3) It makes for a reasonable fit between the formal and material elements of Sidgwick's conception of the good. (4) It also makes sense of Sidgwick's endorsement of the idea that pleasure is the good.

Let us take each point in turn. We noted at the beginning that it was unclear why Sidgwick introduces desire at all in his definition of the good. It is hard to see how a desire could imply a rational dictate because it does not have a logical structure itself and because it is merely a fact about a person. But we can see how desire might be connected to the good on the evidentiary view. Facts can be evidence for propositions. And it is also the case that, though no desire can provide a rational dictate on its own, the totality of rational desires, once systematized, can give us evidence for what we ought to pursue. But we need no longer hold to the view that from the claim that a person has an informed desire we can deduce that he ought to pursue the desired aim.

Furthermore, if our desires are to provide us with evidence of what is good, then it is clear why what is good is independent of what we desire. The desires point to something beyond themselves. Just as observations may be evidence for views about the underlying structure of reality which itself is not characterized in terms of observation, so desires are evidence for what the underlying reality of value is, understood independently of desire. Once we look at the good as something that is independent of desire, then it makes sense to construct a theory of the good that describes features of states of affairs that inhere in the objects themselves. The move to the inherence requirement, which we have seen is absolutely crucial for Sidgwick's argument, is hard to explain otherwise in Sidgwick's view.

The idea that desires provide evidence for what is good fits well with the constraint that we wish to have the most simplified and systematic account of the good. Of course, it may still turn out that we cannot discover a conception of the good that is unitary. But at least we do not have the earlier problem where the fit between the formal and material elements of the conception of the good is purely fortuitous. There is still a problem with the evidentiary account, but it is not as serious.

The evidentiary account also makes sense of Sidgwick's claim that pleasure is the good in the absence of any other better account (*ME*, 406). Sidgwick can be read as saying that, despite the apparent failure to reduce the goodness of every instance of knowledge or contemplation of beauty to their relation to pleasure, we can say that the hypothesis that pleasure is the good is the best hypothesis. We cannot explain every piece of admissible evidence, but our best account is that pleasure is the good.

9. Conclusion

I wish to conclude that the evidentiary view of the relation between desire and the good provides the most satisfying account of their connection in Sidgwick's theory. This is in view of the combination of formal constraints on the notion of an ultimate good and the material element provided by desire. It is hard to see how these two components can be successfully joined into one conception in any other way.

Notes

1 See James Griffin, *Well-Being* (Oxford: Oxford University Press, 1986).
2 It will be important to keep in mind his notion of partial desirability: X is desirable if and only if X "would be desired, with strength proportioned to the degree of desirability, if it were judged attainable by voluntary action, supposing the desirer to possess a perfect forecast, emotional as well as intellectual, of the state of attainment or fruition" (*ME*, 111). We will want to reflect on the relation of goodness to goodness on the whole and how that might relate to the two different accounts of desirability.
3 C. D. Broad, *Five Types of Ethical Theory* (London: Routledge and Kegan Paul, 1930).
4 On a number of other occasions he seems to describe the motivation that is given by the "ought" judgment as an impulse as well (*ME*, 34). And he claims that the impulse that is given by a moral cognition may conflict with other impulses. These morally determined impulses do not seem to be desires, but Sidgwick does not actually differentiate these impulses more than that.
5 I do not think that the test actually does provide a guarantee of temporal neutrality, but this is surely what Sidgwick has in mind. Presumably, temporal neutrality could be insured with an additional antecedent condition such as a temporal veil of ignorance.
6 J. B. Schneewind, *Sidgwick's Ethics and Victorian Moral Philosophy* (Oxford: Oxford University Press [Clarendon Press], 1977), p. 223.
7 The idea of what one would desire were one's desires in harmony with reason seems to be the same, in Sidgwick's view, as the idea of what one would desire insofar as one is a rational being.
8 I do not know how to reconcile this claim with Sidgwick's claim that the maxim that one ought to pursue one's own good on the whole is not tautological (*ME*, 381).

9 Broad thinks that the best way of understanding "desires in harmony with reason" is as "desires that one ought to have." So does J. J. Smart in his "Hedonistic and Ideal Utilitarianisms," in *Midwest Studies in Philosophy*, vol. 3, ed. P. A. French, T. E. Uehling, and H. K. Wettstein (Minneapolis: University of Minnesota Press, 1978).

10 In defense of my claim that Sidgwick understands rational desire in this way, I offer the following evidence: (1) The passage quoted above is the only passage where Sidgwick actually discusses criteria for rational desirability; (2) Sidgwick explicitly mentions comprehensiveness as a feature of his first definition of "good on the whole"; (3) when he discusses Butler's description of self-love he does so approvingly and uses the account to argue against Mill's qualitative conception of utility (*ME*, 94); (4) when he introduces the second definition of "good on the whole", he cites Butler's agreement.

11 There is another interpretation of "considered merely as feeling" that would avoid the objection; that is, that I desire the feeling "considered merely as feeling" if my desire is just for that feeling. This desire I could know about without the representation of other mental states to myself. The trouble is that if I desired that feeling only when it was accompanied by other elements of consciousness such as beliefs and volitions it would be more nearly correct to say that I desired the feeling as a result of its relation to a complex mental state and that I did not desire it by considering it merely as feeling. How would I know that the beliefs and volitions that accompany my feelings do not contribute to the desirability of the feeling? This is similar to what Moore says about Sidgwick's argument in *Principia Ethica* (Cambridge: Cambridge University Press, 1903) but in a different context.

12 Something like this line of reasoning leads Stephen Darwall to question Sidgwick's analysis of pleasure as a feeling. He claims that an objection to Sidgwick's analysis is that in many cases "the object of one's pleasure, that in which one takes pleasure, is not a feeling at all, but rather some state of affairs, some 'objective condition.' . . . And in these cases what is apprehended to be desirable is not the feeling that something is that case, but rather that, as one believes, something is in fact the case" (Darwall, "Pleasure as Ultimate Good in Sidgwick's Ethics," *Monist* 58 [1974]: 481). His argument for this is that "there are cases where it is strained to suggest that a pleasure is an experience. If I learn that the war is over . . . I may well take pleasure in this." He claims that Sidgwick's analysis "suggests that if I am to get pleasure from the news that the war is over then I must apprehend my experience of thinking the war is over to be desirable, *however that experience might come about*. But this is just what is often not the case. Usually one can only take pleasure in thinking that the war is over because one believes one's thinking it to have come about in such a way that one's thinking it is *justified*" (pp. 478–9).

I am more inclined to go along with Sidgwick's characterization of pleasure as a feeling. In defense of Sidgwick, two points can be made here: The above argument seems to confuse logical and psychological conditions of pleasure.

It is no argument against Sidgwick to claim that in order to experience pleasure at the war's ending I must desire the end of the war. Sidgwick agrees that in many cases the experience of pleasure could not come about except as a by-product of the satisfaction of other ends (*ME*, 45). This is consistent with pleasure being defined as an experience that itself is desirable. The second point is that Sidgwick claims that such locutions as "being pleased by" or "taking pleasure in" do not always refer to pleasure at all but to desire or choice. See his remarks on peculiar uses of the word "pleasure" in *ME*, 43–4.

13 Why these, one might wonder? Is there anything that holds them together? They are the classical opponents.

14 Though not always. There are cases where one may get someone to form good habits by enticing them with pleasures. Here, the pleasures could be construed as a means to the achievement of a virtue or some other ideal good.

15 See Richard Brandt, "Two Concepts of Utility," in *The Limits of Utilitarianism*, ed. H. B. Miller and W. H. Williams (Minneapolis: University of Minnesota Press, 1982), for a persuasive argument to this effect.

10

Eminent Victorians and Greek ethics
Sidgwick, Green, and Aristotle

T. H. IRWIN

1. Introduction

Study of the history of ethics includes both an account of previous moral beliefs and practices and a critical evaluation of the theories that describe, explain, or criticize moral beliefs. It therefore requires both historical and philosophical understanding. Serious and self-conscious study of Greek ethics from a historical and philosophical point of view began in the nineteenth century. Here I want to consider two moral philosophers who took Greek ethics seriously, Sidgwick and Green. I am interested in their historical claims about Greek ethics, and especially about Aristotle; and for that reason I will go into some detail about Aristotle. But I am also interested in the philosophical assumptions that they apply to the study of Greek ethics, and the different roles played by Greek ethics in their own moral theories.

Sidgwick and Green were near-contemporaries, shared many intellectual and philosophical interests, and reached sharply opposed philosophical conclusions. Both began as students and teachers of classics; Sidgwick excelled here more than Green ever did. Both turned to philosophy partly in order to make up their minds about the claims of Christianity. Sidgwick became an unbeliever, whereas Green considered himself a sort of believer. Both acknowledged a large debt to Kantian ethics. For Sidgwick, however, this was part of a utilitarian position. Green, on the other hand, was an idealist, believing he could integrate the best insights of Aristotle with those of Kant and Hegel to reach an antiutilitarian conclusion.

Though Green's reputation during his lifetime and for some time afterward was at least the equal of Sidgwick's, their current reputations are quite different. C. D. Broad's foolish attack on Green in defense

In reading several versions of this essay over a number of years I have benefited especially from comments by Christopher Taylor, William Frankena, Nicholas White, Sarah Conly, Richard Kraut, Julia Annas, and David Brink.

of Sidgwick shows that feelings on the issue at one time ran fairly high:
"Even a thoroughly second-rate thinker like T. H. Green, by diffusing
a grateful and comforting aroma of ethical 'uplift,' has probably made
far more undergraduates into prigs than Sidgwick will ever make into
philosophers."[1] Though probably no one now would go quite as far as
Broad, his judgment is perhaps fairly close to the most common view.
Sidgwick is justly respected as a moral philosopher whose work has
more than historical interest. Although Green's reputation may have
begun to rise again after a half-century of general neglect, it still seems
safe to say that his reputation is quite low. His major work on moral
philosophy, *Prolegomena to Ethics*,[2] appears to be little read.[3]

We have several good reasons for expecting that Sidgwick will be a
more reliable guide than Green to the history of Greek ethics. Unlike
Green, he was an excellent classical scholar; perhaps he benefited from
having read classics at Cambridge rather than *literae humaniores* at
Oxford.[4] Though classical scholarship soon became a subordinate interest of his, some of his work in that area is still important and instructive. In particular, his essay on the Sophists remains a more balanced
and sensible treatment of them than anything else that is available.[5]
Green, on the other hand, was never much of a scholar, and his scholarly
projects came to nothing.[6] Moreover, Sidgwick is a clear and precise
thinker and writer, whereas Green's arguments are often more suggestive than rigorous.

I do not want to claim that Green is Sidgwick's equal as a historian
or as a philosopher. Though Broad's criticism is absurdly unfair, one
must admit that it exaggerates some element of truth. Still, I believe
that Green deserves more attention than he usually receives. I hope to
support this claim here, by showing that on some important issues he
has the better of the argument with Sidgwick. For present purposes I
confine myself to some historical questions about the interpretation of
Greek ethics, and in particular of Aristotle. But I hope to show that
the historical issues are connected with some questions of more general
interest.

The nature of this connection is suggested in the most important
modern study of Sidgwick:

Sidgwick's detailed criticism of Green's discussion of Greek morality and moral
philosophy shows both the inadequacies of Green's historical vision and his
failure to enrol Aristotle in a consensus in his favour. . . . Green's admission of
the forward-looking impotence of his principle vitiates his view as to its retro-
spective strength. A moral principle too vacuous to support a method of rational
criticism is necessarily too weak to sustain a method of historical explanation.[7]

I agree with the general principle stated in the last sentence I have quoted; but I do not agree with the verdict on Sidgwick and Green. I believe that on the historical issues Green is broadly right and Sidgwick is broadly wrong.

I will try to show why Sidgwick's rejection of certain possibilities of interpretation reflects his unjustified willingness to dismiss certain philosophical options; conversely, Green's willingness to take certain philosophical options seriously allows him to see why a particular line of interpretation is plausible. If I am right about this, it certainly does not follow that the philosophical options dismissed by Sidgwick deserve to be taken as seriously as Green takes them; but I will suggest that at least the question deserves to be reconsidered.

2. The role of Greek ethics in Green's argument

Greek ethics plays an important role in book 3 of Green's *Prolegomena*, on "The Moral Ideal and Moral Progress"; the discussion of "The Greek and the Modern Conception of Virtue" is part of "The Development of the Moral Ideal," and these chapter titles suggest the direction of Green's interest in Greek ethics and the conclusions he wants to draw from his historical survey. It is easy to see that his concern with Greek ethics is not purely scholarly or philosophically disinterested; on the contrary, he thinks Greek moral philosophy embodies, in undeveloped form, the outlook that Green himself takes to be correct.

Green appeals to Greek ethics to show the apparent conflict between duty and interest. This apparent conflict arises from the ethical theories of Hobbes, Butler, Kant, and Sidgwick; and it appears to force us into the insoluble "dualism of practical reason" that Sidgwick describes at the end of *The Methods of Ethics*. In Green's view, the dualism of practical reason "is a conclusion which, once clearly faced, every inquirer would gladly escape, as repugnant both to the philosophic craving for unity, and to that ideal of 'singleness of heart' which we have been accustomed to associate with the highest virtue" (*Prol.*, 226). The mere fact that the dualism is repugnant does not show that we can escape it; but Green thinks we can escape it, because we can remove any grounds for believing in a genuine and insoluble conflict between duty and interest.

Green thinks that this apparent conflict is soluble, if a person's good is conceived correctly. Green argues: (1) A person's good is his self-satisfaction. (2) Self-satisfaction, adequately conceived, consists in the full realization of a rational agent's capacities. (3) The full realization of one person's capacities requires him to will the good of other people for their own sake. We can show that the dualism of practical reason is avoidable if we can set out a true conception of a rational agent's good.

In Greek ethics Green thinks he finds an attempt to develop and to articulate the true conception of an agent's good. In both Plato and Aristotle, in Green's view, the virtues require the expression of "a will to be good, which has no object but its own fulfilment" (*Prol.*, 251). This is the sort of will in which Aristotle finds a person's good; and therefore he agrees with Green in thinking that duty (the expression of the will to be good) and interest are reconcilable.

It is important to Green that he can find his conception of the good anticipated in Greek philosophy. This is not simply because he likes to appeal to authority, and especially to the authority of the Greeks. His historical argument matters to him because he conceives moral philosophy as a progressive discipline, articulating morality as a rational, progressive system of beliefs and practices. He is not nostalgic for the social and political institutions of the Greek world, or of any other historical period, or for its cultural ideals. On the contrary, he thinks that precisely because the Greeks found the right moral ideal they and their successors down to ourselves have been able to criticize other Greek ideals and practices. For the Greek moralists see that a person's good consists in having the will to be good; and when we understand in more detail what this sort of will pursues, we can explain to the Greeks what is wrong with their more specific views about morality. If Green is right, then we must distinguish the general principles and ideals embodied in Greek moral philosophy from the specific practices and attitudes that the Greeks attempted to justify by reference to the principles and ideals; and we must not assume that the only content that we can ascribe to the principles and ideals is the content that makes sense of the specific practices and attitudes. If Green is right, we must not find that the general principles and ideals are so empty that they cannot possibly conflict with anything; we must find that they provide a basis for rational and justified criticism of those very practices and attitudes that they were intended to support.

This general role that Green sees for Aristotelian ethics leads him in a direction that might well be thought surprising. He focuses especially on Aristotle's account of the particular virtues of character; and this may seem surprising, because it might seem that this is by far the most unpromising part of Aristotle's ethics for any philosopher who wants to restate major Aristotelian doctrines in defensible terms. For although the discussion is full of detail that might interest, and even entertain, the historian of morals, it seems the most evidently outdated part of Aristotle's ethics. The particular virtues are specific traits of character that often seem quite remote from our moral experience, and that often assume social conditions remote from our historical experience.

When I began to think about this aspect of Green, about ten years ago, I think I could have safely said that this part of Aristotle's ethics was neither read nor discussed very often. This is no longer true. Several recent tendencies in moral philosophy have encouraged us to catch up with Green, and to think more seriously about Aristotle's views on the virtues, and not simply about his general views about virtue.[8] Still, I think it remains true that Green's particular approach to this aspect of Aristotle is unusual.

One reason for taking the Aristotelian virtues seriously is strongly antagonistic to Green's main aims. We might observe that Aristotle's general conception of happiness as an activity of the soul in accordance with virtue is quite unspecific; and his familiar claim that virtue of character consists in a mean does not seem to tell us much about which actions and which traits of character actually are virtuous. To supply the necessary content for his theory of the virtues Aristotle introduces the particular recognized virtues that are historically familiar to him; and similarly, we might argue, other philosophers are equally justified in introducing the virtues that are familiar to them. We might argue that this is all we can reasonably expect of moral philosophy; it can articulate the views of a particular society or culture in the light of some general principles, but the principles lack the sort of nonhistorical content that would make them a basis for criticizing one or another historical embodiment of the virtues. On this view, Aristotle's treatment of the virtues will remind us that moral theories are historically conditioned and that it is foolish to look for a nonhistorical point of view from which we can try to criticize the Aristotelian conception of the virtues in contrast to some other conception.

This way of looking at the Aristotelian virtues embodies a degree of historical relativism that Green firmly rejects. In his view, Aristotle reaches his conception of the virtues (1) from his conception of happiness; (2) from some true general principles about how happiness is achieved in different virtues; and (3) from further beliefs, true and false, about the sorts of actions that fulfill these general principles. Green believes that the first and second elements in Aristotle's conception forestall a relativist conclusion. Since the general principles are correct, and since we agree with Aristotle about them, we can use them to criticize the third element in his conception and to show why the virtues require different actions from those that he recommends.

Two different kinds of explanation might be appropriate here: (1) We might argue that the actions Aristotle recommends are in fact the right ones for the historical conditions he has in mind; but for that very reason we might be able to show that different actions (on one way of describing them) are right in the historical conditions we face. (2) We might argue that the actions Aristotle recommends are wrong even for the historical conditions that he has in mind, given the general principles he accepts. Green has both sorts of explanation and correction in mind.

For these reasons Green believes that a historical study of ethics should not be a record of successive moral outlooks that have nothing to say to each other. That would be a historical relativist view. In Green's view, a history of ethics should present a rational development whose rationality can in principle be grasped from the point of view that people take at each stage; this means that we should be able to justify the later stages and correct the earlier, by arguing from principles that are acceptable at the earlier stage.

3. The role of Greek ethics in Sidgwick's argument

In the course of criticizing certain appeals to the traditional cardinal virtues, Sidgwick remarks:

I am fully sensible of the peculiar interest and value of the ethical thought of ancient Greece. Indeed through a large part of the present work the influence of Plato and Aristotle on my treatment of this subject has been greater than that of any modern writer. But I am here only considering the value of the general principles for determining what ought to be done, which the ancient systems profess to supply. (*ME*, 375 n.)[9]

I want to challenge Sidgwick's first claim; I do not think he is in fact "fully sensible of the peculiar interest and value" of Greek ethics. His own views make him peculiarly ill equipped to see what is especially significant about Greek ethics; and in some cases they lead him to misinterpret Aristotle.

Sidgwick agrees with Green in giving a prominent role to Greek ethics, and especially to Aristotle; and he even focuses on the same aspects, including his views on the particular virtues. In contrast to Green, however, Sidgwick uses Greek ethics primarily for a negative, even cautionary, purpose. He thinks that the study of Greek ethics should make us aware of the importance of avoiding certain errors that he avoids in *The Methods of Ethics*.

When Sidgwick claims that Plato and Aristotle have at some points influenced him more than any modern moralist has, he probably has two main points in mind: (1) the discussion of questions in moral psychology in books 1 and 2 of *The Methods of Ethics*; and (2) the discussion of the different moral virtues in book 3. His attitude toward Greek ethics on each of these points is instructive.

Sidgwick agrees with Green in emphasizing the importance of Aristotle's conception of the good, and especially in emphasizing the nonhedonist character of Aristotle's conception. Indeed, he suggests, as many others have, that to translate Aristotle's term *eudaimonia* as "happiness" is to invite confusion between his conception of the good and the conception of those who conceive happiness in hedonist terms.[10] Sidgwick criticizes Dugald Stewart for inviting this confusion in his account of Greek ethics.[11] His criticism, however, seems to be baseless. Stewart is following closely a passage in Reid, where Reid says that the best ancient moralists reduced the whole of morals to a question about "the greatest good" or what is "best for us upon the whole";[12] and there is no reason to think that Stewart means anything different from this in talking about happiness. Stewart seems to see no difficulty or confusion in the use of "happiness" to refer to an ultimate good that need not be conceived in hedonist terms.

Sidgwick's rather possessive attitude to the term "happiness" expresses itself further in his criticism of Mill for speaking of power or fame as "parts" of happiness. Mill's remarks are intelligible if he conceives happiness as something like eudaimonia and understands eudaimonia in partly nonhedonist terms; but Sidgwick attributes the remarks to "a mere looseness of phraseology, venial in a treatise aiming at a popular style" (*ME*, 93,n.1). Sidgwick claims that any nonhedonist conception of happiness involves "manifest divergence from common usage" – though Stewart, Mill, and Green seem to be three counterexamples.

This turns out not to be simply a question about common usage. For Sidgwick does not think a nonhedonistic conception of the good defines a version of egoism that is clear enough to be worth discussion (*ME*, 91–2). Eudaimonism, without further specification, does not define anything that Sidgwick regards as a distinct ethical position:

we must discard a common account of egoism which describes its ultimate end as the "good" of the individual; for the term "good" may cover all possible views of the ultimate end of rational conduct. Indeed it may be said that egoism in this sense was assumed in the whole ethical controversy of ancient Greece; that is, it was assumed on all sides that a rational individual would make the pursuit of his own good his supreme aim; the controverted question was whether this good was rightly conceived as pleasure or virtue or any *tertium quid*. (*ME*, 91–2)

Nor does it help to follow Green in claiming that Aristotle identifies the good with some sort of self-realization. Quite the reverse; Sidgwick thinks an appeal to self-realization introduces further vagueness, since it "seems to be a form into which almost any ethical system may be thrown, without modifying its essential characteristics" (*ME*, 95).

In Sidgwick's view, then, Aristotelian eudaimonism yields no acceptable ethical first principles; for the principles it yields are either trivial or highly controversial, and any controversy has to be settled by appeal to more ultimate principles:

it seems worthy of remark that throughout the ethical speculation of Greece, such universal affirmations as are presented to us concerning Virtue or Good conduct seem always to be propositions which can only be defended from the charge of tautology, if they are understood as definitions of the problem to be solved, and not attempts at its solution. (*ME*, 375–6)

If Aristotelian eudaimonism yields no sufficiently definite first principles, it cannot be expected to fulfill Green's hope of finding an escape from the dualism of practical reason; for nonhedonistic eudaimonism simply conceals questions about the relation of morality to self-interest but does not resolve them. Sidgwick credits Butler with the first attempt to draw a clear and sharp distinction between duty (conscience) and interest (self-love); and he thinks that Butler draws a genuine and sharp distinction where his predecessors had failed to see one:

Butler's express statement of the duality of the regulative principles in human nature constitutes an important step in ethical speculation; since it brings into clear view the most fundamental difference between the ethical thought of modern England and that of the old Greco-Roman world, – a difference all the more striking because Butler's general formula of "living according to nature" is taken from Stoicism, and his view of human nature as an ordered polity of impulses is distinctly Platonic. But in Platonism and Stoicism, and in Greek moral philosophy generally, but one regulative and governing faculty is recognized under the name of Reason – however the regulation of Reason may be understood; in the modern ethical view, when it has worked itself clear, there are found to be two, – Universal Reason and Egoistic Reason, or Conscience and Self-love. (*OHE*, 197–8)

Sidgwick acknowledges Butler as the source of his own formulation of the dualism of practical reason; and he believes that Aristotelian non-hedonist eudaimonism allows us to think we have escaped the dualism simply because we mistake vague and useless formulations for substantive principles with practical consequences.[13] Once we try to say more precisely what a person's good consists in, we will see that we are either assuming some highly controversial claim about the relation of morality to self-love or opening the very gap that Sidgwick calls to our attention.

Sidgwick, therefore, cannot take seriously any attempt to derive practical conclusions from a general conception of happiness such as the one Aristotle accepts; and he cannot endorse Aristotle's attempt (in *Nicomachean Ethics* 9.8) to show that self-love, correctly understood, requires acceptance of morality.

It would have been helpful if Sidgwick had argued more elaborately against the usefulness of nonhedonist eudaimonism. His main reason for rejecting it rests on a demand for clarity that plays a highly controversial role at crucial points in *The Methods of Ethics*. Sidgwick is quite right to point out that unless we accept a hedonist conception of happiness our judgments about when someone is happy, or when one person is happier than another, may not be purely quantitative and non-evaluative; they may actually depend on moral judgments about the value of the activities that we take happiness to consist in. Sidgwick thinks this is a fatal objection to a nonhedonist conception, because such a conception does not allow the ultimate good to play the role that it plays in Sidgwick's theory. But we may not agree that the role he intends for the ultimate good is clearly the right role for it to play; and hence we may not agree that the kind of clarity that Sidgwick demands is necessary or appropriate in this case.

In rejecting nonhedonist eudaimonism Sidgwick rejects a distinctive contribution of Greek moral philosophy to moral thinking. His reasons are insufficient; for they seem to be derived from some highly dubious aspects of his own theory.

The second major influence of Greek moral philosophy on Sidgwick appears in his discussion of common-sense morality. He mentions this influence in commenting on Aristotle's treatment of the particular virtues. In contrast to Green, Sidgwick argues that Aristotle's treatment is simply a detailed and impartial description of common sense; Aristotle, in his view, is not trying to argue systematically from features of happiness to a theoretical account of the virtues, but simply consulting the accepted views of his contemporaries, without trying to reconstruct, revise, or justify them.

In attributing this purely descriptive account to Aristotle, Sidgwick does not mean to write it off as unimportant to moral theory. In fact he thinks Aristotle's conception of his task is, as far as it goes, quite correct, and that it provides an important model for other theorists, including Sidgwick himself:

What he gave us there was the Common Sense Morality of Greece, reduced to consistency by careful comparison. . . . Might I not imitate this? . . . Indeed *ought* I not to do this before deciding on the question whether I had or had not a system of moral intuitions? (*ME*, xix–xx)

In a large part of *The Methods of Ethics* Sidgwick follows what he takes to be Aristotle's example, reviewing common sense without trying to improve on it.

Sidgwick does not suggest that Aristotle's description of the virtues is guided to any important degree by his conception of happiness. Sidgwick's silence may seem surprising, since Aristotle seems to claim that the moral virtues are states that promote the agent's happiness. But it is not really surprising that Sidgwick does not take this claim very seriously. For since he thinks Aristotelian eudaimonism is empty, he cannot suppose that Aristotle's description of the virtues is really controlled by his conception of happiness; an empty conception of happiness could not justify any precise description of the virtues. Since Aristotle offers a relatively precise description of the virtues, the description must come from somewhere other than his conception of happiness; and so Sidgwick infers that it must simply be a catalogue of the traits and behavior approved by common sense. Sidgwick's interpretation of Aristotle's conception of happiness helps to explain his interpretation of Aristotle's description of the virtues.

Though Sidgwick gives credit to Aristotle for the method he follows in his review of common-sense morality, he takes his own aim to be quite different from Aristotle's. He undertakes the review of common sense in order to see whether it rests on genuine intuitions; and he finds that in fact it does not rest on them. Sometimes the principles accepted by common sense turn out to rest on controversial empirical assumptions; sometimes we cannot say what common-sense principles require in this or that type of cause; and in some cases common sense apparently has no advice to offer at all. For all these reasons the principles implicit in common sense cannot embody the intuitions that Sidgwick takes to be necessary for any satisfactory first principles in an ethical system. The only satisfactory first principle is the utilitarian principle; and once we accept this, we can see that it explains and supports common sense to a certain extent but also allows us to supply some of the deficiencies of common sense.

This critical attitude to common sense appears to Sidgwick to be un-Aristotelian; for, in his view, Aristotle records and articulates but does not systematize or criticize. Aristotle's failure to anticipate Sidgwick on these points is not surprising, if Sidgwick is right about Aristotelian eudaimonism; for Aristotle's nonhedonist conception of the good is so indefinite that it cannot be a basis for criticism of common sense.

In contrast to Green, Sidgwick believes that if we study the Aristotelian virtues carefully we will see that they embody ideals that are sharply opposed both to Christian ideals and to the truth. He does not believe that Aristotle criticizes common sense in the light of his principles (since the principles are empty); and he believes that, even if Aristotle had been critical of common sense, the ideals that would have shaped his criticism would not have been those that Green rashly attributes to Aristotle, in the light of his own Christian and Kantian preferences.

This judgment about Aristotle determines his role in moral progress as Sidgwick conceives it. He agrees with Green in thinking of moral philosophy as a rational and progressive discipline. But the progress that he sees consists in replacing false principles with true, not in the gradual statement and clarification of true principles. He believes that progress in moral philosophy is exemplified by, for instance, Butler's formulation of the division between self-love and conscience, and in Bentham's statement of hedonistic utilitarianism. He does not suggest that these statements of principles he accepts are also statements of something that Aristotle vaguely had in mind or was trying to articulate. Moral philosophy advances when philosophers state intuitions that their predecessors overlooked.[14]

Sidgwick sums up his commendation and criticism of Aristotle in this general verdict:

There is enough just and close analytical observation contained in this famous account of virtues and vices to give it a permanent interest over and above its historical value; but it does not seem to be based on any serious attempt to consider human life exhaustively, and exhibit the patterns of goodness appropriate to its different parts, functions, and relations. (*OHE*, 64)[15]

In his own account of common-sense morality Sidgwick tries to avoid these faults that he points to in Aristotle.

Now that I have surveyed some points of disagreement between Green and Sidgwick about Greek ethics, I want to ask who is right. So far, several issues have arisen: (1) Though Sidgwick and Green agree that Aristotle's conception of the good is nonhedonistic, they disagree about whether it has enough content to be useful. (2) More basically, they disagree about what makes a first principle useful. Sidgwick believes that a purported first principle cannot really do its work unless it is intuitively certain and also yields clear enough consequences to allow an answer to practical questions. Green rejects this demand on first principles.[16] (3) They agree in focusing attention on Aristotle's account of the particular virtues. But whereas Green sees here the outline of a systematic account of the virtues that is integrated by a true conception of the good, Sidgwick sees nothing more than a fundamentally unsystematic account of the common-sense morality of Aristotle's own time.

Each of these issues deserves lengthy discussion; but here I will confine myself largely to a brief discussion of the third issue, about the particular virtues.[17] The questions that it raises about Aristotle are quite difficult to answer, and no answer is generally accepted among students of Aristotle. Moreover, the arguments offered by Sidgwick and Green illustrate their different approaches to understanding the history of ethics and allow us to consider what sorts of approaches might be useful and illuminating for what purposes. In particular I think these issues allow us to see the role of philosophical assumptions in interpretative approaches. Though my discussion of these questions will not directly settle the first two issues in dispute between Sidgwick and Green, I think it may contribute something relevant to these issues as well.

4. Green's view of the Aristotelian virtues

Green argues that the Greek moralists found the true principle of morality:

Once for all they conceived and expressed the conception of a free or pure morality, as resting on what we may venture to call a disinterested interest in the good; of the several virtues as so many applications of that interest to the main relations of social life; of the good itself not as anything external to the capacities virtuously exercised in its pursuit, but as their full realization. (*Prol.*, 253)

He recognizes that this statement of the general principle of morality offers no specific guidance for action. But he thinks we can find principles that guide action, if we look at Aristotle's discussion of the particular virtues.

The Aristotelian virtue of bravery is Green's first example; and he sees that it may appear unpromising. For Aristotelian bravery seems to be a virtue that most of us fortunately never have either the need or the opportunity to acquire. Its range is much narrower than the range of courage, as we usually conceive it; for it is confined to citizen-soldiers facing death in battle for their city-state. In restricting the scope of bravery in this way, Aristotle sharply disagrees with Socrates, whose wider conception seems more intelligible to us. Insofar as Aristotle confines bravery to the conventional tests of military valor, he may well seem rather thoughtlessly conservative.[18]

Green, however, takes the initially paradoxical view that Aristotle's narrow conception of the scope of bravery makes it clearer that he is talking about the very same virtue that is displayed by one of Green's own moral heroes, a nonviolent Quaker philanthropist working quietly against all sorts of dangers and obstacles for the relief of suffering (*Prol.*, 258–9). For both the Greek citizen and the philanthropist share a principle that is common to both forms of virtuous action; this is "self-devotion to a worthy end in resistance to pain and fear" (*Prol.*, 258) or, more exactly, "the willingness to endure even unto complete self-renunciation . . . in the service of the highest public cause which the agent can conceive" (*Prol.*, 260).

If this is the principle of bravery, then, Green argues, Aristotle's restriction on the scope of the virtue becomes intelligible and reasonable. For he restricts it to danger in war because this is the highest public cause that he can conceive; and by restricting the scope of bravery in this way, he expresses the general principle of bravery more clearly.[19] In that case, the restrictive conception of bravery in Aristotle actually supports the wider conception of it in Green. Green attends to the historical context of Aristotle's account, in which Aristotle assumes that the survival of a particular political community will depend on the willingness of its citizens to face death in war on its behalf; but he appeals to this historical context in order to show how the Aristotelian virtue can be freed from these particular historical limitations.

Aristotle accepts a narrow conception of temperance, no less than of bravery, and recognizes it only in a limited range of desires and actions. Temperance is not displayed in every sort of self-restraint or appropriate balance in the gratification of appetites; it is confined to the pleasures of the senses, and specifically to the senses of taste and touch (*EN* 1118a23–b8).

In Green's view, however, this restriction is also intelligible. The virtue of temperance, in his view, aims at the good of the community, and the desires that it restrains or modifies are those that are especially dangerous to the common good. Aristotle's restriction on the scope of temperance reflects his view – which we need not share – about which sorts of desires are especially dangerous.

It must be admitted that, when Aristotle treats most methodically of *sôphrosunê*, he does little to specify the particular form of the interest in the *kalon* which he considered to be the basis of the virtue. . . . But to a Greek who was told that the virtue of temperance was a mastery over certain desires, exercised *tou kalou heneka* [sc., for the sake of the fine], there would be no practical doubt what the motive was to be, what was to be the object in which a prevailing interest was to enable him to exercise this mastery. It could only be reverence for the divine order of the state, such a desire to fulfil his proper function in the community as might keep under the body and control the influence of overweening lust. (*Prol.*, 263)

The temperate person's readiness to measure his actions and aims by his conception of the common good insures that he will have the right principle of the virtue.

In the light of this principle we can see why Aristotle attaches the value that he actually attaches to temperance:

It was this character of the motive or interest on which it was supposed to rest, that gave to *sôphrosunê* an importance in the eye of the Greek moralist which, if we looked simply to the very limited range of pleasures – pleasures of the merely animal nature – in regard to which Aristotle supposes the "temperate man" to exercise self-restraint, would scarcely be intelligible. Not the mere sobriety of the appetites, but the foundation of that sobriety in a truly civil spirit, in the highest kind of rational loyalty, gave the virtue its value. (*Prol.*, 263)

If we simply focused on the pleasures that Aristotle connects with temperance, we would find it difficult to see why he should pick this out as an important virtue in its own right. But if we keep in mind his belief that these pleasures are particularly dangerous to the common good, which is the real focus of temperance, then we can see why Aristotle describes the genuine virtue of temperance; and we can see this without accepting his view about the scope of the virtue.

Bravery and temperance are the only two examples that Green describes in any detail. But he intends them as examples to support a general explanatory account of the Greek conception of virtue, and we have to see for ourselves whether the same sort of explanation and revision of Aristotle works for the other virtues as well. In each case Green notices that Aristotle's account of the scope of the virtue seems strangely restricted; and he suggests that in fact the restriction is a clue to the permanent significance and value of Aristotle's account. For Aristotle's restrictions reflect his views about what promotes the common good, and each virtue is a state of character that expresses the agent's identification of his own good with the common good.

To see how far Green's claims can be generalized, we need to evaluate two claims. (1) We are supposed to be able to see the point of Aristotle's description of a virtue if we look at the actions he counts as instances, or primary instances, of the virtue and ask why he counts them as instances of it. (2) Aristotle's general remarks about the moral motive are held to suggest Green's view of the particular virtues. For Green mentions the demand that the virtuous person should act for the sake of the fine (*kalon*), and he takes this demand to acknowledge the intrinsic value of virtuous action; further, he claims that the content of temperance is determined by the connection between the fine and the common good of the community.[20] To see whether Green is right, we must see if Aristotle's remarks really support these two main claims about virtuous action and about the fine.

5. Sidgwick's criticisms of Green's account

Sidgwick argues that Green has exaggerated the degree of system to be found in Aristotle's account, and specifically that he is wrong to treat the common good as Aristotle's standard of ethical approval. Attention to the details of Aristotle's account, he thinks, will reveal features of the particular virtues that do not fit the systematic account that Green tries to impose on Aristotle.

The general attitude to the virtues that Sidgwick finds in Aristotle is a form of "aesthetic intuitionism," which he describes as follows: "We can give only a general account of the virtue – a description, not a definition – and leave it to trained insight to find in any particular circumstances the act that will best realize it" (*ME*, 228). In describing bravery, Aristotle "is merely following closely and impartially the lines of Common Sense, of the ethico-aesthetic sentiment of his society" (*GSM*, 91), and "simply conceives the brave man as realizing moral beauty in his act" (*GSM*, 92). Brave actions need not share any common feature beyond their tendency to provoke the relevant kind of quasi-aesthetic admiration, and Aristotle sees no need to seek any further common feature.

Sidgwick recognizes that a historian might suggest utilitarian features of bravery that would explain its tendency to excite this sort of quasi-aesthetic admiration; but he correctly insists that the historian's explanation should not be confused with a part of the outlook that is being explained. He thinks that common sense displays some degree of "unconscious utilitarianism" (*GSM*, 90; *ME*, 453–7) and that utilitarian considerations might explain some of Aristotle's judgments, but he denies that these considerations constitute any part of Aristotle's own view:

Aristotle sees that the sphere of the virtue of courage (*andreia*), as recognized by the common sense of Greece, is restricted to dangers in war; and we can now explain this limitation by a reference to the utilitarian importance of this kind of courage, at a period of history when the individual's happiness was bound up more completely than it now is with the welfare of his state, while the very existence of the latter was more frequently imperilled by hostile invasions; but this explanation lies quite beyond the range of Aristotle's own reflections. . . . The admiration felt by early man for beauties or excellences of character seems to have been as direct and unreflective as the admiration of any other beauty. (*ME*, 456)

Green is mistaken, then, insofar as he attributes a concern for the common good to brave people themselves (as Aristotle conceives them) and to Aristotle's view of the brave person; such a utilitarian principle properly belongs only to a historian's explanation and not to the view itself.[21]

If we consider some of the details of Aristotle's description of bravery, then, in Sidgwick's view, we can see why Green's account fails to display Aristotle's aesthetic intuitionism. Green's account is too narrow, insofar as it restricts the range of bravery to Greek citizens concerned with the common good of their city, whereas Aristotle remarks that a monarchy as well as a polis honors brave men (*EN* 1115a31–2).[22] For similar reasons it would be absurd to restrict temperance to citizens of a polis.[23] On the other hand, Green's view is too broad for Aristotle's description, because Aristotle does not believe that a brave person displays bravery in sickness or in a shipwreck as he does in war (1115a35–b6), whereas Green's view implies that Aristotle ought to have regarded these as clear examples of bravery.

Sidgwick believes that the same sort of criticism undermines the rest of Green's account of the Aristotelian virtues.[24] A symptom of Aristotle's purely aesthetic attitude to virtuous actions is his view of generosity and magnificence, the virtues concerned with money and other material resources; he does not distinguish self-regarding from benevolent expenditures but simply admires the wealth and power that are displayed in conspicuous consumption, without any necessary reference to the common good. Sidgwick comments:

And an examination of these would show very clearly how simply Aristotle is following the ethico-aesthetic – or even purely aesthetic – sentiment of admiration for certain qualities in the conduct of a Greek gentleman, and how far he is from conceiving self-devotion to a social end as essential to the notion of virtue. For example, his account of liberality is startling to a modern reader from its want of distinction between self-regarding and benevolent expenditure. Compare also his account of *megalopsuchia*. (*GSM*, 96–7)

The attitude that he attributes to Aristotle is similar to the attitude that Sidgwick attributes to the common sense of his own time:

Liberality appears to require an external abundance in the gift even more than a self-sacrificing disposition. It seems therefore to be possible only to the rich; and, as I have hinted, in the admiration commonly accorded it there seems to be mingled an element rather aesthetic than moral. For we are all apt to admire power, and we recognize the latent power of wealth gracefully exhibited in a certain degree of careless profusion when the object is to give happiness to others. Indeed the vulgar admire the same carelessness as manifested even in selfish luxury. (*ME*, 324–5)

Here as elsewhere Sidgwick emphasizes the features of Aristotle that he takes to betray the characteristic limitations of common sense. He sums up his judgment:

the restriction of the sphere of courage to danger in war, and that of temperance to certain bodily pleasures, as well as the want of distinction between selfish and benevolent expenditure in describing liberality, illustrate the fragmentariness and superficiality of treatment to which mere analysis of the common usage of ethical terms is always liable to lead. (*OHE*, 64)[25]

These, then, are the specific objections that Sidgwick urges against Green's attempt to find in Aristotle the outline of a true theory of the good and the moral virtues. One source of the disagreement between Green and Sidgwick is, as I have emphasized, their more general disagreement about what a true theory would be like. But Sidgwick also presents several objections that do not appear to depend on this general disagreement; he suggests that even if Green were right about what we ought to be looking for, he would be wrong to claim that we find it in Aristotle. I will take up some of these more specific objections.

6. Aristotle on the fine

One major disagreement between Green and Sidgwick arises from their sharply divergent, and largely undefended, views about the role of the fine (*kalon*) in Aristotle's conception of virtue. For Green, the connection between virtue and fineness is clear evidence that Aristotle is basically right about the nature of the moral motive and about the connection between the agent's good and the good of others. Sidgwick, however, draws the opposite conclusion; the references to the fine show that Aristotle fails to distinguish strictly moral from purely aesthetic judgments.

It turns out to be quite difficult to say what Aristotle means by saying that virtuous action is fine or that the virtuous person acts "for the sake of the fine." Despite the importance of fineness in the *Ethics*, Aristotle offers remarkably little detailed discussion of it. But I think he says enough to show that Green is essentially right.[26]

It is true that the Greek term that Aristotle uses, *kalon*, is often appropriately translated as "beautiful." But there are good reasons for denying that aesthetic beauty is what he primarily intends when he mentions the *kalon* in connection with the virtues. Several remarks suggest that Aristotle intends the *kalon* to be connected specifically with moral value, and even more specifically with the common good of the relevant community (*koinônia*):

1. What is fine is both intrinsically good and praiseworthy (*Eudemian Ethics* [*EE*] 1248b17–25; cf. *EN* 1101b31–2, 1155a28–31, and *Rhet.* 1366a33–6).
2. Actions that are praiseworthy must be voluntary (*EN* 1109b31; *EE* 1223a9–15); and actions displaying great virtue especially deserve praise (*Rhet.* 1367b28).
3. Actions display great virtue insofar as they especially benefit others (*Rhet.* 1366b3–4;[27] *EN* 1120a11, 1121a27–30, 1123a31–2; *EE* 1231a24).
4. Hence, concern for the fine is contrasted with narrow and exclusive concern for one's own interest (*Rhet.* 1358b38, 1389a32–5, 1389b35; *EN* 1104b31, 1169a6); and when everyone concentrates on fine action, we can expect that to promote the common good (*EN* 1169a6–11).

These remarks strongly support Green's claim that Aristotle intends some systematic connection between virtue, the fine, and the common good of a particular community. It would be wrong to deny that fineness is an appropriate object of some sort of aesthetic admiration in moral contexts; but if the aesthetic admiration is essentially a response to the promotion of the common good, then the promotion of the common good is the essential characteristic of fine actions (states of character, etc.) in moral contexts.

If this is right, then Green cannot fairly be accused of simply reading into Aristotle his own views about the connection between the agent's good and the good of others. On the contrary, he sees that Aristotle intends to argue from his conception of happiness to the conception of a common good as the focus of virtuous action. He expresses Aristotle's definition of happiness as "the full expression or realization of the soul's capacities in accordance with its proper excellence" (*Prol.*, 254) and argues that Aristotle finds the full realization of these capacities in an agent's effective concern for the good of the community.[28] His claim rest on solid Aristotelian support; for Aristotle claims that the happiness of a single person must include the happiness of family, friends, and fellow citizens (*EN* 1097b8–11, 1169b16–19, 1170b14–19). This link between the agent's happiness and the common good explains why a rational agent is justified in valuing the virtues of character that require him to do the fine action for its own sake. Fine action has a justified claim on him because it aims at the common good, and he, as a rational agent aiming at his own good, also has reason to aim at the common good.

7. Bravery

Still, even if Green is right about Aristotle's conception of the virtues and their relation to the fine, he might still be wrong about the particular virtues. It is clear that Aristotle does not fully articulate his general conception, and does not explicitly and emphatically apply it to the particular virtues; if he did these things, we would not have to argue about his views. We might still find that Sidgwick is right to some extent; for perhaps Aristotle fails to argue that the traditional Greek virtues really meet his general conditions for a virtue, and perhaps his description of the particular virtues displays that uncritical acceptance of common sense that Sidgwick attributes to him. To see whether this is so or not, we must return to some of the details that Sidgwick urges against Green.

Aristotle insists that bravery is displayed primarily in the danger of death in war (*EN* 1115a25–9), because this danger is both the greatest danger (because it is the danger of death) and the finest danger (since it concerns death in war). In restricting the scope of the virtue in this way, he departs significantly from common sense. For common sense (both our own and the Greeks') might well be inclined to see bravery in a fearless and dangerous action in a private feud or in a daring crime. The danger may be at least as great in these cases as in the danger of death in war; but Aristotle refuses to count them as cases of bravery, because the danger is not fine. The danger is not fine because it is not undertaken for the common good and therefore does not involve a genuine virtue.

In claiming that virtues aim at the common good, Aristotle does not mean that they aim at maximizing the total good, and to this extent he does not interpret the common good in strictly utilitarian terms. It may be useful for a state if some citizens cheerfully sacrifice themselves for the good of others; but Aristotle does not think this sort of self-sacrifice is necessarily appropriate for the brave person. For he notices that some people may face death because of foolish optimism (*EN* 1115b28), others because of foolish fearlessness (1115b24), others because of shame (1116a18), others because of indifference to their lives – and he remarks rather cynically that the last people will often make the best professional soldiers (1117b17–20). None of these motives, useful though they may be, is characteristic of bravery. In fact, brave people will be less tractable and less useful in some cases, because they will need to be convinced that they are sacrificing themselves for some worthwhile cause; on the other hand, once they are convinced, they will be ready in some circumstances to face hopeless odds that would daunt the professional soldier (1116b15–23). The brave person's discriminating attitude marks the difference between concern for the common good and a tendency to be useful to a community; to this extent Aristotle seems to carry his general views into the details of his description of a particular virtue.

Even among people who have roughly the right sort of motive, Aristotle discriminates in ways that conflict with common sense. Most strikingly, he does not agree that the average citizen-soldier fighting for his city is necessarily brave; if citizens are moved by thoughts of honor, shame, and punishment, these are not sufficient motives for bravery (*EN* 1116a17–20). These restrictions are incomprehensible if Sidgwick is right about the general character of Aristotle's description of the virtues. But if Green is right, they are quite comprehensible; they show that Aristotle insists on the right sort of rational concern for the common good for its own sake in a genuinely virtuous person.

Once we understand what Aristotle is trying to do, we can answer some of Sidgwick's specific objections.

1. When Aristotle says that the brave person does not fully display bravery in sickness or shipwreck, two points are relevant: (1) He presumably refers to private journeys, rather than to naval battles; and so the circumstances do not involve the common good. (2) In any case, Aristotle assumes that the brave person has to face sickness and shipwreck rather passively (*EN* 1115b4–6), so that the circumstances do not offer the opportunity for active pursuit of the common good. If either or both of these explanations are correct, then Aristotle's judgment about these cases can be explained by the sort of general account that Green offers.

2. Contrary to Sidgwick, it probably does not seem at all absurd to Aristotle to claim that, for instance, the subjects of a king fail to display the primary sort of bravery.[29] In fact, he may be thinking of such people when he mentions those who stand firm in danger under compulsion (*EN* 1116a29–b3); and he clearly denies that these people are brave. Sidgwick's objection, if it is sound, applies no less to Aristotle than to

Green's account of him; it actually counts in favor of Green's interpretation rather than against it.

I have discussed bravery at some length, because Green and Sidgwick have most to say about it and because it illustrates their different approaches quite well. Green is certainly careless about details, and we may well suppose that Sidgwick's attention to detail will result in a more accurate account. But this is not what we find. For in fact Sidgwick overlooks those details that strongly support Green's account against his own.

8. Temperance

Temperance raises more difficult questions for Green's account of Aristotle; for though it is fairly plausible to suggest that bravery involves some concern with the good of others, temperance seems more obviously self-regarding. Indeed, temperance may well seem to be so clearly self-regarding that it is not a genuinely moral virtue at all.

Nonetheless, Aristotle claims that temperate people, no less than people with the other virtues, are guided by their view of what is fine when they restrain or indulge particular appetites (*EN* 1119a11–20). To defend this claim, Aristotle needs to show that the temperate person's pursuit of these pleasures is regulated by reference to the fine and the common good. Do his remarks on temperance suggest that he has this sort of regulation in mind?

First, it is relevant to ask why Aristotle focuses on the particular appetites that he takes to be the proper concern of temperance. Though he describes them as the pleasures of touch and taste, he does not actually include all these pleasures (cf. *EN* 1118b4–8). In fact, he refers to the pleasures associated with appetites for food, drink, and sex; and he picks these out because he assumes that the people who pursue them without restraint are especially bestial and slavish (1118b1–4, 10–11). In saying that the intemperate person is slavish, Aristotle means that he is wholly occupied with the pursuit of these particular satisfactions and thinks of everything else as simply a means to promoting these satisfactions. Someone who takes this purely mercenary attitude to rational deliberation attaches no intrinsic value to the exercise of his capacities as a rational agent; and so he cannot be expected to have any intrinsic concern for the common good.

For these reasons, it is fairly plausible to argue, with Green, that Aristotle is concerned with intemperance because of its effects on the common good:

such a check should be kept on the lusts of the flesh as might prevent them from issuing in what a Greek knew as *hubris* – a kind of self-assertion, and aggression upon the rights of others in respect of person and property, for which we have not an equivalent name, but which was looked upon as the antithesis of the civil spirit. (*Prol.* 265)

As Green suggests, wanton aggression (hubris) is a characteristic display of intemperance against other people (*EN* 1129b21), expressed in physical assaults, including sexual assaults (1148b30), and in other attempts to humiliate other people for our own pleasure or gain (1115a22, 1124a26–b6, 1149b20–2). The intemperate person is prone to extravagance, susceptible to flatterers (1121a30–b10), and aggressive in the pursuit of the "contested" goods that people normally fight over (1168b15–19). Such people are aggressive and competitive because they are absorbed in the sort of self-love that is directed to the nonrational part of their souls (1168b19–21); and this is the sort of self-love that conflicts with pursuit of the virtues and the common good. The more intemperate we are, the more likely we are to have desires that conflict with other people's desires, and the less likely we are to cooperate with others (1167b9–16).

If we examine this evidence, we can see why Aristotle thinks temperance is a major virtue, and why he thinks it plays a major role in an agent's rational concern with the common good. He connects intemperance especially with the desires that tend, if they are uncontrolled, to dominate a person and to make him indifferent to his distinctively rational characteristics and therefore tend to make him indifferent to the claims of other people. Only the person who cares about living as a rational agent, and cares about this for its own sake, has good reason to be concerned about the common good for its own sake.

If we believe for these reasons that Aristotle has succeeded in describing a genuine virtue of temperance, we are not forced to agree that he has focused on the right sorts of desires and appetites. His particular psychological claim – that the particular appetites he mentions are the ones that particularly tend to dominate an agent and to make him indifferent to his rational capacities – might well be wrong. But if we have given the right explanation for the fact that he focuses on these appetites, his description of temperance fits readily into the sort of account that Green offers.

Sidgwick once again suggests that Green's account forces Aristotle into a manifestly absurd consequence that Aristotle himself would regard as absurd – that temperance will turn out to be praiseworthy only in a republic (i.e., a Greek polis) where citizens acknowledge that the state pursues their common good (*GSM*, 94). But once again it is not obvious that the consequence is manifestly absurd. It is quite true that other communities besides a polis have reason to cultivate temperance in their members; but it still might be true that only a polis gives an agent reasons to regard temperance as intrinsically valuable and fine. For if virtuous people are to regard an action (e.g.) as fine, and hence as worth choosing for its own sake, they must agree that it promotes a common good that they value as part of their own good. Not every political system makes it reasonable to take this attitude. Green suggests that it is reasonable under "the regime of equal law, the free combination of mutually respecting citizens in the enactment of a common good" (*Prol.*, 263). Why should Aristotle, or we, regard this as an absurd consequence?

In this case also, therefore, study of Aristotle ought to bring us closer to Green's account than to Sidgwick's.

9. Liberality

We should also consider Sidgwick's further objection that, however plausible Green's account of bravery and temperance may be, his view collapses once we try to extend it to the virtues that Green does not discuss. He raises special difficulties about liberality (*eleutheriotês*) and magnanimity.[30]

Sidgwick claims that Aristotle's description of liberality fails to distinguish self-regarding from benevolent expenditure; and it is certainly true that Aristotle discusses both kinds of spending under the heading of liberality. But does this constitute an objection to Green's account?

In many cases it is reasonable for the liberal person to fail to draw a sharp line between self-regarding and benevolent action. A gift to his friend, for instance, will be attractive because it is a source of gratitude and honor; but he will also give it for the friend's own sake, and he cares especially about the gratitude and honor coming from his friend because he cares about his friend for the friend's own sake. In such cases it is not surprising, if an account like Green's is correct, that Aristotle fails to draw the distinction that Sidgwick mentions.[31]

It would indeed be a point in Sidgwick's favor and against Green if Aristotle did not intend the actions of liberal and magnificent people to be guided by reference to the common good. But Aristotle clearly seems to intend the common good to have this regulative function. The magnificent person avoids ostentation even in private expenses, such as building himself a house (*EN* 1123a6–10); he will not want it to be more imposing than public buildings, for instance.[32] Because he thinks about the common good, he will avoid the errors of the ostentatious person who performs his public services in ways that display his wealth but do not benefit the common good (1123a20–7); and when it is appropriate the magnificent person will be moved to positive action by consideration of the common good (1122b19–23, 1123a1–5). The common good guides his choices and actions in just the way that we expect it to if Green's account is correct.

Indeed, the very point that Sidgwick urges against Green is actually a point in Green's favor. For we ought to expect Aristotle to draw a sharp distinction between self-regarding and benevolent actions only if we suppose that a person's self-regarding ends will also be predominantly selfish and that benevolence must be added to, and will probably conflict with, his true conception of his own good. We have seen that this is in fact Sidgwick's view of the relation between self-love and benevolence; he gives Butler credit for having distinguished the two principles sharply enough to allow Sidgwick himself to draw attention to the dualism of practical reason. But Aristotle recognizes no such dualism; if the common good is part of the agent's own good, then self-regarding actions will include benevolent actions, and we need not expect Aristotle to draw a sharp distinction. His failure to draw it is some evidence that Green's sort of account is correct.[33]

10. Magnanimity

Sidgwick is not the only reader who has found Aristotle's account of magnanimity hard to reconcile with our conception of a moral virtue. He probably has these sorts of points in mind:

1. Aristotle's attitude seems to be more aesthetic than moral, insofar as he seems to admire the grand scale of magnanimous action (*EN* 1123b6–8) and refers to morally insignificant details of how the magnanimous person walks and speaks (1125a12–16).

2. The magnanimous person seems rather devoted to himself; and his self-assertive and disdainful pride seems to mark a sharp contrast with any Christian virtue. Whereas Green wants to show that a Christian conscience can accept the Aristotelian virtues, while rejecting Aristotle's views about their extension, Sidgwick argues that magnanimity is a clear counterexample to this attempted reconciliation.[34]

Such objections, however, underestimate the significance of the fact that the magnanimous person is concerned with the fine and the common good. He values his life and does not throw it away cheaply; but he is willing to sacrifice it for the common good in some appropriately worth-while cause (*EN* 1124b6–9, 23–6). He does not guide his life by reference to another person, with the crucial exception of a friend (1124b31–1125a2). He cares about honor, but only for the appropriate sorts of virtuous actions; and since he cares most about acting virtuously, he does not think honor, or any other external good, is very important (1124a12–17).

Without analyzing the rest of Aristotle's description in detail, I hope these points show that magnanimity does not constitute a clear counterexample to Green's account of the Aristotelian virtues.[35] The role of the fine and the common good in the magnanimous person's thoughts and actions confirms Green's general view. In this as in other cases, Aristotle is not content simply to describe the traits of character recognized by common sense as virtuous. He modifies and moralizes common sense, in order to insist on the central role of the virtuous person's correct decision (*prohairesis*) aiming at the agent's own good but also thereby aiming at the fine and the common good.

11. Comparisons between Sidgwick and Green

If Green's view is correct, then Aristotle's conception of happiness is the foundation of a systematic description and defense of the moral virtues. For the specific virtues claim our attention insofar as they aim at the common good; and the common good claims our attention insofar as it is part of our own good. Aristotle needs to show that concern for the common good is part of the fulfillment of a rational agent's capacities, which he identifies with happiness. To see whether Aristotle successfully defends these claims about the agent's good and the common good, we would need to discuss, above all, his account of friendship.[36] But at least I have tried to suggest that Aristotle himself seems to intend the sort of argument that Green attributes to him.

It would be foolish to pretend that this sort of argument is free of difficulty, or that Green satisfactorily answers all the difficulties it raises. In particular, Green makes things too easy by identifying the agent's good with his good will, and by claiming that we fully achieve our own good simply in the exercise of virtues that promote the same good in others. As Sidgwick rightly points out (*GSM*, 94), this conception of the good does not seem to do justice to the account of the good as self-realization; for self-realization seems to involve the actualization of many capacities that do not seem to be exhausted in a person's virtue. Moreover, this conception of the good makes it more difficult to see why we should try to secure for other people the sorts of goods that Green himself thinks we should try to secure for them. For he wants virtuous people to be concerned with the social provision of food, shelter, health, and public amenities; and it seems rather strained to pretend that these are good for people only because they help them to be more virtuous. By attempting to remove any possibility of conflict between the common good and any aspect of the agent's own good, Green actually makes it impossible to give any plausible account of one's own or other people's good.

To admit this, however, is a long way from admitting that Aristotle's theory forces us into Sidgwick's dualism of practical reason. If Aristotle can show that one's own good really includes the sorts of virtues that embody concern for a common good, then he will have shown something important about the relation of morality to self-love. We should not abandon our investigation of this sort of argument simply because we suspect that it will not resolve every possible practical conflict. To be persuaded by these suspicions is to accept Sidgwick's unreasonable demands on ethical first principles.

In this connection it is useful to focus on one questionable assumption that seems to support Sidgwick's confidence that Aristotle – as interpreted by Green – is wasting his time. We noticed earlier that Sidgwick thinks Aristotelian eudaimonism is vague and empty, because it does not give unambiguous answers about happiness that are independent of any further evaluative judgments. His objection to any attempt to derive moral principles from the demands of happiness and self-realization is rather similar. For he claims, quite correctly, that nonhedonist eudaimonism will not yield moral principles that meet his constraints on ethical first principles. But is this a reason for rejecting eudaimonism, or a reason for rejecting Sidgwick's constraints on first principles?

In claiming that first principles must be grasped by intuition and must be capable of resolving moral disputes without reliance on further moral assumptions, Sidgwick intends to reject any role for moral beliefs in specifying the first principles. If this aspect of Sidgwick's moral epistemology is applied to Green and Aristotle, it implies that we cannot rely on any moral beliefs in specifying the content of the human good or of self-realization. We might well agree – or at least concede for the sake of argument – that if moral beliefs are rigorously excluded it will be very difficult to find a conception of self-realization that will vindicate morality in the way that Green expects. But we need not agree that this constitutes a fatal flaw in Green's argument.

A very strong form of foundationalism, such as Sidgwick accepts, would certainly turn us against Green in principle; but if we are unwilling to go as far as Sidgwick goes, we have no reason to reject Green's argument in principle. If we do not reject it in principle, we face the more untidy and piecemeal task of deciding whether the particular sort of moral content that Green may be relying on is the wrong sort for the purposes of his argument. I do not mean to endorse the specific argument that Green offers, or the one that might be offered on Aristotle's behalf; but I want to point out that the reason Sidgwick relies on for rejecting this sort of argument altogether should not strike us as a good reason unless we are willing to accept some highly disputable assumptions in moral epistemology.

This point of disagreement with Sidgwick brings me back to the general issues I raised about the relation between Green's and Sidgwick's philosophical views and their attitudes to the interpretation of Aristotle. Sidgwick is determined to present Aristotle's view as an example of aesthetic intuitionism, and so overlooks the evidence that supports a view of Aristotle different from his own. Aristotle's account of common-sense morality plays an important role in Sidgwick's own argument; seeing the value of an impartial description of common sense, he is ready to find such a description in Aristotle. On the other hand, he is ready to discount the view that Aristotle is really trying to justify and revise common sense in the light of a more systematic account of the good; Sidgwick is convinced that any such attempted justification is a waste of time and that Green is simply reading his own misguided project into Aristotle.

In saying this I do not mean that Sidgwick is being dishonest and deliberately distorting or suppressing evidence. No dishonesty is needed for someone to find his picture of Aristotle appealing. Indeed, it is only reasonable to admit some element of truth in Sidgwick's picture; we need to look more carefully at Aristotle if we are to see that another picture is in fact better supported. Sidgwick does not look for evidence to support this other picture, because he sees that his own picture of Aristotle plays a useful role in his view of the history of ethics.

Even this way of putting it may be unfair to Sidgwick. For it is probably wrong to suggest that he has made up his mind independently of Aristotle about the nature of common-sense morality and about the significance of Greek ethics; it is quite likely that his picture of Aristotle itself influences his views on these other questions. But whatever the order of discovery may have been, the fact that Sidgwick's picture of Aristotle fits into his ethical theory as neatly as it does may well explain why Sidgwick does not see the importance of the aspects of Aristotle that support quite a different picture, and why he wrongly believes that no compelling case can be made in Green's support.

On the other hand, Green's philosophical views allow him to identify central Aristotelian claims about the virtues that are easily missed but are nonetheless essential for understanding Aristotle's position as a whole. Green sees these claims in Aristotle, not because he reads Aristotle more carefully than Sidgwick does, but because he is looking for them to support his own philosophical views. In this case his own philosophical preconceptions are so far from being a handicap in understanding Aristotle that they allow him to understand Aristotle better than many more scholarly readers have understood him.

This is one case in the study of the history of philosophy where efforts to avoid anachronism and philosophical preconceptions may actually limit our understanding. Sidgwick clearly thinks of himself as an impartial historian, in contrast to someone like Green who is evidently grinding his own philosophical axe. But I have tried to show that in fact Sidgwick is no less influenced than Green is by his own philosophical views. Since he thinks the sort of theory that Green finds in Aristotle is open to fatal objections, he does not see the significance of the evidence suggesting that Aristotle holds it; and since he sees some evidence to suggest that Aristotle makes the instructive errors of aesthetic intuitionism, he exaggerates the significance of the evidence supporting this account of Aristotle. In this case we have reasons for being skeptical about Sidgwick's accuracy as a historian of ethics – not because he is ignorant, or careless, or dishonest (for clearly he is none of these) but because some of his philosophical views conceal some of the historical facts from him.

In making these rather sweeping claims about the role of philosophical views in historical understanding, I certainly do not mean to claim that one should simply form one's philosophical views and then impose them on one's favorite philosophers of the past. Still less do I mean to defend the skeptical view that there is no distinction between a historically accurate account of Aristotle and an account that attributes to him the theory that we think philosophically preferable. I am offering a far more limited argument about the heuristic value of approaching historical study with definite philosophical preconceptions. In this particular case, sympathy with a specific philosophical position allows us to see some features of Aristotle's theory that are genuine features of it but whose weight and significance we might well not appreciate if we were not ourselves sympathetic to the position that we see in Aristotle.

Notes

1 *Five Types of Ethical Theory* (London: Routledge and Kegan Paul, 1930), p. 144.
2 I cite the posthumously published *Prolegomena to Ethics* (Oxford: Oxford

University Press [Clarendon Press], 1883), as *"Prol."*, by sections rather than pages. I occasionally cite passages from notes in Green's copies of Aristotle's *Ethics*, in the library of Balliol College, Oxford.

3 There is one recent full discussion of Green: G. Thomas, *The Moral Philosophy of T. H. Green* (Oxford: Oxford University Press [Clarendon Press], 1987). Parts of the *Prolegomena* have been reprinted in *Lectures on Political Obligation and Other Writings*, ed. P. Harris and J. Morrow (Cambridge: Cambridge University Press, 1986).

4 On the difference between their academic careers in classics, compare Thomas, *Moral Philosophy of Green*, p. 9, with *M*, 27–28.

5 This essay is reprinted in his *Lectures on the Philosophy of Kant and Other Philosophical Lectures and Essays (LPK)*.

6 See R. L. Nettleship's biographical essay in *The Works of T. H. Green*, 3 vols. (London: Longmans Green, 1885–8), 3: xxxix: "The preparation for an edition of Aristotle's *Ethics* had no immediate result, though it must have furnished much material for subsequent lectures. He had been occupying himself with Aristotle for some time and had formed a project for editing the treatise *De Anima*. But the great expectations which he had formed of its value and usefulness seem to have been disappointed on a closer acquaintance, and a translation of portions, amounting to somewhat more than half the work, was all that he accomplished. The edition of the *Ethics* was undertaken in conjunction with Edward Caird; it was originally intended to be one of a series of books published by the University Press for use in the university examinations, but this arrangement fell through, and ultimately the work was abandoned. . . .

"It is probable that, if he had been free to choose, he would not have spent on Aristotle so much of his force as a teacher. . . . though for all practical purposes he was a good scholar, he did not move freely in the language, and was constantly haunted by a fear that he was not giving sufficient attention to the detailed interpretation of the text" (p. lxxi).

7 J. B. Schneewind, *Sidgwick's Ethics and Victorian Moral Philosophy* (Oxford: Oxford University Press [Clarendon Press], 1977), p. 411.

8 Interest in the virtues has been partly stimulated by P. Foot, "Virtues and Vices," in *Virtues and Vices* (Oxford: Blackwell, 1978), chap. 1; by J. Wallace, *Virtues and Vices* (Ithaca: Cornell University Press, 1978); and by A. MacIntyre, *After Virtue* (Notre Dame: Notre Dame University Press, 1981).

9 This note is attached to the passage from *ME*, 375–6, quoted later in this section.

10 See *OHE*, 56, n. 2; *ME*, 92.

11 See Dugald Stewart, *The Philosophy of the Active and Moral Powers*, vol. 6 of the *Works*, ed. W. Hamilton (Edinburgh: Constable, 1855), chap. 2, essay 2, p. 219: "As some authors have supposed that vice consists in an excessive regard for our own happiness, so others have gone to the opposite extreme, by representing virtue as merely a *matter of prudence*, and a sense of duty but another name for a *rational self-love*. This view of the subject

was far from being unnatural; for we find that these two principles lead in
general to the same course of action; and we have every reason to believe,
that if our knowledge of the universe was more extensive, they would be
found to do so in all instances whatever. Accordingly, by many of the best
of the ancient moralists, our *sense of duty* was considered as resolvable into
self-love, and the whole of *ethics* was reduced to the question, *what is the
supreme good*? or, in other words, What is most conducive, on the whole
to our happiness?"

12 See Thomas Reid, *Essays on the Active Powers of the Human Mind*, ed. B.
    Brody (Cambridge, MA: MIT Press, 1969), chap. 3, essay 3, p. 211: "the
    best moralists among the ancients derived all the virtues from this principle
    [of a regard to our good upon the whole]. For, among them, the whole of
    morals was reduced to this question, What is the greatest good? Or, what
    course of conduct is best for us upon the whole?"

13 See *ME*, x–xi.

14 Sidgwick's remarks on Butler's alleged failure to ask what precepts we see
    to be ultimately reasonable (*ME*, xi) indicate the same attitude; for Sidgwick
    thinks he has found the intuitive basis that Butler should have been looking
    for.

15 The quotation is continued in Section 5.

16 This is the tendency of the rather complicated and diffuse discussion in book
    4 of *Prol.* on "the application of moral philosophy to the guidance of con-
    duct." Though I cannot find any place where Green states clearly what he
    thinks a first principle can or cannot be expected to do for a theory, it seems
    safe to say that he means to reject Sidgwick's demands.

17 I set aside some further points on which Green is open to justified criticism:
    (1) He thinks he is describing the "Greek" idea of virtue, found not only
    among philosophers, but also among ordinary "Athenians in the period of
    the bloom of Hellas" (*Prol.*, 248). This claim raises many historical questions
    that I will not pursue further. (2) Green thinks his claims hold for the Greek
    moralists in general. Sidgwick rightly criticizes him for ignoring the peculiar
    features of Socrates' moral outlook, to say nothing of the Hellenistic moralists
    (*GSM*, 83). I will consider Green's account with reference primarily to Ar-
    istotle's *Nicomachean Ethics* (*EN*).

18 On Socrates, see Plato, *Laches* 191c–e. Sidgwick might well seem justified
    in remarking that Socrates' approach to the virtues is apparently more con-
    genial to Green's account (*GSM*, 60 n.).

19 Hence, Aristotle has a good reason for refusing to follow Socrates' view that
    bravery is present in every sort of situation where people face danger for
    some worthwhile end.

20 After introducing the conception of a moral motive of "purity of heart" that
    chooses the virtuous action for its own sake (*Prol.*, 251), Green claims that
    Aristotle is describing this motive when he says that acting for the sake of
    the *kalon* is the characteristic motive of the virtuous person. (He quotes *EN*
    1122b6–7 in Greek; his editor translates the passage rather inexactly.) The

connection between the *kalon* and the common good is defended in *Prol.* 256 fin., 263 (partly quoted above).

21 It is not correct to regard Green's remarks about the common good as evidence of utilitarianism; but for the moment I am overlooking the difference (as Sidgwick appears to do).

22 "[E]ven an ordinary Greek would not have denied that a mercenary of the Persian king might be as valiant as possible" (*GSM*, 92).

23 "The idea that *sôphrosunê* would not be laudable except in a republic – which is really what Green's phrase comes to – would have appeared to Aristotle absurd" (*GSM*, 94).

24 On temperance, see *GSM*, 93.

25 This is the continuation of the quotation in Section 3.

26 In the rest of this section I summarize some claims that I have stated and defended at greater length in "Aristotle's Concept of Morality," *Proceedings Boston Colloquium in Ancient Philosophy* 1 (1985), chap. 5. See also Irwin, *Aristotle's First Principles* (Oxford: Oxford University Press [Clarendon Press], 1988), secs. 237–9.

27 Green calls attention to this passage, at *Prol.*, 248.

28 On concern for the good of the community, see *Prol.*, 206 f., 229 f., 240–5.

29 Aristotle is not out of step with Greek common sense and tradition. See Herodotus 7.103.4, 104.4, 210.2.

30 My defense of Green against Sidgwick on these points is derived largely from a note in one of his copies of the *Ethics*: "Liberality really a particular form of the virtue which manifests itself in these general ways. If transformation of false egotism into true is taken as a basis of virtue, then the several virtues can all be developed from a single root. Aristotle fails to develop them because he does not clearly recognize this basis. No unity of principle either in relation of virtues to the person or to the *pathê*. . . . The true view of virtue in relation to egotism most nearly approached by Aristotle in account of *philia* in 8th and 9th books" (*EN*, Copy A, facing p. 61). Green's copies contain very little further comment on *EN* 4, and he does not develop the argument he sketches here. Indeed, he seems less confident here than in *Prol.* that Aristotle grasps the basis of his own account.

31 Sidgwick himself mentions the relevance of friendship in these contexts: "One defect in Aristotle's account of virtue which strikes a modern reader is that benevolence is not recognized, except obscurely in the imperfect form of liberality. The deficiency, however, is to some extent supplied by a separate discussion on the relations of kind affection which bind men together" (*OHE*, 66). The imperfection of liberality is presumably the lack of distinction between types of expenditure that Sidgwick has commented on; and friendship is what supplies the deficiency to some extent.

32 On this sort of ostentation, cf. Demosthenes 3.25–6, 21.158–9, 23.207–8; Isocrates 7.53–4.

33 Green recognizes this point about benevolence: "No doctrine of sympathy

or disinterested benevolence in Aristotle; contrast moralists of last century. This scarcely a drawback. In these moralists taken for granted that man lives either for pleasure or at least for his own good as not consciously identified with that of others. Accordingly they essay [?] to show that there are sympathetic pleasures, in seeking which we please (not = do good to) others; or that self-love may be *balanced* by disinterested benevolence. But Aristotle's fundamental notion is that every [?] one should live for his state. No need then to dwell on benevolence as a balance of selfishness, or on sympathy as a series of pleasures of which pleasure of another is condition" (*EN*, Copy B, on *EN* 8, facing p. 150).

34 "The traits by which Aristotle characterizes in detail this flower of noble life are all the more interesting from their discrepancy with the Christian ideal" (*OHE*, 63). In speaking of the Christian ideal Sidgwick no doubt includes humility, which he describes with something less than enthusiasm (*ME*, 334–6).

35 When Aristotle remarks on the magnanimous person's slow walk and deep voice, he is not necessarily insisting that these are essential to a virtuous person. He wants to show that the content he has ascribed to the virtue makes it intelligible that these features are commonly associated with it; for an appropriately unhurried and unexcitable attitude is suitable for someone who has the right attitude to external goods and does not get flustered about trivialities. In this case the moral content of the virtue explains the apparently aesthetic attitude that people take to some symptoms of it.

36 I have discussed this a bit further in *Aristotle's First Principles*, chap. 18.

11

The attractive and the imperative
Sidgwick's view of Greek ethics

NICHOLAS P. WHITE

1

Sidgwick believed that there are three main differences between Greek ethics and modern ethics. First, he said that in modern ethics the "imperative" or "jural" or "quasi-jural" notions of obligation, duty, and right are central and the focus is on the question, "What is duty and what is its ground?" In ancient ethics, he said, this question is not asked. Instead, it is asked, "Which of the objects that men think good is truly good or the highest good?" And the "attractive" notion of good is central (*ME*, 106).

Sidgwick's second difference is this: "It was assumed on all sides [by Greek writers on ethics] that a rational individual would make the pursuit of his own good his supreme aim" (*ME*, 91–2). The modern view, however, can regard it as rational to take as an ultimate aim something different from and even possibly incompatible with one's own good, namely, right or duty or (in one sense) virtue.

Sidgwick thought that this feature of the ancient view, its acceptance of what I shall call "rational egoism,"[1] is compatible with saying that ancient accounts of conduct are "moralities." On some taxonomies a view does not count as a morality if it either says or is supported by a rationale that says that one's own good is one's ultimate rational end.[2] A taxonomy of this kind holds that such a view is too much like a kind of egoism to be called a morality.[3] Sidgwick, however, identifies the moral with the practically rational and so can count Greek views as moral.

A third difference is closely connected with the second. In taking the

I am indebted to numerous people for helpful comments. Most especially I should thank William Frankena for numerous conversations on these topics, Terence Irwin for his comments at the conference at which this essay was delivered, and also Elizabeth Asmis, David Brink, Stephen Darwall, John Deigh, and Jerome Schneewind. In all cases my responses here have perforce been brief and inadequate, and in some instances the questions raised were so far-reaching that I have had to leave them aside altogether here.

position they did on what a rational individual would regard as his end, according to Sidgwick, the Greeks were maintaining that there is only one "regulative and governing faculty" of reason. But, he said, "in the modern ethical view, when it has worked itself clear, there are found to be two [regulative and governing faculties] – universal reason and egoistic reason, or conscience and self-love (*OHE*, 198). This means that in the modern view a "dualism of practical reason" can arise because the two faculties can conflict, whereas on the ancient view no conflict of this particular sort is possible.

That is not to say that on Sidgwick's account conflict cannot arise within an ancient ethical doctrine. Conflict can indeed arise within the faculty that pursues one's own good, if two things that equally deserve to be called good for oneself are incompatible. Nor have I said that within a modern view conflict *must* arise, since one may believe or hope or postulate that the two faculties do not deliver ultimately incompatible results.[4] Nor would it be right to say that in a modern view all fundamental conflicts must be formulated as conflicts between the imperative and the attractive principles. For conflicting judgments of universal reason and egoistic reason can both be cast as imperatives, or both as attractives, as Sidgwick himself indicates.[5]

These are the three main differences between ancient and modern ethics that Sidgwick claims. There is the one involving imperative and attractive notions, the one involving the claim that ancient ethics takes a person's own good to be the ultimate rational end, and the one concerning the idea that ancient ethics posits one rational principle whereas modern ethics posits two.

In this essay I propose to discuss only the first difference, concerning attractive and imperative notions. Detaching this issue from other aspects of the comparison between ancient and modern ethics is somewhat artificial. Moreover, some may think that only specifically moral imperatives are interesting to discuss and that there is little point in treating imperatives in general. Others, however, join Sidgwick in thinking that the use of specifically imperatival notions is in itself an important feature of modern moral views.[6] I hope that the following discussion shows some reason to take an interest in that idea.

In spite of its initial appeal, the distinction between imperative and attractive notions is extremely puzzling. I intend to raise some problems about it. For one thing, I think that the role of imperative notions in Greek ethics is often underestimated, and I shall point briefly to some places where they figure prominently. For most of the essay, however, I shall press two questions: whether the distinction between imperative and attractive notions is adequate by itself to mark the difference that

Sidgwick had in mind between different types of ethical views, and whether the distinction itself is genuine and important. The adequacy of the distinction is undermined by the existence of another class of notions that Sidgwick ignores (even though they are important in Greek ethics), namely, notions that can be called "repulsive." These are expressed by terms like "ugly," "base," and important uses of "bad." And the genuineness and importance of the distinction are called into question by various considerations that I shall raise, including one advanced against it by Sidgwick himself.

2

Was Sidgwick right that imperative notions are not much attended to in Greek ethics? My answer is, not fully. Here I am not out to show that the Greeks used imperative notions that are *moral*. I believe that indeed they did, but to demonstrate that I would have to discuss the other two differences that Sidgwick claims between ancient and modern ethics. Here I shall try to show only that imperative concepts play significant roles in Greek thinking.

It is easy to cite Stoic ethics against Sidgwick's generalization. But Sidgwick himself recognized this, and because of the Stoics' use of a notion of natural law he regarded them as a "transitional link" between ancient and modern ethics (*ME*, 105; *OHE*, 97). Still, it is worth pointing out that even in the early Stoicism of Chrysippus, and not just in the late Stoicism of the Roman Empire, imperative notions can be very prominent:

> Law is king of everything both divine and human, . . . and must preside over what is honorable (*kalon*) and despicable as ruler and leader. Accordingly it must be the standard of what is just and unjust, and prescribe (*prostaktikon*) what naturally political animals must do (*poieteon*) and prohibit them from what they must not do (*ou poieteon*).[7]

This is about as clear a use of imperative language as one could ask for.

Passages like this do not show, of course, what role the Stoics assigned to imperative language. They do not show, for example, that according to early Stoicism the fundamental reason why one should do a certain thing is that it is prescribed by the law of nature, rather than that conformity to nature is the good or goal for a human being. Sometimes Stoic writings suggest this latter idea instead. So there is room to argue that even the Stoics did not grant imperative notions the same role that they seem to have in some modern doctrines. Still, it would obviously be wrong to say that these notions do not figure importantly in Stoicism, and so if we want to avoid counting it as a flat counterexample to Sidgwick's generalization, we have to call it a transition or anticipation or the like.

At first sight, Aristotle's views would appear to provide a powerful argument that in the classical and clearly nontransitional period of Greek thought imperative notions are not much in play. For one thing, the notion of justice is not given even the kind of prominence that it has in the *Republic* where, as we shall see, it contains imperative elements (Section 3). For another thing, the emphasis right from the first sentence of the *Nicomachean Ethics* is on the notion of the good, and it quickly passes, from *EN* 1.7 onward, to the notion of virtue and the various virtues.

It is wrong, however, to jump to conclusions on this basis. Here I must speak very briefly about a complex issue. In the first place, there is a powerful argument, due to William Frankena, for saying that in Aristotle an imperative notion, the one expressed by the verb *dei*, "ought" or "must," is definitionally basic to his account of moral virtue and hence of happiness, the human good (which is defined in terms of virtue, as activity in accordance with it; *EN* 1098a16–18). Morally virtuous activity is defined in terms of the notion of a mean, which is explained in terms of feeling pleasure and pain "at the times when one ought (*dei*), with reference to objects one ought, toward the people one ought, for the sake of things one ought, and in the way one ought" (1106b21–22). If an ethics of virtue is defined as an ethical doctrine that takes the notion of virtue rather than some imperative notion as definitionally basic, then Aristotle's view does not appear to be an ethics of virtue.[8] Virtues are defined in terms of *dei* or "ought," and not the other way around.

This use of imperative language is no isolated fluke. At the beginning of his discussion of justice (*dikaiosyne*) in *Nicomachean Ethics* 5, Aristotle closely associates general justice, which (unlike special justice) he assimilates to the whole of virtue, with law (*nomos*). Law commands us (*prostattei*), Aristotle says, to do the works of human beings covered by all the special virtues (1029a32–1030a13, esp. 1029b19–27). He says nothing to dissociate the notion of virtue here from the imperative connotations that this discussion introduces.

Undeniable as these facts are, one may wonder what conclusion to draw from them. It still seems true, for what it is worth, that the notions expressed by "ought" or "law" get much less of Aristotle's attention than the attractive notions of good and virtue. Moreover, Aristotle does not investigate the meaning of these terms or the basis of their imperative force. Certainly he does not commit himself to the view that either term here has *moral* force. Still, it is important that he appeals to the imperative notion, *dei*, in a crucial context explaining what virtue is, and does not insist that virtue terms should stand on their own without any imperatival associations.

3

It is interesting to compare Aristotle's view with what Plato says about justice in the *Republic*. Once again I shall have to be very brief.

Unlike Aristotle, Plato does not try to explain notions of virtue in terms of an imperative. On the contrary, the justice of an action – which, as we are about to see, does have an imperative character – is explained in terms of the tendency of an action to promote or preserve a good condition of the soul (*Republic* 443E–444A). By the standard just described, this makes Plato's view in the *Republic* an ethics of virtue.

In addition, Plato gives a preeminence to the notion of good that sometimes seems incompatible with a modern attitude toward the importance of imperative notions. In the *Republic* the good appears to be something like a genus under which justice falls. Justice itself contains a straightforwardly imperative element. It is said to involve a kind of necessity associated with commands, law, and compulsion (519E, 520D–E, 521B, 540B, 540D–E). In particular, the rulers of Plato's ideal city are enjoined to govern the city rather than spending all their time philosophizing. On the other hand, he clearly says that the guide those rulers ultimately use is the good (540A–B; cf. 519C–D), and he does not treat justice as a guide to deliberation independent of the good.

Here we come to an exegetical controversy. Most interpreters, including Sidgwick, understand Plato to be saying that the reason for a person to be just is simply that so being furthers *his own* good. On this interpretation, only what Sidgwick calls egoistic reason is in play. On the other interpretation, which I advocate, Plato believes that the most fundamental reason for a person to be just arises from what Sidgwick calls universal reason, that is, from an understanding of the notion of what is good *simpliciter*, not simply good for oneself, and a realization that justice is a good of that sort.[9] On the egoistic interpretation, the rulers' ground for obeying the injunction to govern the city well, rather than spending their whole lives philosophizing, is that it is just to do so (*Republic* 520A–B, 520E). One's ground for acting justly here is that so doing is conducive to one's own good. On the universalistic interpretation, however, one's ground is that justice is good in a non–self-referential sense.

On the egoistic interpretation the imperative character of justice is entirely superficial. Justice is said to involve injunctions to act in certain ways, but the fundamental ground for obeying them is that doing so is good for oneself – which consideration presumably takes the form, in Sidgwick's terms, of an attractive.

It might seem that on the universalistic interpretation the imperatival character of justice is no less superficial. Here the fundamental reason for obeying dictates of justice is that justice is good and a kind of goodness. That would seem to mean that considerations of justice take on an attractive rather than an imperative cast. But perhaps the shoe is on the other foot. Perhaps we should say that, because the goodness of justice is the reason for following its dictates, that means that goodness is not a purely attractive notion but itself contains an imperatival element. Surprisingly enough, Sidgwick himself sometimes suggests just such a view of goodness, and we shall have occasion to consider it (Section 4).

I shall break off discussion of these historical issues here and turn to examine Sidgwick's distinction itself. I simply reiterate the point that Greek ethics uses imperative notions at some crucial junctures. These junctures need to be examined thoroughly before we conclude finally that the Greeks ignored such notions.

4

Now I turn to the questions that are my main topic. What are the differences between imperative and attractive notions, and between doctrines that stress the one or the other? What did Sidgwick take those differences to be? Are they important?

Sidgwick's own discussions of the matter reveal a curious ambivalence. On the one hand, he presupposes the distinction, especially in contrasting ancient and modern ethics and discussing how the latter arose. On the other hand, as we shall see, he says some things that seem to undermine it.

Some of his explanations of the distinction are problematical and seem strangely off the mark. One is this: In the recognition of an act as "right" there is "an authoritative prescription to do it," but when we judge an act to be "good," "it is not yet clear that we ought to prefer this kind of good to all other good things: some standard for estimating the relative values of different 'goods' still has to be sought" (*ME*, 106). But this does not explain what is distinctive about "right" by contrast to an attractive term. A notion of "best" would do to determine which good is better than all others, but that alone would not make it an imperative notion. Rather, the best thing would simply be rationally the most attractive.

Elsewhere Sidgwick says that the Greeks employed a "generic notion instead of a specific one," so that "virtue or right action is commonly regarded as only a species of the good" (*ME*, 105–6). But although this remark accurately describes much Greek thinking, it clearly cannot explain what is imperative about the one notion and attractive about another. There is nothing inherently imperative about what is specific, or attractive about what is generic.

In addition, I should mention another thing that Sidgwick says about imperative notions, which he rightly does not present as a definition of the class. He proposes that when someone uses the word "ought" he "implies at least the potential presence of motives prompting to wrong conduct; and is therefore not applicable to beings [sc., such as God] to whom no such conflict of motives can be attributed" (*ME*, 217). He also says that a

possible conflict of motives seems to be connoted by the term "dictate" or "imperative," which describe[s] the relation of Reason to mere inclinations or non-rational impulses.... This conflict seems also to be implied in the terms "ought," "duty," "moral obligation," as used in ordinary moral discourse: and hence these terms cannot be applied to the actions of rational beings to whom we cannot attribute impulses conflicting with reason. (*ME*, 34–5)

Sidgwick here claims that the presence of an idea of an actual or potential motive conflicting with the doing of what a term is applied to is a necessary condition of its being an imperative. He does not say, however, that it is a sufficient condition. He thus leaves it open that someone might have a motive conflicting with the indicated action and yet not regard himself as under any obligation. That seems to me like the right result. Certainly we are often subject to conflicting attractions without any sense of obligation, even (I think) when the one is felt as appealing to reason and the other to some nonrational impulse. I shall say a little more about this issue later (Section 9).[10]

Although Sidgwick makes these efforts to explain his distinction, sometimes he says things that tend to cast doubt on it. For one thing, he says that the notion of "that at which it is ultimately reasonable to aim" includes a notion of an obligation or imperative, because "the recognition of an end as ultimately reasonable involves the recognition of an obligation to do such acts as most conduce to the end."[11] Moreover, in his discussion of good he says that, according to common sense, "the calm desire for my good on the whole is *authoritative*; and therefore carries with it implicitly a rational *dictate* to aim at this end, if in any case a conflicting desire urges the will in an opposite direction." And he goes on:

Still we may keep the notion of "*dictate*" or "*imperative*" merely implicit and latent – as it seems to be in ordinary judgments as to "my good" and its opposite – by interpreting "ultimate good on the whole for me" to mean what I should practically desire if my desires were in harmony with reason, assuming my own existence alone to be considered.[12]

It is difficult to be sure what Sidgwick means by saying that we may keep the notion of a dictate "latent." Does its being "latent" mean that it is *present* or not? Each possibility is suggested by some of what Sidgwick says.[13] On balance, though, he seems to me to think that it *is* present.[14] In that case the distinction between attractives and imperatives is blurred, because the attractive notion par excellence, that of good, turns out to contain a latent imperative element.

5

Whatever problems affect Sidgwick's exposition, his distinction has an initial appeal that arises from an idea that his own terminology shows he is aiming at. A rough approximation will have to suffice here, but I think that the following is the fundamental idea. Typical uses of an imperative ethical term are associated with (as I shall loosely put it) a person's regarding himself or someone else as in some way having been *commanded* (usually, but not necessarily, to do some action). By the same token, failure to meet the standard suggested by such a term means being "out of bounds," that is, in a state where one is *forbidden* to be or *commanded not* to be. For brevity I shall sometimes describe this state of affairs very vaguely by saying that the term, or a judgment incorporating it, "conveys" an idea of a person's being or being regarded as having been commanded. By design I am leaving this idea rather unspecific, but I am definitely *not* saying that imperative terms are used only to *issue* commands.[15]

Typical uses of an attractive ethical term – again to oversimplify – are analogously associated with a person's regarding someone, himself or someone else, as *attracted* to something (an object, an action, or a state of affairs). Here a failure to meet the relevant standards means, not being out of bounds, but being in a *less desirable* position than one might be. I shall speak of an attractive term as "conveying" an idea of being attracted. It is important here not to take "being attracted" as equivalent to "desiring." Sidgwick clearly does not intend such an equivalence. I shall not try to explain the difference here except to say that the former is meant to be much broader than the latter.

In saying these things I am not trying to give the entire content of these terms or judgments involving them or to determine whether the relevant judgments report "facts" or, on the other hand, are merely expressive or emotive. Rather, my point merely is that at some level, because of either the content or the way of conveying it, the one sort of term conveys an idea of being commanded and the other conveys an idea of being attracted.[16] In the kinds of uses that Sidgwick had in mind, the ideas will be of rational command and rational attraction, whatever exactly those amount to.

At first sight it certainly does seem that there is some genuine difference between, for example, regarding oneself as having been commanded and regarding oneself as attracted. The sense of that difference must, I think, be the chief cause of the preanalytical thought that imperative notions are different from attractive ones. So far, then, the distinction appears to hold up.[17]

6

Before we examine the distinction further, however, we need to be aware that the distinction we should be drawing is not merely one between imperatives and attractives. To recur briefly to historical matters, we underdescribe Greek ethics if we say that it relies on attractive notions alone. In addition to attractive notions like "good" and "fine," and quite aside from imperative notions like "ought" and "duty," Greek ethics employs notions of another important sort: what I shall call *repulsive* notions like "bad" and "base" and "ugly." Sidgwick forgot about these in this context, and other writers do too. But that is a mistake for both historical and philosophical reasons.[18]

As a philosophical matter it does not appear that the force of repulsive notions is captured by the use of attractive ones alone. In the first place, to say that spitefulness is bad is to say more than that the absence or the contrary of spitefulness is good, because there are things whose absence or contrary is good but which are themselves not bad but only so-so. Nor is the idea caught by saying that the avoidance of spitefuness is good, or even that it is very, very good (which may even be false, even though spitefulness is bad).

In the second place, the force of saying that spitefulness is bad is not captured by saying simply that spitefulness lacks goodness, since that is compatible, once again, with its being simply so-so or neutral. Of course there is a well-known view, which is often attributed to Plato and frequently also to philosophers like Augustine who were influenced directly or indirectly by him, that badness is really the total absence or lack of goodness.[19] Nevertheless, I do not think that this idea touches the point at issue. For all I know, it may be a metaphysical truth that the property of badness (if there is such a thing) is nothing but the property of lacking goodness (if there is such a thing). But in spite of that it seems clearly false to say that the *concept* of badness is just the *concept* of the absence of goodness. In this sense you might say that our concepts of good and bad are Manichaean. Whether by a metaphysical mistake or not, we all use a concept of "affirmative" badness that is not simply the concept of a lack. That the word "evil," with its theological connotations, expresses an affirmative notion in this sense has often been maintained. But the same is just as clearly true of nontheological uses of the word "bad."[20]

The reason for this is easily seen if we accept at face value Sidgwick's description of good as an attractive notion. If an attractive notion can be used, in part, to convey an idea of being rationally attracted to something, then a repulsive notion can be used to convey an idea of being rationally repelled by something. But it seems plain that being repelled by something is not tantamount to any sort of attraction, either to the absence of the thing or to anything else. Being repelled by X is an affirmative reaction to X, not merely a reaction to something else that draws one away from X. This kind of repulsion is what terms like "bad," as well as "ugly," "base," "disgusting," and so forth, often are called on to signal (which is not to say, of course, that repulsion is all that they express).[21]

It is a point of philosophical dispute whether notions of good and bad can be represented, or should be supplanted, by a single notion of preference. Instead of saying that a is good and b is bad, or that a is good compared to b and b is bad compared to a, perhaps we should simply say that a is preferable to b (or, for different purposes, is preferred to b). I propose to ignore this issue here. It seems clear that being attracted to a and repelled by b is different from preferring a to b (which one might do while being attracted by both or being repelled by both). I think that this psychological fact is reflected in a difference between what we can call the notions of goodness and badness on the one hand and the notion of preference on the other. I shall proceed on that assumption.

7

Let me expatiate a little on the historical point, without claiming to give a full account of it. Someone who neglects repulsive notions is omitting something important that is expressed by Greek ethical judgments but not by attractive terms.

As a straightforwardly descriptive matter no one would say that the Greeks restricted themselves to attractive terms alone. Plato and Aristotle used "bad" (*kakon*) as well as "ugly" (*aischron*) to express the opposites of "good" (*agathon*) and "fine," "beautiful" (or however *kalon* should be translated). And both of them also used "badness" or "bad characteristic" (*kakia*, sometimes misleadingly translated "vice") as the opposite of "excellence" (*arete*), and in a way that clearly conveys an affirmatively unfavorable reaction rather than simply the absence of a favorable one.

Nor are the repulsive notions used by the Greeks in a merely tangential way. Aristotle's "Doctrine of the Mean," for example, describes badness of character in patently affirmative terms, as the possession of certain traits in *either* deficiency *or* excess. And Plato's ethics can hardly be said to dispense with the concept of affirmative badness, especially, for example, in his descriptions of various sorts of injustice of the soul in *Republic* 8–9. Indeed, this point seems too obvious to need special defense.

Nevertheless, it is true and extremely important that Greek philosophy tends to treat repulsive notions as though they were *metaphysically* derivative, and attractive notions as though they were metaphysically fundamental. One only has to think here of the role that the Form of the Good plays in Plato's doctrine, a role not balanced by any role given to the Form of the Bad (if he believed in such a thing), or of the way in which the Prime Mover functions in Aristotle's metaphysics, unopposed by any Prime Stopper.[22] One also finds the thought in the Stoics that all badness is purely local and that the universe as a whole is perfectly good, not the other way around.[23]

These facts enable us to understand why historical accounts by Sidgwick and others should have neglected repulsive notions, but they do not show that the Greeks did without those notions. They only show that, even though repulsive notions figure importantly in Greek ethics, their ethical role is not accurately reflected in Greek metaphysics. If you like, the ethical view is sometimes Manichaean in a way in which the metaphysical view is not. In that sense the metaphysical theories of the Greeks are therefore in a certain way not adequate to represent all of the notions employed in their ethics.

8

We can now return to consider the basis of Sidgwick's distinction between imperative and attractive notions, enriched now with repulsive notions, and to the difference between the ideas, conveyed by these terms, of being commanded, attracted, and repelled.

To discuss this difference fully would take us well outside ethics into the philosophy of language and beyond. Sidgwick avoided such excursions into other parts of philosophy, and for the most part I shall imitate him here. Otherwise, we would have to begin a thorough investigation of such questions as how the speech act of saying "Close the door" differs from that of saying "It would be good to close the door" or "Closing the door – *there's* a good thing to do" or the like.

Investigations that have been made into these matters do not say much about such differences. R. M. Hare, for example, treats all evaluative language as involving an imperatival force. He speaks of words like "good" and "ought" as functioning "to commend or in some other way to guide choices or actions" and says that if they are to have this effect then judgments involving them must call forth "assent to some imperative sentence."[24]

J. L. Austin's discussion of speech acts is focused on issues different from the contrast in question. Some of Austin's distinctions, like those between exercitives, commissives, and behabitives, might conceivably be applied to treating the difference between attractives and imperatives, but the application would be extremely indirect and seems to me to offer little prospect of illuminating what concerns us here.[25] Similarly, John Searle's classification of illocutionary acts makes no provision that I can see for the distinction between attractive and imperative notions. Searle's category of "directives" is meant to contain acts whose "illocutionary point" is that they are attempts "by the speaker to get the hearer to do something," but he marks no difference between making the action seem attractive to someone and commanding him to do it. Searle's category of "expressives" contains speech acts, like deploring and welcoming, that might be compared to what is involved in attractive notions, but it also contains many other quite different ones too, like apologizing and condoling.[26]

Something more can be gained from the philosophers of law. One notion of a command, whose principal modern advocate is John Austin,[27] is that of the expression of a desire that someone do something, combined with an indication that the person commanded is "liable to evil . . . in case he comply not with the desire."[28]

Not everyone agrees, however, that a command incorporates such a threat of a "sanction." Thus, H. L. A. Hart says, "To command is characteristically to exercise authority over men, not power to inflict harm, and though it may be combined with threats of harm a command is primarily an appeal not to fear but to respect for authority."[29] In a similar vein, think of Adam Smith, who holds that what motivates us to abide by rules of duty is not the threat of a sanction, even a divine one, but rather a "natural sense of duty" consisting in a "regard" or "reverence" toward general rules of a certain sort.[30] And of course Kant's notion of "respect for the moral law" is similar to this and presumably owes something to it.[31]

It is worth noting, too, that Sidgwick denies that terms like "ought" connote a sanction: "the ideal distinction taken in common thought between legal and merely moral rules seems to lie in just this connection of the former but not the latter with punishment."[32] Whatever imperativeness "ought" contains, therefore, does not, Sidgwick thinks, amount to an Austinian command backed by a threat of a sanction.

9

The foregoing observations offer a way in which someone might argue that the distinction between imperative notions, on the one hand, and attractive and repulsive notions, on the other, must break down. Suppose that an imperative notion carries the idea of a command and that John Austin is right that commands are expressions of a desire that the recipient do something coupled with a threat of some bad consequence if he doesn't. Then it might be proposed that an imperative just amounts to the presentation of a choice: Either you do this or you will suffer (what you will suffer need not be clear). The choice will be so designed as to make the punishment more repulsive than the desiderated action. (As a by-product, this suggestion might do something to explain Sidgwick's suggestion that an imperative thought is always accompanied by the presence of an opposed motivation. The cases where it makes sense for you to want me to regard myself as commanded to do something are the cases where I have some aversion to doing it.)

This idea would yield a rough explanation of imperatives in terms of repulsives, along with the idea of a choice. This does not undermine the distinction between imperatives and attractives, but it attempts to reduce imperatives to the companions of the attractives, namely, the repulsives. And so it might seem to eliminate any important difference between ethical views that focus on imperatives and those that focus on a combination of attractives and repulsives. Thus, it would vitiate Sidgwick's contrast between ancient and modern ethics.

One might combine this idea with a second idea, namely, Sidgwick's suggestion that attractive notions incorporate the idea of a dictate and so are themselves partly imperative (see Section 4). It would then turn out that the respective forces of imperatives and attractives-cum-repulsives could be thought of as mutually explainable in a certain loose sense. For example, to say that a term was rationally attractive would involve saying that it conveyed a notion of a rational imperative to choose it; to say that a term incorporated the notion of a rational imperative would involve saying that it conveyed a sense of being offered a choice between a certain thing and a repulsive alternative; and to say that a term was repulsive would involve saying that it conveyed a notion of a rational dictate to avoid or be repelled by it.

On the other side, however, there are arguments by which one may try to defend Sidgwick's distinction against both of these threats of interexplicability. First, as we have just seen, Sidgwick explicitly rejects the idea that a moral "ought" involves any threat of a sanction (Section 8). As long as he holds that a moral "ought" is like other "oughts" in conveying the notion of a command, therefore, he must reject Austin's view that an idea of being commanded always includes the notion of a sanction. It is not hard to defend that rejection. There is indeed a connection between commands and sanctions, I think, but it is not as simple as Austin held. Sometimes when someone regards himself as commanded his thought is not that punishment will result from disobedience, or even that it could or might, but rather that it *should* result.[33] (I take it that guilt, whatever else it involves, includes this thought.) This seems to me to be true of the kind of command associated with morality and with other kinds as well. But in that case there is no way here to argue that imperative force can be reduced to the force of a choice between an action and a repulsive alternative, since the notion of the sanction is presented as not merely repulsive but also as in some way dictated, so that an imperative notion remains.

Second, one could reject Sidgwick's contention, which I mentioned earlier (Section 4), that the idea of good involves a, perhaps "latent," imperative of reason. He gives no argument for this claim, and I find it implausible. It is not at all obvious why the term "good" should not be said to convey merely the idea of a thing's being attractive to reason rather than that of reason's issuing a command concerning it. Sidgwick says that "the calm desire for my good" is "authoritative" and carries a "rational dictate" to aim at it if a conflicting desire "urges the will in an opposite direction." But it is unclear why he insists on this picture of the situation. Reason could equally well be thought of as acting on the will by attracting it rather than commanding it to move away from the direction in which a conflicting desire tries to get it to go.[34] These are metaphors, I assume, but their force is to tell us what idea is conveyed by various evaluations. And the argument against Sidgwick is that he does not give clear grounds for thinking that the notion of rational good must incorporate or convey a command.

It seems to me that Sidgwick's distinction thus withstands these attempts, including his own, to undermine it. Perhaps it would withstand other attempts too. Everything depends ultimately on, first, how one should say imperatives "convey" the idea of having been commanded and, second, what the nature of a command is. I have indicated that I cannot think of any good way in which these things might be explained, and that fact makes me uneasy. Still, I doubt that anyone who has a sense of the distinction will be moved to reject it simply because it has not been explained, and such a person may think it is simply a brute fact. The next question would be what kind of fact it is, but I cannot answer that question here.[35]

10

The philosophical interest of the historical description of Greek ethics lies primarily in what it shows about possible ways in which our own ethical thinking might be improved by resources drawn from it. Sidgwick was satisfied with most of the overall structure of modern ethical thought as he found it, so he did not think of Greek ethics as a source of suggestions for reforming it. In fact, he probably thought that imperative notions are unavoidable in any adequate ethical view. That may be why he believed that even the notion of good incorporates the idea of a dictate (Sections 4 and 9).

Still, this essay would be incomplete if I did not say something about the reasons, insofar as they are connected with Sidgwick's distinction, for the preference felt by some philosophers, including Victor Brochard, G. E. M. Anscombe, Alasdair MacIntyre, and Bernard Williams, for certain features of Greek ethics over features of modern ethics.[36] There are other reasons for their preference too, particularly objections to characteristics of *morality* as it is now often conceived – and which some or all Greek views are sometimes claimed to lack. These include such features as the idea of impartiality that morality involves, its supposed overridingness or supremacy, and the generality or universality that its deliverances are usually supposed to have. I shall not talk about these matters here and shall continue to confine myself as much as I can merely to issues about imperatives and attractives.

Some of Brochard's and Anscombe's objections are explicitly aimed at the imperative character of notions like obligation and duty. Both think imperativeness is a holdover from the idea of a divine command. One of their main objections focuses on the notion of a command without a commander. They think that modern morality is committed to this notion, and they claim that it is absurd. I am not sure that it is absurd, but I shall leave the matter aside here.

Another objection is that there is something unsatisfactory about an ethical view that relies on the sort of badgering that is often associated with commands and lists of "dos" and "don'ts". And Williams, for example, believes that there is something objectionable both about the kinds of motivations that are required by imperative notions such as respect for law, obedience, and guilt and about the kinds of people who are strongly susceptible to them – a theme that is of course to some degree related to Nietzsche's well-known talk of "slave morality." It is possible to feel that an ethics relying less on imperatives would be more consistent with motivations that would not seem objectionable in this way.

To see whether such an ethics would be feasible as both a theory and an action guide for human beings, one would have to consider several questions. One is whether an ethics that relies on repulsives could seem, to someone who is moved by the considerations just described, more acceptable than one relying on attractives. If I am right, the Greeks do not give us an example of an ethics that relies on attractives alone, even though their metaphysical doctrines make it seem as though they do, and so whatever seems good about Greek ethics cannot be due to its use of attractives alone. In addition, I think one can wonder whether such an ethics is possible for human beings, that is, whether human beings can really be motivated to do very much merely by thinking that certain states of affairs are attractive, and without some notion of what is affirmatively repulsive. Another question is whether the force of imperatives really goes beyond that of repulsives as they figure as "sanctions" in certain choices. There are objections to that claim, as I pointed out (Section 9), but I do not think we can rule it out before we gain more understanding of imperatives and commands than we now have, and particularly of the motivations that support compliance with them.[37] A third question is whether, as Sidgwick sometimes maintained, an attractive notion like good really amounts to a kind of imperative notion. I tentatively rejected that idea earlier (Section 9), but if it is right after all then the differences between the kinds of ethics we are considering come to much less than might at first appear.

Notes

1 I use this phrase to distinguish it from "psychological egoism," which is a psychological theory that many ancients probably accepted, and also – more

importantly in the present connection – from "ethical egoism," which is a view about what makes things ethically right and/or good. Sidgwick did not distinguish these two views.

2 See William Frankena, "Sidgwick and the Dualism of Practical Reason," *Monist* 58 (1974): 449–67, esp. 449–52; and J. B. Schneewind, *Sidgwick's Ethics and Victorian Moral Philosophy* (Oxford: Oxford University Press [Clarendon Press], 1977), p. 228.

3 Frankena himself denies that a morality itself can take one's own good to be the ultimate criterion of what is ethically right, but he allows that a morality could in principle be justified by "rational egoism," i.e., from a rational point of view that takes one's own good as the ultimate rational end. See Frankena, "Is Morality a System of Ordinary Oughts?" *Monist* 63 (1980): 27–47, esp. 44–6.

4 See of course *ME*, concluding chapter.

5 E.g., *ME*, 36.

6 An example is G. E. M. Anscombe, "Modern Moral Philosophy," *Philosophy* 33 (1958): 1–19.

7 *Stoicorum veterum fragmenta* (ed. J. von Arnim) 3.314.

8 I owe this observation to Frankena, in conversation. On the notion of an ethics of virtue, see his "Prichard and the Ethics of Virtue," *Monist* 54 (1970): 1–17, reprinted in *Perspectives on Morality*, ed. Kenneth E. Goodpaster (Notre Dame: University of Notre Dame Press, 1976), pp. 148–60.

9 See my article, "The Rulers' Choice," *Archiv fuer Geschichte der Philosophie* 68 (1986): 22–46.

10 I also would question Sidgwick's claim that the presence of a conflicting motive is even a necessary condition of the use of an imperative notion. It is true that there usually seems to be no reason for someone to issue an imperative unless he thinks that the person to whom it is issued has some motive to act otherwise than as it commands. But an imperative *can* be issued when this condition is not satisfied. And I do not see why a person should not take himself to be commanded to do something even when he has, and knows that he has, no motivation not to do it. Obviously, this point needs further discussion.

11 *ME*, 35; cf. in general *ME*, 34–8.

12 *ME*, 112; emphasis added (except that Sidgwick italicizes "authoritative"). See also *ME*, book 1, chap. 3, esp. pp. 26–8 with 35–6, where he focuses on judgments involving "ought" but seems to be ascribing an imperative character to all moral judgments.

13 That the "latent" notion is not present at all is suggested by Sidgwick's claim, just before these words, that the ideal element involved in the notion of good "does not introduce any judgment of value" but is "entirely interpretable in terms of *fact*, actual or hypothetical" (*ME*, 112; Sidgwick's emphasis). That the "latent" notion *is* present, on the other hand, is suggested by the words that I have quoted, which begin the next paragraph: "It seems to me, however, more in accordance with common sense to recognize – as

Butler does – that the calm desire for my 'good on the whole' is *authoritative*."
Much depends, too, on whether the word "should" in the antepenultimate
line of the page means "would," as Frankena tells me he takes it, or "should"
in a normative sense, as C. D. Broad supposed (see *Five Types of Ethical
Theory* [London: Routledge and Kegan Paul, 1930], pp. 174–7).

14 And certainly that seems to be the clear message of *ME*, book 1, chap. 3,
pp. 34–6.

15 Complications arise here because of the differences between first-person,
second-person, and third-person judgments using "ought" and other imperative terms. Notorious difficulties also arise because of the occurrence of
these terms in clauses embedded within larger contexts. I do not claim that
my present way of talking, even if further developed, would solve these
problems (though it might); I only say that as it is it will allow us to ignore
them for present purposes.

16 This idea will help explain a number of things about the contrast that Sidgwick
draws. (1) It makes clear why obligation terms might seem to presuppose a
contrary motivation, even though virtue terms often do too. The fact that
someone feels a contrary motivation will be an urgent reason for wanting
him to feel commanded. But it can also often be a reason for eliciting his
cooperation by offering to apply a virtue term. (2) Sidgwick also holds that,
whereas to say something is someone's duty is to say that it is "in his power,"
voluntariness attaches "only in a certain degree" to action called virtuous
(*ME*, 219, 224–8). Ordering someone to do something is worth the trouble
only if he can comply reasonably promptly. But doing a virtuous act is
possible only if the requisite trait of character is present, and that trait cannot
be developed on the spot and the act is more likely to be done if it is made
to seem attractive than if it is commanded. One can order someone to
proceed to develop punctuality, say, but issuing a standing order to do so
seems usually less effective than implanting a sense of the attractiveness of
the goal.

17 Even if it holds up it may well not be exhaustive. Elizabeth Asmis urges in
conversation that the psychological condition associated with some Greek
uses of terms like "good" is a sense of being driven rather than a sense of
being attracted. The point is importantly correct. I tend to think, however,
that it can be accommodated by distinguishing different ways of being "attracted" (one of them, for example, being rather like being *dragged*).

18 It might be argued that in addition to imperative notions we also need
permissive ones. Though there are complications that I cannot enter into
here, I take it that being permitted to X is for relevant purposes equivalent
to not being commanded not to X (and being commanded to X is equivalent
to not being permitted not to X), and that for this reason permissive force
can be explained in terms of imperative force.

19 See, e.g., Augustine *De libero arbitrio*.

20 David Brink suggests to me in conversation that "X is bad" might be taken
to be equivalent to "If X obtained, not-X would be good." That would point

to a general way of reducing repulsive to attractive notions (and, presumably, vice versa). But I do not think that the idea will work. It is perfectly possible to think of X as bad while thinking that, if X obtained, nevertheless the obtaining of not-X in and of itself would be not good but merely indifferent. This is because we can readily conceive, in many cases, of a state of affairs that is neither good nor bad but in-between. (A more technical difficulty with the suggestion is that the counterfactual conditional, "If X obtained, . . . ," entails that X does not obtain, whereas "X is bad" does not – alas – entail that.)

21 Here one sees an explanation of the fact, remarked on in the previous note, that a thing can be regarded as neither good nor bad but indifferent. For it is possible to be neither attracted to a thing nor repelled by it.

22 See *Republic* 6–7 and *Metaphysics* 12.7, 9–10, as well as the treatment of the good in *EN* 1. The point about Plato holds whether or not he believed in a Form of Bad, or held that there is no such Form, or held that there is such a Form but it is constructed out of the Good and Difference (all of these are candidate interpretations). The point about Aristotle is not touched by what Aristotle says about matter, which he does not generally think of as resisting the forces that form, moving cause, and purpose bring to bear on it, and certainly does not resist it in the way in which an opposing force would.

23 See, e.g., my paper, "The Role of Physics in Stoic Ethics," *Southern Journal of Philosophy* 23 (1985), supp., 57–74.

24 R. M. Hare, *The Language of Morals* (Oxford: Oxford University Press, 1964), p. 171; cf. p. 30 ("for sentences containing the word as so understood will not be genuine evaluative judgments, because no imperative can be derived from them").

25 J. L. Austin, *How to Do Things with Words* (Cambridge, MA: Harvard University Press, 1962), esp. pp. 150–63.

26 John R. Searle, *Expression and Meaning* (Cambridge: Cambridge University Press, 1979), pp. 12–16; cf. pp. 173–6.

27 It also can be found in Locke and before him, as J. B. Schneewind points out to me, in Suarez.

28 John Austin, *The Province of Jurisprudence Determined*, p. 14. See also Locke, *An Essay concerning Human Understanding*, book 2, chap. 28 – where, however, Locke is talking about "moral good and evil" and not about commands per se, and is certainly not adhering to Sidgwick's distinction.

29 H. L. A. Hart, *The Concept of Law* (Oxford: Oxford University Press, 1961), p. 20.

30 Adam Smith, *The Theory of the Moral Sentiments*, ed. D. D. Raphael and A. L. Macfie (Oxford: Oxford University Press, 1976), pp. 163–4.

31 See the introduction to ibid., p. 31.

32 *ME*, 29. For a criticism of the view of legal rules that Sidgwick here endorses, see Hart, *Concept of Law*, esp. pp. 15–18, 70–6, and passim.

33 Or at least would be *permissible*.

34 As is well known, this is more like the picture that Plato presents us with, except that no "will" seems to enter the picture. Stephen Darwall points out to me that the connection between imperative notions and the concept of the will may well be closer, and more complicated, than I have here suggested that it is.

35 Terence Irwin correctly says that the sense of being attracted and the sense of being commanded can be combined in various ways, and he tends to think that they may really not be ultimately distinguishable. I am inclined to think that they are distinguishable, even though in consciousness they may often be associated almost inextricably. He also suggests that the notion of self-realization might be something that always involves an attractive idea. Conceivably that is correct, but I tend to think that one can have a sense of being commanded to realize oneself (whatever realizing oneself might amount to) just as much as one can have a sense of being attracted to it.

36 Victor Brochard, "La Morale ancienne et la morale moderne," *Revue philosophique* 51 (1901): 1–12; Anscombe, "Modern Moral Philosophy"; Alasdair MacIntyre, *After Virtue* (Notre Dame: University of Notre Dame Press, 1981); Bernard Williams, *Ethics and the Limits of Philosophy* (Cambridge, MA: Harvard University Press, 1985).

37 In fact, there is much more to say than I have space for here about the differences between the various motivations involved in responding to the three kinds of notions that I have discussed. There is room for someone to think that ultimately the differences and relations among them can be explained in terms of those motivations, e.g., the difference between shame and guilt. The reason why I have not pursued that avenue here is that that difference seems to me even more problematical than the ones I have been discussing.

Part IV

History, politics, pragmatism

12

The ordinary experience of civilized life
Sidgwick's politics and the method of reflective analysis

STEFAN COLLINI

Politics is not based primarily upon History but on Psychology: the fundamental assumptions in our political reasonings consist of certain propositions
as to human motives and tendencies, which are derived primarily from the
ordinary experience of civilized life, though they find adequate confirmation
in the facts of the current and recent history of our own and other civilized
countries.

Henry Sidgwick, *The Elements of Politics* (1891)

The only general criticism that occurs to me is that the discussion in these
chapters tends to be rather a discussion of English methods of government,
with occasional references to American methods. If it be possible to generalize the treatment rather more, not making it seem to flow from or follow
the arrangements of England, this would better accord with the scientific
character of the book as a general treatise on politics. But perhaps it is
impossible . . . perhaps there is no writing profitably on ταπολιτικα except
on the basis of experiments of concrete πολιτεια.

James Bryce (1889)[1]

1

From his arrival as an undergraduate in October 1855 until his death in
August 1900, Henry Sidgwick spent only one term away from Cambridge.[2] For the greater part of this period, there were very few other
universities in Britain to which he could have moved, even had he wished
to do so, and in the days before regular sabbatical arrangements, the
varied experience of working at other institutions or even in other countries, which is familiar to the late twentieth-century academic, was no
doubt a rarity. Nonetheless, the sheer geographical and institutional
continuity of Sidgwick's life is not only notable in itself but also calls
our attention to deeper continuities of activity and identity. Beginning

This is a slightly revised version of an essay first published in Stefan Collini, Donald
Winch, and John Burrow, *That Noble Science of Politics: A Study in Nineteenth-Century
Intellectual History* (Cambridge: Cambridge University Press, 1983); I have also drawn
upon some sentences from my *Public Moralists: Political Thought and Intellectual Life in
Britain, 1850–1930* (Oxford: Oxford University Press, 1991).

in this way encourages us to focus on the fact that Sidgwick wrote, thought of himself, and was thought of by others as a don (the more general notion of the career academic only begins to develop in Britain during his lifetime). This identity colored his writing in all his major treatises, but it has, I want to suggest, a special relevance to his work on politics, that least "academic" of subjects in either sense of that now rather bruised word.

It was not, of course, a simple or unchanging identity, and in the historical setting of mid and late Victorian English culture it imposed complex and not always coherent demands. We may catch Sidgwick at a particularly delicate moment in its formation by eavesdropping on the proceedings of a meeting held on November 16, 1872, at the Freemason's Tavern in London to discuss the question of "University Reform." In choosing that venue, the organizers deliberately recalled the historic meeting on June 10, 1864, of university reformers and leaders of Non-conformity to press for the repeal of the Test Acts, thereby opening the ancient universities to those who were not members of the Church of England.[3] By 1872 the focus of attention had shifted rather to the internal organization of the universities and its bearing on what were increasingly recognized as their national functions: Particularly at issue was the conflict between the traditional collegiate tutorial ideal and the newer schemes to promote "research." The publication in 1867 of Mark Pattison's book, *Suggestions on Academical Organization*, and an orchestrated campaign in the *Academy*, a journal founded in 1869 to help promote the cause of "the endowment of research," had insured that the question did not lack for public attention.

Sidgwick, then aged thirty-four and occupying the special post of praelector in moral philosophy at Trinity College, Cambridge, took an active part in this campaign, and it was he who made the opening speech, proposing Pattison as chairman of the meeting. It is, however, to some remarks he made later in the meeting that we must look for a revealing expression of the complexities of the sense of identity, both individual and collective, involved in this newer ideal of academic life. Considerable enthusiasm had been voiced for encouraging research as well as teaching in the natural sciences. Sidgwick could genuinely support this, but went on: "I think it is also important to point out the extreme need of having a body of mature students who can form a body of experts in other studies and departments of thought, those which more immediately relate to practice." These, he argued, were inquiries

which everyone thinks he understands if he has read a handbook upon the subject; I think that these studies deal with subjects upon which confident opinions are expressed every day by half-instructed persons; and opinions, too, which have often had an important effect on practice. Therefore it is of extreme importance that there should always be a body of persons who are able, to a certain extent, to pour the stream of pure science into the somewhat muddy channel of current opinion.[4]

Sidgwick, it is hardly necessary to add, was not a thrilling speaker; it seems unlikely that the gentlemen gathered in the private room of the Freemason's Tavern were brought to their feet by the contagion of his oratory. Even his introduction of an abstraction-leavening metaphor in the last sentence was policed by his usual contingent of "to a certain extent"'s and "somewhat"'s, seemingly fearful lest the metaphor get out of hand and provoke some riotous and disorderly thinking. Even so, the visual image conjured up by those last phrases can hardly have been quite the thought Sidgwick intended to implant in his hearers' minds, since it suggests a rather discouraging picture; clean water added to dirty invariably produces a complete victory for the latter. But perhaps this infelicity was a symptom of a deeper difficulty in the substance of Sidgwick's plea: He evidently envisaged a "body of experts" in various "departments of thought" whose authority "half-instructed persons" would recognize in matters that "immediately relate to practice." Optimism about the growth of the necessary kind of cultural deference seems to be one unmentioned ingredient in this recipe, and confidence about the intimacy of the connection between study and practice might be considered another.

In his own career, Sidgwick increasingly embodied many of the tensions that this new ideal introduced into the lives of late Victorian intellectuals. As a young don in the 1860s, he had been driven to pursue a variety of philosophical and historical studies largely by an always frustrated urge to allay his inhibiting skepticism in matters of religious belief. During this period he participated actively in that flowering of periodical writing that marked the mid-Victorian period, writing on a whole range of topics of general cultural interest. But as he moved into middle age, he tended to concentrate his energies (or, as is so commonly the case, discovered retrospectively that he had already been doing so for some time) in two chief activities: pursuing systematic and technical inquiries in moral philosophy, and contributing to the reform and better administration of Cambridge University.[5] On the publication in 1874 of his first major work, *The Methods of Ethics*, he explained to his mother, as authors are defensively prone to do, why his book would of course be neglected: "I don't expect the 'general public' to read much of my book. In fact the point of it rather is that it treats in a technical and precise manner questions which are ordinarily discussed loosely and popularly." "Indeed," he warned her, "it can scarcely be said to belong to *literature*."[6] His sense that his academic position set him a little apart from the common run of authors was displayed in another way when he wrote to his publisher, Macmillan, objecting to the customary distribution of free copies to distinguished individuals: "Really I believe that sending to distinguished strangers is, for a man in the position of a university teacher, a needless cheapening of oneself."[7] Even when he turned to more obviously "practical" subjects like politics and political economy, he continued, as we shall see, to write in the same "technical and precise manner." As a consequence of this concentration of his energies, his contributions to the general periodicals fell away sharply after the early 1870s. By 1886 he could report to one correspondent that he was not in a good position to advise about opportunities for making a living by one's pen: "Perhaps I ought to say that I am personally now less in the way of knowing about literary opportunities than I was 10 years ago, having eschewed all writing except on professional subjects in an academic way."[8] The stream of pure science was taking an increasingly roundabout course toward the muddy channel of current opinion.

Yet Sidgwick, as we shall also see, was far from being without connection and influence among the late-Victorian political class. It was a world to which he was intimately related in every sense: A man is hardly to be classed as an outsider when one of his brothers-in-law is archbishop of Canterbury and another well on his way to becoming prime minister.[9] He mixed socially with cabinet ministers from both parties; he helped to devise schemes for the education of future Indian administrators. And he was recognized as having some standing as a political economist, at one moment being asked to write an article on socialism "from the Professor's chair," at another being invited as "one of those who have studied economic questions" to be a member of the Royal Commission on the Financial Relations between Great Britain and Ireland.[10] But in addressing these wider audiences, he was conscious that his academic status was both a source of authority and an announcement of the limits of the contribution he could be expected to make. More is involved in such a situation than simply tailoring one's literary tactics to the needs of particular occasions. John Stuart Mill, for example, was conscious of deliberately shifting between registers and levels of abstraction, now pursuing a systematic argument, now engaging in targeted polemic.[11] But he did not do so as one venturing out from his "proper" sphere, or as one deploying an authority that was accorded to an office or institution rather than to an individual. Sidgwick, on the other hand, constantly referred to the obligations of his position, and the title "Professor" became as constitutive a part of his public identity as the name of his diocese is of a bishop's.

We shall need to keep these general considerations constantly in mind as we begin to look at his work on politics in greater detail. In writing in 1887 to a friend living abroad, Sidgwick followed his characteristic survey of the state of national politics – "the outlook is not promising; the sky full of clouds, though none very black just at present" – with this report on his own activities:

> Personally, I am trying to absorb myself in my Opus Magnum on *Politics*. My position is that I seem to myself now to have grasped and analyzed adequately the only possible method of dealing systematically with political problems; but my deep conviction is that it can yield as yet very little fruit of practical utility – so doubt whether it is worth while to work it out in a book. Still man must work – and a Professor must write books.[12]

There is much quintessential Sidgwick here – the sense of duty, the emphasis on analysis and method, the concern with utility, the inhibiting doubt, the conception of a role, the resolutely cheerful conclusion. Even those who know nothing of Sidgwick other than that he lost his faith, hunted ghosts, and wrote *The Methods of Ethics* may find this revelation of a prospective author's state of mind reassuringly familiar. Yet this comfortable response is, at one level, disturbed when one confronts the work that issued from this absorption almost four years later, the "632 rather closely printed octavo pages" in *The Elements of Politics*, which even its author conceded was a "heavy book."[13]

The chief difficulty, apart from a pardonable sagging of the spirits, lies in deciding what kind of book it is. For although it goes into great detail, with chapters on such subjects as "inheritance," "compensation," "relation of judiciary to other organs," and so on, it is clearly not a work of empirical description: It contains practically no proper names, few references to contemporary political events, and no attempts systematically to identify the political institutions and procedures of different states, let alone to produce a comparative survey of them. Even less is it a work of history: Dates are as conspicuously absent as names, there is no account of the growth and development of institutions, and the whole texture of the work is unyieldingly spare and abstract. Yet, on the other hand, neither is it, in any obvious sense of the word, a work of philosophy: There is practically no argued discussion of conceptions of man, the nature of society, the ideal state, and so on, and one reviewer noted, "the author avoids raising philosophical questions which might seem to lie at the basis of political discussions."[14] Sidgwick himself later explained that he had chosen its methodologically neutral title because the book constituted a contribution neither to "Political Philosophy" nor to "Political Science" in the increasingly strict senses given to those terms by the late nineteenth century (*PSR*, 26). Perhaps baffled by its unclassifiability, historians have largely passed by the formidable monument, though even those contemporaries who were critical held it to be "the most comprehensive book on politics by any English writer since Bentham – we might truthfully say by any English writer whatever."[15] Without falling into this sort of guidebook hyperbole, I would suggest that the work *vaut le détour*, in that it was a distinctive, and in some quarters influential, attempt to arrive at a systematic and practical body of political knowledge.

Sidgwick does, moreover, provide a salutary corrective to any tendency to arrange the intellectual developments of the second half of the nineteenth century into overly neat patterns. In particular, his was the most sustained and penetrating criticism of the pretensions of the fashion for the evolutionary and historical treatment of moral and political questions at a time when that vocabulary was at its most coercive; his engagement with the claims of "sociology" in the 1880s and 1890s was an especially important assertion of the incapacity of any putative science to encompass the territory of politics. At the same time, his *Development of European Polity* was one of the most distinguished examples of the genre of "comparative politics."[16] He also produced a highly traditional treatise on political economy when even the continued existence of that enterprise itself was in doubt, treating it, as the younger Keynes later remarked, as "one of a number of subjects which a Moral Philosopher would take in his stride, one Moral Science out of several."[17] And, finally, he (in alliance with Seeley) played the crucial part in obtaining and preserving such a prominent place in the Cambridge curriculum for courses in political science.[18]

One way of placing him – one might even call it the "orthodox" way, did that not suggest that scholarship on Sidgwick's political thought was sufficiently voluminous to admit of division – is to see him as a late, perhaps the last, representative of Utilitarianism, committed to restating the doctrines of that creed (in the form in which he is presumed to have inherited them from Mill) in an increasingly desperate rearguard action against the various anti-Utilitarian strands of thought that gathered strength in the second half of the century.[19] More recent scholarship has already called into doubt both the identification of a unitary, homogeneous Utilitarianism and any easy assumption of its later disappearance: Apart from the various forms which a roughly Benthamite political theory assumed, Hartleian psychology, Austinian jurisprudence, and Ricardian political economy all followed somewhat different trajectories. Still, it was partly as a result of a series of attacks on what was seen as their common deductive method that these theories came to be treated as sharing a common history and a common fate, and when surveying the terms of criticism from the 1860s onward one can readily see why the verdict on Utilitarianism has generally been "death at the hands of the later nineteenth century's obsession with history." But this verdict itself raises difficulties for the attempt to characterize Sidgwick's position. Was he a kind of intellectual Jacobite, refusing to recognize the legitimacy of the new regime and obstinately affirming his old allegiances? Or was he a zealous Whig, proud of the adaptability of his inheritance, eagerly carrying out Mill's unrealized aspirations for the reform of the moral sciences? The answer, it seems to me, is that he was neither – or rather, to maintain the terms of the question, he was an Independent with Tory sympathies who found new and more subtle arguments to justify his traditional loyalties.

Translating the metaphor, the most concise description, with all the attendant dangers of that form, would be to say that his work remained broadly in the Utilitarian mode but still shifted its basis from "science" to "philosophy." Less elliptically, one could say that he conceded the legitimacy of much of the critique of the axioms and methods of classical Utilitariarism which had been made in the name of historical and cultural diversity, and he abandoned the attempt to deduce universally valid precepts from the "laws of human nature" on the overworked model of Newtonian mechanics. Instead, he argued that the essential method of the moral sciences, at least where the drawing of practical conclusions was concerned, was the method of philosophical analysis – "i.e., the method of reflection on the thought we all share, by the aid of the symbolism we all share, language" (*PSR*, 49) – but that such reflective analysis, when combined with a few empirical generalizations indisputably true of the behavior of members of advanced or "civilized" societies, yielded conclusions of a roughly Utilitarian character. It was this conception of philosophy and its role (arguably, a conception of considerable general cultural significance) that underlay Sidgwick's dealings with those branches of the science of politics to which he devoted the greater part of his intellectual energy in the 1880s and 1890s. That he, moral philosopher and university teacher, should in his forties and fifties have invested so much effort in writing on political topics (and his correspondence abounds with evidence of the extent to which it was duty-driven effort rather than the spontaneous promptings of intellectual creativity) is in itself an indication not only of the primacy of "the theory of practice" for Sidgwick, but also of the seriousness with which he regarded the political agency available to an occupant of those traditional stations.

2

The decision to write a treatise on political economy provides a telling example of these concerns. Convinced, as a pillar of the local Charity Organization Society and its precursors, of the utility of the Individualist precepts usually associated with classical political economy; irritated, as a thinker who valued clarity and exactness above all, by the simplistic and dismissive criticisms made by critics like Ingram and Cliffe Leslie; and disturbed, as a cautious and pessimistic political observer, by the possible practical consequences of a public loss of confidence in the subject, Sidgwick turned in the late 1870s from lecturing and writing on metaphysics and moral philosophy to address himself to political economy. The entrepreneurial Morley, ever alert to the value of good controversy for a journal's circulation, snapped up his first efforts for the *Fortnightly* in 1879, since, despite a few polite concessions to Cliffe Leslie's criticisms, Sidgwick's articles were bound to be taken as a more or less intransigent defense of the methods of classical political economy. As his editor smugly pointed out to him, "opinion will regard you as distinctly adverse to Leslie, if not distinctly in accord with Lowe."[20] Although this polemical note was muffled by the encrustation of qualifying clauses in his *Principles of Political Economy*, which appeared four years later (after the effort to finish it, even while on holiday, had made him ill – it was a task that mattered to him), as a political economist Sidgwick certainly represented a tradition on the defensive.

The very conception of the work was intellectually conservative, as he acknowledged, and this in two ways: first, because he adhered to "the older and more popular view of my subject" by including the "art" of political economy, "considered as a department of the general theory of practice," as well as the "science"; and second, because he for the most part upheld "the traditional method of English political economy" rather than adopting either a more historical or a more mathematical approach. In both respects, the model remained Mill's *Principles* upon which, as Sidgwick rather proudly testified, his own work was "primarily founded," though it was Mill modified in the light of Jevons's marginalist theory of value (*PPE*1, 26, 40). In correspondence, he put his position very simply: "I accept Jevons's doctrine as in the main true and as an important addition to the older theory: but I am not prepared to say that the modifications thus introduced into the theory of value as propounded [?] e.g. by Mill is enough to make me regard Jevons's doctrine as a new basis. But I am quite content to be described in general terms as a follower of Jevons."[21] Such ecumenism was an important feature of the work: In his view, the theoretical contributions made since Mill "generally admit of being stated in a form less hostile to the older doctrines than their authors suppose" (a rebuke aimed primarily at the iconoclastic Jevons), and he characteristically represented his own purpose as the elimination of "unnecessary controversy."[22] But by including, as part of the same work, a detailed account of the very limited role for state action in economic matters which was derivable from the premises of classical political economy, Sidgwick was deliberately attempting to confer (or rather restore) the authority of science on a view of politics that remained, for all the qualifications, essentially Individualistic. Similarly, much of his animus against "sociology" surely stemmed from a well-founded fear that the kind of intellectual *compote* with which its proponents often aimed to replace political economy would appear, to less analytical and less cautious minds, to remove what he and many of his contemporaries took to be the chief arguments against the various forms of socialism that were attracting some notice in the 1880s.

At first sight, Sidgwick appears content to replicate the classic discussions by Mill and Cairnes on the abstract nature of political economy's axioms and the consequently hypothetical character of its conclusions. He endorsed the orthodox view that "the human being that political economy assumes to be normal . . . always prefers a greater apparent gain to a less, and prefers to attain any desired result with the least apparent expenditure." (Interestingly, he did not think that this necessarily involved treating labor as a "cost" or "sacrifice"; here was one of the places where he thought that the axioms of classical political economy had been stated in a needlessly unrealistic form, ignoring, for example, the satisfactions of work. However, his own conviction, important as a source of skepticism about the prospects of socialist schemes, was still that "no important part of the labour required for the production of wealth is likely to be carried on to an adequate extent . . . by such beings as men now are, except under the influence of some motive more powerful than the average man's liking for work.") From such premises he went on to deduce, subject to the usual carefully phrased qualifications, "the chief theorems of English deductive political economy," such as that, "where there is open competition, two prices cannot be permanently maintained in one market for the same commodity," and so on. The ceteris paribus clause was duly wheeled into place, with its consequence that "we can draw no positive inference from these theorems without ascertaining how far other things are equal," and thus that, taken alone, they could never provide answers to "particular economic questions of a concrete character." In the by now standard chapter on "custom and habit" he allowed that "we can only learn by a careful study of facts the force of the other motives of which all economists admit the importance and existence; especially of the powerful but unobtrusive impulses which lead a man to what other people do, and what he has done before." Like Maine before him and Marshall after, he chiefly devoted himself to showing that these other motives did not *necessarily* operate to counteract or undermine competition, but he did have to concede that there were "moral or quasi-moral sentiments" which on occasion led groups or individuals to sacrifice the greater gain. The only form in which Sidgwick really considered the operation of these "sentiments" was where individuals are led to modify the economic rationality of their actions (assumed as the basic model) out of attachment to an "ideal" – for which his main example was, revealingly, charity. But this, of course, reduced the potential theoretical difficulties that would be raised by the recognition of the pervasiveness of such motives; having relegated them to this peripheral category, he could plausibly conclude: "I do not, however, think that the effects of these elevated sentiments in modifying the action of economic forces are of fundamental importance in modern societies as they actually exist" (*PPE*1, 37, 44–7, 50; book 2, chap. 12, passim; 392).

The reference to "modern societies" is a reminder that Sidgwick had absorbed enough of the historical school's criticism not to claim that political economy was of all times and all places. But this concession as to the scope of the subject – made commonplace by Bagehot in the late 1870s – was in his case related to a somewhat more interesting departure from the classical account of its method, a departure that had important implications for his later work on politics. For, in his view, the chief method of orthodox political economy was not in fact strictly deductive but "analytical." By this he meant that "it chiefly consists of getting a clearer and more systematic view, through reflective analysis, of general facts which common experience has already made familiar." In his *Principles*, he accordingly gave particular prominence to "the task of defining the cardinal terms of political economy," a task, he defensively remarked, which he had performed "with rather unusual elaborateness." (This was the aspect of the work which its admirers particularly praised: Those less sympathetic dismissed the book as "*reine philologie*.")[23] Apart from the obvious scientific importance of the consistent and systematic use of terms, Sidgwick argued that the process of seeking such definitions, whether successfully completed or not, was the best way to get to grips with the relevant "distinctions and relations of fact." For "in subjects where we cannot present them to the mind in orderly fulness by the exercise of the organs of sense, there is no way of surveying them so convenient as that of reflecting on our use of common terms." This would not involve merely endorsing everyday speech on these matters, for although he thought there were good reasons why, in framing definitions, "we should keep as closely as we can to the common use of language," he recognized that "common usage may be inconsistent" and in other ways inadequate to the task. He emphasized, therefore, that "we should keep carefully distinct the two very different questions, (1) what *do* we commonly mean by the terms Value, Wealth, Money, Capital, etc., and (2) what *ought* we to mean by them – what meaning is it, for scientific purposes, convenient to attach to them?" Sidgwick skirted the somewhat tricky philosophical issues raised by this second question in its general form, content, within the confines of a treatise on economics, to point to the role of such analysis in helping us "to know, contemplate, and as far as possible arrange and systematize, the 'familiar facts of our ordinary experience' " (*PPE*1, 36, 40, 48, 51, 59–62).

It had, of course, been part of the historical school's complaint, in its subtler form, that the "general facts" and "ordinary experience" upon the basis of which the economist formed his concepts were themselves peculiar to certain societies at a particular stage of their development. Sidgwick did not dispute this – indeed, he may even have thought it a necessary truth; but he did not, whether for that or other reasons, regard it as a damaging criticism of the claims of political economy properly understood. As he acknowledged, classical political economy relied not only on "an artificially simplified type of human action," but also on the assumption of the prevalence of certain social conditions: What these conditions actually amounted to, Sidgwick argued, was "a state of things taken as the type to which modern civilized society generally approximates," and this assumption was "incontrovertibly legitimate as corresponding broadly to the facts of modern societies." The method of reflective analysis applied to political economy was to that extent inherently parochial and content to be so. It sacrificed the universalist aspirations of the older theory in order to gain the persuasiveness that attaches to showing how a particular structure of reasoning is implicit in the accepted distinctions of a shared language. Sidgwick, not surprisingly, also drew attention to the educative value of this procedure, that is, its "indirect utility as a means of training the intellect in the *kind* of reasoning required for dealing with concrete economic problems." The extreme historical view, he argued – it was a point he was fond of making against the sociologists also – was from this point of view self-defeating: The more the economic historian insisted that the past was radically different from the present, and hence not to be understood in terms of concepts derived from the present, "the more, *prima facie*, he tends to establish the corresponding independence of the economic science which, pursued with a view to practice, is primarily concerned to understand the present" (*PPE*1, 36, 40, 48). It was, in the end, this focus upon practice that licensed, and even demanded, the introduction of local circumstances into the premises of the theory itself.

3

These features of the method of reflective analysis stand out in still clearer relief in his attempt to write "a great book on Politics,"[24] the germination of which reveals something of Sidgwick's unfashionable intellectual development away from the program laid down in book 6 of Mill's *System of Logic* and toward Bentham's *Constitutional Code*. In a well-known passage of reminiscence, Sidgwick later recalled how in the early 1860s he and his contemporaries, under the spell of Mill and of "Comte seen through Mill's spectacles," aimed, with youthful ardor, at "a complete revision of human relations, political, moral, and economic, in the light of science," and how they took for granted that "this social science must of course have historical knowledge as its basis" (*M*, 39–40, written in 1897). His casual report to a correspondent in 1861 that he had "read through Mill's *Representative Government* in one morning" and found it "extremely good" captures this mood of discipular enthusiasm.[25] But though Sidgwick always revered Mill and his memory, time soon brought distance from his theories: A catalogue of the points on which he came to disagree with his master, often sharply and fundamentally, would make a pretty study in intellectual parricide, and I shall return to some of the more general contrasts between them at the end of this essay. Here it is sufficient to say that Sidgwick seems to have arrived at his own distinctive views on the study of politics, as on ethics and philosophical method generally, by the late 1860s;[26] the decade between graduating in 1859 and resigning his fellowship in 1869 marked his *Sturmjahre*, and thereafter his fundamental views changed very little.

As early as 1865, he reported "designing a treatise on Politics," remarking loftily: "It is very much wanted: G. C. Lewis is miserable; – in fact, everybody has been studying constitutional history lately and ignored Politics. Mill, with characteristic caution, has confined himself to a portion of the subject." (One change that time did bring to Sidgwick's views was that he became a good deal less ready to reproach Mill for his caution.) He was already convinced that "history will have in the future less and less influence on Politics in the most advanced countries. Principles will soon be everything and tradition nothing: except as regards its influence on the form."[27] Such views were, of course, far from being the conventional wisdom of the late 1860s, and they mark the beginning of Sidgwick's protracted and rather lonely battle with the zeitgeist in this area. That they also distanced him even from some of his own earliest admirers is well brought out in a long letter to Alfred Marshall written in 1871, which is particularly rich in matter for the themes of this essay.

As for Evolution, I quite understood the view you expressed last term, but I do not think I agree with you, and I am quite sure I do not agree with Karl Marx. The *Spiessburger* is after all only our old friend the "Bourgeois" for whose wicked selfishness Political Economy is supposed to have been invented: when I first read Socialistic tracts I was much impressed with the breadth of view implied in this contemptuous term: but on reflection the Bourgeois after all appeared to me the heir of the ages, as far as he went: and so of Bentham's Normal Man. I say I do not quite know whether I agree with you: for I do not know whether you mean more than to insist on the *limitations* of Benthamism and the need of supplementing it with some historical sociology. But I certainly do not think it the *special* function of the Philosophy of Jurisprudence to develop dynamical conceptions. On the contrary I feel as if a grasp of the Utilitarian method of determining rules had been of the greatest value to myself, and how few M.P.'s have really got it any critical debate will indicate. It seems to me that the tendency just now, owing to the Positivists, is rather over-historical than otherwise. However, I do not really know if we should disagree: I think I told you that I have worked out principles of constitutional jus – for Bentham's Normal-Mensch – in two or three lectures: so much to my own satisfaction that I am perhaps biassed in favour of the method.[28]

This polite and disarming confession of bias masked, as so often, a deep conviction on Sidgwick's part, a conviction that sustained his struggle over the next two decades to work out the detail of a polity appropriate to Bentham's "Normal Mensch." Struggle it certainly was: As the labor neared its end, he resolved "never again to attempt to comprehend Politics in a single octavo volume of moderate thickness."[29] The sense in which he was attempting to "comprehend Politics," and the source of some of his difficulties with the task, was nicely captured in a despairing reply to some well-meant suggestions from Bryce:

I am partly influenced by the fact that in this chapter I have little to say of concrete interest. For instance, at the very end I have to say something as to Rights of Revolution and Disruption. But I do not find any really useful "media axiomata" on these questions: the generalities I shall utter will amount to little more than that you ought to rebel and disrupt when it is on the whole expedient to do so. Accordingly, to conceal my barrenness of practical wisdom, I take refuge in analysis.[30]

Even making allowances for the exaggerations of an author deep in the toils of composition, this suggests a certain limitation in the "Utilitarian method" and "taking refuge in analysis" and may prove a helpful description to keep in mind when considering *The Elements of Politics* itself.

The primary aim of the political theory that is here to be expounded is not to supply an entirely new method of obtaining reasoned answers to political questions; but rather, by careful reflection, to introduce greater clearness and consistency into the kind of thought and reasoning with which we are all more or less familiar. (*EP*1, 1)

This is hardly the pitch of the natural salesman, yet, as we know from other, more celebrated, historical examples, modest applicants for the post of underlaborer often harbor practically imperial ambitions. For his part, Sidgwick certainly believed that his favored procedure has its political as well as – or even, to some extent, as a result of – its educative value: Though it did not "constitute anything like a complete protection against erroneous practical conclusions," the "systematic effort" to pursue it is "of considerable practical value" (*EP*1, 1–2). And the same marks of the procedure recur in the book itself as in his *Principles of Political Economy*: eliciting "the characteristics that are essentially implied in the commonly received notions" of political discourse, establishing "what we mean or ought to mean" by them, and rendering "somewhat more precise in conception the principles that I find commonly recognized" (*EP*1, 13, 62, 33–4).

At first sight, he may also seem to be pursuing a quite different method, which, with unusual insistence, he lays down (in the passage from which my first epigraph is taken) as the only "rational method" for dealing with "the question of practical politics."

According to my view, it must be a method mainly deductive: we must assume certain general characteristics of man and his circumstances – characteristics belonging not to mankind universally, but to civilised man in the most advanced stage of his development: and we must consider what laws and institutions are most likely to conduce to the well-being of an aggregate of such beings living in social relations. (*EP*1, 8–9)

As in my epigraph, the tone is again one of unassuming confidence and circumspect ambition: While gently coaxing agreement by appealing to lowest common denominators, it makes no attempt, in the manner of more coercive political vocabularies, to go for broke epistemologically. Much, no doubt, is taken for granted. There is the untroubled assumption that "the ordinary experience of civilized life" is in no way opaque, that the identification of the "human motives and tendencies" to be reasoned about is unproblematic, and that "well-being" can be specified in some way that is both uncontentious and nonvacuous. But then, when proposing a method of discussing the solution of "the problems of practical politics" to the educated classes of late nineteenth-century England, it may have been not altogether unreasonable to take these assumptions for granted.

What, in proposing this procedure, Sidgwick is offering amounts to a demure Utilitarianism which has quietly forsaken any claims to be based on a new "science of man." Its pedigree manifests itself most obviously in the examples he cites of the relevant psychological assumptions – Bentham's dicta that, "of two individuals with equal fortunes, he that has the most wealth has the greatest chance of happiness," and that "the excess in happiness of the richer will not be so great as the excess of his wealth," as well as Mill's proposition that "each person is the only safe guardian of his own rights and interests." They were not, Sidgwick urged, "put forward as *exactly* or *universally* true, even of contemporary civilized man; but only as sufficiently near the truth for practical purposes." Indeed, far from their standing being exaggerated, he thought that "at the present time the most prevalent and dangerous mistake" was to neglect their value entirely, a reference not only to the fashion for insisting on historical variation but also to the, sometimes related, socialistic optimism about human nature that he and likeminded mid-Victorian liberals feared was undermining the basis of sound Individualist politics. He acknowledges that, "besides the general characteristics just mentioned," there were the "sentiments and habits of thought and action, formed by the previous history of the nation": The model, once again, turns out to be Utilitarian man as modified – and modified the less, perhaps, the more advanced his society – by national character. So, displaying the same confidence as in the classic accounts of political economy, Sidgwick reiterated that, though "no particular nation is composed of individuals having only a few and simple characteristics" thus isolated, they nonetheless remain "all we can include in our conception of the civilized man to whom our abstract political reasoning relates" (*EP*1, 10–11).

It may help us to understand why Sidgwick felt that the selection of these particular characteristics needed no elaborate justification when we recognize that he was *not*, in fact, pursuing two entirely different methods. For, in his view, a kind of deductive reasoning from such premises *was*, implicity, the basis of everyday political argument: Practical measures were, he pointed out, always partly supported by arguments of an implicitly Utilitarian character even where their advocates explicitly appealed to some other theory. A favorite example was provided by those Individualists – Spencer being only the best known – who held that freedom (or mutual noninterference) was an end in itself: "I cannot directly refute this opinion," Sidgwick wrote in a passage revealing of both his accommodating approach and his gentle tutorial irony, "any more than any other opinion, as to ultimate ends or principles of right conduct; but I think it may be shown to be inconsistent not only with the common sense of mankind, as expressed in actual legislation, but with the practical doctrines – when they descend to particulars – even of the very thinkers who profess to hold it" (*EP*1, 40). It was, therefore, a crucial premise of the book that an analysis of the conclusions to be reached by deduction from Utilitarian axioms would roughly coincide with a systematization of the political views held by "the majority of instructed persons in England at the present day," always the relevant constituency. This was brought out even more clearly in a series of small modifications of the text which he made for the second edition of 1897: For example, he omitted the phrases about the method being "deductive" and based on "psychology" and replaced them with references to "the method commonly adopted in political reasoning" and the assumptions that "we" make, adding, "the present work is an attempt to render this method more systematic and precise" (*EP*2, 11–14). These views themselves, moreover, aspired to derive from more than merely parochial foundations: "Indeed, the least reflection will show that in ordinary political discussions reference is continually made to propositions laid down as true of civilized men generally, not merely of the English species of civilized man." Hence, the value of a training in such reasoning will always transcend the purely local, since "considerations of the general kind with which we shall be concerned must always form an important part of the discussion of any question of practical politics" (*EP*1, 11–12). In Sidgwick's hands, the status of the Utilitarian axioms is revised: No longer presented as the lemmas of a science of man, they figure more modestly as principles implicit in the common political reasoning that it is the task of reflective analysis to systematize. But the scale of the whole enterprise being thus reduced, the apparent modesty of his own contribution assumes a different aspect. And this, surely, is what our opening quotation should have prepared us for: There is nothing very modest, after all, in the conviction that one has arrived at "the only possible method of dealing systematically with political problems."

4

In the course of a generally perceptive review of *The Elements of Politics*, D. G. Ritchie remarked that, although the book was Benthamite in approach, "there is none of Bentham's strong critical antagonism to the institutions of his time. . . . If this is Benthamism, it is Benthamism grown tame and sleek." Tameness and sleekness are, of course, often alleged to be functional adaptations for any intellectual creature that finds itself transplanted into the cozy environs of an academic syllabus, and we always need to remember that Sidgwick was writing with more than half an eye to the needs of students for a reliable text. Still, as Ritchie dryly observed, it is a striking fact that, though Sidgwick was arguing deductively from general propositions, "yet, somehow, the conclusion again and again turns out to be just what we have in the present British constitution."[31] For all his careful discriminations, Ritchie concluded, Sidgwick "nowhere arrives at any conclusion which would differ very widely from that of the average man of the professional and commercial middle-classes at the present day." Though no author relishes being the butt of a reviewer's irony, Sidgwick must have considered this comment – which would have seemed a feeble joke to Bentham, and to Mill a culpable slur – more as an endorsement of his method than as a criticism of it. However, more was involved here than Ritchie's sneer allowed for. To put it in a way that exaggerates the point but brings out its significance, one could say that, as refashioned by Sidgwick, Utilitarianism had become almost inherently conservative in its political hearing. In an obvious sense – so obvious as to amount almost to a tautology – working from the received opinion of the day had a necessary tendency to exclude radically challenging considerations. An example of this is provided by his amplification of Mill's maxim that "each person is the only safe guardian of his own rights and interests." He pointed out not only that the maxim is intended to apply only to sane adults but that "to avoid controversy" he will further restrict it to male adults, "since it is not clear that the common sense of mankind considers women generally to be the safest guardians of their own pecuniary interests." This, he added defensively, "I need hardly say, was not Mill's view"; but neither should such statements be taken as always expressing Sidgwick's own opinion (*EP*1, 9–10).[32] Particularly contentious or eccentric views (in the limited sense in which Sidgwick held such) were set aside in the interests of securing as wide an area of agreement as possible. Since existing views may be (and no doubt usually are) confused and inconsistent, the theorist is not confined merely to repeating current prejudices, but unless some germ of criticism is already present in those views, he has no license for introducing a novel set of criteria.

Moreover, at the level of detail, Sidgwick displayed a Burkean respect for the historically formed shape of existing institutions: Such "particular characteristics," he warned, "may modify to an indefinite extent the conclusions arrived at by general deductive reasoning." His examples, if not the rather clinical detachment with which he presented them, would have warmed the heart of the least Utilitarian of Whig historians.

Thus I may conclude from the point of view of abstract theory, that by taking twelve plain men and shutting them up in a room till they are unanimous, I am likely to get but a blunt and clumsy instrument for the administration of criminal justice: but this defect may be more than compensated by the peculiar confidence placed in this instrument by a people whom the unbroken tradition of centuries has taught to regard trial by jury as the "palladium of its liberties." So again, no one constructing a legislative organ, composed of two chambers, for a newly-founded community of modern civilized men, would propose that membership of the second or revising chamber should be handed down from father to son, like a piece of private property: but in a country that has long been led by a hereditary aristocracy, a chamber so appointed may have a valuable power of resistance to dangerous popular impulses which it may be difficult to obtain by any other mode of appointment. (*EP*1, 11)

Complacency about these particular institutions was hardly a rare commodity in late nineteenth-century England (and one notes again the essentially defensive role assigned to political wisdom). However, Sidgwick, as one might expect, essayed a reasoned justification for a kind of conservatism in matters of detail, though to appreciate its Utilitarian character one has to extrapolate from an argument developed in his much better known work on ethics.

In the course of his examination there of the "method of Utilitarianism" he indicated that although common-sense morality is already to a large extent implicitly Utilitarian, and can in fact be made a *coherent* body of moral rules only by being systematized on an explicitly Utilitarian basis, still it cannot, as it stands, be taken as an entirely reliable guide to the maximization of happiness in the details of conduct (*ME*, book 4, chaps. 3–5).[33] Utilitarians have therefore supposed, he went on, that they need to frame an ideal morality against which the deficiencies of the existing rules could be charted. But to do this, he objected – it is a mark of his distance from his predecessors – it would be necessary to know what kind of human being one was legislating for, since, "whether we consider the intellect of man or his feelings, or his physical condition and circumstances, we find them so different in different ages and countries, that it seems *prima facie* absurd to lay down a set of ideal

Utilitarian rules for mankind generally." A few rather general characteristics could, of course, be assumed, issuing in the kind of hypothetical propositions worked out in his treatise on politics and political economy; but these could only yield very broad imperatives, and it is already established that at this level of generality common-sense morality corresponds roughly with Utilitarian principles. What is at issue is the attempt to bring them into closer correspondence, to improve "the delicacy and precision" with which our moral rules are adapted to "the actual needs and conditions of human life." Nor is the difficulty overcome by confining ourselves to the evidence of "men as we know them, in our own age and country," for such creatures are already in part constituted by their experience and adherence to the existing moral code. An empty, useless abstraction (Sidgwick is here very reminiscent of his fiercest antagonist in moral philosophy, F. H. Bradley) is all that could be produced by attempting to imagine them without the formative power of that experience. In short, "we have to take the moral habits, impulses and tastes of men as a material given us to work upon no less than the rest of their nature, and as something which, as it only partly results from reasoning in the past, so can only be partially modified by any reasoning which we can now apply to it" (*ME*, 467–9).

If, in his views about method, Sidgwick can be seen as representing something of a move from Mill back to Bentham, one could similarly say that in the attitude he wishes to inculcate toward existing institutions and mores, he uses the method of Bentham to arrive at the conclusion of Burke. He urged the Utilitarian to "repudiate altogether that temper of rebellion against the established morality, as something purely external and conventional, into which the reflective mind is always apt to fall when it is first convinced that the established rules are not intrinsically reasonable." Instead, he should "contemplate it with reverence and wonder, as a marvellous product of nature, the result of long centuries of growth," and recognize it as "a mechanism which no 'politicians or philosophers' could create, yet without which the harder and coarser machinery of Positive Law could not be permanently maintained" (*ME*, 475–6). This mood of uncritical reverence – it would seem like antiintellectualism in a less fastidious author – is in fact uncharacteristic; Sidgwick himself felt the philosophical urge too strongly (and respected its office, properly understood, too much) to join in the stock denunciations of the "man of theory" that were so often the accomplishment of these views in nineteenth-century Britain when expressed in a coarser idiom. But he was eloquent that realism in moral and political matters is itself a moral obligation: He became uncharacteristically warm in exposing the self-indulgence and self-deception involved in irresponsible utopianism. The passage where, in *The Methods of Ethics*, he concludes his discussion with the Utilitarian's relation to existing morality can stand, *mutatis mutandis*, as a summary of his sense of the agency available to the responsible realist in politics also.

I hold that the Utilitarian, in the existing stage of our knowledge, cannot possibly construct a morality *de novo* either for man as he is (abstracting his morality), or for man as ought to be and will be. He must start, speaking broadly, with the existing social order, and the existing morality as part of that order: and in deciding the question whether any divergency from this code is to be recommended, must consider chiefly the immediate consequences of such divergence, upon a society in which such a code is conceived generally to subsist. No doubt a thoughtful and well-instructed Utilitarian may see dimly a certain way ahead, and his attitude towards existing morality may be to some extent modified by what he sees. He may discern in the future certain evils impending, which can only be effectually warded off by the adoption of new and more stringent views of duty in certain departments: while, on the other hand, he may see a prospect of social changes which will render a relaxation of other parts of the moral code expedient or inevitable. But if he keeps within the limits that separate scientific prevision from fanciful Utopian conjecture, the form of society to which his practical conclusions relate will be one varying but little from the actual, with its actually established code of moral rules and customary judgements concerning virtue and vice. (*ME*, 473–4)

Remarking on the intellectual and political conservatism of *The Elements of Politics*, several reviewers identified its neglect of the historical and evolutionist approaches as one of its most "old-fashioned" features. On Sidgwick's part the omission was, of course, a deliberate, even polemical, one; in a series of addresses and lectures in the 1880s and 1890s (some of the latter of which were posthumously published in *Philosophy, Its Scope and Relations*), he explained at some length why he thought the expectations commonly held at the time of the "guidance" to be derived from such approaches were greatly exaggerated.[34] He briefly rehearsed these arguments in *The Elements of Politics*, taking care to point out that Mill, despite his announcement in book 6 of the primacy of the pursuit of "the laws according to which any state of society produces the state which succeeds it and takes its place," had, "when he came to treat with a view to practical conclusions the question of the best form of government, . . . certainly dealt with it by a method not primarily historical: a method in which history seems to be only used either to confirm practical conclusions otherwise arrived at, or to suggest the limits of their applicability" (*EP*1, 8).[35]

Sidgwick's affirmation of the essentially secondary or peripheral value of the historical study of politics raises a question which would, were there any substantial body of Sidgwick scholarship, be recognized as "Das Henry Sidgwick Problem", namely, the difficulty of reconciling the fierce antihistoricism of *The Elements of Politics* with the whole enterprise of tracing the historical evolution of the modern state which he undertook in *The Development of European Polity*. After all, complaints about the "comparative uselessness of history" form a recurring motif in his writings,[36] and he certainly did not, in his later years, want for employment of his time. Nor can the problem be explained away by regarding the work as a necessary part of his academic duties: The subject was not, in this form, an essential element of the Moral Sciences Tripos, and it was, anyway, already covered by Seeley's not altogether dissimilar lectures and classes for the Historical Tripos, as well as by several others.[37] Even after editing Seeley's lectures following the latter's death in 1895, he still proposed to publish his own, a task eventually executed by his wife three years after he died. One can well imagine that Sidgwick's more discriminating intelligence found the blunt assertiveness of Seeley's book somewhat unsatisfactory, especially since the latter included a certain amount of what, by Sidgwick's standards, must have seemed rather homely political philosophy; Sidgwick does also seem to have felt – it was a feeling shared by several of his contemporaries – that, notwithstanding the work of Freeman, Seeley, and others, there still existed no usable connected narrative of the development of specifically European forms of polity from ancient times up to the present. Nonetheless, what he hoped to gain from such a purely historical exercise still needs to be explained.

To observe that its author classified *The Development of European Polity* not as a work of history but as a treatment of "an important part of the history of political societies from the point of view of Inductive Political Science" may seem only to redescribe the question, and yet an explanation must begin with the realization that Sidgwick, like so many of his contemporaries, was responsive to the charms of a "science of politics." What, according to him, distinguished this enterprise from "ordinary political history" was "the generality of the object of science." That is, the political scientist, unlike the historian, is aiming not "primarily at presenting facts in their chronological order" but at "ascertaining (1) the classes to which [polities] belong, or the general types which they exemplify, and (2) the causes which have led to the prevalence of this or that general type in different regions at different times." And since political science "aims at bringing together for comparison societies similar in their political characteristics, however widely separated in time," it necessarily involved the use of the comparative method; it "aims like other sciences at ascertaining relations of resemblance among the objects that it studies; it seeks to arrange them in classes, or to exhibit them as examples of types." And as Sidgwick, like any other advocate of the comparative method, acknowledged, the main interest of this morphology was not classification as such but the discovery of "the order of development of political societies" (*DEP*, 1–4). As one may see in the work of both Mill and Maine, the category of "political societies" – the adjective excluded those primitive groups which possessed no discernible government – embraced more than simply the structure and functions of government; even Sidgwick's book included discussion of the development of patriarchal communities out of primitive kingship groups, of the origin and economic foundation of medieval cities, of the nature of theocratic authority, and so on. In other words, as an organizing concept, it had a constant tendency to expand beyond the limits of the conventionally political and to become a way of organizing miscellaneous information about the types of societies.[38]

The fact that Sidgwick could contemplate this conception of political science so benignly renders more puzzling, in turn, his hostility to the at least superficially similar enterprise of "sociology." As one might expect, the puzzle is partly to be resolved by bringing out the considerable differences, at various levels, between the two enterprises as they were then envisaged.[39] One particularly important difference was that political science, strikingly unlike late nineteenth-century sociology, was not primarily constituted by elaborate and implausible articulations of the organic analogy. Seeley, it is true, was given, as one who had been early and lastingly impressed by Comte, to speaking of the state as an organism, but compared to, for example, the rococo variations that Spencer played upon this theme, Seeley's language of "development" and "growth" exhibited positively classical restraint. Moreover, political science stuck, for the most part, to the period of recorded history: The comparative method licensed a limited amount of disciplined conjecture, but did not encompass the wilder shores of speculation characteristic of contemporary sociology, and was scornful of the value of inferences from the behavior of lower animals. Partly related to this, and partly because its exponents tended to be drawn from the university-educated class, the scholarship exhibited in works of political science was not open to immediate and dismissive criticism. As Sidgwick remarked in 1894, it was hardly surprising that "professional students of history" were "likely to distrust the generalisations of the professional sociologist," given that the latter's knowledge "is apt to be distinguished rather by range than by depth or accuracy." Having indicted Benjamin Kidd for a variety of historical errors and misrepresentations in his best-selling *Social Evolution*, Sidgwick clearly lined up alongside the professional historians who, "after reading Mr. Kidd, will be more than ever inclined to draw a sharp line between [their] own methods and those of the would-be sociologist: and will hardly take much interest in any prediction of the future founded on such knowledge of the past as the specimens above-quoted exemplify."[40]

Moreover, the scope and ambitiousness of the claims made by so many of the late nineteenth-century advocates of sociology, presuming at times to settle the perennial problems of epistemology and moral philosophy, were not matched even by political science's most enthusiastic supporters. There are, in fact, subtler complications here, since one must consider the *kind* of guidance which its more moderate exponents like Sidgwick expected from a science of politics during this period, especially the extent to which it authorized any predictions. One must also recognize that political science promised a different and relatively more accessible kind of practical benefit, above all educationally. Overall, the tenor of Sidgwick's response to sociology – a representative and influential response – is well caught in his severe judgment on Franklin Gidding's college textbook: "The analysis is too loose, the generalisations too hasty, there is too much disposition to propound doubtful conjectures as established truths; and, here and there, I find what seem to me curious misrepresentations of familiar historical facts."[41]

Of course, one man's "doubtful conjecture" is another's brilliant hypothesis, and Sidgwick's propensity for remorseless skepticism and his temperamental aversion to bold construction are personal elements in his response that cannot be overlooked. Like many not themselves given to easy generalizations, he was all the more incensed by popular acceptance of the ambitious and confident conclusions of fashionable theorists. He displayed a characteristic mixture of self-knowledge and self-doubt about this tendency. For example, in 1885, while writing the British Association address in which he most authoritatively dissected the claims of sociology, he confided to his journal: "really, in this as in other departments, my tendency is to scepticism," and then went on to the following revealing reflection:

Have been reading Comte and Spencer with all my old admiration for their intellectual force and industry and more than my old amazement for their fatuous self-confidence. It does not seem to me that either of them knows what self-criticism means. I wonder if this is a defect inseparable from their excellences. Certainly I find my own self-criticism an obstacle to energetic and spirited work, but on the other hand I feel that whatever value my work has is due to it.

After delivering the address, his self-reproach was: "it is poor stuff, this sterile criticism, and I am rather ashamed of it: only the pretensions of these people irritate me into the belief that it is a public duty to repress them."[42] There is, of course, a touch of self-irony in this – the "belief," we are allowed to infer, is part rationalization – but also the expression of a genuine if rarefied sense of duty. After his attack on Kidd, he similarly excused what he feared would be seen as the "undue animosity" of his review: "The truth is that I have no ill-will towards Kidd, who is certainly a vigorous and stimulating writer, but I do think that the reviewers are to blame for not having found out how little he knows. I do not mean little compared with most men, but little compared with the pretensions of his book."[43] His own gifts were, need one say, preeminently critical and analytical, and even his major constructive achievement, *The Methods of Ethics*, ends with a frank admission of its inconclusiveness, at least as far as providing any rational proof of the superiority of Utilitarianism to consistent Egoism is concerned. A greater than average suspicion of the aspirations of sociology was perhaps to be expected from a man who, after a 400-page account of the development of the modern state, could muster no more positive conclusion than "I therefore think it not beyond the limits of a sober forecast to conjecture that some further integration may take place in the West European states" (*DEP*, 439).

It is also the case, as this last quotation may suggest, that in execution Sidgwick's contribution to this genre was rather more limited and methodologically temperate than his programmatic endorsement of the general project might have seemed to promise. Although *The Development of European Polity* covered a very long span of time, it stuck closely to the conventional sources for recorded European history, and its taste in explanation and comparison was typically austere; indeed, apart from the first three chapters, there is not all that much to distinguish the book from some of the brisker narratives of orthodox political history. It may be important to recognize that the text as it now stands has a complicated history, and was not, of course, revised for publication by Sidgwick himself. Among the relevant facts of this history are that the first three chapters were written and printed as early as 1889, that the bulk of the rest of the text derives from lectures given in the 1890s, that Sidgwick had not worked on these lectures for several years before his death, and that the section on "imitation," in which he considers objectives which, if accepted, would be fatal to the comparative method, was interpolated in the first chapter by his wife, drawing upon an undated but clearly later note by Sidgwick himself. There is, therefore, some reason for thinking that, had he lived to complete the book himself, Sidgwick might have modified the optimism about what could be inferred from "Inductive Political Science" that characterizes the first three chapters of the book as it now stands. (The material cited in notes 43 and 44 would certainly have given him every reason for much modification.)

That having been said, it is still true that the classification of *types* of stages and a concern with structural rather than chronological connections do make their appearance later in the book, and there is certainly much less about actual political *events* than in most nineteenth-century works of history; but for all that, the book, the first three chapters aside, hardly constitutes a triumphant fulfillment of the promise of "a new science" as heralded by Maine and Freeman. Sidgwick's own cautious reservations about the more exuberant hopes entertained for the application of the comparative method may well have been reinforced by criticisms which he evidently received in the 1890s from his former pupil and present colleague, F. W. Maitland. Some interesting exchanges, for example, must have lain behind Maitland's remark to the historian H. A. L. Fisher about a point "I tried to make in a discussion with Sidgwick in which I endeavoured to convince him that 'inductive political science' is rubbish, and I had far more success than I expected," adding, in a phrase that no doubt provides a model for relations with a revered teacher, "I don't despair of him."[44] The aspect of the topic on which, to judge at least from their published writings, Sidgwick and Maitland disagreed most sharply was the question of the possibility of making any sound induction about the "natural" sequence of political development from the historical records of a variety of unique instances. Maitland denied, and indeed derided, such an enterprise with delightfully informal elegance in his paper "The Body Politic," which was clearly aimed at the very conception of "inductive political science" endorsed, at the insistence, above all, of Seeley and Sidgwick, by the Cambridge Historical Tripos. Sidgwick himself had been no less severe on comparable fallacies when demolishing the grand evolutionary schemes of sociology, and had in fact, as Maitland reported, distinguished "laws" from "trends" and spoken of "the means, the very inadequate means, that we have of foretelling the future of bodies politic" at the meeting of the discussion club immediately preceding that at which Maitland delivered his own paper.[45] And yet, in defending the claims of political science, Sidgwick refused to surrender entirely the hope that it might eventually yield "guidance" for the statesman. Reiterating that such historical inductions could only ever be of secondary importance for politics, he nonetheless affirmed that "the laws of political evolution," which "it must always be the aim and aspiration of Political Science to attain," could at least indicate which political options, given our future development, would be practicable, even if they alone could not determine which of them we should choose (*DEP*, 45–6, 1–2).

A phrase like "the laws of political evolution" seems so much a standard part of the conceptual furniture of late nineteenth-century thought that we are prone simply to let it pass without remark; yet that Sidgwick, of all people, should use it points not only to the coercive power of this vocabulary but also to the implicit model of a science to which the study of politics was now expected to conform. The limited extent to which "the elements and characteristics of our own political society" might be foretold did not, however, exhaust the appeal of such a study. For whereas only very limited inductions could be made about the future of such states precisely because they were seen as being in the van of progress, when "dealing with societies other than their own" (the shift in usage here from "states" to "societies" illustrates the encompassing scope of the central categories of "comparative politics") one could find "instructive analogies . . . in the past condition of societies better known to us." "Analogies" strikes a more modest note than "laws," and, thanks primarily to Maine, the notion that the contemporary condition of, say, India could be illuminated by an investigation of medieval European history had become a commonplace by the 1880s and 1890s. The special interest of these particular comparisons lay, of course, in the fact that these "less advanced" societies were mostly subject to European government, and their futures could thus be affected by the actions of the instructed statesman and administrator. This emerges very clearly from an example that recurs several times in Sidgwick's treatment of this theme, where he argued (again following Maine) that "it might have prevented serious mistakes in our government of India, if the governing statesmen had had before their minds the historical development of land-tenure, as we now conceive it to have taken place in European countries" (*DEP*, 6).[46] Whereas *The Elements of Politics* analyzed the principles raised by "the rational discussion of political questions in modern states," it could be said with pardonable exaggeration that *The Development of European Polity* provided part of the necessary equipment for dealing with the affairs of "nonmodern" societies.

5

Once again, we are reminded of the centrality of "the theory of practice" for Sidgwick, and thereby of his conception of his role and of his audience. After all, he and his colleagues were, to some extent, educating future members of a governing class: This gave added point to a treatment of history in terms of politics, of politics in terms of government, and of government in terms of principles. Sidgwick had at one point characterized his "Opus Magnum on *Politics*" as an attempt "to treat systematically the chief questions for which the statesman has to find answers" and at another, in the passage just cited, as the analysis of "the chief general considerations that enter into the rational discussion of political questions in modern states" (*PSR*, 26). That he could have treated these as equivalent descriptions is revealing. If his work was not a reflection on the problems of politics *sub specie aeternitatis*, not a piece of "political philosophy" in the classical sense, this was in part because it aspired to a more immediate utility, in part because, with that end in mind, it was not unreasonable to take a substantial level of agreement on first principles for granted. The "rational discussion" it was addressed to was that carried on, at its best, equally in parliamentary debates and in the pages of the great reviews: It presumed an elite with some access to power, given to the discussion of current issues as matters of principle and, potentially, of precedent, confronted ultimately with the necessity of making decisions. In these ways it reflected a style of political life to which more than one late Victorian academic was happy to become accustomed.[47]

Sidgwick had become accustomed to it early, and he could not help lamenting its approaching decline, which he was far-sighted enough to regard as inevitable and fair-minded enough to recognize as not, from one point of view, altogether undesirable.

I have a certain alarm in respect of the movement of modern society towards Socialism, i.e. the more and more extensive intervention of Government with a view to palliate the inequalities in the distribution of wealth. At the same time I regard this movement as *on the whole* desirable and beneficent – the expectation of it belongs to the cheerful side of my forecast of the future; if duly moderated it *might*, I conceive, be purely beneficent, and bring improvement at every stage. But – judging from past experience – one must expect that so vast a change will not be realised without violent shocks and oscillations, great blunders followed by great disasters and consequent reactions; that the march of progress, perturbed by the selfish ambitions of leaders and the blind appetites of followers, will suffer many spasmodic deviations into paths which it will have painfully to retrace.

He went on to express his anxiety about "the force of the resistance which [the] machine of party government presents to the influence of enlightened and rational opinion" and concluded, self-mockingly, that "considering all the chances of misfortune that life offers, the chance of having one's railway shares confiscated is not prominent."[48]

Nonetheless, his own world, as I have already remarked, overlapped in several ways with that of the Victorian political class. Since he was in a position to discuss current legislation with cabinet ministers, sit on royal commissions on fiscal policy, and help to devise schemes for the education of future imperial administrators, it is hardly surprising if Sidgwick discovered that working out the best method for dealing with "the problems of practical politics" overrode the claims upon him exercised by his natural bent toward more speculative and more scholarly pursuits.[49] Nor was this concentration of his intellectual energies at odds with his mature political inclinations. Although he had been, as far as his temperament allowed, a Liberal idealist in his twenties, by the 1880s he had, like so many of his generation, become disenchanted with the demagoguery of Gladstonian Liberalism, and soon took the opportunity to board the ferry of Liberal Unionism, bound, eventually and under protest, to be beached on the Conservative shore: In the second 1886 election he voted Tory for the first time, returning from holiday to do so though the seat was a safe one.[50] After spending some days in the previous year at the Balfour family home, surrounded by Tory politicians, he had conceded that "their criticism of the present phase of Radicalism seems to me unanswerable," and he went on to muse on the implications of this concession for his own political identity: "Am I then becoming a Tory? Perhaps, but a strange one. Whoever saw a Tory dressed (symbolically) in sackcloth and ashes, and bewailing the necessity of conserving our glorious constitutions *pro tem*?"[51]

For this kind of half-willing, half-reluctant perception of the rational in the real, Sidgwick was characterized by one contemporary as "an English Hegel."[52] A sense of incongruity and bathos inevitably attends the comparison, though it catches a genuine similarity in some respects: Without referring to the source, one could not immediately be sure whether the aphorism that reading the newspaper was "the morning prayer of the realist" should be attributed to Hegel or to Sidgwick.[53] In the eyes of the latter, it hardly needs to be said, the Hegelian system exhibited too much of that "wonderful earnestness with which the most incomplete solutions of the universe are thrust upon us as complete and satisfying" ever to engage his deeply skeptical sympathies.[54] He had delivered his characteristic and irreversible verdict after an extended bout of wrestling with Hegel (in German) in 1870: "The method seems to me a mistake, and therefore the system a ruin."[55] It is noticeable how, in attempting to assess Sidgwick's influence, his pupils always returned to this question of *method*. It was the note upon which Sorley, his successor as professor of moral philosophy, chose to conclude his encomium: "Sidgwick exerted a powerful influence, both intellectual and moral, upon his pupils. But his temperament was too critical, his

intellect too evenly balanced, to admit of his teaching a dogmatic system.
... What he taught was much more a method, an attitude of mind."
And Maitland, surely his most distinguished pupil, spoke for those,
always the vast majority, who attended Sidgwick's lectures without
thereafter pursuing a philosophical career: "We turned away to other
studies or pursuits, but the memories of Sidgwick's lectures lived on.
The matter of the lectures, the theories and arguments, might be forgotten; but the method remained" (*M*, 306, 308).

That these obituary tributes should have been delivered by those who
were, literally, his pupils and that they should have concentrated on his
teaching was entirely appropriate, for Sidgwick was, as I suggested at
the beginning of this essay, as undeviatingly academic an author as it
was possible at that time to be. His literary manner was correspondingly
self-effacing, always conscious of the obligations of the textbook writer
– of thoroughness and clarity, of balanced summary and judicious resolution of controversy. Textbooks are, inevitably, boring, and so, sometimes, is Sidgwick. Certainly, in his treatises he is deliberately,
ponderously, self-denyingly dull; the playfulness and variety of reflection
that animate his letters and journal are not allowed beyond the gates
of the academy. He felt too intensely the importance of a professor's
being seen to be earnest. There is art, of a kind, in his books, but it is
employed to make his conclusions seem uncontentious: to pour oil,
gently, never to stir. His prose can seem suffocating, not so much because of the weight of qualifying clauses but (partly a consequence of
that) because it comes to seem impossible, or at least ill advised, to
disagree with him. There is such an ostentatiously conscientious effort
on his part to get it right, just right, that the prose comes to seem utterly
impersonal, as if transcribed by the Jeevesian amanuensis of some academic Committee of All the Talents. And in this it was the perfect
medium for the method of reflective analysis, which was intended, after
all, to get our *shared* intuitions straightened out, properly stated,
systematized.

In matters of both style and doctrine, Sidgwick is invariably set alongside, and usually a little below, Mill, and in some ways this is obviously
right. Sidgwick himself clearly felt the weight of the shadow: "Whenever
I have by accident tried to say something that he has said before, without
knowing, his way of saying it always seems indefinitely better."[56] We
might expect Sidgwick to be the more consistent Utilitarian because it
would not surprise us if he proved to be more consistent in his exposition
of any philosophical doctrine, but that only points to the importance of
deeper differences of temperament and role. If it is true to say that Mill
was intellectually and politically the more red-blooded of the two, we

must recognize what that tells us about Sidgwick's tendency to anemia. Mill was far more of a polemicist and a preacher; if he yearned for consensus, he was not above relishing a victory. He was always partisan, always, despite – or perhaps as a cause of – his fondness for altruism and cooperation, a good hater. Sidgwick, by contrast, shunned conflict and regarded no man as an enemy; nuggets of truth could always be extracted from the shale of exaggeration, given good will and a cool head. It is characteristic that in one of his earliest articles the twenty-three-year-old Sidgwick should observe that "what has most hampered political thinkers in all ages is the little free play that has been allowed to their intellects by passion, prejudice, and interest."[57] Mill was by nature the more political animal. Compared to a skillful manager of the Commons or an experienced constituency agent, he was no doubt a naive doctrinaire; but compared to Sidgwick, he was a bonny fighter, even a good party man.[58] Mill was instinctively drawn to politics – oftener to crusades, perhaps, and certainly to manifestos, but to conflict, argument, action of a sort. Sidgwick, like many academics, naturally took the part of the civil servant: That his books often read like committee reports is among their chief drawbacks as books; as a series of minutes they would be outstanding.

As this suggests, the two authors also stood at different heights above the ground, with Mill, perhaps surprisingly, the more elevated. It is true that whereas Mill was strident in declaring his commitment, Sidgwick spoke from the higher ground of disinterested analysis. But, more generally, Mill's vision was limited only by the limits of human progress; he always managed to give the impression that the subject under discussion was but a passing local phase in some much larger development, the outlines of which he, and sometimes only he, could glimpse from his intellectually offshore vantage point. Sidgwick, on the other hand, was a far more apprehensive political traveler, nervously rehearsing the potential mishaps of any journey and made edgy by the uncertainty of the destination; the longer he studied the brochures for utopia, the more he warmed to the idea of staying at home. Nor was this simply timidity or unimaginativeness, though Sidgwick had his share of those qualities; it sprang, rather, from a kind of unshowy moral seriousness about the temptations to self-deception offered by political excitement, and an intellectual conviction that only immediate consequences could be calculated with any reasonable reliability. "Bewailing the necessity of conserving our glorious constitution *pro tem*": He bewailed because he saw its defects, but pro tem – the present having imperatives where the future could only hold out promises – its conservation was a duty.

And this marks not only a personal contrast with Mill but also the distance between the roles and opportunities available in early and late Victorian political life. One can see how Bagehot, for example, stood at a yet further remove from actual veneration of the pieties of Whiggism than Macaulay, even though the latter was already able to regard the glorious constitution with a certain pragmatic detachment.[59] But even Bagehot's identity as a political commentator depended upon those pieties still having some resonance for his audience: Describing politics as "but a piece of business" only acquires its force by contrast with a more sonorous description, and Bagehot relished his role of rug puller because there were still people standing on the rug. Sidgwick was writing for a different audience, a later as well as a more academic one, and this called for a different voice; whereas Macaulay seemed to be addressing the House and Bagehot chatting in the club, Sidgwick was always lecturing in the classroom. This also means that none of the earlier political labels is now appropriate. Though a Utilitarian, he was hardly a Philosophic Radical, in part because he was, temperamentally, so little of any kind of radical, just as his lack of any felt emotional continuity with the shibboleths of Whiggism meant that he was not really a philosophic Whig, either. Even the more clearly mid-Victorian political identities are inexact: Too much of a skeptic to be a Liberal enthusiast, too much of a realist to be a Tory diehard, he could perhaps best be classed, in this vocabulary, as an intellectual Peelite, intent on getting on with the business in hand while maintaining a principled aloofness.

Party labels, however, are necessarily inappropriate to capture the character of someone with so little sectarian feeling. One reviewer slyly remarked that Sidgwick's work exhibited "good sense intensified almost to the point of genius."[60] Sidgwick presumably approved of, even savored, the "almost"; certainly, he must have been pleased that he had managed to make the divisive problems of politics appear amenable to "good sense." He realized, of course, that there was more to politics, potentially, than "the ordinary experience of civilized life" allowed for, but it was part of his conception of his role to insist upon that experience as the only practical starting point for responsible scientific treatment.

Notes

1 Bryce to Sidgwick, while reading the proofs of *The Elements of Politics*, February 15, 1889. Bryce MSS 15. 139, Bodleian Library, Oxford.

2 The Lent term of 1883, just prior to his election to the Knightbridge chair; see *M*, 366.

3 On this campaign, see Lewis Campbell, *The Nationalization of the Old English Universities* (London: Chapman and Hall, 1901).

4 The printed minutes of the meeting, headed "The Reorganization of Academical Study," are in the Henry Sidgwick Papers, Wren Library, Trinity College, Cambridge University; Add. MSS c. 97.23 (quotation at p. 8).

5 "His truest monument is . . . the difference between Cambridge as it is now and the Cambridge of forty years ago." *Pilot*, September 15, 1900 (cutting in Sidgwick Papers, Add. MSS c. 104.13).

6 Sidgwick to his mother, July 11 and December 28, 1874; Sidgwick Papers, Add. MSS c. 99. 177 and 180.

7 Sidgwick to Alexander Macmillan, December 12, 1874; Macmillan Papers, British Library, Add. MSS 55159/6.

8 Sidgwick to A. J. Patterson, July 26, 1886, Sidgwick Papers, Add. MSS c. 98.9. Not, of course, that the discontents endemic to the academic life were unknown to him: On his fiftieth birthday he confided to his journal the desire to leave Cambridge and "the desire of literary independence, to be able to speak when I like as a man to men, and not three times a week as a salaried teacher to pupils" (*M*, 489).

9 His sister was married to E. W. Benson; Arthur Balfour was his wife's brother.

10 H. J. Paton (editor of the *Contemporary Review*) to Sidgwick, March 10, 1886, Sidgwick Papers, Add. MSS c. 95.2; Sidgwick, *M*, 457, 561. Paton's phrase may have been an allusion to the so-called *Kathedersozialisten* who were receiving a lot of attention in Germany at the time.

11 See Collini, *Public Moralists: Political Thought and Intellectual Life in Britain, 1850–1930* (Oxford: Oxford University Press, 1991), chap. 4.

12 Sidgwick to J. A. Symonds, December 1, 1887, *M*, 481.

13 C. G. Ritchie, "Review: *The Elements of Politics,* by Henry Sidgwick," *International Journal of Ethics* 2 (1891–2): 254–7; Sidgwick to Symonds, November 2, 1887, *M*, 480.

14 Ritchie, "Review," p. 254.

15 Ibid., p. 257; cf. Hastings Rashdall, "Review of *Elements of Politics*," *Economic Review* 2 (1892): 275–8.

16 For this genre, see Stefan Collini, Donald Winch, and John Burrow, *That Noble Science of Politics: A Study in Nineteenth-Century Intellectual History* (Cambridge: Cambridge University Press, 1983), essay 7.

17 J. M. Keynes, in *Memorials of Alfred Marshall*, ed. A. C. Pigou (London, 1925), p. 57.

18 See Collini, Winch, and Burrow, *That Noble Science*, essay 11.

19 E.g., William C. Havard, *Henry Sidgwick and Later Utilitarian Political Philosophy* (Gainesville: University of Florida Press, 1959), passim.

20 John Morley to Sidgwick, November 8, 1878, and January 15, 1879, Sidgwick Papers, Add. MSS c. 94. 144–7. The article in question, entitled "Economic Method," appeared in the *Fortnightly Review* 31 (1879): 301–18.

21 Sidgwick to H. S. Foxwell, November 21, 1886, Foxwell Papers, in the possession of R. D. Freeman.

22 The first chapter of *PPE*1, "The Present State of Economic Controversy in

England and the Special Aim of the Present Work," contains a judicious account of the English *Methodenstreit* and of Sidgwick's relation to it.

23 For the first response, see, e.g., J. N. Keynes, "Henry Sidgwick," *Economic Journal* 10 (1900): 588, and W. R. Sorley, "Review of Alfred Marshall's *Principles of Economics*," *Mind*, o.s. 16 (1891): 1213. For the second response, see Sidgwick to Lady Welby, August 11, 1891: "It is a difficult matter to persuade a plain man to go through the process necessary to attain precision of thought: it requires great literary skill in presenting the process. I tried to do something of this sort in my *Principles of Political Economy* but I fear I bored the reader horribly. A German student of political economy told Mr Ashley . . . that he tried to read my book but found it '*reine philologie.*' " Sidgwick Papers, Add. MSS 98.64.

24 "I want to write a great book on Politics during the next ten years, and am afraid it will be too academic if I do not somehow go into the actual struggle. But how?" Journal entry, April 4, 1885, *M*, 407.

25 Sidgwick to H. G. Dakyns, May 1861, *M*, 66. "Though," he added, "I cannot get over my scepticism as to the elaborate Hare-ian scheme."

26 The best, and indeed the only, discussion of the development of Sidgwick's thinking on ethics and philosophy generally is the excellent study by J. B. Schneewind, *Sidgwick's Ethics and Victorian Moral Philosophy* (Oxford: Oxford University Press, 1977); see esp. pp. 40–62.

27 Sidgwick to Oscar Browning, September 27, 1865, *M*, 131–2. Cf. his remarks in the previous year about how "history will always be subsidiary to Politik," and the following year his announcement: "Take notice that I have finally parted from Mill and Comte – not without tears and wailings and cutting of the hair"; *M*, 124 and 158.

28 Sidgwick to Alfred Marshall, July or August 1871, Sidgwick Papers, Add. MSS c. 100.96.

29 Sidgwick to Bryce, April 19, 1891, Bryce MSS 15.70.

30 Sidgwick to Bryce, April 28, 1891, Bryce MSS 15.76. Compare Mill's admission while writing book 5 of the *Principles* on "the province of government": "I have felt the same difficulty you do about the *axiomata media*. I suspect there are none which do not vary with time, place, and circumstance. I doubt if much more can be done in a scientific treatment of the question than to point out a certain number of *pro's* and a certain number of *con's* of a more or less general application, and with some attempt at an estimation of the comparative importance of each, leaving the balance to be struck in each particular case as it arises." Mill to John Austin, April 13, 1847, *Works*, vol. 13, *The Earlier Letters of John Stuart Mill, 1812–1848*, ed. Francis E. Minera (London: Routledge and Kegan Paul, 1963), p. 712.

31 Ritchie, "Review," pp. 254–7. Hastings Rashdall made a similar complaint: "We do feel that in this bulky treatise a little more might have been done to express the idea that the ultimate end of government is not served by just maintaining the status quo – carrying on the business, so to speak, which it

has inherited, in a respectable and dignified manner." Rashdall, "Review of *Elements of Politics*," p. 278.

32 In the present case, given Sidgwick's efforts on behalf of the education of women and similar causes, this almost certainly did not represent his own considered view.

33 The general argument of this section of the book is carefully discussed in Schneewind, *Sidgwick's Ethics*, esp. chaps. 9 and 12, though Schneewind does not deal with its political implications.

34 These criticisms, and the contemporary expectations to which they were addressed, are briefly discussed in Stefan Collini, *Liberalism and Sociology: L. T. Hobhouse and Political Argument in England, 1880–1914* (Cambridge: Cambridge University Press, 1979), pp. 193–6, where full references are also given.

35 For its application to Mill, see Collini, Winch, and Burrow, *That Noble Science*, p. 156.

36 The phrase is taken, in this instance, from his journal entry for January 1, 1886, *M*, 435.

37 On the place of "Inductive Political Science" in the Cambridge curriculum, see Collini, Winch, and Burrow, *That Noble Science*, essay 11; Sidgwick acknowledged the use of Seeley's (then unpublished) lectures in *EP*1, vii.

38 These observations apply with particular force to Seeley – see esp. his *Introduction to Political Science: Two Series of Lectures* (London, 1896), pp. 1–39. See also the discussion in Collini, Winch, and Burrow, *That Noble Science*, pp. 228–30, and for Mill and Maine, see pp. 133–4, 215–18.

39 For a discussion of "sociology" as understood in late nineteenth-century Britain, see Collini, *Liberalism and Sociology*, pp. 187–206.

40 Henry Sidgwick, "Political Prophecy and Sociology" (1894), reprinted in *MEA*; quotation at pp. 226–7. See also the discussion in Collini, *Public Moralists*, chap. 6.

41 Henry Sidgwick, "Review of *The Elements of Sociology*," *Economic Journal* (1899): 411. On the influence of his criticisms, see Abrams's remark: "Sidgwick's argument . . . became the orthodox basis for resistance to sociology – above all for academic resistance." Philip Abrams, *The Origins of British Sociology, 1834–1914* (Chicago: University of Chicago Press, 1968), p. 82. Seventy years later, the first professor of sociology at Cambridge could still take Sidgwick's criticisms as his reference point: J. A. Barnes, *Sociology in Cambridge* (Cambridge: Cambridge University Press, 1970), passim.

42 Journal entries, July 15, August 11 and 22, 1885, *M*, 417, 421, 422.

43 Sidgwick to Miss Cannon, January 1, 1895, *M*, 533.

44 F. W. Maitland to H. A. L. Fisher, December 16, 1894, in *The Letters of Frederic William Maitland*, ed. C. H. S. Fifoot (Cambridge: Cambridge University Press, 1965), p. 128. The "point," a criticism of the possibility of inference from the materials of political science, had been made by Fisher in his article "Modern Historians and Their Methods," *Fortnightly Review* 56 (1894): 810.

45 F. W. Maitland, "The Body Politic," in *The Collected Papers of Frederic William Maitland*, ed. H. A. L. Fisher, 3 vols. (Cambridge: Cambridge University Press, 1911), 3:285–303. It is not known when Maitland's paper was delivered – Fifoot's guess is May 1900 (*Letters*, p. 213), though it may have been earlier – but he had obviously been making its essential point to Sidgwick for some time; consider, e.g., Maitland to Sidgwick, February 28, 1896 (*Letters*, p. 148), criticizing Freeman and, by implication, the whole enterprise of comparative politics.

46 Cf. *PPE*, 48.

47 There is a helpful treatment of Sidgwick as an "academic liberal" in Christopher Harvie, *The Lights of Liberalism: Academic Liberals and the Challenge of Democracy, 1860–1886* (London: Lane, 1976), on which see also Stefan Collini, "Political Theory and the 'Science of Society' in Victorian Britain," *Historical Journal* 23 (1980): 203–31.

48 Journal entry, March 17, 1886, *M*, 441–2.

49 The *Memoir* abounds with evidence of his intimacy with cabinet ministers of both parties: aside from the Balfour circle, Bryce and Trevelyan were among his leading informants. For his part in designing the new scheme of entrance examinations, which came into effect for both the Indian Civil Service and then the Home Civil Service in the 1890s, see Collini, Winch, and Burrow, *That Noble Science*, pp. 353–7.

50 Journal entry, July 3, 1886, *M*, 449. The evolution of Sidgwick's political allegiances requires more careful analysis than can be given here; there is some useful material in Harvie, *Lights of Liberalism*.

51 Journal entry, January 26, 1885, *M*, 398–9.

52 Ritchie, "Review," p. 255.

53 The remark is quoted in Shlomo Avineri, *Hegel's Theory of the Modern State* (Cambridge: Cambridge University Press, 1972).

54 Journal entry, December 22, 1884, *M*, 395.

55 Sidgwick to Roden Noel, September 8, 1870, *M*, 238; emphasis in original.

56 Journal entry, August 9, 1885, *M*, 420–1; cf. 133–4.

57 Henry Sidgwick, "Alexis de Tocqueville" (1861), *MEA*, 368.

58 See the discussion in Stefan Collini, "The Member for Westminster: Doctrinaire Philosopher, Party Hack, or Public Moralist?" *Utilitas* 2 (1990): 307–22.

59 See Collini, Winch, and Burrow, *That Noble Science*, esp. pp. 172–3.

60 Rashdall, "Review," p. 275.

13

Rethinking tradition
Sidgwick and the philosophy of the via media

JAMES T. KLOPPENBERG

Although Henry Sidgwick is doubtless best known for his role in the reformulation of utilitarianism, he also played an important part in a broader transatlantic community of discourse. Having written elsewhere about Sidgwick's ideas in the context of that more general transformation of American and European philosophy and political theory,[1] I will concentrate in this essay on the relation between Sidgwick's ideas and those of the American pragmatists William James and John Dewey. Both James and Dewey admired Sidgwick, and James knew him well not only as a philosopher but as a fellow member of the Society for Psychical Research. After Sidgwick's death in 1900, James wrote a moving tribute to Sidgwick's widow describing the "flawlessness in quality" of his character as well as his genius as a philosopher. In Dewey's estimation, Sidgwick stood as a "monument" to all that was best in the British liberal tradition because of his "simplicity, openmindedness, absolute fairness and sincerity."[2] But it was not merely Sidgwick's personality that attracted James and Dewey. They were drawn equally to Sidgwick's incisive criticism of prevailing options available in late nineteenth-century thought: idealism and positivism in epistemology, Kantian intuitionism and Benthamite utilitarianism in ethics, and revolutionary socialism and laissez-faire liberalism in political theory. Like James and Dewey, Sidgwick worked to create alternatives to such positions not only because he was by nature a moderate – although he surely was that – but because he genuinely believed that more fruitful philosophical and political arguments lay between, or beyond, those poles. He sought synthesis, for reasons and in ways that I will suggest here, not for convenience but from conviction.

When James died in 1910, Dewey assessed his impact on modern thought in terms that can be extended to Sidgwick as well. Reaching

This essay is based on the discussion of Sidgwick in James T. Kloppenberg, *Uncertain Victory: Social Democracy and Progressivism in European and American Thought, 1870–1920* (New York: Oxford University Press, 1986).

intellectual maturity in the late 1860s, the generation of Sidgwick and James (born, respectively, in 1838 and 1842) faced the prospect of choosing between a lingering Hegelian or romantic idealism and emerging forms of scientific naturalism. Confronting such mutually exclusive world views, James set out to find what Dewey called "a *via media* between natural science and the ideal interests of morals and religion." At first, Dewey wrote, "James stood practically alone – a voice crying in the wilderness." Slowly, however, "the temper of imagination changed," and by the dawn of the twentieth century James found himself riding the crest of the zeitgeist.[3] James recognized as clearly as Dewey that a process of intellectual convergence was transforming the transatlantic world of ideas. In a letter he wrote to the English philosopher F. C. S. Schiller about Dewey and his associates at the University of Chicago, James expressed his belief "that from such opposite poles minds are moving toward a common centre, that old compartments and divisions are breaking down, and that a very inclusive new school may be formed."[4] Because Sidgwick, like James and Dewey, drew explicitly from the traditions of idealism and empiricism, I will follow Dewey's lead and designate them the philosophers of the via media, although I should stress that I am not trying to argue that they occupied identical positions on all issues. Because Sidgwick died before James and Dewey completed much of their most important work, he wrote less about them than they did about him. Nevertheless, the resonances among the three thinkers' ideas may add an intriguing dimension to our understanding of Sidgwick's historical significance, and their comparison also reveals Sidgwick's crucial importance in the development of pragmatism.

Sidgwick's misgivings about Christianity paralleled James's, as did his persistent fascination with the phenomenon of religious faith. Though both remained interested in, and even sympathetic toward, various unconventional forms of belief, Sidgwick felt compelled to acknowledge "the provisional character of the structure of thought" to which faith belonged, and he refused to cover his doubts with the veneer of confidence demanded by propriety but unwarranted by his own experience. His perspective left room for hope but excluded certainty that reason could solve the most difficult problems we face. As he put it in the concluding passage of the first edition of *The Methods of Ethics*, "the prolonged effort of the human intellect to frame a perfect ideal of rational conduct is seen to have been foredoomed to inevitable failure" (*PSR*, 243; *ME*1, 473). We must proceed, Sidgwick advised, without knowing – or pretending to know – that our answers are correct, relying on experience and hoping it will shave the edge of despair from our uncertainty. Sidgwick shared with James and Dewey the conviction that, although our knowledge can only be provisional, we can use the compass of accumulated cultural experience to help us choose among the options open to us. In these thinkers' historical sensibility, the weight of the past and the potential of the future are held in delicate balance, for individuals collectively must determine their own values and decide their course, recognizing as boundaries human experience rather than God's or nature's law. When they cut the moorings to certainty, the philosophers of the via media simultaneously liberated the imagination and imposed an awkward responsibility on those who could presume to provide guidance in such an uncertain universe of ideas.

Though Sidgwick traced his roots to the tradition of British empiricism, he was uneasy with various aspects of that tradition. He denied, first of all, the adequacy of associationism's mechanistic model of causality as a basis for understanding how we know. He insisted that "no attempt to give a physical explanation of Cognition, or even to analyse it completely into more elementary psychical facts, has succeeded or is likely to succeed" (*GSM*, 3). The root of this difficulty lay in the rigid separation of subject from object posited by associationists, a separation that James in particular sought to end by the more fluid conception of experience he presented first in *The Principles of Psychology* (1890) and developed in his later writings. Beyond that dualism lay an equally basic inconsistency that Sidgwick traced to the materialism of scientific psychology. From the Greek atomists onward, materialists have found it difficult to justify intuited principles according to empirical procedures. Sidgwick pointed out that empiricists since Locke had relied on the mind's ability to establish relations among discrete sensations, yet they had discovered no empirical foundation for that claim. Similarly, the principles of inference underlying the central process of association and guiding the construction of knowledge out of sense data rested on no satisfactory empirical grounds. These elements of empirical psychology, Sidgwick concluded, had no firmer basis than the claims of metaphysical intuitionists such as T. H. Green, whom hardheaded scientists scorned for their wishful thinking. Though Sidgwick surely considered himself an empiricist, he demanded that empiricism divest itself of dogmatic materialism and admit the inadequacy of scientific naturalism as a satisfactory model for understanding human knowledge. In an unpublished essay probably written about 1870, in which he articulated the impulse that drove James's inquiry into – and uneasiness with – psychology, Sidgwick put this crucial point succinctly: "We are impelled to science by a desire to get knowledge, to philosophy by dissatisfaction with the knowledge we have got."[5] A large part of that dissatisfaction, Sidgwick believed, stemmed from the tendency of empirical psychologists to focus so narrowly on the sources of experience that they neglected to investigate its meaning. In his awareness of the centrality of value to the texture of human sensibility, Sidgwick likewise identified a theme that was to be of great importance for James and Dewey.[6]

Like James and Dewey, Sidgwick was an eclectic on principle as well as by temperament. He resisted efforts to account for knowledge by either a "physical explanation" or a flight from experience toward idealism. In his essay "The Criteria of Truth and Error" (1900), Sidgwick argued that neither rationalist nor empiricist methods taken in isolation could provide "the ultimately valid basis" for epistemology. He suggested the consideration of two complementary approaches, intuitive verification and discursive verification, which relied on the emergence of consensus to resolve nagging questions that could not be answered by any other methods of testing knowledge. Although Sidgwick emphasized the "special and preeminent importance" of discursive verification, which derived from empiricism, he claimed that "the special characteristic of *my* philosophy is to keep the importance of the others in view." The dead ends encountered by each epistemological tradition could be avoided only by creatively selecting different approaches for the different kinds of knowledge we require (*GSM*, 3).[7] A similar endorsement of creative selection marked James's *Pragmatism*, in which he counseled drawing on both "tender minded" rationalism and "tough minded" empiricism to overcome the inadequacies of both. These philosophers of the via media were among the first to appreciate what scientists as well as critical theorists now take for granted: the relation between the results and the methods of investigation. By opting for flexible and open-ended combinations of intuition and empiricism, Sidgwick helped inaugurate the nonfoundationalist pragmatism that James and Dewey later helped make a central feature of twentieth-century intellectual life.

These renegades emphasized the continuity between this new conception of knowledge and practical activity. Feeling, judging, and willing together constitute only the first stage of a process that is completed in action. The idea that rational choices are not merely a matter of reflection but must issue in purposive action is most closely identified with Dewey's philosophy, and it is true that it was the cornerstone of his instrumentalism. Yet he was hardly alone in emphasizing the need to fuse the processes of reflection and activity, which Western philosophers had tended to keep separate since the Greeks distinguished *theoria* from *praxis*. An epigrammatic entry in Sidgwick's journal of 1867 expressed his opposition to the conventional spectator theory of knowledge in words that could have served equally well as a manifesto for James or

Dewey. "Theory ∞ Practice. Let every effort be used to form this chain. Practise [*sic*] alone can correct theory. Theory alone can inform practice." If everyone, all at once, were to act upon what they claimed to think and believe, Sidgwick continued, "to what great grief we should come in details! but how rapidly we should improve not only in Practice but in Theory."[8] This emphasis on the interdependence of contemplation and action, on the completion of theoria in praxis, signaled a dramatic departure from the image of the mind as mirror prevalent in Western philosophy since Descartes, and it was tied to these thinkers' antidualist conception of experience. When the subject and object are perceived as related immediately rather than as two distinct substances, the gap separating external reality from the thinking process vanishes. It is then only a short step to the conclusion that we must act upon our environment, not simply think about it. Though that conclusion may appear to echo Marx's challenge to Feuerbach, these thinkers doubted their ability to provide blueprints for appropriate forms of individual or social activity.

Indeed, the same spirit of uncertainty that characterized Sidgwick's scattered comments on epistemology flowed through the ethical writings of these philosophers of the via media. Dewey argued in 1907 that although the fundamental postulate of Sidgwick's *Methods of Ethics* "was the basic identity of happiness and duty," when Sidgwick found these values "discrepant" in the world of experience, he conceded his doubts about the possibility of reconciling the contradictory demands of the good and the right. Sidgwick "combined the scientific, inductive and empirical interest with great personal sensitiveness to ideal and spiritual aspirations, and he found himself to the last unable satisfactorily to reconcile the two tendencies." In its attempt as well as its failure to achieve that reconciliation, Dewey concluded, Sidgwick's *Methods of Ethics* exemplified "one of the most characteristic features of recent thought."[9] Sidgwick's frank admission of uncertainty in the face of the irreconcilable demands of "happiness and duty" was his most important contribution as a moral philosopher, at least from the perspective of James and Dewey. Sidgwick is properly classified as a utilitarian, but it is worth emphasizing that he designed *The Methods of Ethics* to synthesize the best from both the utilitarian and intuitionist schools of ethics. To use Sidgwick's own image, the truth lies between the Scylla and the Charybdis of intuitionism and utilitarianism. He maintained that the utilitarians' standard of maximizing pleasure must supplement the principles of common-sense morality, namely, justice, prudence, and benevolence, because he judged such precepts to be frayed around the edges. Although "perfectly adequate to give practical guidance to common people in common circumstances," these principles provide inadequate guidance in difficult cases. Moreover, when they contradict one another, no principle of reconciliation appears satisfactory. Sidgwick concluded that no intuited ethical maxims provided "clear and precise principles for determining the extent of duty in any case." He contended that Kant's categorical imperative was too loose and that a volition consistent with that precept "may after all be wrong." Kant's ethics, like intuitionism in general, was overly formal. There are certain absolute practical principles, Sidgwick wrote, that are manifestly true, "but they are of too abstract a nature, and too universal in their scope, to enable us to ascertain by immediate application of them what we ought to do in any particular case (ME, 361, 262, 210, 379). To supplement these principles, Sidgwick returned to utilitarianism, and in his own ethical theory he tried to compensate for the weaknesses of each system.

Sidgwick was careful to distinguish his universalistic utilitarianism from the egoistic utilitarianism of Bentham. Reflecting the distance separating Sidgwick from his predecessors, Dewey classified him with Green and James Martineau under the rubric of "Intuitionism,"[10] and Sidgwick's treatment of utilitarianism in *The Methods of Ethics* seems to substantiate Dewey's argument. Sidgwick repeatedly criticized the reduction of ethics to simple calculations of pleasure and pain, and he insisted that "it is manifestly possible that our prospect of pleasure resulting from any course of action may largely depend on our conception of it as right or otherwise." It was over this central question of the desire for pleasure as the root of motivation that Sidgwick explicitly parted company with Bentham's psychological egoism:

Our conscious active impulses are so far from being always directed toward the attainment of pleasure or the avoidance of pain for ourselves, that we can find everywhere in consciousness extra-regarding impulses, directed towards something that is not pleasure, nor relief from pain; and, indeed, a most important part of our pleasure depends upon the existence of such impulses.

Moreover, the desire for personal pleasure tends occasionally to conflict with the desire to satisfy our extra-regarding impulses, and this incompatibility "is no doubt specially prominent in the case of the impulse toward the end which most markedly competes in ethical controversy with pleasure; the love of virtue for its own sake, or desire to do what is right as such." Sidgwick's use of Kant and Bentham to supplement each other was deliberate, and he insisted that he adopted that synthetic position only after reflecting on the inadequacies of the intuitionist and utilitarian traditions when judged against the evidence he derived from experience (ME, 40 f. 52).[11]

Dewey's early writings on ethics illustrate not only this convergence of ideas regarding the inadequacy of both intuitionism and utilitarianism in general but also the special importance of Sidgwick's *Methods of Ethics*. In *Outlines of a Critical Theory of Ethics* (1891), Dewey challenged hedonism on the grounds that it substituted individual pleasure for the "fulfillment of human powers and functions." Hedonists reduced the sense of satisfaction from social action to "mere having, to bare feelings or affections eliminating the element of doing." Dewey derived that part of his analysis as much from Aristotle's idea of praxis as from Sidgwick, and he supplemented it with references to critiques of utilitarianism advanced by Green and James. But in his sections of the *Ethics* (1908) that he coauthored with James Tufts, Dewey repeatedly cited Sidgwick's *Methods of Ethics*, and he compiled the various arguments Sidgwick leveled against Benthamite utilitarianism into a comprehensive list of its difficulties. After using James on the social self and the desire for approval as a source of motivation, and Green on the confusion of the desire for goodness and the desire for pleasure, Dewey invoked Sidgwick on the absence of any empirical foundation for the definition of happiness as the ultimate good.[12]

Dewey followed Sidgwick in criticizing both of John Stuart Mill's revisions of utilitarianism as inconsistent with the fundamental tenets of Bentham's philosophy. Although both Dewey and Sidgwick considered the introduction of a qualitative standard to be a necessary revision, they pointed out that such a standard rested on an a priori judgment incompatible with psychological hedonism. As Sidgwick wrote, "In order to work out consistently the method that takes pleasure as the sole ultimate end of rational conduct [i.e., ethical hedonism], Bentham's proposition [that "pushpin is as good as poetry"] and all *qualitative* comparison of pleasures must really resolve itself into quantitative." To be consistent, one must accept psychological hedonism as well as ethical hedonism. When other qualifications are introduced, which experience compels us to do, "then we are clearly introducing a non-hedonistic ground of preference: and if this is done, the method adopted is a perplexing mixture of Intuitionism and Hedonism." Sidgwick in fact opted for a similar, albeit more straightforward, mixture in his own ethical theory, but he forthrightly acknowledged its reliance on principles that departed from hedonism. Second, Dewey and Sidgwick offered the familiar criticism that Mill failed to establish the desirability of the general good on hedonistic grounds. Mill argued that each individual ought to desire the general good rather than individual pleasure, yet as Sidgwick pointed out,

This proposition is not established by Mill's reasoning, even if we grant that what is actually desired may be legitimately inferred to be in this sense desirable.

For an aggregate of actual desires, each directed toward a different part of the general happiness, does not constitute an actual desire for the general happiness, existing in any individual; and Mill would certainly not contend that a desire which does not exist in any individual can possibly exist in an aggregate of individuals.

Although Sidgwick endorsed the principle that the individual ought to desire the general welfare, he noted that there was a gap in Mill's argument that could be filled only by "some such proposition as that which I have tried to exhibit as the intuition of Rational Benevolence" (*ME*, 94–5, 388).[13] In short, as Dewey maintained, there is "no *direct road* from individualistic hedonism" or "private pleasure" to "universalistic" hedonism or "general pleasure." Like Sidgwick, Dewey adopted a universalistic utilitarian standard. He conceded that a similar, "thoroughly socialized ideal of happiness is the most characteristic feature of Mill's ethics. It is noble," he concluded, "but it is not hedonism."[14]

Contemporary moral philosophers may be tempted to overlook or even deny Sidgwick's synthetic purpose in *The Methods of Ethics*, an unfortunate but understandable tendency given the peculiar publishing history of the book. In its original form, the book included numerous historical references illustrating Sidgwick's deliberate attempt to bring together ideas from different sources. Each successive edition, however, contained fewer of these historical references. Sidgwick's discussion of his revision of Kantian ideas, to cite a notable example, all but disappeared after the first edition. Sidgwick believed ethics to be a progressive discipline, and he thought that consideration of the historical debate and the gradual emergence of a consensus within the community of ethical philosophers was of crucial importance. Each time he revised the book, however, he covered more carefully the tracks of the traditions he followed, and as a result the later editions of *The Methods of Ethics*, including especially the seventh edition that is most widely used today, only partly reflect his concern with history and his synthetic intent.[15]

"Hedonism and Ultimate Good," an essay Sidgwick wrote three years after publication of *The Methods of Ethics*, demonstrates his conviction that philosophers were moving toward the acceptance of certain basic ethical principles. Sidgwick described developments in "Intuition, Utilitarianism, and Evolutionism" that pointed toward agreement, and he concluded that "this convergence of several distinct arguments has had, I think, a considerable effect on contemporary thought; and probably a large majority of reflective persons are now prepared to accept 'Common Good' as the ultimate end for which moral rules exist." In "Hedonism and Ultimate Good," Sidgwick described how the principles of justice, prudence, and rational benevolence drew together intuitionist and utilitarian ethics:

The fundamental intuitions of conscience or the practical reason on which one school (Kantians and intuitionists) have always laid stress, are merely the expression in different aspects or relations of that ideal subordination of individual impulses to universal ends on which alone Utilitarianism, as a system of ethics, can rationally rest. Thus the essence of Justice or Equity, insofar as it is absolutely obligatory, is that different individuals are not to be treated differently, except on grounds of universal application: which grounds, again, are given in the principle of Rational Benevolence, that sets before each man the good of all others as an object of pursuit no less worthy than his own.[16]

Yet the principle of rational benevolence may not entirely resolve the conflict between the principles of justice and prudence. The reasonable requirements imposed by the self do not always neatly coincide with the reasonable requirements of one's sense of equity. This difficulty, rooted in the two dimensions of the individual as a private consciousness and a member of a community, admits no easy solution, and Sidgwick agonized over it throughout his career. Sidgwick's anguished conclusion to *The Methods of Ethics* reveals his uncertainty. He denied that he could offer any "practical solution of this fundamental contradiction," and he admitted that the ultimate reconciliation of duty and self-interest extends beyond the limits of practical reason. In cases of genuine conflict, he suggested, we can at best accept as a moral imperative the duty to maximize general happiness, a hybrid hypothesis "logically necessary to avoid a fundamental contradiction of one chief department of thought." He declined to speculate on the validity of metaphysical or religious claims to verify that hypothesis. Instead, he compared it revealingly to the "edifice of physical science." Sidgwick admitted that those who accept scientific propositions as ultimately true might legitimately demand an equally solid basis for their ethical principles, but then he abruptly turned the tables on such self-confident and tough-minded empiricists. If, Sidgwick suggested in his tortured closing sentence,

we find that in our supposed knowledge of the world of nature propositions are commonly taken to be universally true, which yet seem to rest on no other grounds than that we have a strong disposition to accept them, and that they are indispensable to the systematic coherence of our beliefs, – it will be more difficult to reject a similarly supported assumption in ethics, without opening the door to universal scepticism. (*ME*, 508–9)

Sidgwick appreciated what recent antifoundationalists have claimed about the fiduciary aspect of all claims to knowledge, scientific as well as ethical. *The Methods of Ethics* thus culminates in an acknowledgment of the limits of human reason and the assertion of a Jamesian "will to believe" in the principle of benevolence rather than an irresistible demonstration of its validity.

James's scattered writings about ethics strongly resembled Sidgwick's arguments in *The Methods of Ethics*. In "The Moral Philosopher and the Moral Life," James emphasized the antagonism "between the ethics of infinite and mysterious obligation from on high, and those of prudence and the satisfaction of merely finite need." Like Sidgwick, he denied that the conflict between those demands could be resolved in the absence of a religious appeal, but James was less reluctant to proclaim the attractiveness of faith for pragmatic moral purposes: "The strenuous type of character will on the battle-field of human history always outwear the easy-going type, and religion will drive irreligion to the wall." James offered as his final conclusion that "the stable and systematic moral universe for which the ethical philosopher asks," and in which self-interest and duty might be reconciled, "is fully possible only in a world where there is a divine thinker with all-enveloping demands."[17] James, like Sidgwick, denied the possibility of solving the problem without recourse to a nonhuman truth.

That much of James's ethics is familiar. The full extent of his debt to Sidgwick has not been recognized, however, perhaps because the link establishing the connection appears in a book moral philosophers rarely read, *The Principles of Psychology*, rather than in any of James's essays that focus specifically on ethics. In "Aesthetic and Moral Principles," the penultimate section of his final chapter, James attempted to account for ethical decisions, and his analysis followed Sidgwick's precisely. He argued that moral judgments can be reduced neither to mere habit nor to the force of public opinion. What then is the source of moral judgment? Consider the judgments of justice, or equity, James suggested. "Instinctively, one judges everything differently, according as it pertains to one's self or to someone else. Empirically one notices that everybody else does the same." Gradually, however, one comes to realize that "nothing can be right for me which would not be right for another similarly placed," that the "fulfillment of my desires is intrinsically no more imperative than that of anyone else," and that "what it is reasonable that another should do for me, it is also reasonable that I should do for him." With that dawning judgment, James concluded, "the whole mass of the habitual gets overturned."

James cited as the only source for this analysis the section of *The Methods of Ethics* in which Sidgwick advanced the principles of justice, prudence, and rational benevolence in their clearest form. It should be apparent, although it has not received much attention, that James modeled his discussion of moral judgment on Sidgwick's formulation of these principles. James also echoed Sidgwick's analysis of the conflict between the principles of justice and prudence and the impossibility of reconciling them satisfactorily in the principle of rational benevolence. He contrasted the "logical stickler for justice" with "the man who goes by tact and the particular instance," and he maintained that each is right in some cases. In short, there is no easy reconciliation of duty with desire; no general rule can provide an answer in cases of genuine conflict.[18] Some commentators have claimed that James sacrificed the demands of justice, or equity, for the rights of the individual. But as his discussion of the contrast between the easygoing and the strenuous moods in "The Moral Philosopher and the Moral Life" and his treatment of the demands of prudence and justice in *The Principles of Psychology* indicate, he recognized the depth of the difficulty. Like Sidgwick, James denied that philosophy could solve the problem of reconciling individual pleasure with the common good; he attributed a more modest capacity to practical reason.

James and Sidgwick claimed that an irreconcilable conflict looms between the dictates of personal desire and the common good. Dewey, on the other hand, believed that such tensions could be eased if not entirely dissolved, because he considered individual happiness impossible outside the context of social responsibility. Like T. H. Green, Dewey defined ethical behavior in terms of self-realization, by which Dewey meant the continuous refinement of desire to bring personal wants into conformity with social needs. Whereas James dismissed such attempts as "mere postulates of rationality," the possibility of that identification was essential to Dewey's, and to Green's, ethical theories. Denying Sidgwick's distinction between justice and prudence, Green contended that all virtues are really social; "or, more properly, the distinction between social and self-regarding virtues is a false one."[19] Virtuous activity both satisfies the agent and benefits society. If it fails to meet either of those criteria, Green refused to classify it as virtuous.

Sidgwick acknowledged the attractiveness of Green's conception of virtue; yet as Sidgwick pointed out, the argument was unclear. Green tended to swing between wider and narrower conceptions of the good, describing it first in broad, sociopolitical terms, then treating it as a function only of the goodness of the individual will. When Green emphasized the noncompetitive character of his ethical ideal, he referred to such practical duties as securing the "real opportunity of self-development" for the poor. If individual virtue is the key to ethics, Sidgwick maintained, then the most unrelenting competition cannot interfere with the exercise of virtue on the part of the weakest and most disadvantaged competitor. If, on the other hand, ethics requires the realization of all scientific and artistic capacities, as Green sometimes claimed, then the quest for such realization constitutes "the main motive of the keen struggle for material wealth which educated and refined persons generally feel themselves bound to keep up, for their children even more than for themselves." If virtue is conceived as wholly personal, competition presents no problem, and yet that moral ideal exhibits as abstract a quality as Kant's categorical imperative. Alternatively, if the range of true goods includes the development of artistic and scientific ability and the unending pursuit of knowledge of all kinds, it is difficult to imagine a noncompetitive good.[20] Some real goods can by virtue of their scarcity be distributed only unequally, as Green seems to have admitted in his treatment of justice. Thus, the problem of reconciling personal desires and the desires of others reappears. Sidgwick admitted his failure to resolve this conflict; he also denied that Green succeeded where he had failed.

Undaunted by the disagreements between Sidgwick and Green on the question of personal development, Dewey tried to resolve this problem in his ethics. Perhaps no better illustration of the convergence of ideas among the philosophers of the via media exists than Dewey's ultimately futile efforts, which he abandoned in his later work, to harmonize the modified utilitarianism of James and Sidgwick with Green's ethics of self-realization. In both Dewey's "*Outlines of a Critical Theory of Ethics* and his and Tuft's *Ethics*, he approached ethical issues with an eye toward synthesis, discussing various theorists' contradictory analyses and attempting simultaneously to minimize and reconcile their differences. This strategy led Dewey to cite both Green and Sidgwick as sources for his ideas on various issues without admitting the extent to which their ideas differed. Dewey's chapter on "Conduct and Character" in *Ethics* typifies his approach. He first contrasted Kant's emphasis on the pure will with the utilitarians' focus on consequences. He then tried, following Sidgwick's *Methods of Ethics*, to combine these two, but his synthesis at this stage of his thinking owed more to Green than to Sidgwick. Dewey offered the idea of self-realization as a solution to the difficult problem of weighing motives against intentions: "The distinction of 'inner' and 'outer' is one involved in the *growth of character and conduct.*" Only if character were not changing constantly, only if conduct were a fixed because isolated thing, "should we have that separation of the inner and the outer which underlies alike the Kantian and utilitarian theories." By hitching character to the dynamic process of self-realization, and by placing ethics within the framework of his conception of immediate experience, Dewey believed he could end the long-standing division between the right and the good.[21]

In light of his persistent efforts to draw together Sidgwick's and Green's ethics, it is hardly surprising that Dewey considered the conflict between individual interest and the common good a pseudoproblem. The moral end, he wrote, is entirely social. Responding to Sidgwick's challenge to Green, Dewey asserted that "intellectual and artistic interests *are themselves* social, when considered in the completeness of their relations." In short, all real goods, including intellectual and artistic development, must involve "interest in the well-being of society."[22] By that sleight of hand, however, Dewey merely reaffirmed Green's position without directly confronting the problem of the unequal distribution of scarce goods. Given his conceptualization of the issue in terms of individual development instead of pleasure, he did not meet the force of Sidgwick's argument. That disagreement, whether rooted in honest or willful misunderstanding, distinguishes Dewey's ethics and his social theory from the ideas of Sidgwick and James, and it points toward one of the perennial questions of politics: Is individual character sacrificed or fulfilled in the integration of the personal will with the common good?

Dewey and Green believed that self-realization requires the progressive growth of character through ethical action motivated by a desire to advance the common good *and* carefully calculated to advance social goals effectively. Only by following the principle of rational benevolence can the individual realize his full moral potential. Dewey stated this ethical postulate concisely: "In the realization of individuality there is found also the needed realization of some community of persons of which the individual is a member; and, conversely, the agent who duly satisfies the community in which he shares, by that same conduct satisfies himself." Obligation, as Dewey conceived it, corresponds to social satisfaction, whereas freedom provides self-satisfaction. Not only do they not conflict, they are interdependent and inseparable. The individual can find fulfillment only "as a member of a community. In this fact are found both freedom and duty."[23]

From the perspective of James and Sidgwick, that analysis seemed a naive attempt to solve an intractable problem by defining it away. Concluding his treatment of ethics in *The Principles of Psychology*, James wrote, "Where harmonies are asserted of the real world, they are obviously mere postulates of rationality, so far as they transcend experience. Such postulates are exemplified by the ethical propositions that the individual and the universal good are one, and that happiness and goodness are bound to coalesce in the same subject." Though such propositions assume harmony, experience presents us with painful choices, and in every genuinely forced moral decision there is a sacrifice of one cherished principle in order to satisfy another. When the demands of prudence collide with the demands of justice, there is no choice that does not exact a tragic price. In the deliberately stark image James used in "The Moral Philosopher and the Moral Life," in every moral decision "some part of the ideal is butchered."[24]

In ethics as in epistemology, the via media led James and Sidgwick away from the comfort of familiar systems and toward the uncertainty of constant experimentation. Whether applying the principle of rational benevolence would help resolve conflicts between the right and good remained an open question to be answered not a priori but only in experience. In unpublished lecture notes from 1888–9, James stated his synthetic purpose and acknowledged the tragic choices that he considered unavoidable. "I firmly believe that we have preferences inexplicable by utility," he wrote, "preferences for certain kinds of behavior, as consistency, veracity, justice, nobility, dignity, purity, etc., etc." Like Sidgwick, James believed that such intuitive preferences derive from immediate experience; they are apparent to us "from a *psychological* point of view." The problem, as James admitted, again following Sidgwick, emerges from the collisions between competing preferences, "for many of them exclude each other. The whole difficulty of the moral life consists in deciding, when this is the case, which good to sacrifice and which to save."[25] James recognized in the evidence of historical development a progression from a more individualistic toward a more social orientation in moral philosophy, a gradual movement from prudence to justice. Still, he refused to counsel the adoption of any abstract, universally applicable standard by which individual activity could be judged. Morality must grow from experience. It cannot be imposed dogmatically, since history, which James described as "an experiment of the most searching kind," has "proved that the laws and usages of the land are what yield the maximum of satisfaction to the thinkers taken all together." For that reason, he concluded, "the presumption in cases of [ethical] conflict must always be in favor of the conventionally recognized good."[26] That argument paralleled the case Sidgwick made for grounding his utilitarianism firmly on the everyday principles of common sense.

Both Sidgwick and James believed that we can never hope to attain any ultimate moral ideal, and even their conception of ethics as progressively more inclusive remained deliberately indefinite. Within those limits, the standard provided by history, a standard available for all critical students of ethical development to explore, remained the best available normative measure, because history discloses how people create values. We do not find values in being but bring them into being and test them in experience. Ethics is thus an empirical and historical discipline, whose provisional truths are disclosed gradually through a process of trial and error, and it must be critical in much the same way that epistemology must be critical. Moral philosophers cannot penetrate beyond experience in order to uncover unchanging ethical principles in ontology; they can aspire only to relative certainty.

The tendencies toward mediation and doubt likewise characterized the writings of James and Sidgwick on the subject of politics. In the chapter "Justice" in *The Methods of Ethics*, Sidgwick noted the persistent conflicts in nineteenth-century thought between the "Individualistic and the Socialistic Ideals of a political community." Liberals elevate "the realization of Freedom as the ultimate end and standard of right social relations," but their notion of freedom is too shallow to yield a solid basis for social construction because it violates our sense of justice. Socialistic ideals, on the other hand, appeal to our intuition of fairness, but they are too utopian and imprecise to guide social policy. Whereas most political theorists merely projected their personal preferences as universal truths, Sidgwick argued that a constructive social reformer cannot possibly hope to begin *"de novo* either for man as he is (abstracting his morality), or for man as he ought to be and will be. He must start, broadly speaking, with the existing social order, and the existing morality as part of that order." Not surprisingly, this approach ruled out cataclysmic change as a method of attaining political goals, and at the opposite end of the spectrum it also denied that history conforms to an unalterable pattern. The only tendency history exhibits is the tendency to build upon itself as a long-term project of pragmatic truth testing by trial and error. In Sidgwick's words, theorists trying to settle the question of "divergence" from the social code "must consider chiefly the immediate consequences of such divergence" (*ME*, 293–4, 474).

Not surprisingly, Sidgwick judged revolution a utopian fantasy that turns into a practical disaster, and he believed that only moderate reform stands any chance of success. He dismissed Marx as an economist, judging the labor theory of value to be a quaint and romantic notion displaced by the marginal utility theory of William Jevons and Alfred Marshall. Marx's conception of change was deduced from his philosophy of history, Sidgwick believed, not derived from careful analysis of economic development. Neither did Sidgwick accept the invisible hand of the classical liberals' political economy, which he considered an equally unwarranted attempt to elevate a set of abstract propositions beyond experience and enshrine them as eternal truths. The nineteenth century was running away from the false utopia of laissez-faire, Sidgwick argued, and those who tried to halt its progress labored in vain. In *The Methods of Ethics*, Sidgwick described the conflict between defenders and critics of the status quo as "permanently latent in the very core of Common Sense," and he was no more optimistic about resolving it once and for all than he was about easing the tension in ethics between the demands of prudence and the demands of justice. When he counseled that we should "balance one set of advantages against the other, and decide according to the preponderance," his judgment was as honest – or evasive – as it was in his discussion of the ethics of rational benevolence (*ME*, 447–8).[27]

Sidgwick adopted a moderate reformist stance that he considered consistent with the uncertain, experimental, pragmatic, and historically sensitive spirit of his epistemology and his ethics. In his essay "The Economic Lessons of Socialism" (1895), he sketched out the principal features of his position. Liberal political economy had learned much from socialist economic theory, Sidgwick wrote, and the two schools were no longer as far apart as they once were. Adam Smith and his disciples had promulgated a gospel with two parts, one concerning the production, exchange, and division of wealth independent of government interference, and the other purporting to demonstrate that this process naturally led to the most desirable consequences. As a result of its collisions with socialist ideas, and with the realities of industrialization and democratization, liberal theory had been forced to concede that the two principal tenets of its creed had no necessary logical connection with each other. The description of economic processes now had to be distinguished from the justification of their effects. This gradual development culminated in the writings of John Stuart Mill. In the later editions of Mill's *Principles of Political Economy*, Sidgwick pointed out, Mill was "completely Socialistic in his ideal of ultimate social improvement." Sidgwick then quoted a passage from Mill's *Autobiography*: "I look forward to a time," Mill wrote, "when the produce of labour, depending, in so great a degree as it now does, on the accident of birth, will be made by concert on an acknowledged principle of justice."[28] As Sidgwick correctly perceived, the apostasy of James Mill's son, and Bentham's prize pupil, held enormous significance for the future of liberal theory. When the author of *On Liberty* endorsed in principle the ideal of socialism, he signaled as no other individual could have done the convergence of the values of individualism and community that Sidgwick himself carried at least one step farther forward.

Although neither James nor Sidgwick was committed to radical social reform, it would be a mistake to portray them as uncritical apologists for the existing order. Their moderation was in part temperamental and in part a consequence of their principled uncertainty about knowledge and values. Their sensitivity to historical variation made them politically broad-minded, perhaps to a fault. As Sidgwick explained in his *Elements of Politics* (1891), "There is scarcely any widely spread political institution or practice – however universally condemned by current opinion – which has not been sincerely defended as conducive to human happiness on the whole" (*EP*, 40). Or, as James put it in *The Will to Believe* (1897), "There is indeed nothing which someone has not thought absolutely true, whilst his neighbor deemed it absolutely false."[29] That perception of diversity is valuable as an antidote to fanaticism, but unless accompanied by some substantive political values it can be incapacitating. These thinkers' doubt was as much a part of their legacy as their detachment, and its consequences ultimately proved less salutary.

In short, neither James nor Sidgwick was a reformer. Dewey played a more active and prominent political role, but a discussion of his mature political writings is beyond the scope of this essay. Though the importance of James's and Sidgwick's bourgeois status in shaping their attitude toward politics should not be minimized, neither should their conception of their responsibility as intellectuals be ignored. From the perspective of thinkers more committed to political struggles, their contributions of speeches, essays, and well-reasoned letters to the editors of popular newspapers and magazines seemed decidedly timid. They were part of a transitional generation wedged between the preachers who preceded them – and who were, in the cases of Green and Sidgwick and, in a sense, James, their fathers – and the more politically active intellectuals who followed them. They protected their independence as a matter of principle, but they did not limit their writing to matters of limited technical concern, as did the academic philosophers who completed the professionalization of higher education. It is instructive that philosophy and social science diverged, both institutionally and intellectually, shortly after this generation died. Philosophers in the Anglo-American world gravitated increasingly toward the study of language and logic and left the questions of value and society largely to social scientists, who in turn gradually shifted their focus from broader philosophical questions to the description of individual, social, and political behavior. The heart of political philosophy, the analysis of the connections between knowledge and responsibility and politics, was for a time all but abandoned.

Sidgwick and James shared the ambivalence of many Victorian social critics concerning the virtues and vices of democracy. The blend of enthusiastic reformist sentiment and elitist reserve that characterized James's scattered musings about politics also shows up in the more systematic writings of his friend Sidgwick, whom James invited to Harvard in 1899 specifically to lecture on economics and politics instead of more narrowly defined philosophical questions. In his *Elements of Politics*, Sidgwick emphasized the importance of instilling in legislators "a keen *concern* for the interests of the various elements of the community for which they legislate," an aim to be attained by more frequent elections and the use of the initiative and referendum. Undercutting the apparently democratic sentiments prompting such recommendations, however, Sidgwick argued that members of Parliament still ought not be paid. In that way, "the class of persons who possess a moderate amount of wealth may have a practical influence on legislation out of proportion to their numbers," thereby securing the fusion of oligarchy and democracy that Aristotle recommended to minimize class conflict. Sidgwick claimed that his general view of politics derived from the writings of Bentham and J. S. Mill. Given his understanding of Mill's shifting attitudes toward both democracy and socialism – recall that he favored plural voting by the more educated members of society so that their more enlightened views might carry greater weight – Sidgwick's ostensibly revealing admission slips back into the ambiguity of Mill's own problematic mixture of cultural elitism and economic democracy (*EP*, 357–8, 373–4, 590–2, v–vi).[30]

Although Sidgwick did not contribute as significantly as did Green to the revision of liberal theory in Great Britain, neither was he as uncritical an exponent of individualism as is sometimes supposed. Fabian socialists admired his commitment to reform and recommended his books to members of the society; Sidney Webb judged Sidgwick superior to Marx as an economist.[31] Though it would be a mistake to classify Sidgwick himself as a socialist or even as a social democrat, neither was he altogether content with the liberalism that prevailed in late nineteenth-century England. He was, as Stefan Collini has argued, sympathetic toward socialism yet drawn even more powerfully toward an idiosyncratic variety of conservatism.[32] He reasoned, in much the same way that Green did in his celebrated lecture "Liberal Legislation and Freedom of Contract" (1880), that property holding had become sufficiently concentrated to restrict the freedom of others: "The institution of private property as actually existing goes beyond what the individualistic theory justifies. Its general aim is to appropriate the results of labour to the laborer, but in realizing that aim" it put the propertied classes "in a position of diminishing the opportunities of the unpropertied in a manner which . . . renders a demand for compensation justifiable on the strictest individualistic grounds." Sidgwick's call for compensation thus rested on his conviction that individuals must be able to exercise their rights in fact rather than merely possess them in theory. He broadened his conception of property rights to include what has been called "the right not to be excluded by others," and he drew an interesting distinction between the freedom to use and the freedom to own. "If the freedom is understood strictly," Sidgwick contended, "I do not see that it implies more than [a property owner's] right to non-interference while actually using such things as can only be used by one person at once." He distinguished that right from "the right to prevent others from using at any future time anything that an individual has once seized," which he deemed "an interference with the free action of others beyond what is needed to secure the freedom, strictly speaking, of the appropriator." That limitation on the extent of property rights, although as vague in its implications for policy as Green's argument concerning liberty as "a positive power or capacity of doing or enjoying something worth doing or enjoying," nevertheless directly challenged the liberal conception of freedom (*EP*, 156; *ME*, 276–9).[33]

In *The Methods of Ethics*, Sidgwick provided a clear statement of the question that troubled all of the philosophers of the via media when they turned their attention to politics: "Can it be fair for any class of persons to gain competitively by the unfavourable economic situation of another class with which they deal?" Sidgwick answered that question in the negative. "And if we admit that it would be unfair," he asked, then "Where do we draw the line?" (*ME*, 288). The drawing of that line represented to these thinkers the principal challenge of modern politics. They could all agree that the concept of individual property rights must be broadened, but how far the range ought to be extended, how radically conditions ought to be altered, and by what means, this generation failed to resolve. In his essay "What Makes a Life Significant?" James insisted that society must "pass toward some newer and better equilibrium, and the distribution of wealth has doubtless got to change." He restated that conviction, which united the philosophers of the via media, in "The Moral Equivalent of War." "I devoutly believe," he wrote, "in the reign of peace and in the gradual advent of some sort of socialistic equilibrium."[34]

Neither James nor Sidgwick adequately translated these abstract principles, which rested on a broadened conception of liberty requiring progressive social and economic equalization, into specific political programs. They believed that the form of the emerging society should be determined by democratic means, and they therefore denied in principle that the final shape of such a polity could be outlined in advance. Taken together, their broader conception of property rights, their idea of effective freedom, and their commitment to the gradual equalization of social conditions did suggest certain implications for policy, but the two options that presented themselves, although they appeared to be mutually reinforcing, were not necessarily consistent. The first was a modest redistribution of wealth, to be achieved principally through progressive taxation. The second involved the various regulatory, insurance, and income-support mechanisms that have come to be associated with the welfare state. The latent conflict between these two strategies, which these thinkers did not clearly perceive, was to become a focal point in the writings of a later generation of social democrats and progressives.

As a means of equalizing the burden of government and at least potentially redistributing wealth through a gradual process, progressive taxation exerted a strong appeal. As Sidgwick argued in *The Elements of Politics*, for example, its equity and efficacy could hardly be denied. Yet he repeatedly expressed the ambivalence that has become a standard feature of twentieth-century politics, and his doubt was emblematic of his generation's attitude toward the proper means of translating their principles into policy. Sidgwick feared that, given prevailing values and the likely persistence of selfishness, excessive taxation to equalize wealth might impair production by reducing incentives, and thus the equality of incomes effected by such redistribution might become "an equality in poverty." This "danger of loss to the whole community," he reasoned, necessitated a gradualist approach to the problem of inequality. Successfully balancing the goals of equity and productivity seemed to him a delicate project, and for that reason he remained uncertain about such redistribution (*EP*, 173–4, 151–2).[35] Yet even provisional support for progressive taxation marked a clear break from the liberal creed, a departure resting on the heretical claim that in industrial societies wealth is not a personal but a social product.

Use of the state to cope with problems stemming from industrialization and interdependence originated in Germany between 1883 and 1889 and slowly spread to England and the United States. Through a process too complicated even to trace here, such measures as industrial regulation and insurance against sickness, old age, unemployment, and disability gradually became part of modern government. These measures did not necessarily contribute to the kind of solution anticipated by Green or Dewey, James or Sidgwick. For, as Burke argued in theory and Bismarck proved in practice, the essence of conservatism is timely reform, and the welfare state has tended only to mask, and thereby to perpetuate, the institutionalized inequalities the philosophers of the via media recognized as the core of modern social conflict. Committed to democratic procedures and to a strategy of gradualism in political reform, they called for a new conception of rights and for progress toward greater political, social, and economic equality. The welfare state was in its infancy when they wrote, so they did not discuss it in any detail, yet both James and Sidgwick endorsed the general expansion of state responsibility. Their recommendations concerning the best course of action, however, re-mained vague. That vagueness derived only in part from their uneasiness regarding the consequences of progressive taxation and the provision of social services by the welfare state. Their ambivalence also had deeper roots, extending from their conception of experience as social, historical, and value-laden, and from their conviction that individual life involves the interweaving of sensation and reflection, thought and action. They were skeptical of efforts to remove from individuals the responsibility to make their own choices and to act; consequently, they resisted the larger claims of those who looked to the state for straightforward answers to social and political problems. In their politics as in their epistemology and ethics, they tried to mediate between extremes, and their recom-mendations manifested a similar degree of uncertainty.

Sidgwick's *Principles of Political Economy* and *Elements of Politics* typified this approach. In much the same way that he used the principles of utilitarianism and intuitionism to supplement one another in *The Methods of Ethics*, so he invoked the principles of socialism for those cases in which "the individualistic basis" of liberalism tended "to be inadequate to produce the attainable maximum of social happiness." Because he believed that individuals can care for themselves better than governments can, he ruled out all comprehensive schemes of social reconstruction, and he endorsed the extension of state authority as a "supplementary and subordinate element in a system mainly individu-alistic." Sidgwick discussed three methods of coping with poverty: reg-ulated alms giving, which he associated with France; public relief, the typical English response; and compulsory insurance, which Germany adopted under Bismarck. Characteristically, he recommended "a careful combination of the three methods" as "the practically best plan." Choices among these options, he advised, should depend on "the actual extent and effectiveness of voluntary association among the citizens" and on the amount of "philanthropic effort and sacrifice habitually de-voted by private persons to the supply of social needs." Though such counsel may seem less than enlightening, Sidgwick considered anything more specific undesirable, because political answers cannot be deter-mined in advance from any set of abstract guidelines. Policies must be grounded in experience and tested and refined in practice. Freely ac-knowledging his failure to provide "general principles on which the nature and extent" of collective action such as welfare legislation or nationalization might be determined, he defended caution as the best policy. "It would hardly be possible to work out a system of detailed practical rules on the basis of these principles," he confessed. But he judged that feature of his politics a strength rather than a weakness, because it reflected his recognition of "the extent to which the construction of such a system ought reasonably to be influenced by the particular social and political conditions of the country and time for which it is framed" (*EP*, 39, 139; *PPE*, 533–44, 158–9, 530, 418).

That conclusion, methodological rather than substantive in its approach to the political process, was consistent with the enlarged empiricism and the historical sensibility Sidgwick shared with the other philosophers of the via media. They were committed to flexibility not because they lacked convictions about political issues but because they considered the willingness to adapt a virtue, an indication of intellectual honesty rather than an evasion of responsibility. They believed in experimentation in questions of social policy not because it was expedient but as a matter of principle, as the political corollary of their epistemology and their ethical theory. Politics begins and ends in the uncertainty of experience, not in abstractions, and these thinkers unflinchingly faced the realization that reformers could no longer proceed effectively with elaborate agendas made up in advance. Unlike conservatives who shared their caution, they were committed to progressive change; unlike revolutionaries who shared their ideals of genuine freedom and greater equality, they were committed to a strategy of incremental and peaceful reform.

Sidgwick believed that the fundamental questions of life are irreducibly philosophical, and thus, like James, he denied that such questions as competition, at root an ethical problem of balancing the claims of prudence and justice, can ever be settled once and for all by social policy. Life inevitably presents us with a series of dilemmas, and no course of action, taken either by individuals or by society, can prevent the sacrifice of one genuine good in order to satisfy another. Sidgwick doubted that a workable scale could ever be devised for accurately measuring desert. In the absence of such a measure, social peace would be impossible, because nearly everyone would feel either inadequately rewarded for his own special contribution to the common good or dissatisfied with the system of preexisting inequalities that could prevent less advantaged members of society from sharing its rewards. Though James conceded in *The Varieties of Religious Experience* that a just community, "in which there would be only sympathy and fairness" instead of competition and inequality, would be perfectly adapted to the virtues of a saint, he remained skeptical whether human society could ever reach a condition in which saints might thrive rather than suffer. "We have, in short," Sidgwick wrote, "to give up as impracticable the construction of an ideally just social order, in which all services are rewarded in exact proportion to their intrinsic value." For no such "intrinsic value" is disclosed in experience; we have only clashes among competing and incommensurable interpretations of it. Moreover, Sidgwick concluded regretfully, common sense "scarcely holds such a method to be possible: for though it considered Ideal Justice to consist in rewarding Desert, it regards as Utopian any general attempt to realize this ideal in the social distribution of the means of happiness" (*ME*, 289–90).[36] That sober judgment reveals Sidgwick's doubt, a doubt James shared, about the possibility of attaining the degree of social harmony that Green and Dewey cherished and anticipated. James and Sidgwick favored progressive social change, but they believed that the meaning and value of life relate to its physical conditions as color relates to form. They maintained that life is imbued with meanings that flow from history and culture, and its value is determined less according to material conditions than by individual will and activity.

The philosophers of the via media thus expressed their political ideas in the distinct keys of anticipation and skepticism. But none of them counseled inaction, because they considered social change desirable, although not inevitable. Though they disagreed about the prospect for attaining harmony, they agreed about the general course of action most likely to lead in that direction. They challenged the identification of politics with economics, insisting that a broader conception of autonomy required the destruction of liberals' identification of freedom with unrestricted property rights. Just as they linked individual experience with social and cultural context and individual responsibility with community membership, so they conceived of politics as the attempt to achieve, as nearly as possible, the harmonious integration of autonomous individuals. They conceived of autonomy, however, not in the standard liberal terms of acquisitiveness and independence from the threatening forces of corruption represented by government, but instead as citizenship, an ideal involving positive freedom secured by an active, democratic state designed to provide a context of equality for the moral development of all of its members.

This vision of politics, of course, was hardly new. It mirrored the classical image of the correlative rights and duties of the republican citizen. What was new about it, and what made it radical philosophically and ambiguous politically, was its deviation and its limits. It originated not in a priori notions of reason, virtue, or justice but instead in a new conception of experience and new awareness of uncertainty. Using the tools of radical empiricism and the experimental method of pragmatism, the philosophers of the via media fashioned a theory of social action stressing the reciprocal relation between individual choices and historically developing cultural values. According to that theory, moral and political principles are not brought by reason to experience but grow from it; like all ideas, they are subject to endless testing in practice. Change, which according to the classical republican view signaled decline, these thinkers interpreted as a sign of vitality. Flexibility and innovation, based on collective experience but expressing the imagination of reflective individuals, they considered methodological principles consistent with the ongoing quest for the most satisfactory way of organizing social life. Expediency they judged a matter of principle, responsiveness to new demands a responsibility. Steady, incremental change through the democratic process, with all its confusions and imperfections, the philosophers of the via media deemed the political expression of this philosophical creed. These ideas, moderate, meliorist, democratic, and sensitive to the possibility that no perfect reconciliation of liberty and equality can be attained, are the consequences of pragmatism for politics.

Notes

1 James T. Kloppenberg, *Uncertain Victory: Social Democracy and Progressivism in European and American Thought, 1870–1920* (New York: Oxford University Press, 1986).

2 William James to Mrs. Henry Sidgwick, Henry Sidgwick Papers, Wren Library, Trinity College, Cambridge University; John Dewey, review of *M*, first published in *Political Science Quarterly* 22 (1907): 133–5, reprinted in Dewey, *The Middle Works, 1899–1924* (hereafter cited as *MW*), vol. 4, 1907–9, ed. Jo Ann Boydston (Carbondale: Southern Illinois University Press, 1977), pp. 242–4.

3 Dewey's appreciation of James first appeared in the *Independent*, September 8, 1910; it is reprinted in *MW*, 10:91–7.

4 James's comments on Dewey appear in a letter to F. C. S. Schiller, April 8, 1903, reprinted in Ralph Barton Perry, *The Thought and Character of William James*, 2 vols. (Boston: Little, Brown, 1935), 2:375.

5 Sidgwick, "The Coherence of Empirical Philosophy," *Mind* 7 (1882): 533–43. The quotation is from an unpublished, untitled essay in the Sidgwick Papers. See also his essay "Is Philosophy the Germ or Crown of Science?" (also in the Sidgwick Papers), in which he develops a similar argument; and cf. the discussion of these issues in Jerome B. Schneewind, *Sidgwick's Ethics and Victorian Moral Philosophy* (Oxford: Oxford University Press [Clarendon Press], 1977), pp. 52–3.

6 I discuss this issue in greater detail in *Uncertain Victory*, pp. 95–114. See

also the essay on Sidgwick by Jerome Schneewind in *The Encyclopedia of Philosophy*, ed. Paul Edwards (New York: Macmillan and Free Press, 1967), 7:434–46.

7 See also Schneewind, *Sidgwick's Ethics*, pp. 58–62.

8 Sidgwick's journal for 1867 is in the Sidgwick Papers.

9 Dewey, review of *M*, in *MW*, 4:244.

10 Dewey, "Intuitionism," in *Johnson's Universal Cyclopedia*, ed. Charles Kendall Adams (New York, 1894), 4:657–9; reprinted in John Dewey, *The Early Works, 1882–1898* (hereafter cited as *EW*), vol. 4, 1893–4, ed. Jo Ann Boydston (Carbondale: Southern Illinois University Press, 1971), pp. 123–31.

11 See also Sidgwick's autobiographical notes in *ME*, xvii; and Schneewind, *Sidgwick's Ethics*, pp. 42 f.

12 Dewey, *Outlines of a Critical Theory of Ethics*, in *EW*, 3:259 f., 254. Dewey and Tufts, *Ethics*, in *MW*, 5:85–6, 269–70, 265 n., 281–4. Dewey and Tufts identified their individual contributions in the book's preface.

13 See also Dewey, *Outlines*, *EW*, 3:270–1, 274–5, where he relies on T. H. Green's *Prolegomena* and distinguishes Sidgwick from Mill.

14 Ibid., p. 276; and Dewey, *The Study of Ethics: A Syllabus*, *EW*, 4:284–5. For further criticism of Mill along similar lines, see James's lecture notes from 1888–9, in the William James Papers, Houghton Library, Harvard University, Cambridge, MA.

15 *ME*, 379. On the publishing history of the seven editions of *The Methods of Ethics*, see Schneewind, *Sidgwick's Ethics*, pp. 412, 424. Sidgwick's own "genetic account" of the book, published as a preface to the sixth and seventh editions, partly compensates for the alterations in the text by recounting his intellectual development from John Stuart Mill through Whewell, Kant, Butler, and Aristotle, and by revealing the importance of different ethical traditions in the shaping of his ideas.

16 Sidgwick, "Hedonism and Ultimate Good," *Mind* 2 (1877): 32, 31.

17 James, "The Moral Philosopher and the Moral Life," *The Will to Believe*, in *The Works of William James*, ed. Frederick H. Burkhardt et al. (Cambridge, MA: Harvard University Press, 1979), p. 161.

18 James, *The Principles of Psychology*, 2 vols. (New York: Holt, 1890), 2:672–5. See also James's extensive marginal notations in his copies of Sidgwick's *Methods of Ethics* and *Outlines of the History of Ethics*, both of which are in the Philosophical Library of William James, James Papers.

19 T. H. Green, *Lectures on the Principles of Political Obligation*, in *The Works of T. H. Green*, 3 vols., ed. R. L. Nettleship (London: Longmans, Green, 1885–8), 2:550.

20 Sidgwick first launched his attack on Green's notion of a noncompetitive ideal in his review of Green's *Prolegomena*, which appeared in *Mind* 9 (1884): 169–84. He expanded it in his *Lectures on the Ethics of T. H. Green, H. Spencer, and J. Martineau*, from which these quotations are taken; see *GSM*, 65–72.

21 Dewey and Tufts, *Ethics*, *MW*, 5:221–40.
22 Dewey, *Outlines*, *EW*, 3:315; cf. pp. 292 f., 300.
23 Ibid., pp. 322, 327.
24 James, *Principles*, 2:675; "Moral Philosopher," p. 154.
25 James's lecture notes from 1888–9 are in the James Papers.
26 James, "Moral Philosopher," pp. 155–6.
27 See also Sidgwick's preface to *PPE*, v; and "The Economic Lessons of Socialism," *Economic Journal*, September 1895; reprinted in *MEA*, 237. For Sidgwick's interpretation of the fate of laissez-faire ideals in the nineteenth century, see *DEP*, which Eleanor Sidgwick edited for publication after Sidgwick's death.
28 Sidgwick, "Economic Lessons," *MEA*, 235–48. See also *PPE*, 499–517, in which Sidgwick offers a similar analysis. The passage from Mill appears in his *Autobiography* (New York: Columbia University Press, 1960), p. 162.
29 James, *Will to Believe*, p. 23. For an incisive discussion of the personal and political reasons for Sidgwick's nonpartisanship, an account that places less emphasis on his philosophical reasons than I do here, see Stefan Collini's essay in Collini, Donald Winch, and John Burrow, *That Noble Science of Politics: A Study in Nineteenth-Century Intellectual History* (Cambridge: Cambridge University Press, 1983), pp. 305–7, a revised version of which appears as Chapter 12, herein. Other treatments of Sidgwick's political ideas include Eric Hobsbawm, "Dr. Marx and the Victorian Critics," in *Labouring Men: Studies in the History of Labour* (London: Weidenfeld and Nicholson, 1976); William C. Havard, *Henry Sidgwick and Later Utilitarian Political Philosophy* (Gainesville: University of Florida Press, 1959); and D. G. James, *Henry Sidgwick: Science and Faith in Victorian England* (Oxford: Oxford University Press, 1970).
30 See James's letters to Sidgwick dated March 22 and April 30, 1899, in the James Papers.
31 See Kloppenberg, *Uncertain Victory*, pp. 202, 223, 241, on Sidgwick and the Fabians. For a recent discussion of the principle of redistribution that acknowledges Sidgwick's contribution to establishing this basic premise of the welfare state, see Stein Ringen, *The Possibility of Politics: A Study in the Political Economy of the Welfare State* (Oxford: Oxford University Press, 1987), p. 140 n. 30.
32 Collini, Winch, and Burrow, *That Noble Science*, pp. 302–3.
33 See also *M* 441–2; and Collini, Winch, and Burrow, *That Noble Science*, p. 302, n. 60, on Sidgwick's ambivalence regarding property. On Green and property, see Kloppenberg, *Uncertain Victory*, pp. 180–2.
34 James, "What Makes a Life Significant?" in *Talks to Teachers on Psychology: And to Students on Some of Life's Ideals* (New York: Holt, 1901), p. 189; "The Moral Equivalent of War," in *Memoirs and Studies* (New York: Longmans, Green, 1911), p. 286. In *Will to Believe*, p. 156, James lamented "the abuses which the institution of private property covers, so that even to-day

it is shamelessly asserted among us that one of the prime functions of the national government is to help the adroiter citizens to grow rich."

35 See also *PPE*, 560–71; and "Economic Socialism," in *MEA*, 200–15. Given the enormous productivity of liberal capitalism, despite the inequalities it generates, this has continued to be a legitimate concern. For a recent attempt to solve it, see John Rawls, *A Theory of Justice* (Cambridge, MA: Harvard University Press, 1971), p. 302. Although Rawls is generally critical of Sidgwick, part (a) of his second principle of justice echoes Sidgwick's reservations concerning the relation between production and distribution.

36 James, *The Varieties of Religious Experience*, 2d ed. (New York: Random House [Modern Library], 1929), p. 366. On the incommensurability of competing conceptions of justice, which remains a central theme in contemporary political philosophy, see James T. Kloppenberg, "Why History Matters to Political Theory," in *Science and Reform*, ed. Ronald Walters (Baltimore: Johns Hopkins University Press, forthcoming).

Index

wick problem," 352–8; *see also* ethics; freedom; politics; sociology; *and individual moralists*
excellence, see duty; intuition; perfectionism; virtue
externalism/internalism, 35–6, 202–6, 235n6, 241–4, 244–7; affects interpretation of egoism, 206, 235n9; contrast between affects interpretation of utilitarianism as rational benevolence, 202–3, 235nn7–8; and dualism of practical reason, 153, 202–6, 235n8; and dualism of practical reason in history of ethics, 185–6, 195–7; interpretations of S, 35–6, 116–17, 192–7, 202–6, 234n4, 241–4, 258n2, 258n4; and intuitionism, 235n5, 235n8, 204–6; and I. Kant v S, 191–2, 251–2; J. Mackie criticizes T. Nagel's account of, 170–2; R. Price's internalism, 187; S and I. Kant v D. Ross and H. A. Prichard on, 244; J. B. Schneewind on S on, 116–17; as theme in history of ethics, 195–7, 241–4; *see also* benevolence; dualism of practical reason; egoism, rational and ethical; intuition; motive; reason

faith, *see* Christianity; religion; theology
feeling: can only be judged by person who feels, 268; and definition of pleasure, 268, 277nn11–12; desirability of a counterfactual judgment, 268–9; emotions or passions, against reason, 175–98, 241–4; and objective conditions, 268–9, 277nn11–12; *see also* desire; good; hedonism
Fenelon, Archbishop: incineration of as problem for utilitarianism, 172–3
fidelity, *see* duty; good faith
fine, the, 293, 295–7; affirmative badness as opposite of, 321; and bravery, Aristotle on, 297–9; T. H. Green on Aristotle on, 295–7, 308n20, 309n27; and liberality, 301–2; and magnanimity, 302–3; S on Aristotle on, 295–7; and temperance, 291–2, 299–301; translated as "beautiful," 296; *see also* common good; motive; perfectionism; virtue
firmness, *see* temperance; virtue
Fisher, A. L.: and inductive political science, 357, 366n44
Forbes, Duncan, 119n26
formal and material rightness, see good; right
fortitude, *see* bravery; temperance

foundationalism, *see* cognitivism; ethics; intuition; knowledge; philosophy; reason
Fowler, Thomas, and J. M. Wilson: on history of ethics, 88, 90n31
Frankena, William, 10–11, 35, 48n4, 51n17, 52nn21–2, 53n37, 57n68, 327n8, 327n13; on "dei" as imperative in Aristotle, 314; earlier works of on dualism of practical reason, 175, 197n2; as externalist, 35–6, 196, 327n3; and moral point of view, 196; offers internalist interpretation of S, 35–6, 57n70, 234n4
freedom, 52n31, 54n40, 336, 338, 340–4, 384–92; and contract/property, 384–92; as ideal good, 270–1; Spencer's law of equal freedom, 73–4, 348; *see also* determinism; free will; individualism; justice; political economy; politics
Freeman, Edward A., 364n21
Freeman, Richard, 353, 357, 367n45
free will, 111–12; Coleridge on, 96; in connection with justice and desert, 111–12; and independence of ethics, 7, 40; *see also* Cambridge moralists; determinism; freedom; justice; moral theory
Frey, R. G., 53n38
friendship: Aristotle on 309nn30–1, 309n33; *see also* common good; virtue

Gash, N., 119n26
Gauthier, David, 149
Gay, John: as theological utilitarian, 66, 185
general agreement, as condition of philosophical intuitionism: apparent rather than real in common-sense morality, 17, 128–9; stringency of such condition, 15, 28–32, 35–6, 41–2, 128–9; W. Whewell on, 128–9; *see also* intuition
general good, *see* common good; good
generosity, *see* magnanimity
Gibbard, Alan: on S on self-evident principles, 53n38, 56n61; utilitarianism of, 32, 53n38, 56n61
Giddings, Franklin: S criticizes sociology textbook of, 355
Gizycki, Georg: on dualism of practical reason, 116, 121n98
Gladstone, W. F., 135–6, 360
Gleig, George: first English history of ethics, 87, 90n26
God, *see* Christ; Christianity; moral order; religion; theology
Godwin, William: compared to J. Bentham, 34–5; utilitarian argument on

son and, 175–77, 286–7, 309n33, 311–12; egoism of, 110, 175–8, 177, 285–90, 309nn30–1, 309n33, 311–12, 315–16, 326n1; T. H. Green on uniformity of, 308n17; T. H. Green v S on, 279–306 passim; as Manichean in ethics, 320, 321; and moral progress, 282–3; serious study of began in 19th century, 279; S on importance and influence of, 284–5; S on vacuity of, 285–90, 304–5; S's hedonism leads him to reject distinctive contribution of, 10, 287; Stoics transitional from, 10, 175, 313–14; and virtue as the will to be good, 281–3; *see also* egoism, rational and ethical; ethics; good; intuition; perfectionism; virtue

Green, T. H., 47, 65, 71–2, 89n11, 279–306 passim, 379–81; argues Greeks found true principle of morality, 290; and Aristotle on bravery, 290–1, 297–99; on Aristotle on the fine, 295–7; on Aristotle on temperance, 292–3, 299–301; as classicist, 279–81, 307n6; collaboration with E. Caird, 307n6; on common-sense morality in Greeks, 308n17; compared to S, 279–81, 284–90, 293–306, 379–82, 385, 386–7; contrast with S on Aristotle, 284–90, 293–306; current reputation of, 279–81; and empiricism, 371; on hedonism, 71–2, 379–81; as liberal reformer, 71–2, 379–82, 385; R. L. Nettleship on, 307n6; notes on copy of Aristotle's *Ethics*, 306n2, 309n30, 309n33; *Prolegomena to Ethics* little read, 280, 307n3; rejects historical relativist interpretation of Aristotle, 283–4; S criticizes vacuity of, 280–81; self-realization ethics of, 71–2, 279, 281–4, 290–3, 303–6; similarities to J. Dewey, 379–82, 385; and S on interpretation of Aristotle as aesthetic intuitionist, 293–5; against utilitarianism, 279, 293–306 passim, 375; and virtue as will to be good, 282, 292–3, 386–7

Griffin, James, 52n31, 53n38

Grote, John, 94, 118n1, 120nn56–69, 120n72, 121n99; on J. Butler and dualism, 116–17; and Cambridge Moralists, 105–7; on history of ethics, 93; and W. Whewell on religious basis of ethics, 106; *see also* Cambridge moralists

Grotius, Hugo, 184

happiness, *see* desire; good; hedonism; perfection; utilitarianism; well-being

Hardin, Russell, 15, 20–1, 32, 143–60;

collective action, 159n19; on limits of formal decision theory, 20–1; utilitarianism of, 32, 53n38, 57n74, 143–60, 158n4

Hare, Julius, 94; friend of S's, 119n25, 119nn27–30, 365n25; on progress, 99–100, 114, 118n7; *see also* Cambridge moralists

Hare, R. M., 23, 53n38, 54n42, 196; evaluative language has imperatival force, 322, 329n24; universal prescriptivism leads to utilitarianism, 172

Hart, H. L. A., 54n40, 322–3

Hartley, David: as theological utilitarian, 185

Harvard University: S declines to visit, 385–6

Harvie, Christopher, 48n5, 367n47, 367n50

Havard, W., 48n5, 49n8, 364n19, 394n29

Hayek, F. A., 158n4

Hayward, F. H., 4, 5, 8, 49n8, 51n17

hedonism: absurdity of egoistic hedonism of present, 58n77, 236n11; and agent-weighted theory, 211–12; allows systematization, 13, 52n31, 270–1, 287, 304–5; J. Butler on, 265; S. Coleridge, 96–8; and comprehensiveness requirement, 271–3, 274; contemporary dismissal of, 13, 32, 52n31; and contemporary utilitarianism, 52n31, 200–1; and counterfactual judgment, 234n1, 268–9; J. Dewey on J. S. Mill on, 375–6; ethical, 8–10, 13, 30, 52n31, 67–70, 71–2, 115, 124, 201, 234n1, 261, 266–73, 304–5, 374–6; and evidentiary view of desire, 274–6; and feeling, 71–2, 266–73; as functional state, 200–1; and generality requirement, 262, 266–8, 274; and good, ultimate good, good on the whole, 8–10, 13, 52n31, 71–2, 165–9, 234n1, 266–73, 273–4, 277n11–12, 309n33; J. Grote, 105–6; and ideal goods, 52n31, 201, 234n1, 267, 269–73, 278n13; and mean of virtue, 314; in J. S. Mill, 277n10, 375–6; and moral theory of ancients, 10, 13, 177, 270–1, 284–90, 304–5, 309n33; and objective circumstances, 268–9, 277n11–12; and person slices, 216; pleasure as means to virtue, 278n14; pleasure as qualitative mental state, 200–1, 268; psychological, 374; and rejection of Aristotelian eudaimonism, 52n31, 287, 304–5; S as preference hedonist, 201, 216, 234n1; simple v preference, 200–1; S on value

Liberal party: and academic reform, 135–6; S and, 360, 363
liberty, *see* freedom; individualism; political economy; politics
Locke, John, 184, 371; and commands, 329nn27–8; on personal identity, 220; and S's intuitionism, 243
love, *see* benevolence; charity

Macaulay, T. B.: on J. Mill, 67–8; as public moralist, 363
MacIntyre, Alasdair: and virtue ethics, 51n20, 159n23, 307n8, 325
Mackie, John, 3–4, 52n31; on G. E. Moore's criticism of S, 37, 51n18; on S on egoism, 37, 163–74; on theological solution to dualism of practical reason, 163–4, 170, 173–4
Mackintosh, Sir J.: first book-length history of ethics, 87; influence on C. Darwin, 75–6, 89nn6–7; J. Mill on, 68
Macmillan, A.: S's publisher, 336
magnanimity: Aristotle on, 302–3, 309n32, 310n35; S criticizes T. H. Green's account of Aristotle on, 294–5; *see also* common good; virtue
Maine, Henry S.: *Ancient Law* and historical school, 88, 354, 357, 358; and classical political economy, 342
Maitland, F. W.: criticizes S on inductive political science, 357; on S as teacher, 361
Mandeville, Bernard de, 156
Marshall, Alfred: and non-self-interested motives, 342; and S on marginalism, 383; S to on political economy, politics, 342
Martineau, James, 70, 80, 88, 90n30, 119n25; on "Cambridge Theology," 98; J. Dewey on S and, 374; S writes to about B. Jowett, 141n11
Marx, Karl: S on, 345, 383
materialism: S's rejection of, 109, 371–2
Maurice, F. D., 83, 90n20, 94, 100–2, 103, 118n7, 119nn31–42, 120n72; stresses importance of knowledge of God, 102–3; *see also* Cambridge moralists
maxims, *see* acts; axioms; judgment; methods of ethics; motive; principles; reason
merit, *see* desert; justice
metaphysics, *see* moral theory; personal identity; philosophy; theology
methods of ethics, 6–7, 12–13, 14, 27–8, 42–3, 46, 76, 113–14, 123, 129, 192–5,

202, 235n8, 373–4; Aristotelian perfectionism as, 10, 13–14, 281–306 passim; and basic moral notion, 8–11, 251–8; contribution to independence of moral theory, 6, 12–3; and demands of practice, 23–7, 76–86, 372–92; dispute over number of basic methods, 13–14, 49n13; egoism, 6, 13, 18, 26, 33–5, 43–7, 66, 76, 163–74, 175–8, 192–6, 374; and ends, 82, 124; T. H. Green v S on, 308n16; intuitionism, 13, 14–27, 28–31, 76–86, 123–5, 127–9, 204–5, 235n8, 241–3, 256–8, 304–5, 372; Kantian constructivism as, 14, 27–8, 49n13, 59n82, 59n84; logical criteria and, 12, 235n8; principles and, 12, 52n28; some confusion over definition of, 12–13, 52n28, 192–5, 235n8, 251; three basic methods, 13–14, 76; utilitarianism, 13, 26, 33–5, 76–83, 123, 143–60, 350–2
Methods of Ethics, The, absence of utilitarian casuistry in, 131–5; addressed main question that troubled via media, 387; central accomplishment of, 76; central thought of, 11, 123; change of last line in, 34, 116, 163–5, 174, 370; as conservative in its reverance for common-sense morality, 19–22, 158, 350–2; J. Dewey on, 373–4; does not prove common-sense morality has utilitarian basis, 143; dominance of, 66; early impact of, 87; editions of, 3, 35, 163–6, 376, 393n15; as establishing dualism of practical reason, 33–7, 41–8, 76–7, 115–18, 152–8, 163–74, 192–6, 202–6, 356, 376–7; and evolutionary theory, 76; externalist/internalist readings of, 35–6, 116–18, 195–7, 202–6, 245–7; as greatest work in British intuitionist tradition, 3, 241; index of, 82; influence of Plato and Aristotle on, 284–5, 287–90; W. James's marginal notes on, 393n18; on justice, 383–92; leaves dogmatic intuitionism unmolested, 128–9; as modern moral theory, 5–7, 49n11; object of, 3–7, 17; plan of, 131; reception of, 335–6; as revealing S's antipathy to W. Whewell, 130–1; tension between reform and conservatism as central to as dualism of practical reason, 384; as theological investigation, 6–7, 107–18; widespread misconceptions of, 3, 5, 49n8, 93–4, 107–8; writing of, 2, 42, 44, 108–18; writing of common-sense morality section, 113
Mill, James, 67–8; and analysis of